LOVE, POVERT

CHRISTOPHER HITCHENS is a widely pub........ ....quent radio
and TV commentator. He is a contributing editor to *Vanity Fair* and visiting
professor of liberal studies at the New School in New York.

'[Hitchens] can write and speak beautifully, overpoweringly, iconoclastically.'
Yasmin Alibhai-Brown, *Evening Standard*

'An exceptional political polemicist… He might end up as the best literary
and cultural critic of his generation.' David Herman, *Prospect*

'A truly joyous literary compendium.' Brian Hennigan, *Glasgow Herald*

LOVE, POVERTY AND WAR

JOURNEYS AND ESSAYS

CHRISTOPHER HITCHENS

Atlantic Books
London

First published in trade paperback in the United States of America in 2004 by Nation Books, an imprint of Avalon Publishing Group Inc., 245 West 17th St., 11th Floor, New York, NY 10011, USA.

First published in 2005 in Great Britain by Atlantic Books, an imprint of Grove Atlantic Ltd.

This paperback edition published in Great Britain by Atlantic Books in 2006.

ISBN 978 1 84354 452 4

A CIP catalogue record for this book is available from the British Library.

13 14 15 16 17 18 19

Designed by Maria E. Torres and Paul Paddock
Printed and bound by CPI Group (UK) Ltd, Croydon, CR0 4YY

Atlantic Books
An imprint of Grove Atlantic, Inc.
Ormond House
26–27 Boswell Street
London
WC1N 3JZ

For Martin Amis

CONTENTS

INTRODUCTION   xi

I. LOVE

THE MEDALS OF HIS DEFEATS   3

A MAN OF PERMANENT CONTRADICTIONS   29

THE OLD MAN   43

HUXLEY AND *BRAVE NEW WORLD*   55

GREENELAND   69

SCOOP   77

THE MAN OF FEELING   87

THE MISFORTUNE OF POETRY   99

THE ACUTEST EAR IN PARIS   109

JOYCE IN BLOOM   123

THE IMMORTAL   131

AMERICANA

IT HAPPENED ON SUNSET   143

THE BALLAD OF ROUTE 66   155

THE ADVENTURES OF AUGIE MARCH   179

REBEL GHOSTS   191

AMERICA'S POET? BOB DYLAN'S ACHIEVEMENT   201

I FOUGHT THE LAW IN BLOOMBERG'S NEW YORK   211

FOR PATRIOT DREAMS   219

II. POVERTY

MARTHA INC.   229

SCENES FROM AN EXECUTION   235

IN SICKNESS AND BY STEALTH   247

THE STRANGE CASE OF DAVID IRVING   255

WHY AMERICANS ARE NOT TAUGHT HISTORY   265

A HUNDRED YEARS OF MUGGERY   279

UNFAIRENHEIT 9/11: THE LIES OF MICHAEL MOORE   289

VIRGINITY REGAINED   301

THE DIVINE ONE   305

THE DEVIL AND MOTHER TERESA   309

BLESSED ARE THE PHRASEMAKERS   319

JEWISH POWER, JEWISH PERIL   323

THE FUTURE OF AN ILLUSION   333

THE GOSPEL ACCORDING TO MEL   339

III. WAR

BEFORE SEPTEMBER

THE STRUGGLE OF THE KURDS   351

THUNDER IN THE BLACK MOUNTAINS   365

VISIT TO A SMALL PLANET   373

HAVANA CAN WAIT   387

THE CLINTON-DOUGLAS DEBATES   397

AFTER SEPTEMBER

WE'RE STILL STANDING   403

THE MORNING AFTER   407

AGAINST RATIONALIZATION   411

OF SIN, THE LEFT, & ISLAMIC FASCISM   415

A REJOINDER TO NOAM CHOMSKY   421

BLAMING BIN LADEN FIRST   429

THE ENDS OF WAR   433

PAKISTAN: ON THE FRONTIER OF APOCALYPSE   437

SADDAM'S LONG GOOD-BYE   451

A LIBERATING EXPERIENCE   463

INTRODUCTION

An antique saying has it that a man's life is incomplete unless or until he has tasted love, poverty, and war. O. Henry, in whose eponymous yet pseudonymous Irving Place tavern I so pleasurably wasted some of my early evenings in New York, once wrote a short story entitled "The Complete Life of John Hopkins," in which a guileless citizen manages to undergo the whole trinity of these phenomena while stepping out of his cramped city apartment in search of a five-cent cigar. O. Henry's considered view was: "It seems that the wise executive power that rules life has thought it best to drill man in these three conditions, and none may escape all three." I haven't the smallest belief in any supreme executive power, let alone in a wise one (I don't believe in Her, in other words) but it would be idle to deny the element of perspicacity here.

Most thoughtful or sensitive people would presumably like to say that we have too little of the first of these "conditions," and a surplus of the second and the third. Both George Orwell and Joseph Heller registered strong disagreement, arguing vigorously that money is far more important than love. (And even that it is more important than health which—as Heller reminded us in *Something Happened*—"won't buy you money.") This in turn may have been an over-reaction to poverty, itself often falsely praised by the spiritually-minded as something ennobling but now widely marked down for having the contrary effect.

War, too, has a bad press in general yet seems able to win glowing reviews in retrospect: retrospect being the very department where love lets you down the most. One might phrase it like this—and I am sincerely sorry if the address here is too masculine, but there is no help for it. Men wish that they *had been* warriors, or are proud that they once were. They wish that they were in love *now*. And they like to view poverty as something that they overcame, or at least could have overcome. The full-time fighter is a rarity (as indeed is the full-time lover). But the man who stresses his early struggles with want and scarcity is to be found practically everywhere, and will go on emptying rooms until the end of time.

To state my own case baldly: I come from a longish line of naval and military types on my father's side, and was brought up on and around bases, and within earshot of tales of stoicism and even courage. I was very glad, during the long peace that followed the "boom" of my babyhood, to be the first Hitchens for a few generations who did not even have to contemplate donning a uniform. Great Uncle Harry, whose ship went down in freezing seas at the Battle of Jutland in 1915, saved not only himself but also the Maltese messwaiter. The bar-bills were lost for ever. I remember being touched to be told that I resembled his oil-painted portrait, but I wanted to hold it right there. I also remember being entirely astonished, several years ago, when my father took the highly unusual step of ringing up to congratulate me on an article I had written. It was about the civil war in Beirut. "Thought it was rather brave of you to go," he said, before hanging up as if he'd thought better of it. I have, since then, been a witness to warfare several times but never in such a way as to leave no convenient avenue of escape. My father's lightly-armed cruiser, HMS *Jamaica*, delivered the *coup de grace* to quite a serious Nazi battleship named the *Scharnhorst* in December 1943, a much better and riskier day's work than I have ever done, or will ever do. I experience the same feeling of mingled reverence and embarrassment when I briefly travel with correspondents and photographers—John Burns, Ed Vulliamy, James Nachtwey, Sebastião Salgado, Isabel Hilton—who consistently and yet modestly expose themselves to the heat and burden of the day.

Concerning love, I had best be brief and say that when I read Bertrand Russell on this matter as an adolescent, and understood him to write with perfect gravity that a moment of such emotion was worth the whole of the rest of life, I devoutly hoped that this would be true in my own case. And so it has proved, and so to that extent I can regard the death I otherwise rather resent as laughable and impotent.

Poverty is relative as well as absolute, as my own case would prove. My parents were haunted by the shortage of money not by the absence of it: I grew up knowing that waste was unpardonable and extravagance unthinkable and education—by means of deferred gratification—probably the solution. (Not a bad way in which to be reared, though not all that much fun, either.) I have often been broke but never been desperate. Now in my mid-fifties, I at last make more income than I require for the immediate exigencies, and I make it by writing and speaking, which are the only things I was ever able to do or desirous of doing. I live in a very agreeable apartment in the center of the capital of the United States. My three children are all beautiful, intelligent, and humorous. (I shall say nothing about their mothers except this: to have been lucky with women is to have been lucky *tout court*.) I have the ideal parents-in-law. My appearance and physique could benefit from a lot of work, or even from a little, but I have never had a serious illness or injury, and I am well-insured if such should befall. If I want to express my views publicly, I have more than a fair chance of doing so. I have traveled to several dozen countries. I hold a passport from the European Union, giving me work and residence rights in two dozen democratic and developed nations, and can hope to become an American citizen. Reviewed briefly by any reader, these elements must place me in the most fortunate one percent of all those now living, let alone of all those who have passed on to join the large majority in which my other version of materialism believes. Nobody would have any patience with my complaints, in other words.

And yet, I wake up every day to a sensation of pervading disgust and annoyance. I probably ought to carry around some kind of thermometer or other instrument, to keep checking that I am not falling prey to premature curmudgeonhood. Was it always this way? I ask myself. Did politics always seem to be a sordid auction between banal populists, and did a visit to the movies or the theater most often reward me with a sense of insult? Was publishing always a racket run by the meretricious? I am relieved to find, leafing back through previous collections, that at least I was just as curmudgeonly when I was younger. Since I have now seen more mornings and evenings than I am going to see, it may be that Erich Fromm's concept of "the struggle against pointlessness" is more resonant than it once would have appeared. But the enemies still look and feel much the same—especially that most toxic of foes, religion: the most base and contemptible of the forms assumed by human egotism and stupidity. Cold, steady hatred for this, especially in its loathsome jihad shape, has been as sustaining to me as any love. It deserves a "Poverty" section of its own, not just for the parasitic relationship it bears to disease and ignorance and misery, but also in the sense intended by Marx when he spoke of "the poverty" of some philosophy.

There came a point a few years ago, after I'd published a series of short attacks on such despicable figures as Bill Clinton, Henry Kissinger, and "Mother" Teresa, when nice old ladies in bookstores would ask me worriedly if there wasn't anyone or anything I *liked*. I was naturally sorry to have given this deplorably negative impression. I haven't exactly set out to correct it, either, but I may hope in what I have written about some authors here to show that I do think there is a gold standard, and that literature establishes and maintains it. I had begun to resolve, after the end of the cold war and some other wars, to try to withdraw from "politics" as such, and spend more time with the sort of words that hold their value. Proust, Borges, Joyce, Bellow—if you ask me why there's no Nabokov the answer is quite simply because I am not *ready*. This is a love that matures in the cask, if you will, and deepens with time. In common with other loves it is difficult to phrase in words, but I have found the effort worth making, and I'd be happy if I succeeded even slightly in delighting others as well as myself.

Then there is the rather awkward question: Can one love a country? In the England of my youth, this would have come under the heading of the superfluous: some things just don't need to be affirmed publicly and there is something suspect about those who get too strenuous on the point. I'll go this far, though. The United States of America has been very kind and hospitable to this immigrant, and I would calmly affirm that, in case things should ever become desperate enough for anyone to have to care, my adopted country has found a defender in me. This necessarily broad and vague allegiance came to a tungsten-sharp point in the fall of 2001, when my favorite city in all the world—and a favorite city *of* the world—was foully assaulted, as was my hometown of Washington D.C., by barbaric nihilists. I at once realized, with somewhat greater force, what I had always known and often lazily said: that there *is* no refuge from political engagement, and that if you try and hide from public life, it will assuredly come and invade your precious private sphere. I have been slandered here and there for what I wrote at the time, and so have taken care to reprint it, in the raw stages in which it first appeared, so as to try and show how my feelings gradually became more like thoughts. That was a condensed day of love, poverty, and war, all right. The fraternal solidarity helped overcome the damage and the loss, but we received a real glimpse of the horrors of peace, as well, and of the fatuity of letting only one side be ruthless and organized, let alone self-confident. It is civilization and pluralism and secularism that need pitiless and unapologetic fighters.

For rescuing me from curmudgeonhood, I must thank my graduate students at the University of California in Berkeley and at the New School—as I still call it—in New York. They may have been through an intellectually impoverished education system that was designed to bore them to death with second-rate and pseudo-uplifting tripe, but they had apparently managed to conserve their wit and curiosity and tough-mindedness. Then it seems that there are always editors, in publishing and journalism, who live to disprove the prophecy that everything is destined to dissolve into mediocrity. I have been fortunate beyond my deserts with Carl Bromley of Nation Books, who deftly steered this old tub into harbor. Graydon Carter, Aimee Bell, and David Friend of *Vanity Fair*, Ben Schwarz at the *Atlantic Monthly*, Victor Navasky and Katrina vanden Heuvel of *The Nation*, Lewis Lapham at *Harper's Magazine*, Jacob Weisberg at *Slate*, Jody Bottum of the *Weekly Standard*, Peter Stothard at the *Times Literary Supplement*, James Miller at *Daedalus*, and Simon Winder and Michael Millman at Penguin Books are the sorts of editor that I hope my students are one day lucky enough to meet. I reserve a closing mention for my friend and editor Michael Kelly of the *Atlantic Monthly*, who in April 2003, while I was skulking in the rear on the Iraq/Kuwait border, gave something like a full measure of devotion to his craft and calling, and lost his life on the outskirts of Saddam Hussein International Airport, a place which was long overdue to be renamed.

CHRISTOPHER HITCHENS
WASHINGTON, D.C.
SEPTEMBER 2004

I. LOVE

THE MEDALS OF
HIS DEFEATS

I n the fateful spring and early summer of 1940 the people of Britain clustered around their wireless sets to hear defiant and uplifting oratory from their new Prime Minister, Winston Churchill. On May 13, having just assumed the burden of office from a weak and cowardly Neville Chamberlain, Churchill promised a regime of "blood, toil, tears and sweat." On June 4, after the evacuation of the defeated British army from Dunkirk, he pledged, "We shall fight on the beaches." On June 18 he proclaimed that even if the British Empire were to last for a thousand years, this would be remembered as its "finest hour." Over the course of the ensuing months Britain alone defied the vast conquering appetites of Hitlerism and, though greatly outclassed in the air, repelled the Luftwaffe's assault with a handful of gallant fighter pilots. This chivalric engagement—"The Battle of Britain"—thwarted Nazi schemes for an invasion of the island fortress and was thus a hinge event in the great global conflict we now call World War II.

The foregoing paragraph could appear without much challenge in almost any English or American newspaper or magazine, and versions of it have recently seen print in the reviews of *Churchill: A Biography*, by the British Liberal statesman Lord Jenkins of Hillhead. One might, however, call attention to some later adjustments to this familiar picture.

- The three crucial broadcasts were made not by Churchill but by an actor hired to impersonate him. Norman Shelley, who played Winnie-the-Pooh for the BBC's *Children's Hour*, ventriloquized

3

Churchill for history and fooled millions of listeners. Perhaps Churchill was too much incapacitated by drink to deliver the speeches himself.

- Britain stood alone only if the military and economic support of Canada, Australia, South Africa, India, and the rest of a gigantic empire is omitted. As late as October of 1940, furthermore, the Greeks were continuing to resist on mainland Europe and had inflicted a serious military defeat on Mussolini. Moreover, the attitude of the United States, however ostensibly neutral, was at no time neutralist as between a British versus a German victory.

- The Royal Air Force was never seriously inferior, in either men or machines, to Hermann Göring's Luftwaffe, and at times outgunned it. British pilots were mainly fighting over home territory and, unlike their German opponents, could return straight to duty if they parachuted down. The RAF had the advantage of radar and the further advantage of a key to the Nazi codes. The Royal Navy was by any measure the superior of the Kriegsmarine, and Nazi surface vessels never left port without exposing themselves to extreme hazard.

- The German High Command never got beyond the drawing-board stage of any plan for the invasion of Britain, and the Führer himself was the source of the many postponements and the eventual abandonment of the idea.

A close reading of the increasingly voluminous revisionist literature discloses many further examples of events that one thinks cannot really be true, or cannot be true if the quasi-official or consecrated narrative is to remain regnant. Against which nation was the first British naval attack directed? (Against a non-mobilized French fleet, moored in the ports of North Africa, with the loss of hundreds of French lives.) Which post-1940 air force was the first to bomb civilians, and in whose capital city? (The RAF, striking the suburbs of Berlin.) Which belligerent nation was the first to violate the neutrality of Europe's noncombatant nations? (The British, by a military occupation of Norway.) But these details, not unlike the navels and genitalia in devotional painting, are figleafed in denial. They cannot exactly be omitted from the broader picture, nor can they be permitted any profane influence on its

4

sanctity. Meanwhile, who made the following broadcast speech to the British people in 1940?

> We are a solid and united nation which would rather go down to ruin than admit the domination of the Nazis . . . If the enemy does try to invade this country we will fight him in the air and on the sea; we will fight him on the beaches with every weapon we have. He may manage here and there to make a breakthrough: if he does we will fight him on every road, in every village, and in every house, until he or we are utterly destroyed.

That was Neville Chamberlain, who (albeit in his rather reedy tones) delivered the speech himself. And how many casualties did the RAF suffer during the entire Battle of Britain? A total of 443 pilots, according to official sources cited in Richard Overy's cool and meticulous revisiting of the story.

I was brought up on the cult of Winston Churchill. In the declining post-imperial 1950s and 1960s the Homeric story of 1940, and of its bulldog-visaged protagonist, was at once a consolation for many disappointments and an assurance of Britain's continued value to the world. Even then it was sometimes difficult to swallow Churchill whole, as it were. A sort of alternate bookkeeping was undertaken, whereby the huge deficits of his grand story (Gallipoli, the calamitous return to the gold standard, his ruling-class thuggery against the labor movement, his diehard imperialism over India, and his pre-war sympathy for fascism) were kept in a separate column that was sharply ruled off from "The Valiant Years." But even the many defeats and fiascoes and dishonors added in some numinous way to his stature. Here was a man who had taken part in a Victorian cavalry charge at Omdurman, in the Sudan, to avenge the slaying of General Gordon by a messianic mullah, and who had lived to help evolve the design and first use of thermonuclear weaponry. He was not a figure in history so much as a figure *of* history. (Invited by Adlai Stevenson to contribute something to the English-Speaking Union, he gruffly replied, "I *am* an English-speaking union." In anyone else this would have been solipsism, rather than charm commingled with truth.) And because in 1946 he had effectively founded the Anglo-American "special relationship" in its cold war form, at Fulton, Missouri, his enormous specter seemed to guarantee Britain a continued role as a junior superpower, or at least as a superpower's preferred junior.

In the early 1970s I was working at *The New Statesman*, in London, very near the Public Record Office, when a fresh tranche of Churchill's wartime papers was released. These covered the discussions between Churchill ("Premier," as the official papers called him) and Stalin about the future of postwar Eastern Europe. It was already known that Churchill had proposed, on the back of an envelope, a deal with Stalin for 90 percent British control of Greece in exchange for an equivalent communization of the Balkans. But it was not quite clear whether he had also deliberately traded Poland into Stalin's "sphere of influence." The matter had moral as well as historical importance, since it was in defense of Poland that Britain had finally declared war on Hitler, in September of 1939. A. J. P. Taylor prompted me to examine the documents, but the authorities informed me that the entries for Anglo-Soviet discussion of wartime Polish policy had been unaccountably mislaid. That sort of thing happens a lot in a state with an Official Secrets Act, but this was flagrant; and Poland had recently begun to stir and shift again as an actor for itself in European politics. "They always say that when it's important," Taylor told me about the "loss" of the critical records. I briefly considered titling my *New Statesman* article "The Churchill-Stalin Pact" but swiftly appreciated that this would make me look like a crank. There was no Churchill-Stalin Pact. There *could not have been* a Churchill-Stalin Pact. The necessary three words could not be brought into apposition. Heroic and improvised pragmatism— yes. Degraded and cynical statecraft? Not yet thinkable.

The Churchill cult in England, however, is mild and reflective in comparison with the Churchill cult in the United States. (I don't think any British school would be so artless as to emulate the Winston Churchill High School in the upscale D.C. suburb of Potomac, Maryland, which has a yearbook titled *Finest Hours*.) The aftermath of September 11 only reinforced a series of tropes that were already familiar to students of ready-made political rhetoric. "We will not waver, we will not tire, we will not falter, and we will not fail," President Bush proclaimed as the bombing of Afghanistan began. "We shall not fail or falter; we shall not weaken or tire," Churchill said—somewhat more euphoniously—sixty years before. Secretary of Defense Donald Rumsfeld has outdone even his Churchill-obsessed predecessor Caspar Weinberger, announcing to the staff of the Pentagon on September 12, "At the height of peril to his own nation, Winston Churchill spoke of their finest hour. Yesterday, America and the cause of human freedom came under attack." Only a week earlier, this time speaking in favor of a missile-defense system, Rumsfeld had informed a Senate committee, "Winston Churchill once said, 'I hope I shall never see the day when the forces of right are deprived of the right of force.' " On September 25, asked whether the Defense Department would be authorized to deceive the press in prosecuting the war, he unhesitatingly responded, "This conjures up Winston Churchill's famous phrase when he said . . . sometimes the truth is so precious it must be accompanied by a bodyguard of lies." Mayor Rudolph Giuliani, later to be described as an American Churchill, laid the groundwork for his own plaudits by announcing, just after the aggression of September 11 against his city, that he was reading a book about Churchill's wartime premiership "and nothing is more inspirational than the speeches and reflections of Winston Churchill about how to deal with that." Ronald Reagan hung a portrait of Churchill in the Situation Room of the White House soon after taking power; the first President Bush allowed Jack Kemp to compare him to Churchill during the Gulf War; the second President Bush asked the British embassy in Washington to help furnish him with a bronze bust of Churchill, which now holds pride of place in the Oval Office. The legacy-obsessed Bill Clinton can only whimper at the lack of Churchillian analogy to his own tenure, but the rest of us might wish that if the United States is going to stand for something, it (or its overpaid speechwriting class) would try to come up with some mobilizing rhetoric of its own.

This prevailing line, which teeters between grandeur and kitsch, is followed with reasonable fidelity by American historians and commentators. A few weeks before September 11 a fairly banal development earned a front-page story and an editorial in the *New York Times*. It became known that William Manchester, debilitated by two strokes, would not be completing his trilogy on the life of Churchill. This trilogy, generically titled *The Last Lion*, had run to two volumes, *Visions of Glory* and *Alone*. If these titles are insufficient to convey the flavor, one might cite, as did the *New York Times* in its editorial, the closing staves of the second and now-to-be final book: "And now, in the desperate spring of 1940, with the reins of power at last firm in his grasp, he resolved to lead Britain and her fading empire in one last great struggle worthy of all they had been and meant, to arm the nation, not only with weapons but also with the mace of honor, creating in every English breast a soul beneath the ribs of death."

Never in the field of human biography can metaphor have been more epically mixed. Yet the *New York Times* regarded the lack of a sequel as a cultural event worthy of reverent coverage and a deferential editorial. The latter, unsigned, described the incomplete work as leaving "Churchill somehow suspended, poised in the midst of a great arc whose outcome we know but whose details we would like to savor over again in Mr. Manchester's words." Or, to put it another way, there can never be too much reinforcement of a familiar and useful morality tale. In the quite recent past at least two books have been published to general acclaim—*Churchill: A Study in Greatness*, by Geoffrey Best, and *Five Days in London, May 1940*, by John Lukacs, which assist in this ramming home of an already near unassailable myth. And these, together with Lord Jenkins's tome, only continue a process begun by Churchill himself when he annexed the papers of his time in office to write his own version of events. He could emerge as a historic figure—as he put it in one of his many and likeable moments of self-deprecation—by making sure of writing the history himself. The names of his early research assistants and drafters—Alan Bullock, F. W. Deakin—are testimony in themselves to what might fairly be called a conscription of the historians' professional mainstream. Yet upon reflection one might perhaps decide that the term "conscription" is unfair. "Churchill the historian," said the late Sir J. H. Plumb, "lies at the very heart of all historiography of the Second World War and will always remain there." Donald Cameron Watt commented dryly seven years later, in 1976, "For the bulk of the historical profession in America, Sir Winston Churchill's view of British policy before 1939 has hardly required a moment's critical examination." It would be no insult, then, to describe certain authors not as conscripts but as volunteers.

Manchester's series proposed itself modestly as only the condensed (or large-print) version of the *ur*-text of approved Churchilliana: the eight-volume official biography, by Sir Martin Gilbert, the doyen of Churchill historians.

Unlike the grave and measured work of which it is the flickering Platonic shadow, Manchester's unfinished labor is overwrought in the sentimental, para-historical Camelot style that its author helped to originate. Once again, action is judged by reputation rather than reputation by action. In an extraordinary gesture Manchester rendered Churchill's wartime speeches as blank verse, with carefully incised line breaks and verse settings. This was to make explicit what had been latent heretofore, and it was also to pay Churchill the compliment he would probably have most valued and desired. (Remember that he received his 1953 Nobel Prize for literature.) In the English-speaking world, at any rate, his lapidary phrases and rolling flourishes have achieved the familiarity and renown enjoyed by some passages of the King James Bible, the Book of Common Prayer, and the "kingship" plays of William Shakespeare. These excerpts or verses have the peculiar and potent faculty of recurring to our minds in time of trouble or when they seem relevant or poignant (or simply useful). And they are associated above all with fortitude, staunchness, and stoicism, salted with a little gallows humor. Imperishability of that sort descends on human beings very rarely indeed. And the audience does not mind a little exaggeration if the aim is flattering to the groundlings. "After he had spoken to them in the summer of 1940 as no one has ever before or since," Isaiah Berlin wrote in this magazine, in one of his many courageous stands for the conventional wisdom, "they conceived a new idea of themselves which their own prowess and the admiration of the world has since established as a heroic image in the history of mankind." How true. In bidding a gracious farewell to Neville Chamberlain, Churchill nobly called him "the packhorse in our great affairs." Accepting the compliment, Chamberlain pointed out that the line comes from *Richard III* and not, as Churchill had alleged, from *Henry VI*. But no matter. The thing is not to be right about Shakespeare. The thing is *to be Shakespearean*. Blood, toil, tears, sweat—and some immodest populism.

In the flush of the "finest hour" in 1944 Laurence Olivier produced and starred in his own patriotic movie version of *Henry V*. This film constituted (and still constitutes) subliminal propaganda of a high order. Shakespeare, Saint George, and the Almighty are yoked together against minatory Continental power. Some deference to contemporaneous Gallic sensibilities resulted in a downplaying of the original quarrel over the Salic law and the

French throne, and the scene at Agincourt involving the ruthless massacre of all Prince Hal's civilian and military prisoners was thoughtfully excised. Indeed, who today cares about the true foundation of Henry's opportunistic claim, or about the heaps of dead on both sides, or the eventual ruin of his plan for the mainland? What is this when set beside the marvelous evocation of the Feast of Crispin, or the five-to-one numerical odds against the English at Agincourt ("we few, we happy few"), or the splendid words in which the terms of surrender are twice refused by Harry, or the glorious and seductive notion that sacrifice and wounds are to be envied and that "gentlemen in England, now a-bed / Shall think themselves accurs'd they were not here"?

These very words were muttered by living (and dying) men on the shores of Dunkirk and Dieppe and Normandy, along with the whispered accompaniment that those absent would "hold their manhoods cheap whiles any speaks / That fought with us upon Saint Crispin's day." And for at least a generation after World War II they had a stilling effect on all politicians who had apparently temporized about the last—or, indeed, the next—European conflict. In a secondhand form they exist in our vernacular as taunts about "Munich" or "appeasement"; the Munich analogy having extended itself through the "Iron Curtain" address in Fulton as a reproach to all those who were soft on communism. Manhood was the least of it; the taint of treason lay behind the suggestion of a want of virility.

In his time Churchill was very "soft," as well as very hard, on both fascism and communism. His protean, volatile character has allowed him to escape most of the moral and political consequences. So it must count as a minor irony of history that his reputation and rhetoric, both of them highly serviceable to conservatives, have come under sustained attack from a determined school of British right-wing historians—for the intelligible reason that the salient grievance of these historians is the loss of the British Empire. Nevertheless, some American circles retain anti-Churchill suspicions, because of Churchill's lifetime role in embroiling the United States in European wars. And beneath all this is a more utilitarian critique that simply inquires whether World War II could or should—because of its appalling cost—have been averted.

I earlier employed the term "profane," knowing that I should be in need of it again. The argument about World War II and its worthwhileness is the most apparently settled and decided of all major questions in our culture. There may be an occasional flinch (about the obliteration of Dresden, say, or the incineration of Nagasaki, or the wisdom of demanding unconditional surrender). But the evidence adduced at Nuremberg has the effect of retrospectively annulling all such doubts. Even the standby argument of some anti-Churchill Tories (and others, including George Orwell), about the callous collusion between Churchill and Stalin, seems almost anachronistic in view of the eventual implosion of the Soviet system. Finally, nostalgia for the British Empire is not so strong either in Britain or in its former colonial possessions as to evoke much rancor or regret at the loss of dominion.

Churchill and his right-wing critics, from John Charmley to David Irving, have something in common. They unite around the two propositions that communism was to be opposed and British imperialism was to be upheld. For the first few decades of his political career Churchill was happy to be counted an extremist—if not, indeed, a fanatic—on both these counts. He helped to organize the brutal, abortive invasion of Lenin's Russia in 1918, and published at least one subsequent article blaming the Jews for Bolshevism. He also wrote and spoke until quite late in the day (though more as an anti-Communist than an anti-Semite) in favor of Mussolini, Franco, and even Hitler. His fundamentalism about India, and the racist language in which he opposed the smallest concession to the Indian independence movement, were among the many reasons for the wide distrust that hampered him in the 1930s, and for his exclusion from the Tory Cabinets of that decade. Thus we face an intriguing question when we ask ourselves how it was that he came to embrace a cause that not only transcended those two elemental commitments but eventually negated them.

The hagiographer and the hatchet man are in unspoken agreement here. William Manchester and David Irving lay considerable stress on the near eclipse that overtook Churchill in the mid-1930s. The consensus politics of the so-called National Government had no appeal for him, and no need for him either. He was popularly (and correctly) regarded as one of those whose calamitous earlier policies had made coalition and compromise so necessary. And he was further distrusted as one who was predisposed toward grand-opera or militaristic solutions. Already in his sixth decade, Churchill was also (as some have a tendency to forget) on the verge of bankruptcy. Locust years indeed, in which Churchill ("so surfeit-swell'd, so old, and so profane . . .") was more Falstaff than Hal. The blunt conclusion, encouraged by a reading of Manchester no less than of Irving, is that the Last Lion needed a last hurrah— a campaign issue that allowed him scope for all his talents and energies.

Confronted by the enemy's herald, who warns him that he faces annihilation if he brings his sick and shabby force onto the field of battle, King Henry V retorts with pugnacity but without overmuch bravado: "We would not seek a battle as we are / Nor, as we are, we say; we will not shun it." This was not unlike the wager that Churchill made in his campaign against the Baldwin and Chamberlain governments in the late 1930s. He accused them of being militarily unready while simultaneously urging them to risk battle. The contradiction is forgiven in light of eventual triumph, as it was in the case of Agincourt. But the political underlay was epigrammatically understood by Churchill as early as 1934. Writing about the reactionary press baron Lord Rothermere, who was enthusiastically pro-Nazi *and* pro-empire, he said, "He wants us to be very strongly armed & frightfully obsequious at the same time." The left, he added with equal acuity, wanted Britain to remain "disarmed & exceedingly abusive." The central paradox of the epoch has never been better phrased. We are almost conditioned to forget that many of the anti-Churchill Tories were busily committed to rearmament, but regarded Churchill's constant drumming on the subject as vulgar and alarmist (as, indeed, it sometimes was).

The historian David Dutton seeks to rehabilitate Chamberlain and to write about Churchill as if he were, at last, approachable as a mere mortal. But in doing so he understates the way in which the Tory establishment of the time was subjectively, as well as objectively, pro-Nazi.

On closer examination the image of Churchill as the resolute and unwavering opponent of the 1930s' dictators—a reasonable basis from which to launch an assault upon Neville Chamberlain—begins to dissolve. His contemporary criticism of the aggression of totalitarian regimes *other than Hitler's Germany* was at best muted. When Japan invaded Manchuria in 1931 Churchill declared that there would be a general unwillingness to fight or to "make any special exertions in defence of the present government of China." Similarly, his record over Ethiopia and the Spanish Civil War failed in reality to place him in a distinctly different camp from Chamberlain and the National Government. Nor did Churchill rush to denounce the Anglo-German Naval Agreement of 1935. As late as 1937 he even seemed willing to give Hitler the possible benefit of the doubt. Accepting that history was full of examples of men who had risen to power by "wicked and even frightful methods" but who had gone on to become great figures, enriching the "story of mankind", he held out the possibility that "so it may be with Hitler" . . . Before 1938 his most significantly outspoken criticism of government policy related to its failure to uphold Baldwin's pledge to maintain air parity with Germany. The government, however, had come to admit its failure in this respect and to begin to increase the pace of rearmament. [*Italics added*]

This is true enough in the formal sense. But one might as readily have summarized Lincoln's hesitations and evasions on the matter of slavery and abolition, and his long and tortuous attempts to avoid war, and his preference for the survival of the Union over other questions of principle. Yet when the arrogant exorbitance of "The Slave Power" compelled a confrontation, there was no length to which Lincoln would not go; no abolitionist group, however fanatical, that he would not befriend; and no extremity of pitiless violence to which he would not resort. His gift—better to say his instinct—for unifying and spirited phrasing promoted him well above the sordid battlefields for which those phrases were carpentered. Churchill (who in his writings actually betrayed a sympathy for the Confederacy) strikes me as a politician of that kind—a statesman who could use terms like "destiny" and "the Almighty" without seeming self-conscious; a Hegelian figure capable of entirely fusing himself with what he conceived as a fateful hour. In his contradictions he contained multitudes.

The word "appeasement" obscures some elements of this realization now, as it did then. It was the vague term chosen by the Tories themselves to mask a collaboration with fascism and also their candid hope that the ambitions of Hitler could be directed eastward against Stalin. It is as easy to imagine the RAF helping the Wehrmacht in the Caucasus—had things occurred in a slightly different order—as it was difficult for my gruff, reactionary Royal

Navy father to find himself, under Churchill's orders, running guns to Stalin via Murmansk. In their neglected book *In Our Time: The Chamberlain-Hitler Collusion* (to which I should confess I wrote the introduction), Clement Leibovitz and Alvin Finkel deploy an arsenal of documents to argue that sympathy for the Nazi Party prevailed in the highest British circles even after the declaration of war in September of 1939. It wasn't at all that the British rightists were vacillating and pacifistic—an absurd notion to begin with. It was that they thought they could save their empire by a tactical alliance with Berlin. One simple proof of this can be adduced: British colonial and naval officials were historically very jealous of their country's predominance in the Mediterranean, which extended from the Strait of Gibraltar to the shores of Palestine. Mussolini's maritime challenge to this hegemony was vastly strengthened by Franco's advance in Spain, and British ships visiting Republican ports were actually sunk by Italian planes and submarines during the Spanish Civil War. Yet the cheers for Franco on the Tory benches never died away. Quite obviously, these people thought they saw in fascism a future ally and not a future rival.

Thus Professor Dutton is ungenerous to Churchill. He partly acknowledges as much, in the small concession above on the threat from Germany, which was qualitatively as well as quantitatively different from that posed by Italy or Spain or even—Churchill's greatest failure of prescience—Japan. But he omits to credit the *way* in which Churchill broke from his previous sympathy for fascism and the "appeasement" of it, and also the stern, memorable words he employed to make the breach. It was actually the realization about Britain's position in the Mediterranean, and not any sympathy for Republican Spain, that impelled him to recant his long-standing support for the Franco side. But when he made the switch, he made it wholeheartedly. The British ambassador in Paris did not especially object to Churchill's inviting Léon Blum to dinner during his unofficial stopovers (the leader of the *Front Populaire* was also an honored guest at Churchill's own country house at Chartwell). But he did put his foot down when Churchill asked him to produce some French Communist guests. Writing to a colleague about "The Focus," that loose-knit group of politicians and journalists and socialites that informally coordinated anti-appeasement information and activity in the late 1930s, Churchill once described it as a coalition seeking support especially from "those of the 'left.' " As a back-bencher with no official position, he repeatedly invited Stalin's ambassador, Ivan Maisky, to his home to discuss political strategy.

It is difficult to exaggerate the difference between this and all his previous stances. And so it is indeed strange, given the heavy emphasis placed by chroniclers on Churchill's sheer magnitude of personality, that the ingredient of pure ambition should be so much ignored or even disallowed. Churchill knew he had but one chance to put himself at the head of affairs. He was more than willing to amend or abandon all his previous allegiances in order to do so. To take only one example, Churchill had rashly enlisted on the side of King Edward VIII and Mrs. Simpson against Stanley Baldwin. He made such a fool of himself in the process (even Lord Jenkins concedes urbanely that he must have been hopelessly drunk at the crucial moment) as to jeopardize his newfound anti-Nazi connections. Yet only a short while later he jettisoned all his romantic and high-flown nonsense about being "a King's man" and rejected the absurd former monarch as if he, Churchill, were Hal and the King the cast-off jester. Rereading this record, and surveying the ever multiplying fund of fresh sources, we find ourselves reviewing the career of a vaulting prince of opportunists.

Here one must negotiate the toxic figure of David Irving. If Sir Martin Gilbert's work is the quarry from which the wagons of orthodoxy continue to trundle away, laden with the building blocks for lesser edifices of loyalism, then Irving's projected trilogy *Churchill's War* is the dynamite that lies still unexploded around the quarry. Two volumes have so far been published, bringing the story up to 1943, with the Battle of Kursk balanced by the impending invasion of Sicily. Since his first volume was published, to some acclaim, in 1987, Irving has been reduced to publishing and marketing his books himself. The reason for this is now well understood. Both in his public life as a fringe speechmaker and in his career as a freelance archivist and historian, Irving has tainted himself with the one thing of which no serious person can even be suspected: a sympathy for the Nazi cause. Much of this taint is the consequence of an unsuccessful libel lawsuit against the Holocaust specialist Deborah Lipstadt.

Anyone who reads his first two Churchill volumes with open eyes will see at once that Irving invites, if not enjoys, his reputation as an untouchable.

Whenever he mentions Nazi defectors or mutineers or anti-Hitler plotters (and the frigid reception given to such men by Chamberlain and Lord Halifax was yet another clue to their real sympathy for the Führer), he refers to them as "traitors." He repeatedly describes Churchill as a front man for "the Socialists" and for (variously) "the Zionists" and "the Jews." He has an unconcealed contempt for mongrel America, and for the wiles of Roosevelt as he schemed to poach the wonderful British Empire. Yet in the text Irving often refers to Churchill as "Winston." (Irving, as those who study him will know, has a tendency to mix the oleaginous with the aggressive.) About halfway through Volume One, describing the tit-for-tat raids by which, he maintains, Hitler was first induced by Churchill to bomb London in September of 1940, he summarizes his essential position.

> This first attack had killed 306 Londoners. It was the first lurch towards the holocaust. Now Churchill and Portal needed no further justification for what they proposed—to unleash a new kind of war, in which ultimately one million civilians in Germany as well as hundreds of thousands of French, Poles, Czechs and others would die under the trample of the Allied strategic bomber forces.

("Holocaust" literally means a devouring by fire, so the term may be technically allowed, but you see what I mean.) Irving has a great facility for innuendo; its most successful application is the repeated suggestion that Churchill used his foreknowledge of German air raids sheerly for grandstanding purposes. On the nights when he knew that Göring's bombers would overfly London on their way to, say, Coventry, he would make a point of standing on the Air Ministry roof, or of taking a stroll in the Downing Street garden, thus impressing his staff and subordinates with his pluck and daring and sangfroid. On the nights when Enigma gave him private information about a raid on London itself, he would decamp to the country house of a wealthy friend. This accumulation of detail is so subversive of the legend as to make a greater difference in the mind of the reader than many more-serious shortcomings of generalship. The allegation has now been in print for fifteen years, and I have never seen it addressed by the Great Man's defenders, let alone rebutted.

So visceral is his contempt for Churchill that even the later revisionist historians handle Irving with tongs. Clive Ponting's study *1940: Myth and Reality*, published in 1991, does not acknowledge Irving's existence except in the bibliography. John Charmley's first book on Churchill, *Churchill: The End of Glory*, was published in 1993 (while Charmley held the chair at, of all places, Fulton, Missouri), and his second book, *Churchill's Grand Alliance*, appeared in 1995. The name David Irving is only briefly cited in either text or index. (This method is employed in turn by Lord Jenkins, who awards Charmley a single reference *en passant*, doesn't even credit Irving in his bibliography, and in general writes as if all "second thoughts" about Churchill are beneath his, and our, notice.) Yet internal evidence strongly suggests that Ponting, Charmley, *and* Jenkins have read Irving with keen attention, and have used him to enlarge their narratives without appearing to bow to his influence.

I would not consider as qualified in the argument about Churchill anybody who had not read Irving's work. In those pages one may read, without the veil of discretion or constraint that descended like a thick velvet curtain after 1945, what Churchill's colleagues and subordinates really thought about him at the time. What they often thought—ambassadors, private secretaries, generals, air marshals—was that he was a demagogue, a bluffer, an incompetent, and an inebriate. Some of those cited are jealous subordinates, and others are military men with a pre-war sympathy for fascism. But here, for instance, is Lord Hankey, one of the leading professional civil servants during both world wars, writing in May of 1941, when he had the job of coordinating Britain's secret services:

Churchill has great gifts of leadership, and can put his stuff over the people, Parliament, his Cabinet colleagues and even himself. But he is not what he thinks himself, a great master of the art of war. Up to now he has never brought off any great military enterprise. However defensible they may have been, Antwerp, Gallipoli and the expedition to help the White Russians at the end of the last war were all failures. He made some frightful errors of judgment between the two wars in military matters, e.g. obstructing the construction of new ships in 1925 . . . his false estimates of the value of French generals & French military methods . . . It was he who forced us into the Norwegian affair which failed; the Greek affair which failed; and the Cretan affair which is failing.

All of this, and more, is true. Yet even as the disaster in Crete was becoming evident, and Churchill was wondering how to break the news of another calamity, the Nazi flagship *Bismarck* was found in the North Sea (with the help of an "unofficial" American spotter plane), disabled by a hastily dropped torpedo, and sunk. Triumph. If Churchill was a Hegelian figure, and if Hegel described Bonaparte as "history on horseback," then Churchill is the most exemplary illustration of one of Bonaparte's maxims about generalship: he was lucky. The Norwegian fiasco—a fiasco of his own making—led to the vote of confidence in Parliament that deposed Neville Chamberlain. The defeat of France, which negated Churchill's dogmatic and dangerous belief in the efficacy of the Maginot Line and the Maginot mentality, allowed him to launch an enormous domestic "unity" campaign that stilled his critics and neutralized his rivals. The sudden frightening indebtedness and impoverishment of Britain gave him room to be sole mediator with Roosevelt, who agreed for a price to be his banker and armorer. At almost every point Churchill was allowed by events to flaunt the medals of his defeats.

There were times when this was not so, but they have been airbrushed from the received record. Not only did Churchill entirely lack foresight (or even ordinary prudence) about the ambitions of Japan, but in the early days of his prime ministership he gave orders for the closure of the Burma Road, the supply route by which Nationalist China had received the means of resistance. This was an overt capitulation to Hirohito's demands—an abject act of "appeasement" and one that was, interestingly enough, opposed as such by none other than the now despised Lord Halifax. Yet when, not long afterward, Singapore was encircled by the Japanese, Churchill raged incoherently about the failure of his generals to warn him of the threat, spoke terrifyingly of the need to uphold "our country and our race," and gave the direct order "There must at this stage be no thought of saving the troops or sparing the population . . . Commanders and senior officers should die with their troops." Read out of context, this hysterical directive could have been a telegram to either commander in the Battle for Stalingrad. It was discreetly countermanded by Archibald Wavell, who permitted the odious General Percival to capitulate. (The story of this outburst is rendered no prettier by the fact that Churchill was hoping, in his own words, to impress the Americans by a great human sacrifice.) Lord Jenkins, I must confess, surprised me in only one way: he freely admits Churchill's continual worry that the British soldiers were not as good, or as worthy of his militancy, as the soldiers of the other side. This insecurity about the unworthiness of the rank and file for great deeds or great sacrifices was of course shared by at least two of the other three wartime overlords.

Scouring the increasingly meticulous and assertive and well-sourced revisionist literature, I felt a sensation I had experienced only once before, while reading Josephine Tey's minor masterpiece, *The Daughter of Time*. As fellow addicts of this book will know, it begins with an acceptance of the standard view of Richard III—"Crookback Dick," the usurper, and the murderer of the Little Princes. Then, by slow forensic degrees, it demonstrates that every aspect of this story is an accumulation of lies and later courtier propaganda. The chronicle of Holinshed, the memoir of Sir Thomas More, the drama of Shakespeare himself—all are pitilessly uncovered as the merest conjury and fraud. Even for a reader who has no stake in Tudor spin-doctoring, the effect is a vertiginous one, with all the cargo in the hold slowly turning over. Is one to be left with no illusions? Is the whole pageant a cruel put-up job?

There is an increasing scholarly understanding that only when Hitler made the mistake of fighting the Soviet Union and the United States simultaneously did he condemn himself to certain defeat. The overall British contribution to that defeat has been diminished by the years and with the unsealing of more and more international archives. Yet the legend of 1940 has persisted, and has survived the opening of even the British archives on the period. A sort of cognitive dissonance is in operation. The records show, for example, that in secret Cabinet discussions that spring and summer Churchill more than once favored limited negotiations with Hitler, while Chamberlain at least once voted against them. Nobody in the government was in favor of surrender; nobody, including Churchill, was in favor of rejecting all negotiation with Hitler on principle. But some, including Churchill, were too much committed to a war to turn back without risking ridicule or obloquy.

For an instance of the tenacity of the traditional view, by which one historian underwrites and reinforces the conventional efforts of another, I cite this excerpt from John Lukacs's November 2001 review of Geoffrey Best's *Churchill: A Study in Greatness.*

> One of the stunning phrases in Churchill's history of World War I is his description of the First Fleet leaving Portsmouth for Scapa Flow on July 28, 1914, through the English Channel: "Scores of gigantic castles of steel wending their way across the misty, shining sea, like giants bowed in anxious thought." Best ends his book with Churchill's funeral, on January 30, 1965, "the great cranes along the south side of the stretch of the river between Tower Bridge and London Bridge, dipping their masts in tribute as [Churchill's funeral launch] went by, 'like giants bowed in anxious thought.' " This is the mark of a great historian.

It is by no means the mark of a great historian. It is the mark of a recycler of familiar rhetorical themes, and of stale rhetorical expressions ("wending their way") at that. But Lukacs is committed to this style in precisely the way he is committed to its corresponding substance, which admits of no demurral. Just as it's easy to shock someone whose knowledge of World War II comes from the movie *Casablanca* by mentioning the obstinate fact that the Roosevelt administration recognized Vichy even during the war with Germany, or the equally obstinate fact that it never declared war on Hitler but waited for Hitler to declare war on the United States, so it is easy to upset the Lukacsian world view with a couple of incontrovertible observations: In 1940 the Churchill government did not even surrender the Channel Islands. It evacuated them, beaches and all, and permitted an unopposed Nazi occupation. Churchill himself was quite ready to discuss Hitler's demand for some German colonies in Africa if that would help to buy time, and even contemplated the cession of some British colonies, such as Malta and Gibraltar.

Indeed, it is fascinating to notice how often the colonial "periphery" was deemed the essential theater for avoiding an all-out war between Europeans. Chamberlain had cared far more about India (a much more faraway country) than about Czechoslovakia, whereas Churchill was willing to use imperial outposts as bargaining chips with both Roosevelt and Hitler; and in dealings with Washington the British were forced to mortgage what they actually held—in the Caribbean especially—as a down payment on Lend-Lease. It seems almost unbelievable now that the British should have panicked at the "prospect" of a Nazi invasion of Ireland, but it remains the case that Churchill (who had helped to fix the Partition of Ireland in 1921) offered to hand over Protestant Ulster to Eamon De Valera in exchange for the use of Irish ports. Hoping to preserve good relations with food-producing Argentina, the British considered relinquishing their dubious historical claim to the Falkland Islands.

Nor is this colonial dimension a sidebar to the main event. If anyone were to write a serious book about the moment when Britain and Churchill crossed the Rubicon and convinced those at home and abroad that there was no alternative to a war to the finish, the relevant time would not be the days of equivocation in May of 1940. It would be July 3 of the same year, when the order was given to destroy the French fleet in the port of Mers el-Kébir, or Oran, in Algeria. Having vastly and repeatedly overstated the will and the ability of the French to resist Hitler, and having nearly lost an entire British army on this delusion at Dunkirk, Churchill became his own polar opposite and decided that the surviving French naval force was in imminent danger of being grafted onto the German fleet. As it happened, Franklin Roosevelt and Cordell Hull were expressing precisely the same anxiety, at exactly the same time, about the *British* fleet. In none too delicate a fashion they suggested that Churchill dispatch the Royal Navy across the Atlantic for safekeeping. As late as June 27 Hull had proposed this very course, before being checked by an indignant reply from Churchill.

It can confidently be asserted, based on numerous records and recollections, that the British bombardment of the French navy put an end to this period of vacillation. In Parliament, Churchill's earlier and more famous speeches (which he did at least give in the chamber, leaving Norman Shelley to handle the airwaves) had been greeted by the Tory members with sullenness or sarcasm—with what one Minister described at the time as a "sinister" lack of enthusiasm. But the news from Mers el-Kébir precipitated the first real ovation of his stewardship as Prime Minister. It was also employed by him to rub in a very salient point: "I leave the judgment of our action, with confidence, to Parliament. I leave it also to the nation, and I leave it to the United

States. I leave it to the world and to history." There was to be no more talk of compromise: "We shall on the contrary prosecute the war with the utmost vigor by all the means that are open to us until the righteous purposes for which we entered upon it have been fulfilled. This is no time for doubts or weakness. It is the supreme hour to which we have been called."

"Supreme hour" is just as effective as "finest hour," but this is one speech that has not come down to us by way of the Churchill school of historians. Why not? After all, it rallied opinion, spat defiance, dissolved factional differences, and mightily impressed both Washington and Moscow. It was also an unarguable act of war rather than an act of verbiage. It was a burning of the boats. Ah, but the boats were French. And so were the many hundreds of those who died in them. Moreover, no evidence has ever been produced to suggest that the French would have given over their fleet to the Nazis, and there is much evidence the other way: the ships had been moved to North Africa in the first place to avoid their impressment by Germany, and no surviving Vichy vessel was ever transferred to German control. The British commander who was ordered to open fire on a fleet that lay at anchor—Admiral James Somerville—confessed himself nauseated by the task. The French never forgave the incident. Chroniclers prefer to skate over it or, where possible, elide it altogether.

Yet here, if you will, is the Shakespearean or biblical element at work again. If Churchill would so cheerfully slay and humiliate his recent ally, as an earnest of his ruthlessness and resolution, then what might he not do? This was a much more literally and vividly "Churchillian" moment than most. It's just not—if I may put it like this—the sort of thing they teach you in school.

At the end of his almost parodically orthodox book Geoffrey Best asks himself why Lyndon Johnson did not attend Churchill's funeral, in 1965, and decides to leave this wounding question as an open one, almost incapable of rational explanation. Well, Churchill very pointedly did not attend Franklin Roosevelt's obsequies in 1945, and even Lord Jenkins allows one to speculate—in view of Churchill's addiction to Atlantic crossings and White House hospitality—that this was determined by pique, including pique at Roosevelt's repeated refusal to visit Britain during the war. Several years ago I read through the entire Churchill-Roosevelt correspondence and was astonished to find how much the two men had disliked and distrusted each other. Astonished, too, by the clarity and candor of this mutual disaffection, and by the way that official history, most notably Churchill's own volumes, downplayed the fact. The resentment on Roosevelt's side was rather petty: he did not forget being snubbed by Churchill at their first meeting, in 1918; did not care for his endless importunacy; and was often appalled by his alcoholism. For Churchill's part there was the detestation that is often felt by the mendicant; he hated having to be polite to the man he was asking for a loan. And to this was added the humiliation of the terms: Roosevelt always exacted payment, in gold or in bases, in advance, and was once described by his victim as "a sheriff collecting the last assets of a helpless debtor."

One might feel more sympathy for this complaint if Churchill had not employed precisely the same lofty and arrogant method with his own mendicants. The French and the Poles, much more injured in their pride and in their territory than the British (and this often as a result of listening to British promises), were bluntly and sometimes thuggishly told to know their place and to keep their mouths shut. One does not have to reopen the tattered conspiracy theory about the death of General Sikorski. But it is morally impossible to read Churchill's brutal injunction to Sikorski—that he drop the subject of the Soviet massacre of the Polish officer corps at Katyn—without reflecting that many more deaths were much more cynically covered up. (No serious British official doubted the truth or the justice of Sikorski's complaint, though Churchill continued to smokescreen the issue even in his memoirs.)

Roosevelt's case was slightly different. He was determined not to repeat the Wilsonian mistake of involving America in secret diplomacy; he was fighting the last war. But then, so was Churchill in his way. The issue foremost in Churchill's mind was the entanglement of the United States in the combat. He and his admirals regularly joked about the happy possibility that the German navy would provoke a confrontation with an American vessel in the North Atlantic. During the hunt for the *Bismarck* and its consort, *Prinz Eugen*, Churchill announced that "it would be better for instance that she should be located by a U.S. ship as this might tempt her to fire on that ship, then providing the incident for which the U.S. government would be so grateful." He may have been too jaunty about the second part of the hypothesis. But the evident reference was to the notorious sinking of the *Lusitania*, in 1915, which occurred during his first tenure at the British Admiralty. The official historian of British Naval Intelligence, Patrick Beesly, has already written about this as follows:

> For my part, unless and until fresh information comes to light, I am reluctantly driven to the conclusion that there *was* a conspiracy deliberately to put the *Lusitania* at risk in the hope that even an abortive attack on her would bring the United States into war. Such a conspiracy could not have been put into effect without Winston Churchill's express permission and approval.

Those who like to refer to Churchill as an adventurer or a swashbuckler or a buccaneer do not like to hear their words come back to them in this fashion; the Beesly history is invariably omitted from the authorized version. But I venture the prediction that the next wave of Churchill revisionism will focus more and more acutely on this and similar incidents. If he has a titanic place in history, it is largely because he was instrumental in engaging the United States in two world wars, and thus acted as (inadvertent) midwife to the successor role of America as an imperial power. The disagreeable and surreptitious element of this story cannot indefinitely remain unexamined. (There is more than a hint in some recent work that the paranoid American right may be mistaken in its ancient belief that "FDR knew" about the imminence of Pearl Harbor. FDR probably did not know. But Churchill quite possibly did.) At any rate, Churchill got his wish, for a wholehearted American commitment to the war. But in exchange he had to sign a virtual British "Declaration of Dependence," on everything from currency to colonies.

Churchill's role in advancing the career and power of Joseph Stalin is the second guarantee of his enduring historical importance. In many of his communications and confidences one gets the distinct sense that he admired the great despot not in spite of his cruelty and absolutism but because of it. (He told Ivan Maisky of his admiration for Stalin's annihilation of the Trotskyists. And that was before the outbreak of war.) Thus, when he mounted the podium at Fulton and spoke of an "Iron Curtain" extending from the Baltic to the Adriatic, Churchill at least possessed the authority of someone who had done much to bring that curtain down. In his other character, as Anglo-American imperialist, he had also helped to determine Washington's role as guarantor of the other side of the curtain. Finally, he had helped to share the atomic secret as partial payment for a permanent seat for Britain at all superpower negotiations. A colossus by any measurement, if not the part avuncular and part growling figure depicted by those who trade in reassurance.

It is truth, in the old saying, that is "the daughter of time," and the lapse of half a century has not left us many of our illusions. Churchill tried and failed to preserve one empire. He failed to preserve his own empire, but succeeded in aggrandizing two much larger ones. He seems to have used crisis after crisis as an excuse to extend his own power. His petulant refusal to relinquish the leadership was the despair of postwar British Conservatives; in my opinion this refusal had to do with his yearning to accomplish something that "history" had so far denied him—the winning of a democratic election. His declining years in retirement were a protracted, distended humiliation of celebrity-seeking and gross overindulgence.

Some recent work on Hitler, notably by Ian Kershaw, has disclosed a banal but nonetheless awful thought: The Führer always "knew" that he did not have long to live. He embarked on rash or hectic or suicidal enterprises not because he believed that his Reich would last a thousand years but because he sensed that it would not. (Those of his intimates who came to realize this were in possession of one of the most ghastly insights in human history.) Even without this awareness no actuary would have insured Hitler's life for an extra decade, or even five years. In retrospect this terrible knowledge might seem to vindicate the appeasers and those who, like pre-1941 Roosevelt, were ready to wait and see. A holding operation, or a compromise, could have perhaps resulted in Hitlerism's giving way to a successor regime or possibly being overthrown in favor of one. The Final Solution, which did not begin until the night and fog of war obscured it, might have been averted or at least attenuated. Millions of other Europeans and Americans might not have been burned or starved or tortured to death. We might not be living under the minute-by-minute menace of nuclear extinction.

I can think such thoughts, and even adduce evidence for them, and feel all the cargo in my hold slowly turning over again until there is no weight or balance left. Stephen Jay Gould, reviewing the evidence of the fossil record in the Burgess Shale, offered the dizzying conclusion that if the "tape" of evolution could be rewound and run again, it would not "come out" the same way. I am quite sure that he is correct in this. But history really begins where evolution ends, and where we gain at least a modicum of control over our own narrative. I find that I cannot rerun the tape of 1940, for example, and make it come out, or wish it to come out, any other way. This is for one purely subjective reason: I don't care about the loss of the British Empire, and feel that the United States did Britain—but not itself—a large favor by helping to dispossess the British of their colonies. But alone among his contemporaries, Churchill did not denounce the Nazi empire merely as a threat, actual or potential, to the British one. Nor did he speak of it as a depraved but possibly useful ally. He excoriated it as a wicked and nihilistic thing. That appears facile now, but was exceedingly uncommon then. In what was perhaps his best ever speech, delivered to the Commons five days after the Munich agreement, on October 5, 1938, Churchill gave voice to the idea that even a "peace-loving" coexistence with Hitler had something rotten about it. "What I find unendurable is the sense of our country falling into the power, into the orbit and influence of Nazi Germany, and of our existence becoming dependent upon their good will or pleasure."

Those who write mournfully today about the loss of the British Empire must perforce admit that the Tory majority of 1938 proposed to preserve that empire on just those terms. Some saving intuition prompted Churchill to recognize, and to name out loud, the pornographic and catastrophically destructive nature of the foe. Only this redeeming x factor justifies all the rest—the paradoxes and inconsistencies, to be sure, and even the hypocrisy. But then his last political initiative, and his final excuse for declining to make way for a successor, was in 1953-1954, when he reversed course and proposed a major summit with Stalin's heirs to try to avert a cold war. That was, in light of his past, paradoxical and inconsistent and hypocritical also. Yet it hurts to read of the contempt and condescension with which Dwight Eisenhower and John Foster Dulles treated this greathearted effort. Even Best and Jenkins are ruefully at one on this episode. For those then in power the Churchill legend was quite satisfactory as it was, with the instrumental metaphors of Munich and Dunkirk and Fulton always at hand.

Earlier I mentioned the stand of the Greeks in 1940. On October 28 of that year, having received an ultimatum from Mussolini to capitulate or face immediate occupation, they responded with the single word "*Ochi*"— "No!"—and mounted an extraordinary resistance that at first drove the forces of Italian fascism well back into Albania. The day is a national holiday in Greece, and "*Ochi*" can be seen cut into the side of more than one Greek mountain. When the Nazis joined Italy to punish this intransigence, and exerted overwhelming force, a Greek editor wrote an imperishable front-page article saying that Greece, which had once taught men how to live, would now show them how to die. There was much brave mention of Thermopylae and Marathon. It's a good and an inspiring story. However, and in fact, Greece at the time was ruled by a particularly crude homegrown Fascist dictator named Ioannis Metaxas. He almost certainly never uttered the pungent word "*Ochi*,"—replying, rather, to a demarche from the Italian ambassador by saying "*Enfin—c'est la guerre*." The relatively brief Greek holdout led eventually to appalling reprisals and a cruel famine, and made very little difference to the outcome of the war. (Though it is an article of belief among many Greeks that the savagely protracted defense of the island of Crete, invaded from the air where once Daedalus and Icarus had soared, delayed the start of Operation Barbarossa and thus contributed to Hitler's fatal collision with the Russian winter.) The story's ending is distinctly inglorious, with Winston Churchill arriving in liberated Athens in 1944 and ordering the British General Scobie to treat the Red-dominated population as if he were in a conquered city (and meanwhile trading Greece itself for Poland, with Stalin).

Yet would one want to be without that story of Greek defiance, even if it proved illusory, or the defiance futile? People fight, as Kant and Hegel and Nietzsche have emphasized, for dignity and for "recognition" just as much as for their "real" interests. Cold and detached revision has removed the aura of heroism from many luminous and legendary events, including the storming of the Bastille, the fall of the Winter Palace, and the publication of the Emancipation Proclamation. Yet new tales arise continually to replace the exploded ones. We seem to have a need, as a species, for something noble and lofty. The task of criticism could be defined as the civilizing of this need—the appreciation of true decency and heroism as against coercive race legends and blood myths. The application of this winnowing and discriminating process to the Churchill cult is more urgent and more relevant—and more feasible—than any reconsideration of Agincourt or Thermopylae. In common with these epics, though, it will be found to have survived in its Platonic essence, quite independent of any evidence or testimony. On the wall of the folkish cave it retains a refracted light and life of its own. Satirizing the too-much hymned Greek war against the Emperor Darius, Robert Graves once wrote a poem called "The Persian Version," which reduced Marathon to its proper proportion as a fleeting skirmish on an imperial periphery (and, by doing so, slyly and implicitly reinstated it in its impossible glory). Graves's work helped us to see that the antique gods and emperors were mere mammals like ourselves. But it is another of Graves's titles, this time a modern one, that furnishes the necessary condition for future Churchill scholarship.

THE ATLANTIC, APRIL 2002

A Man of

Permanent Contradictions

A review of *The Long Recessional: The Imperial Life of Rudyard Kipling*
by David Gilmour

I n his generous and beautiful elegy for William Butler Yeats, W. H. Auden
affirmed, "Time that is intolerant," nonetheless "Worships language and
forgives / Everyone by whom it lives." Putting this poetic faith to what
he evidently regarded as a strenuous test, he asserted,

> *Time that with this strange excuse*
> *Pardoned Kipling and his views,*
> *And will pardon Paul Claudel,*
> *Pardon him for writing well.*

But the relation between time and tolerance turns out to be more uneasy
than that. When he was alive many critics thought Kipling to be a bad writer,
and also a bullying and jingoistic one, and many readers today agree. Moreover, much of Kipling's work, inarguably, was hasty and poorly written. Dick
Heldar, in *The Light That Failed* (1890), says, "Four-fifths of everybody's work
must be bad," and one feels Kipling speaking more truly than he knew when
his character adds, "But the remnant is worth the trouble for its own sake."
A great deal of his fiction is still a chore or an embarrassment (never mind
the "politics") and he overproduced verse in a quite promiscuous manner,
often for the most short-term and propagandistic motives. The shock effect
of some of Kipling's compositions has actually faded; they now afflict the
reader more with a sense of faint amusement than with horror or disap-
proval. There is the beery sentimentality; the gruff, husky, and rather painful

male bonding; the agonizing affectation of demotic or plebeian speech; the writhe-making racial condescension. But there is also this:

> *What is a woman that you forsake her,*
> *And the hearth-fire and the home-acre,*
> *To go with the old grey Widow-maker?*

I paid a call on Jorge Luis Borges in Buenos Aires in late 1977, and fell into a trap from which I had no desire to escape. He was blind and lonely, and said he liked my voice, and asked me if I would stay and read to him for a while. He knew exactly where on the shelf to find the Kipling, and on what page I would find "Harp Song of the Dane Women."

> *She has no house to lay a guest in—*
> *But one chill bed for all to rest in,*
> *That the pale suns and the stray bergs nest in.*

"Long sips, please—more slowly," the old man beseeched as I reached the lines

> *Yet, when the signs of summer thicken,*
> *And the ice breaks, and the birch-buds quicken,*
> *Yearly you turn from our side, and sicken—*
> *Sicken again for the shouts and the slaughters,—*
> *You steal away to the lapping waters,*
> *And look at your ship in her winter quarters.*

I had never read the poem with such attention before. And, though I knew it expressed something profound and eternal about men and women and warfare, I had not noticed until then that it is made up of Old English words. It was a leathery old aficionado of Anglo-Saxon, sitting in a darkened room many leagues below the Equator, who lovingly drew this to my attention.

Twenty-two years later in Hong Kong, as I witnessed the closing moments of the British Empire, a Royal Guards band struck up the perfect hymn: "The Day Thou Gavest, Lord, Is Ended." Those who do not know this modest yet stirring feature of the Anglican or Episcopalian evensong may also not know the words or the music to "Eternal Father, Strong to Save," sometimes titled "For Those in Peril on the Sea." But if by chance you do know the latter anthem, you can hum the opening staves of Rudyard Kipling's "Recessional."

> *God of our fathers, known of old,*
> *Lord of our far-flung battle-line,*
> *Beneath whose awful Hand we hold*
> *Dominion over palm and pine—*
> *Lord God of Hosts, be with us yet,*
> *Lest we forget—lest we forget!*

When he was living among the whores and shore-leave drunks on the Thames Embankment, by Charing Cross (and writing *The Light That Failed*), Kipling used to go to music halls and pick up the melodies of the masses. When he was keeping company with regiments overseas, he would attend church parade, and attend to the hymnal. During the Boer War he was made to feel slightly uneasy when Sir Arthur Sullivan (partner of Sir William Gilbert) set one of his patriotic doggerels to music. But his entire success as a bard derived from the ability to shift between Low and High Church, so to speak. He was a hit with the troops and the gallery because of the very vulgarity that Max Beerbohm despised, Oscar Wilde rather envied, and Henry James could only admire. But he was also, because of his capacity for sonority and high-mindedness, the chosen poet of the royal family and the *Times*. (In my opinion, he declined the laureateship so that he could keep one foot in each camp.)

There is something about twilight that appeals to the English, and that expresses itself in the Beating of the Retreat, the singing of "Abide With Me," the bugles calling the Last Post, the shades lengthening over cloisters and cricket grounds, and the melancholy "drawing-down of blinds" so perfectly caught by Wilfred Owen. "Recessional"—the dying music of the evensong choir as it withdraws—has all this netted in one word. To those born or brought up in England after 1914, let alone 1945, the sense of a waning day is part of the assumed historical outcome. It was Kipling's achievement to have sounded this sad, admonishing note during the imperial midday, and to have conveyed the premonition among his hearers that dusk was nearer than they had thought. David Gilmour's title is therefore exceptionally well chosen, because between the first chill of realization and the eventual recognition there falls—or fell—a shadow.

Gilmour's admirable book is written slightly too much on the defensive. He maintains that Kipling was not, as the smug moderns believe, a racist or an imperialist or a sadist or an anti-Semite or a repressed homosexual—and there is sound evidence, in his writing and in his life, to counter any such simplistic interpretations. But there is also much evidence, drawn from the same sources, to suggest that Kipling *was* all of the above. It is far preferable to approach this author, as Gilmour often does, as a man of permanent contradictions.

Kipling's most celebrated poem, which is also the proof of his durability as a poet who can above all else be recited, is "If—." The whole scheme is based on the reconciliation of opposites.

> *If you can dream—and not make dreams your master;*
> *If you can think—and not make thoughts your aim;*
> *If you can meet with Triumph and Disaster*
> *And treat those two impostors just the same;*

And (more significant for Kipling's own trajectory)

> *If you can talk with crowds and keep your virtue,*
> *Or walk with Kings—nor lose the common touch . . .*

In Kipling's lifetime this became the favorite poem of José Antonio Primo de Rivera, the founder of Spanish fascism, and of President Woodrow Wilson. It was apparently written in honor of Leander Starr Jameson, a British colonial pirate who led an aggressive raid into Boer territory, precipitating the horrible South African war by acting as a "deniable" provocateur for Cecil Rhodes. Gilmour comments dryly that the lines in commendation of fortitude and stoicism sat ill with "the man who blundered impatiently into the Transvaal, surrendered rather quickly when surrounded by armed Boers, and was led weeping into captivity." But perhaps those very lines, which illustrate T. S. Eliot's gallant distinction between "verse" and "poetry" (with Kipling just on the right side of the demarcation), were inscribed with these short-comings in mind.

Robert Philip Hanssen, meet Aldrich Ames, Kim Philby, Greville Wynne, and Gordon Lonsdale. Kipling's most successful and polished achievement in prose, *Kim* (1901), is also dependent on the idea of a double life. The boy is an orphan, raised to believe he is half-caste, and is "passing" for Indian. (His father was an Irish soldier and his mother, we learn, a white camp follower.) The whole action of the story hangs on dissimulation and duality. Some friends of mine once employed the epigraph to Chapter Eight as an epigraph to a study of Kim Philby, the most accomplished double agent of all time.

> *Much I owe to the Lands that grew—*
> *More to the Lives that fed—*
> *But most to Allah Who gave me two*
> *Separate sides to my head.*

This is drawn from a Kipling poem titled "The Two-Sided Man." As if to underline its message, Kipling added,

> *I would go without shirt or shoe,*
> *Friend, tobacco or bread,*
> *Sooner than lose for a minute the two*
> *Separate sides of my head!*

If one were to assemble a balance sheet of Kipling's own explicit contradictions, it would necessarily include his close relationship with the Bible and the hymnal, and his caustic anti-clericalism; his staunch Anglo nationalism, and his feeling that England itself was petty and parochial; his dislike of nonwhite peoples, and his belief that they were more honest and courageous; his love-hate relationship with the Irish; his contempt, and deep admiration, for the United States; his respect for the working class, and his detestation of the labor movement; his exaltation of the empire, and his conviction that its works were vain and transient.

A similar approach could be taken to the study of Kipling's psyche. From childhood he was both repelled and attracted by cruelty. He manifested an extreme fear and loathing of homosexuality—vulgarly regarded as telltale. (Gilmour flatly dismisses Martin Seymour-Smith's suggestion that Kipling was gay, but Angus Wilson was probably right in supposing him to have been in love with the young writer Wolcott Balestier, whose sudden and early death appeared to drive him to distraction. Those friends, including Henry James, who attended his bizarre, hasty wedding to Wolcott's mannish sister Caroline—where it might almost be said that the funeral baked meats for the brother did coldly furnish forth the marriage table—were somewhat at a loss to explain it any other way.) Ultimately, Kipling's two greatest literary and emotional attainments—the ability to evoke childhood and the capacity to ennoble imperialism—contradicted themselves too flatly and painfully, and culminated in the shattering sacrifice of his beloved son, John, on the Western Front in 1915. This was enough inner contradiction for several lifetimes.

One learns from Gilmour that Kipling's first Indian stories, *Plain Tales From the Hills* (1888), were considered subversive in their day. E. M. Forster's *A Passage to India* still lay in the future, with its even more unsparing depictions of racial and sexual hypocrisy, but Lord Curzon, the viceroy and governor-general of India, felt obliged to soothe Queen Victoria by countering "the unfair and rather malevolent impressions that have gone abroad and have received some colour from the too cynical stories of Rudyard Kipling." It is important to note also that part of Kipling's animus against the Christian missionaries in India arose from his indignation at their destructive puritanism. Anglican clerics and pious generals forbade legalized prostitution for British soldiers, which led inevitably to a heroic rise in the incidence of venereal disease; Kipling later wrote that he wished he "might have six hundred priests— Bishops of the Establishment for choice—to handle for six months precisely as the soldiers of my youth were handled." Kim, it is fairly obvious from the opening passages of the story, has done some discreet pimping in Lahore in his time. The facts of life and the sexual motive are not hidden from our gaze as we follow him along the Grand Trunk Road (Forster regarded this as the best writing any Englishman had done on India), where Kim and his lama later meet a Church of England clergyman who looks out "with the triple-ringed uninterest of the creed that lumps nine-tenths of the world under the title of 'heathen.' "

Kipling, it could be argued, did not like it when other people patronized Indians. But that did not inhibit him from patronizing them himself. His distaste for Hinduism in particular—like most British occupiers, he preferred Muslims—overstepped the bounds of his ostensible objection to forced marriage and became vitriolic. He drew many an unkind picture of the ways in which educated Indians tried to ape British customs. And, though he reserved to himself the right to praise Indians as equals ("Gunga Din" is the best-known example), he was always a ferocious and intemperate foe of any talk of self-government, let alone independence. To his ineffaceable shame, he even applauded General Dyer's massacre of unarmed demonstrators in the city of Amritsar in 1919, though one must remember that he had become unhinged by World War I. Gilmour is quite right to argue that the phrase "lesser breeds without the Law," in "Recessional," is not a racial reference but an allusion to the pagan arrogance of powers like Germany. He is equally correct in saying that there is no bow to apartheid in the lines about "East is East, and West is West, and never the twain shall meet"—lines that actually celebrate mutual respect. However, it is impossible to maintain that the essence of "The White Man's Burden" is not a belief in the concept of race-childhood, and therefore in the supposed corollary of racial tutelage, even if this stern condescension did mandate a self-sacrificing commitment and a responsibility on the part of the "white man."

A comparable ambivalence is to be found when we see Kipling writing about his countrymen. In one breath the British or the English are the descendants of Saxon and Dane and Norman, and the heirs to a new Rome. In another they are an effete breed given overmuch to mindless games ("the flannelled fools at the wicket or the muddied oafs at the goals") and too lazy to do much more than draw their dividends. In *Stalky & Co.* (1899) the boys mock and jeer at a Tory politician—"an impeccable Conservative"—who comes to orate and to find recruits. The speaker presumes that many of them desire no more than the heady experience of "leading their men against the bullets of England's foes." The sour view of his youthful audience is that he is simply a "Jelly-bellied Flag-flapper." Yet Kipling himself was a fierce partisan of conscription, a frequent speaker at rallies for recruitment, a zealot for Baden-Powell's Boy Scout ethos, and a rabble-rouser for the most flag-flapping faction in British history, the Ulster Orange loyalists. It's a testimony to his art that he could put the opposite case with equal flair, but Gilmour is dead wrong in trying to acquit him of the charge of chauvinism.

Yet where Kipling excelled—and where he most deserves praise and respect—was in enjoining the British to avoid the very hubris that he had helped to inspire in them. His "Recessional" is only the best-known and most hauntingly written of many such second thoughts.

> *Far-called, our navies melt away;*
> *On dune and headland sinks the fire:*
> *Lo, all our pomp of yesterday*
> *Is one with Nineveh and Tyre!*

There is also "The Lesson," a poem designed to rub in the experience of defeat in Africa, and (though it is abysmal as poetry) "Fuzzy-Wuzzy," a tribute to the fighting qualities of the Sudanese. "Arithmetic on the Frontier" is a memorable, sardonic warning against imperial overstretch in Afghanistan. Even in some of his verses from World War I—his most gung-ho and overwrought period—Kipling tried to hedge himself and his cause and to avoid overweening arrogance. Though he much esteemed his friend Cecil Rhodes, he was cautious about echoing Rhodes's grandiose fantasies of annexation and expansion. (In two short stories, though, he depicts a scheme to repopulate Kashmir with English and Eurasian settlers—a reverie that now makes one reflect.) It is also notable that he had a lifelong distrust of Winston Churchill, despite their many points of rhetorical and political agreement about India, Ireland, and Germany. Here again it may be that when listening to another alarmist patriot, Kipling had the grace and integrity to suspect his own motives and effects as well as the other's. This capacity, as he might himself have put it, is not given to all men.

A book to study in tandem with Gilmour's would be George Dangerfield's small masterpiece *The Strange Death of Liberal England* (1935). In the first fourteen years of the twentieth century British politics was almost completely remade by the three forces of organized labor, Irish nationalism, and female suffrage. This triumvirate, representing a potential new majority as well as a new democratic ethos, was checked and thrown back by the cataclysmic and catastrophic outbreak of a continental war. (It still gives me a tremor to recall that although the vote on Irish Home Rule passed Parliament in 1914, it was not enacted, owing to World War I.) The figure of Rudyard Kipling could be taken as the emblematic reactionary of this period, and Dangerfield deployed him as such on at least one occasion. Though, by still another paradox, Kipling himself was partly the product of liberal England. He was related on his mother's side to the Pre-Raphaelite painter Edward Burne-Jones, and his aunt Georgiana Burne-Jones had rescued him from the appalling cruelty of the boardinghouse described in "Baa, Baa, Black Sheep," his fictionalized memoir of childhood misery and deprivation. Kipling's contempt for the aesthetes and socialists who had cared for him in extremity was sometimes expressed in an exaggerated distaste for the William Morris types and the "arty" in general. But he also loathed and despised the coal miners and railwaymen who were, as he saw it, undermining orderly society. This banal prejudice did not "hurt him into poetry," as Auden memorably said that Ireland had done for Yeats. The Irish question stirred Kipling to produce some of the worst political verse ever written. It also moved him to support a shameful Tory mutiny against parliamentary rule. His speeches and poems from this period are hysterical in their anti-Catholicism and their invocation of blood and conspiracy. This is from "Ulster," published in April of 1912, as the Orange militias were arming and drilling to defy the vote that would have gone against them.

We know the wars prepared
On every peaceful home,
We know the hells declared
For such as serve not Rome—

This was a direct negation of the core of "Recessional": if there was one colony where the British had every need to be modest about their conduct (and also every reason to be so), it was surely Ireland.

Yet when Kipling needed a romantic or daredevil or charmingly coura-geous character in fiction or ballad, he almost unfailingly selected an Irishman (or at any rate an Irish name). This stock-in-trade stuff—either the Hibernian broth of a boy or the shifty, priest-ridden thug—is to be con-demned, if only as a cliché, or perhaps better say two clichés. The tension between the two became acute for Kipling himself when his only son was denied a commission in the army in 1914—he had inherited his father's extremely poor eyesight—but managed with paternal string-pulling to find a risky place with the Irish Guards. After the boy's death Kipling forced himself to write the official history of the regiment, as a form of atonement. He knew an irony, or a contradiction, when it bit hard enough.

Deeply hostile to the extension of the franchise, he composed one of his better efforts—"The Female of the Species"—as a sort of teasing satire. (Some say it was written as a reply to the female suffrage movement.) Like many quasi-misogynists, Kipling took refuge in the idea of woman as stern, pure, majestic, and decisive: "more deadly than the male." It was this innate, lethal superiority, he insisted, that debarred women from the higher counsels of state, where detachment, reason, and compromise were required. So it's somehow unsurprising that when war came, he was especially fond of citing rape victims in Belgium as the prime reason why English boys should flock to the colors and refuse all talk of peace.

The paradox underlying all of Kipling's work, whether it be his letters, his poetry, or his stories, is a horror of democracy combined with an exaltation of the common man. He always ostensibly preferred the grunt or the ranker to the officer, the humble colonial servant to the viceroy, the stoker and the sailor to the admiral. His songs about engineers and artificers—of which "McAndrew's Hymn" is a sterling example—show, moreover, a real appreciation of modernity and innovation, and may explain why he attracted the attention of the Nobel committee when, as critics sniffed, Swinburne, Meredith, and Hardy were still alive, and a "blacksmith" should not have been preferred to a "goldsmith." Probably no compliment could have delighted him more. Yet in his heart he disliked industrialism and the mass civilization that it brought in its smoky train.

This paradox extended to his odd encounter with America—alternately hailed as young, brash, and experimental, and excoriated as vulgar, cynical, and acquisitive. It can't be said that Kipling was the first Englishman to register this contrast, or to fail to reconcile it, but his oscillations were unusually volatile. In different moods he could compose a poem accusing the rebels of 1776 of stabbing the motherland in the back or a paean to the magnificence of Teddy Roosevelt. He affected to adore Mark Twain, and then wrote a virtual manifesto for Twain's least favorite cause, the Spanish-American War of 1898 (that was "The White Man's Burden": an eloquent plea for the colonization of the Philippines). Hoping, like Cecil Rhodes, for the reclamation of America as a part of Anglo-Saxondom, he helped to administer the famous scholarships. But in a later poem, "The Question," he more or less accused the United States of betraying civilization by following Wilsonian principles.

Gilmour is obviously right to stress the "Roman" element in Kipling. He believed that the barbarians were always mustering on the frontier, and that order and good government could be maintained only by a stoic, disciplined, self-conscious, and self-sacrificing minority. This was both a saving solution for the outlying provinces of the empire and an insurance against sloth and corruption and decay at home. One of his most celebrated lines inquires, "What should they know of England who only England know?" Thus Kipling's most agonizing paradox was his gnawing fear that the cost of empire would prove too great for the complacent and selfish English, and that they would throw away what they had won. (In a further fold of contradiction, he also disliked the bloodlust of both the London press and the stay-at-home patriots: a contempt amply, and equally, expressed in *The Light That Failed.*) He always represented the empire as a drain and a sacrifice. The idea that it could make a profit, or was an economic system at all, never really engaged his interest. What caught and held his attention was the figure of the lone white district officer, holding the line against flood and cholera and rescuing resentful "natives" who would never be grateful. One such civil servant, John Holden in "Without Benefit of Clergy," becomes involved with a Muslim woman and reflects, "The drawbacks of a double life are manifold." In one of the finer poems, "The Roman Centurion's Song," a recalled officer begs to be allowed to "stay on" as the legions withdraw, and help continue to civilize the British.

Kipling was true to this stern ideal in his way. He knew that his beloved son was essentially unfit for military service, yet he felt it would be indecent to hold him out of the ranks when other boys were going. But the long-awaited conflict with Germany, and young John's consequent death, nearly abolished his sense of balance and proportion, and therefore of fruitful contradiction. The notorious short story "Mary Postgate," in which a shriveled spinster experiences an orgasmic charge after deliberately refusing help to a wounded German airman, is entirely lacking in the chiaroscuro of the Indian tales; it shows us Kipling giving utter vent to the distraught, repressed, and sadistic side of his nature.

When I was a schoolboy in England, the old bound volumes of Kipling in the library had gilt swastikas embossed on their covers. The symbol's "hooks" were left-handed, as opposed to the right-handed ones of the Nazi *hakenkreuz*, but for a boy growing up after 1945 the shock of encountering the emblem at all was a memorable one. I later learned that in the mid-1930s Kipling had caused this "signature" to be removed from all his future editions. Having initially sympathized with some of the early European fascist movements, he wanted to express his repudiation of Hitlerism (or "the Hun," as he would perhaps have preferred to say), and wanted no part in tainting the ancient Indian rune by association. In its origin it is a Hindu and Jain symbol for light, and well worth rescuing.

To return to where I began: Kipling was not long gone when Auden wrote his farewell to Yeats, the closing staves of which begin, "Earth, receive an honored guest: William Yeats is laid to rest." In "The Charm" Kipling had written, "Take of English earth as much / As either hand may rightly clutch." This near repetition of meter was possibly a compliment of a kind, however subconscious. After closing Gilmour, I picked up *Kim* and re-read it in one session, marveling again at how fine it is. Bengali babus are mocked gently in what we might now call a "stereotypical" way, but the English are painted from the viewpoint of the conquered, and the joke is very often at their expense. The intimacies of racism are well understood: when Colonel Creighton tells Kim to beware of white boys "who despise the black men," Kim reflects that this hatred is most vile when expressed by half-castes. And then I came across this everyday police problem in the Great Game: "It was a wry-necked matter of unauthorised and incendiary correspondence between a person who claimed to be the ultimate authority in all matters of the Mohammedan religion throughout the world, and a younger member of a royal house who had been brought to book for kidnapping women within British territory."

It's all there: the image of the jihad megalomaniac combined with that of a spoiled and sulky princeling (plus Kipling's perhaps deliberate use of the disrespectful term "Mohammedan"). It gave me a vertiginous feeling to be reading this at a moment when British soldiers, self-consciously shouldering an Anglo-American burden, were back on the Afghan side of the forbidding Khyber Pass—this time neither as conscripts nor as conquerors.

THE ATLANTIC, JUNE 2002

THE OLD MAN*

Two images have been with me throughout the writing of this essay. Between them they seem to show the alternative paths for the intellectual. The one is of J. M. Keynes, the other of Leon Trotsky. Both were obviously men of attractive personality and great natural gifts. The one the intellectual guardian of the established order, providing new policies and theories of manipulation to keep our society in what he took to be economic trim, and making a personal fortune in the process. The other, outcast as a revolutionary from Russia both under the Tsar and under Stalin, providing throughout his life a defense of human activity, of the powers of conscious and rational human effort. I think of them at the end, Keynes with his peerage, Trotsky with an icepick in his skull. They are the twin lives between which intellectual choice in our society lies.

—ALASDAIR MACINTYRE, "BREAKING THE CHAINS OF REASON,"
IN *OUT OF APATHY* (1960)

Yet, precisely like a personage in classical tragedy, Trotsky did not act to arrest, to defeat, the dangers he foresaw. Clairvoyance and policy drew apart, as if doom, seen as a historical process, had its irresistible fascination. He stumbled on, majestic. One thinks of Eteocles going clear-sighted to the death gate in Seven Against Thebes, *refusing the plea of the chorus for evasion or liberty of action:*

> *We are already past the care of gods.*
> *For them our death is the*
> *admirable offering.*
> *Why then delay, fawning upon*
> *our doom?*

—GEORGE STEINER, "TROTSKY AND THE TRAGIC IMAGINATION" (1966)

Alasdair MacIntyre and George Steiner—the authors, respectively, of *After Virtue* and *Antigones*—have both evolved a good deal since they wrote those lines. But if either of them was again to need a figure to represent dissent and defiance, or the fusion of the man of ideas with the man of action, or the wandering internationalist, he might be drawn once more to the character of Trotsky. Of no other participant in the Bolshevik-Marxist battles of the twentieth century could this really be said to be the case. Lenin is stranded in time and place, as are Mao and Ho Chi Minh. Stalin is

*A review of *The Prophet Armed: Trotsky 1879—1921; The Prophet Unarmed: Trotsky 1921–1929; and The Prophet Outcast: Trotsky 1929–1940* by Isaac Deutscher.

annexed to the general study of pathological dictatorship. Combative and brilliant intellectuals such as Rosa Luxemburg, Antonio Gramsci, and Nikolai Bukharin are for specialists, and were localized before they were defeated. Fidel Castro has at least made it into the twenty-first century, but at the price of becoming a bloated and theatrical caricature. Only Che Guevara retains a hint of charisma, and he made no contribution whatsoever to the battle of theories and ideas.

The three succeeding portraits on the covers of this trilogy (which originally appeared volume by volume in 1954, 1959, and 1963) show the ardent young radical journalist and activist, the more mature Soviet tactician and commander of the Red Army, and the snowy-headed exiled sage. To have had a part in two revolutions, wrote Thomas Paine, was to have lived to some purpose. Trotsky took a leading part in the Russian revolutions of 1905 and 1917, and also in many other political and military upheavals, from the Balkans to China, and was perhaps the most prescient writer of his day in warning of the true menace of National Socialism. Yet his most enduring and tenacious battle was against the monstrous regime that had resulted from his earlier exertions.

It is this, combined with the revolutionary credentials that he possessed, that helps explain the large footprint of Trotsky and Trotskyism among intellectuals. To start with a few American examples, Trotsky makes a magnetizing appearance in Saul Bellow's *The Adventures of Augie March*. He caused Mary McCarthy to write one of her most penetrating essays ("My Confession"), about herd behavior in the radical smart set. Clement Greenberg partly founded his seminal article "Avant-Garde and Kitsch" on a passage from Trotsky's *Literature and Revolution*. Norman Mailer acknowledges as his own political inspiration a Trotskisant maverick named Jean Malaquais. Shift the scene a little, and we have no difficulty deciphering the figure of Emmanuel Goldstein in Orwell's *Nineteen Eighty-four*, or in recognizing the secret "book within a book" in that novel (*The Theory and Practice of Oligarchical Collectivism*), as a derivative of Trotsky's *Revolution Betrayed*. Nearer the present time, the hero of Milan Kundera's *The Joke* has only to write "Long Live Trotsky!" on a postcard in order to find out precisely how, why, and when a "joke" under communism has gone too far.

Nor was this the only nervous establishment that found him a specter difficult to exorcise. Winston Churchill, in an acidulated portrait in *Great*

Contemporaries, depicted Trotsky even in impotent exile as having been the "ogre" of international subversion. (He perhaps could not forgive one of the two men to have outgeneraled him in the field, the other being Kemal Atatürk.) A. J. P. Taylor tells the story of how an Austro-Hungarian minister, upon being warned by a nervous colleague that a too-precipitate war with Russia in 1914 might mean revolution, demanded to know who would lead this revolution: "Herr Trotsky of the Café Centrale?" (Trotsky's time in the cafés of Vienna was not wasted.) In late 1939 the French ambassador Robert Coulondre had his last meeting with Hitler before the coming of war. The Führer was in a boastful mood, Coulondre recalled in his memoir, having just concluded a pact with Stalin, and spoke of the inevitability of further triumphs. The ambassador sought to sober him by warning of the unintended consequences of conflict. "You are thinking of yourself as victor," Coulondre said, "but have you given thought to another possibility—that the victor may be Trotsky?" Hitler leaped to his feet, as if "he had been hit in the pit of the stomach," and yelled that this threat was reason enough in itself for Britain and France to capitulate at once. It would be amusing to know if Churchill ever learned of this conversation.

Most haunting of all, perhaps, was the moment when Trotsky, hounded from country to country, was ordered by the Norwegian government in 1936 to move on. An agitation against him had been started by Moscow's agents, who had not yet made their pact with Hitler, and by Vidkun Quisling, the leader of the Norwegian Fascists, whose name would later become synonymous with collaboration. The invertebrate Social-Democratic government of Trygve Lie, who was subsequently the founding secretary-general of the United Nations, caved in and told Trotsky to stop writing or else submit to deportation. Trotsky told these gentlemen,

> This is your first act of surrender to Nazism in your own country. You will pay for this. You think yourselves secure and free to deal with a political exile as you please. But the day is near—remember this!—the day is near when the Nazis will drive you from your country, all of you.

"After less than four years," as Isaac Deutscher records in relating this episode, "the same government had indeed to flee from Norway before the

Nazi invasion; and as the Ministers and their aged King Haakon stood on the coast, huddled together and waiting anxiously for a boat that was to take them to England, they recalled with awe Trotsky's words as a prophet's curse come true."

I find I want to add Deutscher's comment on the memoir of Ambassador Coulondre mentioned above: "Thus, the master of the Third Reich and the envoy of the Third Republic, in their last manoeuvres, during the last hours of peace, sought to intimidate each other, and each other's governments, by invoking the name of the lonely outcast trapped and immured at the far end of the world." This is majestic and sonorous; written in the stern and judging manner of the Talmudic scholar that Deutscher had been and the Marxist polymath that he became, and of Thomas Carlyle, whose study of Cromwell he so esteemed. (One must also marvel at the way in which Deutscher mastered the English language almost as late in life as his fellow Pole Joseph Conrad.) The *Prophet* trilogy strives to reconcile the materialist conception of history with the importance of the "great man," and though the trope of prophecy armed and unarmed is taken from the sixth chapter of Machiavelli's *Prince*, it would be a dull ear that did not also detect the cadences of the Pentateuch.

To re-read this magnificent trilogy today, however, is to be overcome by a sense of melancholy and waste. Writing just as official "de-Stalinization" was spreading across Russia and Eastern Europe, Isaac Deutscher was sure that Trotsky would be vindicated by history and rehabilitated in the Communist world. Nothing of the sort was to happen: communism proved itself able to adapt but not to reform, and "Trotskyism" remained one of the few unpardonable heresies of which a dissident on the other side of the Iron Curtain could be accused. Deutscher himself could not abandon the idea that the nations of the Warsaw Pact represented some version of progress—a quasi new order worth defending until the day when the workers recovered their senses and demanded "real" Bolshevism instead. Of the actual rebellions against Stalinism, in East Germany, Hungary, and Poland, he was contemptuous, writing "Eastern Europe found itself almost on the brink of bourgeois restoration at the end of the Stalin era; and only Soviet armed power (or the threat) stopped it there."

In the theoretical magazine of the post-Trotskyist *groupuscule* of which I was once a member, a learned commentary on this and other writings of his appeared, titled "The End of the Road: Deutscher's Capitulation to Stalinism." Deutscher did not live to see the events of 1968 in Czechoslovakia (he died in the fall of 1967), but I think by then he might have preferred even "bourgeois restoration" to the communism of the Panzers.

Thus this mighty work of reflection and engagement is to a large extent the record of great debates that apparently no longer matter to us. The split between Menshevik and Bolshevik, the dispute over collectivization and industrialization, the polemics concerning Karl Kautsky and Georgi Plekhanov and Otto Bauer—all of these have come to appear as arcane as the strife over the Nicene and Athanasian Creeds. There are some haunting and visceral moments to be added to the ones I cited above: the massacre of the oppositionists in the gulag and the hunting down of Trotsky's most distant relatives was exhaustively examined by Deutscher long before many modern historians had taken the full measure of Stalinism. And two major episodes, one of them under-represented and one of them described beautifully, repay more-intense scrutiny.

The first of these is Trotsky's coverage of the Balkan Wars of 1912–1913. Writing at a time when Titoism appeared secure, Deutscher devoted little space to the ethno-nationalist bloodbaths that had convulsed the region and helped to bring on the great catastrophe of the First World War. He gave a rather spare account of Trotsky's work in the area, which was undertaken as a journalistic project for a liberal Russian newspaper at a time when Trotsky himself had not become a full-fledged Bolshevik. These dispatches from the front lines in Serbia, Romania, and Bulgaria are actually among the finest war-correspondent files of all time. Trotsky was first of all most suspicious of the pan-Slavic prejudices of his "own" side, and hastened to inform Russian readers of the cruelties inflicted by the people of the Orthodox cross on the people of the Turkish crescent. He lampooned Russian and Bulgarian chauvinism as it had not been lampooned since Tolstoy ridiculed it in *Anna Karenina*. (The great examples of Russian literature were never far from his mind, though I can't be sure of any direct influence in this case.) But when the tide went the other way, and it was the turn of Bulgarians to suffer, he was no less trenchant and truthful. He saw that all parties in the conflict were being manipulated by the "Great" Powers in a cynical rehearsal for a larger war, and he believed that in all the contending countries there were healthy democratic and socialist elements that could rise above crudity and superstition. At the time, this was not merely a sentimental opinion. There actually were such forces. Their panic and capitulation in 1914, and the Europe-wide surrender of the Social Democrats to kings and emperors and generals, was for Trotsky the greatest imaginable tragedy, even if it did provide the opportunity for revolution.

Trotsky's second great moral moment was to occur during a repeat performance of this capitulation, which occurred nearly two decades later. As Hitler was advancing toward power in Germany, the European left once again abandoned its nerve and its principles, and declined to make common cause. The most depraved offender was Stalin's Communist International, which insisted that the Social Democrats were a greater enemy than the Nazis, and which implied that a victory by Hitler would merely clear the way for a Communist triumph. In a series of articles that really do vibrate with the tones of Cassandra, Trotsky inveighed against this mixture of ugly realpolitik and cretinous irresponsibility. The late Irving Howe once described those articles collectively as the finest polemic of all time. I am not sure that I would go so far, but it is very difficult to re-read them even today without a tingling in the scalp and a lump in the throat. Better than Freud or Reich (or Churchill), Trotsky intuited the sheer psychopathic element that underlay the mass appeal of fascism. Much of what he wrote was by analogy, and reflected his old obsession with the decay of the French Revolution ("Fascism is a caricature of Jacobinism"). But as the full seizure of power by the Nazis became imminent, and as Stalin colluded with it more and more openly, he abandoned mere class analysis, as in the following passage:

> Today, not only in peasant homes but also in the city sky-scrapers, there lives alongside the twentieth century the tenth or thirteenth. A hundred million people use electricity and still believe in the magic power of signs and exorcism . . . What inexhaustible reserves they possess of darkness, ignorance and savagery! Despair has raised them to their feet; fascism has given them the banner. Everything that should have been eliminated from the national organism in the . . . course of

the unhindered development of society comes out today gushing from the throat: capitalist society is puking up the undigested barbarism. Such is the physiology of National Socialism.

Trotsky would have scorned to stress his own Jewishness in this situation. When he wrote that "Einstein has been obliged to pitch his tent outside the boundaries of Germany," he was alluding to the vulgar Nazi contempt for disinterested, rational scientific endeavor. But he partly understood that anti-Semitism was a harbinger, or predictive symptom, of something much worse than unchecked warfare. He had experienced the same premonitions in some of Stalin's viler attacks on him. Now, he thought, there was a real danger of a war not of mass destruction alone but of mass extermination.

His essays from this terrifying moment are worth re-reading not just for their prescience. (When Neville Chamberlain later signed a deal with Hitler at Munich, Trotsky was the only one to predict that this would lead directly to another pact—the one between Hitler and Stalin.) They are above all a moral warning against the crass mentality of moral equivalence. He wrote, "The wiseacres who claim that they see no difference between Bruning and Hitler are in fact saying: it makes no difference whether our organizations exist or whether they are already destroyed. Beneath this pseudo-radical verbiage hides the most sordid passivity."

Deutscher was so committed to the defense of Trotsky's honor, in this desperate situation and in the ones that preceded and followed it, that he could never quite accept the obvious: Trotsky was so much an intellectual that in the final analysis, Marxism was not quite enough for him. He always had the Russian classics in mind, and though these did seem to invoke the committed life as the highest calling, they also supplied ample warning of defeat and disappointment, if not despair. George Steiner cites a favorite passage of mine from Trotsky's *History of the Russian Revolution*. It describes one of his escapes from Siberian exile, in which he succeeded in boarding a train under his real name, Lev Davidovitch Bronstein.

In my hands, I had a copy of the *Iliad* in the Russian hexameter of Gnyeditch; in my pocket, a passport made out in the name of Trotsky, which I wrote in it at random, without even imagining that it would become my name for the rest of my life . . . Throughout the journey, the entire car full of passengers drank tea and ate cheap Siberian buns. I read the hexameters and dreamed of the life abroad. The escape proved to be quite without romantic glamour; it dissolved into nothing but an endless drinking of tea.

History, too, might have endings and ironies that are simply inscrutable, or that do not yield to any known dialectic. In spite of the most appalling discouragements and reverses and persecution, Trotsky did continue almost to the end in a belief that the workers would rise again, and that Hitlerism and Stalinism and imperialism would be overthrown by a self-aware and emancipated class. It was this that led him to his only truly banal or farcical initiative: the proclamation of a Fourth International to succeed the Social-Democratic and Communist ones. But at the very end of his life, cut off in Mexico and aware of his own declining health, he admitted, after the outbreak of the Second World War, that the conflict might just end without a socialist revolution. In that event the whole Marxist-Leninist project would have to be abandoned:

> We would be compelled to acknowledge that [Stalinism] was rooted not in the backwardness of the country and not in the imperialist environment, but in the congenital incapacity of the proletariat to become a ruling class. Then it would be necessary to establish in retrospect that . . . the present USSR was the precursor of a new and universal system of exploitation.

Being Trotsky, he could not admit that in the event socialism "petered out as a Utopia," there would be nothing left worth fighting for. On the contrary, "it is self-evident that a new minimum program would be required—to defend the interests of the slaves of the totalitarian bureaucratic system."

Isaac Deutscher disapproved so much of this closing statement—it came only months before Stalin's envoys of murder got past Trotsky's few dedicated bodyguards—that he almost failed to cite it, and shrouded it in his own verbiage about new "cycles" of postwar revolution, to be set in motion by Stalin's absorption of Eastern Europe. Professor George Lichtheim, who did unearth the article and who quoted it in an essay critical of Deutscher in 1964, went on to say that although Trotsky himself retained an element of grandeur, Trotskyism was completely finished as a political phenomenon, even a marginal one.

In point of fact, Trotskyism, or a variant of it, did have a brief blaze of revival in the Europe-wide *annus mirabilis* of 1968. The goateed face of "the Old Man" was on banners and posters as the Fifth Republic of Charles de Gaulle was shivered and shaken, and as worse dictators in Spain, Portugal, and Greece were assailed. That year there were also active Trotskyists in the seminal stages of the worldwide movement against the Vietnam War, and in the civil-rights campaign that put an end to the long domination of Orange Unionism in Northern Ireland. None of these activists had much in the way of a lasting effect. But the historical record ought to show that they exerted a certain force in Eastern Europe as well. The two best-known intellectual dissidents of the Polish movement of 1968, Jacek Kuron and Karel Modzelewski, both had "Trotskyist" pasts, and both went on to help form the KOR (Workers Defense Committee), which became the nucleus of Solidarnosc. In Czechoslovakia the Trotskyist Petr Uhl was the longest-serving political prisoner of the Red Army's occupation regime, and earned wide respect for his courage and principle. When the longest-serving Yugoslav detainee—a Kosovar—was released, he proposed naming a street in Pristina after Trotsky, because of the latter's principled defense of Albanian minority rights: this street would have been the only one in Europe so named. A couple of years ago I had a reminiscent lunch with Adam Michnik, one of the intellectual inspirations of the 1989 transition and a distinguished figure in the new Poland, and we compared and contrasted the activity of various Trotsky-ish sects in the events that leveled the Berlin Wall. It wasn't a completely quixotic or ironic conversation; the epigones of the Old Man had, partly inadvertently, carried out his final wish by taking part at last in a successful revolution—against communism.

Even today a faint, saintly penumbra still emanates from the Old Man. Where once the Stalinist press and propaganda machine employed the curse of Trotskyism to criminalize and defame the "rotten elements" and "rootless cosmopolitans," now the tribunes of the isolationist right level the same charge at neoconservatives and the supporters of regime change. In Patrick Buchanan's vituperations, and in a plethora of related attacks on a hidden American "cabal," it is openly said that the cunning members of a certain ethnic minority are up to their old tricks of "permanent revolution," and even that the arcane figure of Leo Strauss is the partial reincarnation of Trotsky. Intended as a mortal insult, and wildly, not to say laughably, mistaken in point of any theoretical resemblance, this charge might yet have a faint tincture of interest to it. As Alan Wald helped demonstrate in his brilliant if orthodox 1987 study *The New York Intellectuals: The Rise and Decline of the Anti-Stalinist Left From the 1930s to the 1980s,* there is an occluded relationship between Trotsky and the founding editors of *Commentary, Dissent, The Public Interest,* and *Partisan Review.* Harold Isaac's *The Tragedy of the Chinese Revolution*— once the best-known book in America on a seismic event—was first published in 1938 with an introduction by Trotsky himself. (It was later, in less congenial times, republished without that contribution.) If any young scholar were now possessed of equivalent daring, a biography of the protean, scintillating revolutionary and cold war sage Max Schachtman could be an intellectual Rosetta stone for the story of mental and moral combat in the modern American mind. Sometimes the kinship is merely an anecdotal or autobiographical one: Saul Bellow was once an admirer of Trotsky's and became close to Allan Bloom; the philosopher Martin Diamond did move from Trotskyism to Straussianism. In other instances the relationship is more paradoxical: in 1989 the Communist world was convulsed by a revolution from below, whereas "revolution from above" (Trotsky's inadequately satirical comment on Stalinism) might be a closer description of the design, at least, of the American intervention in Iraq.

Until we are done with the ironies of history (because they will never be done with us), the image of Trotsky will not dissipate. Of all his essays, the one that has stayed longest with me is "The Struggle for Cultured Speech," a little-known commentary on the vileness and obscenity of Russian cursing, full as this was of the accreted inheritance of serfdom and racism and self-hatred. Of all the descriptions we have of Trotsky, the most vivid is that furnished by Isaac Babel in his story "Line and Color," where at the close of a fatuous speech from Kerensky, Trotsky mounts the podium, twists his mouth, and confidently begins, "Comrades! . . ." The tenderest—if the word may be excused—is from Mary McCarthy, at the end of her account in "My Confession" of the intellectual bullying that she received as a consequence of having taken Trotsky's part more or less by accident.

His shrug before the unforeseen implies an acceptance of consequences that is a far cry from penance and prophecy. Such, it concedes, is life. *Bravo,* old sport, I say, even though the hall is empty.

THE ATLANTIC, JULY/AUGUST 2004

ldous Huxley absolutely detested mass culture and popular entertainment, and many of his toughest critical essays, as well as several intense passages in his fiction, consist of sneers and jeers at the
cheapness of the cinematic ethic and the vulgarity of commercial music. He
chanced to die on the same day as the assassination of President Kennedy in
November 1963 (being cheated of a proper obituary notice as a result, and
sharing the date of decease with C. S. Lewis, chronicler of Narnia) so he missed
the televisual event which once and for all confirmed the "global village." But
if he were able to return to us, and cast his scornful and lofty gaze on our
hedonistic society, he would probably be relatively unsurprised at the way
things are going. Sex has been divorced from procreation to a degree hard to
imagine even in 1963, and the current great debates in the moral sciences concern the implications of reproductive cloning and of the employment of fetal
stem-cells in medicine. The study of history is everywhere, but especially in
the United States, in steep decline. Public life in the richer societies is rou-
tinely compared to the rhythms of spectacle and entertainment. A flickering
hunger for authenticity pushes many people to explore the peripheral and
shrinking worlds of the "indigenous." This was all prefigured in _Brave New
World._ So, in a way, was the "one child" policy now followed in Communist
China, where to the extent that the program is successful we will not only see
a formerly clannish society where everyone is an only child but a formerly
Marxist one that has no real cognate word for "brotherhood." Interconti-
nental rocket travel has not become the commonplace Huxley anticipated

but its equivalents have become a cliché: jumbo jets do the same work of abolishing distance for the masses even though, in a strange moment of refusal, the developed world has stepped back from the supersonic Concorde and reverted to the days of voyaging comfortably below the speed of sound.

No, what would astonish laconic old Aldous would be the discovery that his photograph is among those on the album cover of *Sergeant Pepper's Lonely Hearts Club Band*—perhaps the least cacophonous of the signature records of pop and rock—and that Jim Morrison of the Doors had named his group after Huxley's later and proto-psychedelic book *The Doors of Perception.* In America, as Joan Didion once wrote, people who say "No Man Is an Island" think that they are quoting Ernest Hemingway: the fans who still make a shrine of Morrison's grave in Paris probably don't appreciate that Huxley was himself borrowing from William Blake. Nonetheless, literary immortality often depends on such vague but durable misunderstandings, and the three words "Brave New World" (themselves annexed from Miranda's speech in Shakespeare's *Tempest*) are as well known as "Catch-22" or "Nineteen Eighty-Four"—virtual hieroglyphics which almost automatically summon a universe of images and associations.

English literary society in the twentieth century was a fairly small pond, and the English class system tended to mean in any case that a limited number of people kept running into each other. (This is one of the bonding yet realistic elements in the splendid novel sequence written by Anthony Powell.) However, that Aldous Huxley should have taught George Orwell at Eton, which was also Anthony Powell's old school, seems to strain the natural serendipity of coincidence. Having originally hoped to become a physician, Huxley contracted a serious eye infection as an adolescent, lost a good deal of his sight, and until he could launch himself as a writer was compelled to be a rather diffident and reluctant teacher of French. In his class were Stephen Runciman, later to become the grand historian of Byzantium and the Crusades, and Eric Blair, later to metamorphose into George Orwell. Runciman remembers that "Blair" admired Huxley's command of French culture and that he detested those boys who took advantage of the schoolmaster's myopia.

Orwell never referred to this personal connection in print, as far as I know, when *Brave New World* was published in 1931 and when its dystopic metaphors entered the conversational and social bloodstream. He suggested at one point that Huxley had "plagiarized" from an earlier anti-Utopian novel, Evgeny Zamyatin's *We*. But since he acknowledged that work as an inspiration of his own, the allegation may have been no insult. He didn't get around to reviewing *Brave New World* until July 1940, when Britain seemed to have more urgent problems than the supposed nightmare of too much free sex and narcosis:

> Here the hedonistic principle is pushed to its utmost, the whole world has turned into a Riviera hotel. But though *Brave New World* was a brilliant caricature of the present (the present of 1930), it probably casts no light on the future. No society of that kind would last more than a couple of generations, because a ruling class that thought principally of a "good time" would soon lose its vitality. A ruling class has got to have a strict morality, a quasi-religious belief in itself, a *mystique*.

For some decades after this review was written, many people might have been inclined to say that Orwell was right, and that the "true" threat was one of jackboots, tanks, bombs, and bullies. Nonetheless, Huxley never went out of style. Something about his work seemed to tug at our consciousness.

One could also point out that, in the picture of Mustapha Mond with which Huxley opens the work, we are in fact introduced to a self-conscious ruling class with ideas of its own. Mond is not represented as wanting a "good time" for himself, after all. He is the chilly, objective theorist of the idea that social engineering and the wide distribution of easy pleasure will keep the masses in line. And two further things are made plain at once, both of which may have influenced Orwell more than he knew. We are told quite early on, in the flashbacks that occur during Mond's address to the awestruck students, that the brave new epoch began after the "Nine Years War," in which weapons of mass destruction (including "anthrax bombs": a superbly modern detail) had been employed. And we are also reminded of the crucial role played by amnesia in the maintenance of power. Mond takes the great capitalist Henry Ford at his word:

> "History," he repeated slowly, "is bunk."
> He waved his hand; and it was as though, with an invisible feather whisk, he had brushed away a little dust, and the dust was Harappa, was

Ur of the Chaldees; some spider-webs, and they were Thebes and Babylon and Cnossos and Mycenae. Whisk. Whisk—and where was Odysseus, where was Job, where were Jupiter and Gotama and Jesus? Whisk—and those specks of antique dirt called Athens and Rome, Jerusalem and the Middle Kingdom—all were gone. Whisk—the place where Italy had been was empty. Whisk, the cathedrals; whisk, whisk, King Lear and the Thoughts of Pascal. Whisk, Passion; whisk, Requiem; whisk, Symphony; whisk. . . .

This combination, of annihilating war and the subsequent obliteration and erasure of cultural and historical memory, is almost exactly what Orwell later relied upon to set the scene for his *Nineteen Eighty-Four*. But he was writing about the forbidding, part-alien experience of Nazism and Stalinism, whereas Huxley was locating disgust and menace in the very things—the new toys of materialism, from cars to contraceptives—that were becoming everyday pursuits. Perhaps that is why his book still operates on our subconscious.

There must indeed be an explanation for this, because I have to say that the fine passage quoted above is not completely typical. Huxley was thought rather snobbish even in his own generation, and often tended to condescend to the reader, as much of the dialogue in *Brave New World* also tends to do. It is didactic and pedagogic and faintly superior: indeed you might say it was the tone of voice of an Etonian schoolmaster. It is also somewhat contradictory and even self-defeating. Clearly, Huxley disdained socialism and the idea of equality: why then give the name of Bernard Marx to the only dissident in his awful system? And why call one of the few natural and spontaneous girls Lenina? This is stodgy and heavy rather than ironic, and it becomes absurd when we meet a sexy little child named Polly Trotsky in the opening chapters. (It's elsewhere stated that all citizens must be named from a pool of officially authorized surnames: the hedonistic regime either wants to abolish interest in history or it does not, and in neither case will it tempt fate by naming millions of its subjects after revolutionaries.)

Huxley came from revolutionary stock, but of a different kind. His grandfather was T. H. Huxley, a celebrated naturalist, who was a partisan and friend of Charles Darwin. It was the elder Huxley who first coined the term "agnostic" and who vanquished the Victorian Bishop Wilberforce in the famous debate between evolution and creationism at Oxford University. On his mother's side, Aldous could claim Matthew Arnold, author of *Culture and Anarchy,* as a maternal uncle. His own views were to fluctuate between the affirmative importance of high culture and the necessity of skepticism. His favorite philosopher was the ancient Hellenic thinker Pyrrho, who argued that judgment be suspended on any matter concerning the truth. Every position may be held to be equally right as well as equally wrong.

It's worth knowing this about Huxley, who often held and expressed diametrically opposite opinions, and who described himself as an "amused Pyrrhonic aesthete" in the introduction he wrote to the twentieth-anniversary edition of *Brave New World.* In the novel itself, one can often detect strong hints of a vicarious approval of what is ostensibly being satirized. For example, when Mustapha Mond invites the medical students to "try to imagine what 'living with one's family' meant," he goes on:

Home, home—a few small rooms, stiflingly over-inhabited by a man, by a periodically teeming woman, by a rabble of boys and girls of all ages. No air, no space; an understerilized prison; darkness, disease and smells.

Huxley was never at all impoverished as a boy (and in any case we can recognize the denunciation above from any study of Victorian or now "Third World" domestic conditions), but his mother died of cancer when he was fourteen and his brother committed suicide two years later, so he knew that even upper-class family life could be distraught. The above passage combines this insight with a fastidious disdain for the masses.

The study of eugenics was popular among the governing and intellectual classes of Britain in the Victorian epoch and subsequently (indeed it was an aspect of what has been termed "Social Darwinism"), and we learn from his biographer Nicholas Murray that Aldous Huxley was highly interested in "breeding," in both the aristocratic and the scientific sense of the term. I know from Huxley's own essays that he fell straight for the early theorists of IQ, who believed in its distribution by heredity. To this he added that it was important to encourage "the normal and supernormal members of the population to have large families," while preventing the subnormal "from having any children at all." So it was very clever of him—as well as quite Pyrrhonic—both to mobilize his own feelings on this subject, and then to harness them for a satire on the planned economy. One need not object to his having things both ways, as long as one notices the trick being performed.

In rather the same way, Huxley thought that free love and infidelity were all very well for people like himself (he and his first wife had an open marriage and even shared the bed of the same female lover, Mary Hutchinson). But still, when he came to describe the mindless and amoral sex lives of the men and women in *Brave New World,* he wrote with a curled lip. In an article describing the "jazz age" in California in the late 1920s, he had relished the profusion of nubile young girls and wrote that: "Plumply ravishing, they give, as T. S. Eliot has phrased it, ' promise of pneumatic bliss.' " Eliot spent his critical and poetic energy in the attempt to revive, in a more specifically Catholic and conservative form, the values of Matthew Arnold. So it is again amusing to note that the coarse word "pneumatic," used throughout *Brave New World* by both its male and female characters as a cheap synonym for good sex, derives from this rather disapproving source, as well as expressing Huxley's own divided view of the subject.

The influence of T. S. Eliot can also be felt in the depiction of "World Controller" Mustapha Mond, described as possessing "a hooked nose, full red lips, and eyes very piercing and dark." Martin Green has drawn attention to the resemblance to Mustapha Kemal, better known as Atatürk, who was a commanding figure when Huxley was writing. Sir Alfred Mond, the founder of the giant chemical multinational known as ICI (Imperial Chemical Industries), was also a power-celebrity of the period, and Eliot often alluded to him as the prototypical cosmopolitan Jew. (Huxley's few references to Jews were also often disobliging: he blamed them for the mercantile sleaziness of Hollywood, among other things. As if to rub this in, there's also a somewhat repellent character in *Brave New World* named Morgana Rothschild.) And we catch another prefiguration of *Nineteen Eighty-Four,* when the Director of Hatcheries and Conditioning finds himself nervous in Mond's presence, because "there were those strange rumors of old forbidden books hidden in a safe in the Controller's study. Bibles, poetry—Ford knew what." Did Orwell half-remember this when he created the looming figure of O'Brien and the Inner Party's secret book? If so, his review of *Brave New World* was again unfair to Huxley.

I find the tracing of these contemporary influences to be valuable, because Huxley was composing *Brave New World* at a time when modernity as we know it was just coming into full view. He later reproached himself for not mentioning nuclear fission, about which he was quite well informed, but this element of the literal hardly matters. Readers then and since have filled in many gaps for themselves: they knew and they know what Huxley was driving at. Can the human being be designed and controlled, from uterus to grave, "for its own good"? And would this version of super-utilitarianism bring real happiness?

Huxley himself conceded that his fictional characters were no more than puppets to illustrate his points, and this lack of characterization (truly a drawback in his earlier and later novels, most especially in *Island*, his last and most self-consciously Utopian effort) is paradoxically rather a help in *Brave New World*. The marionettes do their stuff, giving us a very rapid and complete picture of mindless bliss and its usefulness to power. Then they begin, or some of them are authorized by their carpenter to begin, to experience vague but definite feelings of discontent. They find themselves asking: Is this all there is? The three deficiencies they feel, often without knowing how to name them, are Nature, Religion, and Literature. With only chemical and mechanical and sexual comforts provided to them, they sense the absence of challenge and drama and they fall prey to *ennui*. With no concept of a cosmos beyond the immediately human, they are deprived of the chance to feel awed or alienated. And with nothing but sensory entertainment (Huxley might not have been the best of movie critics, given his near-blindness, but he used this disadvantage to imagine "the feelies" as the culmination of "talkies" and "movies") they have no appreciation for words.

Huxley's expression of this dilemma, and of its resolution, is again very didactic. He allows some of his prefabricated figures to feel the stirrings of sexual jealousy and its two accompaniments: the yearning for monogamy and the desire to bear one's own child. He permits them the aspiration to experience the wilderness, even if it is only a reservation, and to take the requisite risks. And he leaves a tattered copy of Shakespeare lying around. (I'm sorry to keep doing this, but when Winston Smith in *Nineteen Eighty-Four* awakes from a haunting dream of a lost pastoral England, he does so to his own surprise "with the word Shakespeare on his lips.")

The possessor of the Shakespeare edition is The Savage, and it is he who wreaks revenge on the overprotected and superinsulated creatures who stumble upon his existence. This revenge is partly accidental, in that his own need for authentic emotion is enough in itself to cause convulsions in the society that adopts him as a fearful curiosity or freak. Huxley later said that if he could rewrite the novel he would have given The Savage more warning of what to expect. This shows that fiction writers do well to leave their creations alone and spare them from second thoughts: it is the effect of The Savage upon others that makes the dramatic difference, and it is his very naïveté and simplicity that make a quasi-Calvary out of the final chapter. Huxley was fairly indifferent to Christianity as a religion (and his satire on the Church of England and the "Arch-Community-Songster of Canterbury" has since been easily surpassed by the fatuous degeneration of that Church itself), but he was not immune to its metaphors, and the seeker for truth in the wilderness is only one of these. We can always be sure of one thing—that the messengers of discomfort and sacrifice will be stoned and pelted by those who wish to preserve at all costs their own contentment. This is not a lesson that is confined to the Testaments.

In a way, I have been arguing that *Brave New World* was both ahead of, and behind, its time. And Huxley was—shall we say?—a reactionary modernist. He had this quality in common with Evelyn Waugh, who also took his tone from Eliot's "The Waste Land" and who dilated about eugenics and euthanasia while carrying a burden of unpurged religious guilt. The disguised presence of original sin is reimagined in *Brave New World* when Huxley, in the most absurd of his scenarios, shows us little children being sleep-conditioned to consume, and to use up material goods and opportunities with as much abandon as possible. Here one must ask, who but a member of the comfortable or agnostic classes imagines that people need to be brainwashed into being greedy? The acquisitive instinct, perhaps initially supplied by Satan himself in one interpretation, is after all fairly easily engaged. It was Karl Marx and not Bernard Marx who wrote that, in relation to his victims, the capitalist "therefore searches for all possible ways of stimulating them to consume, by making his commodities more attractive and by filling their ears with babble about new needs." Marx also thought, as is usually forgotten or overlooked, that this impulse led to innovation and experiment and to the liberating process of what has sometimes been called "creative destruction." In other words, it is a means of arousing discontent with the *status quo*, not a mere means of stupefying the masses. Our own contemporary world suggests that the energy of capital is not easily compatible with *stasis*.

Having never wanted for much himself, Huxley was quicker to miss this point than he might have been. And, in his Pyrrhonic way, he was also quicker to surrender to the blandishments of Nirvana, in its consumer-capitalist form, than most. This is what makes *Brave New World Revisited* into a disappointment. Once again, the clue is to be found in an exchange with Orwell, who sent Huxley an advance copy of *Nineteen Eighty-Four*. In late 1949, Huxley wrote back to say "how fine and profoundly important" the book was. However, he was convinced that future rulers would discover that:

> infant-conditioning and narco-hypnosis are more efficient, as instruments of government, than clubs and prisons, and that the lust for power can be just as completely satisfied by suggesting people into loving their servitude as by flogging and kicking them into obedience . . . the nightmare of *Nineteen Eighty-Four* is destined to modulate into the nightmare of a world having more resemblances to that which I imagined in *Brave New World*. The change will be brought about as a result of a felt need for increased efficiency.

Perhaps it is partly Orwell's fault, since his descriptions of the Thought Police and Room 101 are so annihilatingly and memorably ghastly, but it does deserve to be said that his own fictionalization of absolutism does not depend exclusively upon the power of fear and violence. The masses are not handed *soma* to tranquilize them, but they are given plentiful cheap gin. Lotteries are staged for their amusement and excitement, and cheap pornographic literature is freely available to all proles. The cinema is depicted as an orgy of distraction and propaganda, on Colosseum lines, admittedly, rather than of exquisite sensation. The *Nineteen Eighty-Four* regime is one of scarcity rather than abundance, but the traditional bribes of materialism and indeed of conditioning cannot be said to have been overlooked.

When he came to publish *Brave New World Revisited* almost a decade later, in 1958, Huxley nonetheless opened with a long contrast between his own vision and the Orwellian one; a contrast very similar to the one he had sketched in his letter of 1949. He rightly pointed out that in the Soviet Union the need for rationalization of the economy had produced some alleviation of the totalitarian system. However, his general obsession with eugenics once again caused him to replace the emphasis elsewhere:

> The United States is not at present an over-populated country. If, however, the population continues to increase at the present rate (which is higher than that of India's increase, though happily a good deal lower than the rate now current in Mexico or Guatemala), the problem of numbers in relation to available resources might well become troublesome by the beginning of the twenty-first century. For the moment over-population is not a direct threat to the personal freedom of Americans. It remains, however, an indirect threat, a menace at one remove. If over-population should drive the underdeveloped countries into totalitarianism, and if these new dictatorships should ally themselves with Russia, then the military position of the United States would become less secure and the preparations for defense and retaliation would have to be intensified. But liberty, as we all know, cannot flourish in a country that is permanently on a war-footing, or even a near-war footing. Permanent crisis justifies permanent control of everybody and everything by the agencies of the central government. And permanent crisis is what we have to expect in a world in which over-population is producing a state of things, in which dictatorship under Communist auspices becomes almost inevitable.

In no respect is this a paragraph of prescience. The geopolitical sentences are both too detailed and too vague. One might note, also, that the chief demographic problem of the United States in 2003 is its aging population, with the "graying" process somewhat delayed or postponed by legal and illegal immigration. Scholars, such as Amartya Sen in particular, have come up with multiple refutations of Malthus. "Population bomb" theorists, most notably Paul Ehrlich, have seen their extrapolated predictions repeatedly fail to come true—at least partly because they are extrapolations. Finally, it would appear from his remarks about Mexico and Guatemala that Huxley suddenly isn't all that much in love with the primitive adobe and cactus natives, or not as much in love as he affected to be in *Brave New World*.

One element of that ancestral culture had, however, quite bewitched him in the years that separate the writing of *Brave New World* and *Brave New World Revisited*. His Lawrentian sojourns in California, New Mexico, and elsewhere—he was the editor of D. H. Lawrence's letters—had exposed him to the psychedelic properties of peyote and mescaline and their derivatives, such as LSD (the "Lucy in the Sky with Diamonds" of the *Sergeant Pepper* smash hit). I don't mean to be too "judgmental" about this: Huxley was almost blind and was entitled to any colorful voyage of the imagination that he could get his hands on. But there is something almost promiscuously uncritical in his *Brave New World Revisited* recommendation:

> In LSD-25 (lysergic acid diethylamide) the pharmacologists have recently created another aspect of *soma*—a perception-improver and vision-producer that is, physiologically speaking, almost costless. This extraordinary drug, which is effective in doses as small as fifty or even twenty-five millionths of a gram, has power (like peyote) to transport people into the other world. In the majority of cases, the other world to which LSD-25 gives access is heavenly; alternatively it may be purgatorial or even infernal. But, positive or negative, the lysergic acid experience is felt by almost everyone who undergoes it to be profoundly significant and enlightening. In any event, the fact that minds can be changed so radically at so little cost to the body is altogether astonishing.

Huxley became a friend of Dr. Timothy Leary, a man of great charm and wit (as I can testify from experience) and a truant Harvard scientist whose advocacy of LSD trips made him an emblem of the "Sixties." It was this comradeship that attracted the attention of the Beatles and Jim Morrison. But again one must pause and notice a contradiction. Leary believed that the use of mind-altering drugs was essentially subversive, and would help individuals both to evade and erode "the system." The authorities appear to have agreed with him on this, pursuing and imprisoning him (at one point in a cell adjacent to Charles Manson) and making it highly illegal to follow his advice, not just concerning LSD but also cocaine and marijuana. What becomes, then, of Huxley's belief that such hallucinogens, analgesics, and stimulants are the ideal instrument of state control? The "war on drugs" is now being extended to a state-sponsored campaign against tobacco and alcohol and painkillers: if the ruling class wants people to be blissed-out it has a strange way of pursuing this elementary goal. In our time, the symbol of state intrusion into the private life is the mandatory urine test.

A map of the world that does not show Utopia, said Oscar Wilde, is not worth glancing at. In *Brave New World,* and in his closing novel *Island,* Huxley tried to fix Utopian cartography in our minds. In the first setting, sex and drugs and the conditioning of the young are the symptoms of un-freedom and the roots of alienation and anomie, while in the second they are the tools of emancipation and the keys to happiness. The inhabitants of *Brave New World* have no external enemies to keep them afraid and in line; the *Island*-people of Pala have to contend with an aggressive neighboring dictatorship led by Colonel Dipa, a Saddam/Milŏsevíc type who seems to think, and with good reason, that the traditional methods of club and boot and gun are still pretty serviceable. We should, I think, be grateful that Aldous Huxley was such a mass of internal contradictions. These enabled him to register the splendors and miseries, not just of modernity, but of the human condition. In his essay "Ravens and Writing Desks," written for *Vanity Fair* in 1928, he said:

> God is, but at the same time God also is not. The Universe is governed by blind chance and at the same time by a providence with ethical pre-occupations. Suffering is gratuitous and pointless, but also valuable and necessary. The universe is an imbecile sadist, but also, simultaneously, the most benevolent of parents. Everything is rigidly predetermined, but the will is perfectly free. This list of contradictions could be lengthened so as to include all problems that have ever vexed the philosopher and the theologian.

Aware perhaps that this teetered on the edge of tautology, the old Pyrrhonist wrote elsewhere in his essay on the great Spinoza:

"Homer was wrong," wrote Heracleitus of Ephesus, "Homer was wrong in saying: 'Would that strife might perish from among gods and men!' He did not see that he was praying for the destruction of the universe; for if his prayer was heard, all things would pass away."

The search for Nirvana, like the search for Utopia or the end of history or the classless society, is ultimately a futile and dangerous one. It involves, if it does not necessitate, the sleep of reason. There is no escape from anxiety and struggle, and Huxley assists us in attaining this valuable glimpse of the obvious, precisely because it was a conclusion that was in many ways unwelcome to him.

FOREWORD TO *BRAVE NEW WORLD*
BY ALDOUS HUXLEY 2003

M any of the admirers of Graham Greene—those of us, that is, who chose to spend some part of our reading lives in voluntary exile in the exotic locale colloquially known as "Greeneland"— became familiar with the whims of the president of this remote yet familiar territory. One of those whims (benign enough, as befitted a rather lenient and tolerant authority) was the division of his fictions into novels and "entertainments." And the first-born of the latter category was *Orient Express* or, as it has been variously titled, *Stamboul Train* or *Stamboul Express*. Dr. Samuel Johnson once remarked that only a fool wrote for anything but money, and Greene himself was bracingly candid about the motives for his bifurcation. As he informed the audience of his autobiography, *Ways of Escape:*

> That year, 1931, for the first and last time in my life I deliberately set out to write a book to please, one which with luck might be made into a film.

The law of unintended consequences is designed in part for authors who make decisions in this way under the lash of financial exigency: one need only think of those works of Greene's which were translated into film but which did not begin life as potential scripts. *The Third Man* (which he actually did write as a treatment) would be preeminent, followed by *Brighton Rock,* but one should also tip one's hat to *The Comedians, Travels with My Aunt, Our Man in Havana, The Power and the Glory,* and *The Quiet American.* The "entertainment" of *Orient*

Express—as I shall call it from now on—was designed and ready-made for motion pictures but nonetheless counts as Greene's worst filmic flop. Indeed, as he himself so wryly put it, continuing the quoted sentence above:

> The devil looks after his own and in [*Orient Express*] I succeeded in both aims, though the film rights seemed at the time an unlikely dream, for before I had completed the book, Marlene Dietrich had appeared in *Shanghai Express,* the English had made *Rome Express,* and even the Russians had produced their railway film, *Turksib.* The film manufactured from my book by Twentieth Century-Fox came last and was far and away the worst, though not so bad as a later television production by the BBC.

When Graham Greene employs a well-worn phrase such as "the devil looks after his own" one does well to look for the trace of irony. Although this book does not belong at all in the category loosely known as his "Catholic" novels, it does contain the themes of self-sacrifice and betrayal, and a sort of Gethsemane as well as a sort of Calvary. Its disgrace as a movie was, in his mind, a partial revenge for its catch-penny intentions. But this turns out to be a useful if not fortunate failure, because it enables us to read the book without having to do so through the prism of any later celluloid distortion.

Subsequent images nonetheless do color the way in which we approach it. Agatha Christie's *Murder on the Orient Express,* the drama of *The Lady Vanishes* and Ian Fleming's *From Russia with Love* have all put the continental express at the center of modern romance and adventure. I used to work, in an even lowlier capacity than the one in which Greene had once toiled, at the offices of the *Times* in Printing House Square, and until it was demolished I always derived a thrill from the chiseled stone facings of the Blackfriars station opposite, which listed the destinations of Berlin, Warsaw, and St. Petersburg. Even in this register, the name of Istanbul, or Stamboul, or Constantinople, would come out top. The Golden Horn, the Bosphorus, the Sea of Marmara, the dome of Saint Sophia . . . these evocations have spelled "romance and adventure" since before John Buchan's *Greenmantle* (which Greene avowed as an early and decisive influence on his own imagination).

The essence of Greeneland, if one may dare to try and define it, is the combination of the exotic and the romantic with the sordid and the banal. Those who travel or depart, says the poet Horace, only change their skies and not their condition. The meanness of everyday existence is found at the bottom of every suitcase, and has in fact been packed along with everything else. Nonetheless, it is sometimes when they are far from home and routine that people will stir to make an unwonted exertion of the spirit or of the will.

This isn't obvious at first in this case, because both Myatt and Coral Musker have embarked for mundane reasons (a business crisis and a job opportunity, respectively) and because there are ways in which trains conspire to suspend animation:

> In the rushing reverberating express, noise was so regular that it was the equivalent of silence, movement was so continuous that after a while the mind accepted it as stillness. Only outside the train was violence of action possible, and the train would contain him safely with his plans for three days . . .

At the time it was written, this would have recalled to many minds the famous image coined by Winston Churchill, of Lenin being carried like a "bacillus" in a "sealed train" from Germany to St. Petersburg. And on the Orient Express, also, there is infection and illness. It is this which throws Coral Musker together first with the Communist Dr. Czinner, who is on his own private mission of revolution, and then with Myatt, the self-conscious Jew. The encounter with Czinner gives Greene the chance for a beautiful moment of inversion or "transference": Coral awakens from a swoon to see the physician's face, and imagines for an instant that it is she who is ministering to him:

> He's ill, she thought, and for a moment shut out the puzzling shadows which fell the wrong way, the globe of light shining from the ground. "Who are you?" she asked, trying to remember how it was that she had come to his help. Never, she thought, had she seen a man who needed help more.

Her piercing insight is no delusion. It is registered also, but with much more cynicism, by the hard-bitten yellow-press reporter Mabel Warren, who knows for a fact that Dr. Czinner needs help but is prepared to throw him to the wolves for a good story. How perfectly Greene catches the ingratiating tone of the desperate journalist: "Her voice was low, almost tender; she might have been urging a loved dog towards a lethal chamber."

Greene could be accused of peopling his train novel (or train script) with stock characters—the showgirl who's seen it all; the political exile and conspirator traveling incognito; the butch lesbian with a weakness for drunken sentimentality—and the charge of stereotype has been leveled with especial force against his portrayal of Myatt. The bitter controversy over anti-Semitism touches an extraordinary number of the novels, poems, and essays written during the 1920s and 1930s (it continues to inflect all discussion of Greene's early hero John Buchan, for example, but it extends through Ezra Pound, T. S. Eliot, and even Thomas Mann). And *Orient Express* was written just as the Nazi Party was preparing to take power. So one ought not to postpone a confrontation with the question. Michael Shelden, Graham Greene's biographer, states roundly that Myatt is a deliberately ugly caricature of Jewishness, and that this conforms to other bigoted opinions expressed by Greene in his film reviews. In reply, the novelist David Lodge has argued that Greene disliked the vulgarity of Hollywood, and that it was difficult for him not to mention the preponderance of Jewish executives in this milieu. ("The dark alien executive tipping his cigar ash behind the glass partition . . ." as Greene phrased it in the London *Spectator* as late as 1937.) As for Myatt, Lodge maintains that he is represented as a Good Samaritan rather than a Shylock or a Fagin. (I am paraphrasing his point of view without, I hope, misrepresenting it.)

I trust the reader to decide for himself or herself about this, and I don't like splitting the difference between the two opposing views, but it does seem to me that to take the points in random order, the reference to the executive above is a cliché at best and a slur at worst. Furthermore, Greene did slightly amend *Brighton Rock* after the Second World War to make the racetrack gangs seem somewhat less palpably Semitic, and he presumably would not have done this unless prompted by some sort of uneasy conscience. But as for Myatt, I would submit the following excerpt, unmentioned by either Shelden or Lodge. Coral Musker cannot believe that a Jew is offering her his own berth in a first-class sleeping compartment:

Her disbelief and her longing decided him. He determined to be princely on an Oriental scale, granting costly gifts and not requiring, not wanting, any return. Parsimony was the traditional reproach against his race, and he would show one Christian how undeserved it was. Forty years in the wilderness, away from the flesh-pots of Egypt, had entailed harsh habits, the counted date and the hoarded water; nor had a thousand years in the wilderness of a Christian world, where only the secret treasure was safe, encouraged display; but the world was altering, the desert was flowering; in stray corners here and there, in western Europe, the Jew could show that other quality he shared with the Arab, the quality of the princely host, who would wash the feet of beggars and feed them from his own dish; sometimes he could cease to be the enemy of the rich to become the friend of any poor man who sought a roof in the name of God. The roar of the train faded from his consciousness, the light went out in his eyes, while he built for his own pride the tent in the oasis, the well in the desert. He spread his hands before her.

Whatever this is, it is not anti-Jewish. Indeed the problem may be the reverse: it might be too strenuous a demonstration of sympathy to be altogether convincing. In setting out to counter received opinion, Greene deployed some clichés of his own (the Mosaic wanderings, the blooming of the desert, the stage-Jew spreading of the hands) and lazily repeated the word "princely." Most of all, however, one notices with a pang that Jews are supposed to feel safe at last, in "western Europe"—in 1931! Still, the plain intent is to defend Jews from defamation, and the taunting anti-Semite on the train—a ghastly specimen of English suburban womanhood—is furthermore consistently represented as vulgar and mean. If this all seems like trying too hard, there is a fine and redeeming one-liner when Myatt, shocked at Coral's hoarding of yesterday's sandwiches and milk, exclaims "Are you Scotch?" Another good instance of inversion, or table turning.

The novel deals with class consciousness in two ways. During this epoch it was possible to judge any English person the moment he or she uttered a syllable, and Greene catches this with a most acute ear. All the Brits on the train are either stressing the more refined pronunciations they have acquired with such labor, or making too much of being plain-spoken and unaffected. Not for an instant are they free of the hidden traps of social stratification. An oblique testament to this pervading sensitivity came in the form of a lawsuit brought against the novel by Mr. J. B. Priestley, now rather deservedly forgotten but in those days the very model of the pipe-smoking, no-nonsense bluff man of the people. He claimed, quite rightly as far as I can see, to be the model for the affected novelist Q. C. Savory, a mildly fraudulent character who positively relishes the democratic manner in which he drops his own aitches. ("May I draw a red 'erring across your argument?") This was the first of many libel actions that paid their own compliment to Greene's realism.

And then there is class consciousness in the Marxist sense of the term, exemplified by Dr. Czinner. This man—with his surname that of the fallen Everyman—stands for all the idealistic leftists who were then being ground under by what it would be no cliché to call the forces of reaction. All of Greene's sympathy for the underdog, or perhaps more exactly for the losing side, is mobilized in his portrait:

> He had his duty to his patients, his duty to the poor of Belgrade, and the slowly growing idea of his duty to his own class in every country. His parents had starved themselves that he might be a doctor, he himself had gone hungry and endangered his health that he might be a doctor, and it was only when he had practised for several years that he realized the uselessness of his skill. He could do nothing for his own people; he could not recommend rest to the worn-out or prescribe insulin to the diabetic, because they had not the money to pay for either.

Czinner is represented as an atheist, but in what I believe to be the key to this novel he is returning home in order to offer himself as a sacrifice. Confronted in his train compartment and seeing that the mysterious intruder is wearing a silver crucifix, "For a moment Dr. Czinner flattened himself against the wall of a steep street to let the armoured men, the spears and the horses pass, and the tired tortured man. He had not died to make the poor contented, to bind the chains tighter; his words had been twisted." Greene became a Catholic in 1926, five years before he wrote this novel, and had previously had a flirtation with Communism. In *Orient Express* he synthesized the two impulses as he was later to do in several books, perhaps most notably *Monsignor Quixote*. Just as he often satirized Catholicism and Communism, so he was ridiculed in his turn for these allegiances. (Entering a *New Statesman* competition for a Greene parody under an assumed name, he found his submission winning third prize. John Fuller and James Fenton, in their "Poem Against Catholics," lampooned his work as one where "Police chiefs quote Pascal/Priests hit the bottle/Strong Men repent in Nijni-Novgorod.")

But Greene could lampoon his own loyalties. He was to see his work placed on the Vatican's once-notorious Index of banned books, and when he wished to be sardonic about the Left he could give Coral's mental response to Czinner's admission of Communist beliefs:

> She thought of him now as one of the untidy men who paraded on Saturday afternoons in Trafalgar Square bearing hideous banners: "Workers of the World, Unite," "Walthamstow Old Comrades," "Balham Branch of the Juvenile Workers' League." They were the killjoys, who would hang the rich and close the theaters and drive her into dismal free love at a summer camp . . .

However, a moment of decision is imminent and when it comes, Coral Musker sticks by Dr. Czinner against his tormentors. This is the consequence of a blunder and a misunderstanding, but it is nonetheless a test and she passes it, by declining to leave the sad stranger alone to face his martyrdom. Meanwhile, Myatt also has to confront his own responsibilities. He is given a chance to make it easy on himself, and we are told that "he knew suddenly that he would not be sorry to accept the clerk's word and end his search; he would have done all that lay in his power, and he would be free." (It is, by the way, in this very paragraph that he reflects upon the alternative chance "to set up his tent and increase his tribe"—the words most complained of by Michael Shelden.) However, he persists in a rash course of rescue until he can decently persuade himself that he *has* done all that he can. There's a thief and a murderer, too, at the end, and some brutal soldiers, too: I think we are being invited by Greene to a subliminal Passion Play where the moment of cockcrow is postponed for as long as is humanly possible—which is as much as to say, not for very long.

Betrayal itself is reserved for the closing chapter in Constantinople, where a false atmosphere of gaiety and luxury and seduction banishes the disquieting memories of the hard voyage, and where everybody can be convinced that all is for the best. "A splinter of ice in the heart," Greene once wrote, is a necessity for the novelist. One must see unblinkingly into the pettiness and self-deception of the human condition. Innocence is another word for prey. Survival is the law. Praising the work of his rival in personal frailty, and its relation to faith, Evelyn Waugh said that, with Greene's prose: "the affinity to the film is everywhere apparent . . . it is the camera's eye which moves." Behind this sometimes protective lens, the author of *Orient Express* could deprecatingly present a piece of pitiless objectivity as an "entertainment."

INTRODUCTION TO *ORIENT EXPRESS*
BY GRAHAM GREENE 2004

Three years before his death in 1966, Evelyn Waugh wrote, in *Basil Seal Rides Again,* a prefiguration of his own literary obituary:

> His voice was not the same instrument as of old. He had first assumed it as a conscious imposture; it had become habitual to him; the antiquated, worldly-wise moralities which, using that voice, he had found himself obliged to utter, had become his settled opinions.

The very rotundity here is its own cumbrous self-criticism: if Evelyn Waugh later became a byword for port-sodden Blimpery it was because his face shaped itself to fit a mask. Yet let us not forget the face, and the voice, that predated that heavy, bilious terminus. In the pages of *Scoop*, we encounter Waugh at the mid-season point of his perfect pitch; youthful and limber and light as a feather. In fact:

> Feather-footed through the plashy fen passes the questing vole . . .

No sooner has one imbibed this journalistic "intro," from the fertile yet innocent pen of "William Boot, Countryman," the editor of "Lush Places," than one enters or re-enters a world of delight and imagination, freighted in its depiction with just enough of the sinister and the cynical to escape the charge of sentimentality.

The figure of the innocent abroad, or the Candide or Pinocchio, is such a familiar device as to require the most delicate handling. Waugh solves this problem brilliantly, and from the first page, by having not one but two innocents abroad, and by focusing initial attention on the wrong one. In a seriously heartless sentence he introduces John Boot, conceited citizen of the Republic of Letters:

> He had published eight books (beginning with a life of Rimbaud written when he was eighteen, and concluding, at the moment, with *Waste of Time,* a studiously modest description of some harrowing months among the Patagonian Indians), of which most people who lunched with Lady Metroland could remember the names of three or four.

I personally can never scan that passage without thinking of the vastly overrated society traveller Bruce Chatwin: there has always been someone in London who fits the description and as Waugh cleverly intuited, there always will be. This Boot—pale and ineffectual and sycophantic—flaps his gossamer wing in peevish discontent and, all unknowing, creates a typhoon in far-off Boot Magna and in even remoter Ishmaelia.

It's quite permissible to read the entire Waugh canon as an original use of original sin. When he decides to play with an innocent character, that character stays played with. The Book of Job is an over-ornate trifle when set beside the caprice visited on poor little Lord Tangent, for example, in *Decline and Fall.* But the other John Boot, the timid and bucolic near-herbivore who is forcibly mutated into "Boot of the Beast," is the most satisfying and, in every sense of the term, the most "finished" of Waugh's fictional victims.

Were I asked to reminisce and expatiate at one of Lord Copper's infamous dinners, I could become suitably boring and prosaic about the brave days of Fleet Street. I could enlarge on the origins of its three colloquial names: "The Street of Adventure," "The Street of Dreams," and "The Street of Shame." As one who briefly held the title of foreign correspondent at the old *Daily Express,* and who still held it when the Aitken family sold out to some property developer or other, I can argue with room-emptying conviction that my own broken person represents that of the last Beaverbrook "fireman." I remember that pseudo-deco dark-glassed palazzo, so near to Ludgate Circus and the plaque to Edgar Wallace; a building known half-admiringly as "The Black Lubyanka." And I remember the thrill of its lobby and its commissionaires, as well as the surge that went through my system when taking a taxi from there to Heathrow airport; a wad of traveler's checks at the ready and an exotic visa stamp in the old blue-and-gold hardback that was then our passport.

Was it true that the standby slogan of the *Express* foreign desk, for any hack stumbling on to a scene of carnage and misery, was "Anyone here been raped and speaks English?" I regret to say that it was. Is it true that an *Express* scribe in some hellhole, his copy surpassed by a *Daily Mail* man who had received an honorable flesh-wound, received a cable: "MailMan shot. Why you unshot?" I never saw the cable itself, but I did see a front-page, complete with dashing photograph of the embattled correspondent, confected from whole cloth about a world-shaking event which the intrepid hack had irretrievably missed. And there wasn't anyone at the bar—the "mahogany ridge" from which so many fine stories were filed—who did not have his version of the following:

Why, once Jakes went out to cover a revolution in one of the Balkan capitals. He overslept in his carriage, woke up at the wrong station, didn't know any different, got out, went straight to a hotel, and cabled off a thousand-word story about barricades in the street, flaming churches, machine guns answering the rattle of his typewriter as he wrote, a dead child, like a broken doll, spreadeagled in the deserted roadway before his window—you know.

The "you know" there is positioned to perfection. Yes, indeed we did know. There was also the matter of alcoholic etiquette:

The bunch now overflowed the hotel. There were close on fifty of them. All over the lounge and dining-room they sat and stood and leaned; some whispered to each other in what they took to be secrecy; others exchanged chaff and gin. It was their employers who paid for all this hospitality, but the conventions were decently observed—"My round, old boy." "No, no, my round!" "Have this one on me." "Well, the

next is mine!"—except by Shumble, who, from habit, drank heartily
and without return wherever it was offered.

At gatherings in the Europa in Belfast, in the Commodore in Beirut, at
Meikles in old Rhodesia, and even in the Holiday Inn in Sarajevo I have heard
this banter repeated, sometimes self-consciously. The names of Waugh's
morally hollowed-out hacks are perhaps a bit Dickensian, but that can be
overlooked in a near-flawless sentence like this one:

> Shumble, Whelper and Pigge knew Corker; they had loitered of old on
> many a doorstep and forced an entry into many a stricken home.

I once met a man, in the Punch Tavern opposite the old *Beast* building, who
fondly explained to me that one required a solid colleague when calling on
the recently bereaved. "They'll always offer a cup of tea, see, and want to talk
about the crash or the accident or the murder. So your mate offers to help in
the kitchen and that'll give you nice time to go in the drawing-room and
swipe the photos from the mantelpiece." But, you notice, it takes me three
times as long to explain as it did for Waugh to conjure the scene. His little
story is replete with exquisite asides of the same sort, some of them short
("One native whom they questioned fled precipately at the word 'police' ")
and some requiring a longer run-up to attain the pressure-point where mirth
explodes:

> They were bowling up the main street of Jacksonburg. A strip of
> tarmac ran down the middle; on either side were rough tracks for
> mules, men, cattle and camels: beyond these the irregular outline of
> the commercial quarter; a bank, in shoddy concrete, a Greek provisions
> store in timber and tin, the Café de la Bourse, the Carnegie Library, the
> Cine-Parlant, and numerous gutted sites, relics of an epidemic of arson
> some years back when an Insurance Company had imprudently set up
> shop in the city.

The last clause, with its answer-back between "insurance" and "prudence,"
both completes the scene and collapses the scenery. We are in Absurdistan.

The first chapter of Book Two is probably the finest evocation of Absurdistan ever composed. One yearns to quote or excerpt the whole of it, from which I select the fate of those missionaries who ventured into Ishmaelia:

> They were eaten, every one of them: some raw, others stewed and seasoned—according to local usage and the calendar (for the better sort of Ishmaelites have been Christian for many centuries and will not publicly eat human flesh, uncooked, in Lent, without special and costly dispensation from their bishop.)

A lesser writer might have made more of the rhythm that is furnished by the remorseless succession of public ... human ... uncooked ... in Lent. But here we touch on a sensitive ganglion. Is Mr. Waugh, by employing the "stereotype" of the cannibal stewpot, not reaching for the baser instincts of his readers? Do his characters not also use words like "darky" and "coon" and even "nigger" without evident compunction? Well, there's no real point in trying to acquit Mr. Waugh in front of the sort of modern jury he would have despised or ignored. But he himself employs no term of hatred or contempt; his main fools and dolts are English or Swedish or German, and his villain—the memorably-sketched Dr. Benito—is a suave and elegant and fluent black man. The most subhuman portrayals are of British youths back in southern England (a theme to which I want to return). One might add that the only authentic cannibal in Waugh's fiction is Basil Seal and—a detail from Absurdistan, but a true detail none the less—that in the 1960s the exiled leaders of the Pan-African Congress wrote to Waugh at his Somerset home in Combe Florey, asking if they could annex the name "Azania," from his novel *Black Mischief,* for the future liberated South Africa! (The title "Azania" survives now in lapidary form on the gravestone of Steve Biko.)

I've done the best I can: Evelyn Waugh was a reactionary and that's that. But he combined in the same person an attachment to modernism. (Lines from "The Waste Land" occur in the title of one of his novels, and in the text of another one.) Like Eliot, his prejudices were in some way his muse: how brilliant of him to have awarded Bloomsbury names to the leaders of Ishmaelia's Jackson dynasty:

It had been found expedient to merge the functions of national defence and inland revenue in an office then held in the capable hands of General Gollancz Jackson; his forces were in two main companies, the Ishmaelite Mule Tax-gathering force and the Rifle Excisemen, with a small Artillery Death Duties Corps for use against the heirs of powerful noblemen.

These five detachments are described as returning from their expeditions "laden with the spoils of the less nimble"—a deft and near-perfect anticipation of what would later be called "kleptocracy" in post-colonial Africa.

The manners and *mores* of the press, however, are the recurrent motif of the book and the chief reason for its enduring magic:

> William and Corker went to the Press Bureau. Dr. Benito, the director, was away but his clerk entered their names in his ledger and gave them cards of identity. They were small orange documents, originally printed for the registration of prostitutes.

Later:

> "Once and for all, Salter, I will not have a barrier erected between me and my staff. I am as accessible to the humblest . . ." Lord Copper paused for an emphatic example . . . "the humblest *book reviewer* as I am to my immediate entourage."

This world of callousness and vulgarity and philistinism (who was it who called aloud in those days for Providence to "drain the Rother Mere and dam the Beaver Brook"?) also introduces us to yet a third Candide of the action. Mr. Salter, the hapless underling of the hateful Lord Copper, is never even given a first name. He is the plaything of fate. Best-known perhaps as the nervous utterer of the over-used phrase "Up to a point, Lord Copper," he deserves more recognition than he has so far received. To William Boot, it is the big city that represents *partibus infidelium,* and once there and installed against his will in a vile modern hotel he asks for a toothbrush "and presently a page with a face of ageless evil brought it on a tray." This hideous boy is further described as "the knowing midget." To Mr. Salter, it is the rural dominion that suggests terror and cruelty; upon arrival at the despond-infested platform of Boot Magna Halt he encounters "a cretinous native youth who stood on the further side of the paling, leant against it and picked at the dry paint-bubbles with a toe-like thumb. When Mr. Salter looked at him, he glanced away and grinned wickedly at his boots." Converse proves arduous: "Mr. Salter's voice sounded curiously flutey and querulous in contrast to the deep tones of the moron." This interlude of what I would describe as life-affirming heartlessness is rounded off deliciously when the idiot lad overturns his truck, burying Mr. Salter's hand-luggage in an avalanche of slag. The butler brings the news:

> "He overturned the vehicle in the back drive."
> "Was he hurt?"
> "Oh, yes, sir; gravely."

I have always thought Sam Peckinpah's *Straw Dogs* to be the finest counterpoint to the apple-blossom propaganda of the countryside idyll. It is followed closely by *Withnail and I,* in which two Londoners go "on holiday by mistake." ("Stop saying that, Withnail! *Of course* he's the fucking farmer.") But Evelyn Waugh had both of these two hellish expeditions mapped out in advance:

> There was something un-English and not quite right about "the country," with its solitude and self-sufficiency, its bloody recreations, its darkness and silence and sudden, inexplicable noises; the kind of place where you never know from one minute to the next that you may not be tossed by a bull or pitchforked by a yokel or rolled over and broken up by a pack of hounds.

Indeed, Waugh seems to confirm this *noir* version at the close. "Maternal rodents pilot their furry brood through the stubble," writes William Boot in his resumed "Lush Places" column. "Outside the owls hunted maternal rodents and their furry brood," notes the author in laying down his pen. And are not Shumble and Whelper and Corker and Pigge, in the last instance, peasant names? William at this point has lately emerged from a reverie about Katchen, the entirely unsuitable girl to whom he had lost his heart in Jacksonburg.

Frailty, it might be said, thy name is Katchen. (Though the divine Julia Stitch can also play a pretty devious hand when it suits her.) The German girl's utter and transparent and mercenary indifference to all interests save her own, and her complete disregard for William's tender feelings, demonstrate how flayed Waugh still felt where women were concerned, and how easily a few careless words can first inflict pain and then generate bitterness. As with the owls and the rodents, and the poor, enthusiastic cub reporter who greets the returning Boot at Victoria station, life is random and unfair, and sin, however original, largely unpunished.

Perhaps aware that he might be in danger of letting cynicism or despair pollute his most sprightly fiction, Waugh summons the most literal *deus ex machina*. "Mr. Baldwin," first encountered on an aeroplane, alights again like an angel from the skies over the endangered shanties of Jacksonburg, and allows William to confirm his accidentally-acquired status as "Boot of the *Beast*." And from then on, the reign of good humor is restored. Even William's depraved Uncle Theodore, with his "dark and costly expeditions to London," ends the book with a reasonable chance of getting laid.

Lest I offend by the above vulgarism, I should point out that *Scoop*, though written by one who affected infinite contempt for America, pays its own tribute to modernity and Americanism. For all the dated "Bright Young Thing" slang ("Wasters" for *Waste of Time*: "Foregonners" for "foregone conclusion"— the same trick or tic that made Rugby Football into "rugger" and Association Football into "soccer") the New World is visible over the horizon. Lord Copper in Chapter Two finds that he has "gotten a new angle" on Mrs. Stitch's charisma. The expression "poor hick" is used early on to describe William, who is further depicted as a potential "sucker" when visiting General Cruttwell (in my opinion a potential original for Ian Fleming's boffin-like "Q") for his legendary outfitting. Most amazing of all, "When Corker and his friends" make a certain discovery about a ticket collector on their Ishmaelite train, "they felt very badly about this." Felt very badly? This may be one of the earliest usages of this barbarous neologism, and I felt ungood about it, as I did on noticing the novel's one other stylistic blemish: the repetition of "chafing dish and spirit lamp" at Boot's first dinner with Mr. Salter and at Mr. Salter's first and last dinner *chez* Boot.

These are spots on the sun. For all its marvellous fantasies and intricacies,

Scoop endures because it is a novel of pitiless realism; the mirror of satire held up to catch the Caliban of the press corps, as no other narrative has ever done save Hecht and MacArthur's *Front Page* and, to a smaller extent, Michael Frayn's *Towards the End of the Morning*. "Staunchly anti-interventionist," mutters Corker in robotic journalese after being reviled by an Ishmaelite landlady. "Doyenne of Jacksonburg hostesses pans police project as unwarrantable interference with sanctity of Ishmaelite home." In Moscow in the waning days of Communist rule, colleagues of mine discovered that the pre-Gorbachev ruler Konstantin Chernenko had died. But they got the tip from the cleaning ladies appointed to prepare the hall for the lying-in-state. Unwilling to give such lowly sources for their scoop, and deciding that everyone in the Soviet Union ultimately worked for the regime, they attributed the rumor to "low level government employees." While only the other day, the Toronto press reported that the wife of Conrad Black, himself a Megalopolitan type, had summoned a female reporter to her home. After some brisk questioning, she exclaimed: "But you're not the one I asked for." And so Elena Cherney discovered in time that she had been mistaken for Louisa Chialkowska ("the other one"). It still goes on, all right.

INTRODUCTION TO *SCOOP*
BY EVELYN WAUGH, 2000

THE MAN OF FEELING

A review of *LUCKY JIM*
by Kingsley Amis

I n *That Uncertain Feeling* (1955), one of Kingsley Amis's lesser novels, the narrator, John Lewis, is watching some young women play tennis, and decides to examine himself on an important question: "Why did I like women's breasts so much? I was clear on why I liked them, thanks, but why did I like them *so much*?" It's surprising, in a way, that Amis didn't capitalize those last words, as he was apt to do when he required any savage or emotional emphasis in his correspondence with Philip Larkin. (George Du Maurier's *Trilby*, for example, "might be a lot worse," he wrote. "AND A LOT BETTER.") But he seldom permitted any such heaviness to pervade his novels, and it is this very delicacy that allows one to answer the sensitive and dangerous question not Why is *Lucky Jim* funny? (daunting enough as an essay topic) but Why is it *so* funny?

I happened to be in Sarajevo when Kingsley Amis died, in 1995. I was to have lunch the following day with a very clever but rather solemn Slovenian dissident. She knew that I had known Amis a little, and she expressed the proper condolences as soon as we met. Feeling this to be not quite sufficient, however, she added that the genre of "academic comedy" had enjoyed quite a vogue among Balkan writers. "In our region zere are many such satires. But none I sink so amusing as ze *Lucky Jim*." This, delivered with perfect gravity in the lugubrious context of the Milosevic war, made me grin with inappropriate delight. How the old buzzard would have gagged, with mingled pride and disdain, at the thought of being so appreciated by a load of Continentals— nay, foreigners. And what the *hell* can his masterpiece be like when rendered into the Serbo-Croat tongue?

Just try to suggest a more hilarious novel from the past half century. Something by Joseph Heller? Terry Southern? David Lodge or Malcolm Bradbury? Yes, the Americans can be grotesque and noir; and the Englishmen have their mite of irony. (In fact, the "academic comedy" is now a sub-genre of Anglo-Americanism.) But even so. The late Peter de Vries—much admired by Amis for his *Mackerel Plaza*—depended too much on the farcical. No, the plain fact is that Amis managed in *Lucky Jim* (1954) to synthesize the comic achievements of Evelyn Waugh and P. G. Wodehouse. Just as a joke is not really a joke if it has to be clarified, I risk immersion in a bog of embarrassment if I overdo this; but if you can picture Bertie or Jeeves being capable of actual malice, and simultaneously imagine Evelyn Waugh forgetting about original sin, you have the combination of innocence and experience that makes this short romp so imperishable.

"The most powerful card in the hand of the novelist interested in character drawing," Amis once said, cleverly restating the obvious, "is differentiation by mode of speech." Well, we knew that from Dickens, didn't we? But Dickens never managed to convey in a few opening lines the pulverizing tedium and irritation provoked by our first-paragraph encounter with Professor Welch.

> "They made a silly mistake, though," the Professor of History said, and his smile, as Dixon watched, gradually sank beneath the surface of his features at the memory. "After the interval we did a little piece by Dowland," he went on; "for recorder and keyboard, you know. I played the recorder, of course, and young Johns . . ." He paused, and his trunk grew rigid as he walked; it was as if some entirely different man, some impostor who couldn't copy his voice, had momentarily taken his place; then he went on again . . .

Immediately one recognizes the lineaments ("you know," "of course," and "young Johns") of the practiced and uninterruptible bore. The absolute proof is delayed for a page or so, until Welch actually *is* interrupted—by a respectful and relevant question at that—and "his attention, like a squadron of slow old battleships, began wheeling to face this new phenomenon." At this moment, when our palms are getting slightly damp and our toes beginning to curl,

Welch's academic subordinate, the luckless Jim Dixon, has already mobilized his inner resources. He will when next alone "draw his lower lip in under his top teeth and by degrees retract his chin as far as possible, all this while dilating his eyes and nostrils," he promises himself. "By these means he would, he was confident, cause a deep dangerous flush to suffuse his face." Other "faces," denominated rather than described, include the shot-in-the-back face, the consumptive face, the tragic mask face, the mandarin, the crazy peasant, the Martian invader, the Eskimo, the Edith Sitwell, the metaphysical, the lemon-sucking, the mandrill, the lascar, the Evelyn Waugh, and the face that denotes "sex life in ancient Rome." Private faces in public places. All these are still to come, but we realize at once that if Dixon dared to wear an outward label, it would read "Warning: Contents Under Pressure." And as Chekhov stipulated, no gun that is onstage in the first act will be undischarged by the end. In other words, we are swiftly possessed by a sense of anticipation.

Not yet daring to play a subversive Sancho Panza to Welch's prolix Don Quixote, Dixon has also to register embarrassment of the most acute sort when he reflects upon the ghastly Margaret, a colleague to whom "he'd been drawn by a combination of virtues he hadn't known he possessed: politeness, friendly interest, ordinary concern, a good-natured willingness to be imposed upon, a desire for unequivocal friendship." This exposes him to such questions as "Do you like coming to see me?" "Do you think we get on well together?" "Am I the only girl you know in this place?" and—as the horror mounts—"Are we going to go on seeing so much of each other?" Dixon has to light cigarettes he cannot afford at the mere recollection of this. Having already recalled Paul Pennyfeather, in *Decline and Fall*, tyrannized by the cranky and solipsistic Dr. Fagan, he now puts me very much in mind of Bertie Wooster when confronted by the simpering Madeleine Bassett. Except that Madeleine Bassett was pretty and innocent, whereas Margaret (as Amis deftly conveys to us while keeping it from Dixon) is designing and sinister as well as ugly and frigid. It is only through a chance meeting with another man, Catchpole, that the decent and ingenuous Dixon eventually discovers just how designing and sinister she is. As with the faces, where Amis is confident that the reader will do much of the work in imagining how they might look (and feel), he can reliably convey character in just a few strokes.

Without overdrawing his picture of powerlessness and entrapment, Amis awards Dixon a mediocre physique ("on the short side, fair and round-faced, with an unusual breadth of shoulder that had never been accompanied by any special strength or skill"). He further gifts him with shabby clothes, a lack of funds, provincial manners, and a cramped room in a dismal boarding-house. Expert in the uses of humiliation, Amis takes only a sentence to intro-duce Michie, the most intimidating student in Dixon's sorely neglected class, who had "commanded a tank troop at Anzio while Dixon was an RAF cor-poral in western Scotland."

And how immediately one is ready to detest and abominate Bertrand, the pseudo-aesthete and bully who is the spoiled son of the vapid Professor Welch and his hard-boiled wife. Not only does he have a bad beard and an affectedly metropolitan manner, but this gargoyle pronounces the word "see" as " *sam*." The extremely trying noise comes out like this:

> The vowel sound became distorted into a short "a," as if he were going to say "sat." This brought his lips some way apart, and the effect of their rapid closure was to end the syllable with a light but audible "m."

I pause to note two things. The first is that this invention owes much to Amis's gift for poetry, and to his superlative qualities as a mimic. The second is that having coined it, he pushes it no further than it ought to be pushed. At evenly spaced intervals we and Jim Dixon hear Bertrand say "you sam," "hostelram," "got mam?," "this is just how I expected things to bam," and (most tellingly, in my view) "obviouslam." Again we feel a warm thrill of anticipation, realizing that someday Bertrand will say "you sam" once too often.

Metaphors and details are inserted so deftly that one scarcely notices how they push the action along. "Fury flared up in his mind like forgotten toast under a grill." A fellow lodger of Dixon's is described as employing a new pipe around which to train his personality "like a creeper up a trellis." A bellowing bandleader sounds like "an ogre at the onset of aphasia." The hideous Welches, at a musical recital, serve "coffee and cakes, intended to replace an evening meal." By these and further hints we build up a picture of Amis's atti-tude at the time, his genius for provincial and small-scale subversion.

Like the burned sheets and scorched but nonetheless "valuable-looking" rug that confront Jim in his nadir of hung-over disgrace at the Welches', the threadbare phrase "Angry Young Man" doesn't quite cover it. Dixon's rebellion arises from two simple elements of the servile condition: "real, over-mastering, orgiastic boredom, and its companion, real hatred." There are one or two political hints. Margaret turns out to sing for a local Conservative club, and Jim's first quarrel with Bertrand concerns the non-virtues of the rich. Thinking about his laughable scholarly project on medieval shipbuilding techniques, he reflects,

> Those who professed themselves unable to believe in the reality of human progress ought to cheer themselves up, as the students under examination had conceivably been cheered up, by a short study of the Middle Ages. The hydrogen bomb, the South African Government, Chiang Kai-Shek, Senator McCarthy himself, would then seem a light price to pay for no longer being in the Middle Ages.

And Mrs. Welch is represented as hostile to the welfare state. It's odd, and useful, to remember that when he was writing *Lucky Jim*, Amis was not yet completely through with the Communist Party. Yet one sees also the first symptoms of his famous turn toward the conservative world view. He shows a fine disdain for the new college system, where, as one of his more sympathetic characters puts it, "All right, we'll lower the pass mark to twenty percent and give you the quantity you want, but for God's sake don't start complaining in two years' time that your schools are full of teachers who couldn't pass the General Certificate themselves, let alone teach anyone else to pass it."

I don't know if I can claim to be the first reader to notice that there are a number of suggestive correlations between *Lucky Jim* and George Orwell's *Keep the Aspidistra Flying*. Jim Dixon and Gordon Comstock both have jobs they hate, and authorities to whom they must truckle. They are both oppressed by sterile and burdensome chunks of "work in progress." They both measure the days in cigarettes, often smoking one reserved for sometime next week. They both attack alcohol without compunction when given the chance, or the spare change, and both register penitential hangovers. They both live in grim furnished lodgings for bachelors. They both suffer from difficulties, or luck-lessness, with women. Each has a rich patron capable of acting as a *deus ex machina*. Moreover, the prettiest girl in Dixon's class (she is of course the partner of the self-assured Michie) is named Eileen O'Shaughnessy, as was Orwell's first wife. So it is perhaps possible to "locate" *Lucky Jim* in a tradition of English underdog writing, just as it was later plausible to "situate" it along with the work of John Osborne, John Wain, and other authors of postwar England. The difference, it is scarcely necessary to emphasize, is that *Lucky Jim* is wildly and anarchically funny, and that Dixon, so far from lapsing into anomie, is capable of seizing opportunity when it comes and making, literally, the best of it.

In October of 1954, an influential review in *The Spectator* announced the arrival of a "Movement," composed of Amis, Wain, Elizabeth Jennings, Thom Gunn, D. J. Enright, and Iris Murdoch, among others. The article's author, J. D. Scott, summarized the putative membership as "bored by the despair of the forties, not much interested in suffering, and extremely impatient of poetic sensibility, especially poetic sensibility about 'the writer and society.' "

> So it's goodbye to all those rather sad little discussions about "how the writer ought to live," and it's goodbye to the Little Magazine and "exper-imental writing." The Movement, as well as being anti-phoney, is anti-wet; sceptical, robust, ironic, prepared to be as comfortable as possible.

Amis's immediate reaction was to write to Philip Larkin and say, "Well, what a load of bullshit all that was in the *Spr* about the new movt. etc." And Evelyn Waugh wrote a rather grand letter of rebuke to the magazine the following week, concluding, "Please let the young people of today get on with their work alone and be treated to the courtesy of individual atten-tion. They are the less, not the more, interesting, if they are treated as a 'Movement.' " But it seems that critics need aggregates, and prefer to deal with writers in packs. They also appear to require some form of semiotics. Robert Conquest—the actual founder of "The Movement" as a poetic phe-nomenon—later wrote an essay for *Critical Quarterly* titled "Christian Sym-bolism in *Lucky Jim*," which was an obvious spoof from the very first page, citing "The Phallus Theme in Early Amis" and other learned articles. The magazine received so many serious and literal-minded letters, disputing some of the hermeneutic points, that the editors felt compelled to publish a disclaimer in the next issue, thus anticipating the *Social Text* hoax by some decades. Humor, as I was trying to say earlier, becomes distinctly less hysterical the more it has to be explained.

There is one element in the creation of *Lucky Jim* that has received insufficient attention and might (I suppose) gratify some of those critics who believe in collective or collaborative authorship. The novel was, quite evidently, co-written with Philip Larkin. At the onset of their Oxford friendship it was Larkin who wanted to be, and was, a novelist, and Amis who hoped to be, and was, a poet. One of the many charms of *The Letters of Kingsley Amis* (2000), which has been edited in masterly fashion by Zachary Leader, is the way in which the collection demonstrates the slow transformation of this symbiotic relationship, whereby each man took on some of the qualities of the other and mutated rather nicely into a counterpart rather than an opposite. Larkin's early novel *Jill* was a satire on low-level academic miseries, and he was the dedicatee of *Lucky Jim* at a time when he was too little known to be included in the roundup of The Movement.

We know, because Amis tells us in his memoirs (1991), that the idea for the novel came from a visit to Larkin's roost at University College, Leicester, where he lived on Dixon Drive. From the same pages we learn:

> In 1950, or so, I sent him my sprawling first draft and got back what amounted to a synopsis of the first third of the structure and other things besides. He decimated the characters that, in carried-away style, I had poured into the tale without care for the plot: local magnate Sir George Wettling, cricket-loving Philip Orchard, vivacious American visitor Teddy Wilson . . .

(Thank Christ for that, one hears oneself murmuring, even though Amis would have reproved the incorrect use of the word "decimate" by anyone else.) Larkin also prohibited the novel from being titled *Dixon and Christine* . But the debt is much deeper and more subtle, as the *Letters* gradually discloses.

Writing to the man he loved (there's no question about it), Amis describes the terrible imposition of his father-in-law (model for Welch) and says, "Whenever his face was turned away from mine, I screwed my own into a dazzle-pattern of hatred and fury." A month later he confides:

> If the style of this epistle becomes a little stiff and ungainly, or even incoherent, that will not be, I am sorry to say, because I am drunk, but because I mustn't light another cigarette until 11.30 A.M., and it is now 11.20 A.M., and I want to light a cigarette now, but I mustn't do that, because I have so little money to spend, and if I light a cigarette now, the packet that must last me for two days won't. You might tell me, by the way, what was good in my postscript.

The postscript, like the cigarette rationing, turns out to be part of the scheme for *Lucky Jim*. In a subsequent letter, dated September 8, 1952, Amis rehearses almost every facet of the novel in accordance with Larkin's instructions. The paragraphing is the result of a meticulous collaboration, with sequence headings ("the library," "the lecture," "the job," "Bertrand's pass," "Mediaevalism") that addicts will easily recognize as the eventual core ingredients. In all instances Amis was happy and grateful for trenchant advice. Then there is an appeal based on pure friendship and trust.

> Would it be asking too much to ask you to skim quickly through the typescript, making marginal indications of anything that displeases you? ("Bad style," "damp squib," bad bit of dialogue & so on, to prevent me using them again.)

Two months later he was promising Larkin to restart the novel—by this time titled *The Man of Feeling*—from scratch. By March of 1953 he was more or less finished, altering only a few curlicues ("I have changed 'his Indian beggar face' to 'his Evelyn Waugh face' ").

This is not only a very moving acknowledgment—Amis freely donated these letters to posterity—of the invaluable influence of a fellow author. It is also, unless I am quite deluded, the clue to an underappreciated aspect of the novel. Extensive tracts of *Lucky Jim* are not humorous at all—deliberately not humorous, if you follow me. Bleakness obtrudes, especially in the many discussions and depictions of unhappiness, mediocrity, failure, and even suicide. Most of Dixon's inoffensive friends (he's always called Dixon) are as much doomed to disappointment and indigence as he at first seems to be. And his disasters and triumphs are rendered in such a way as to put us in mind of manic-depressive mood swings. (At one point he feels like a man who while fighting a policeman sees another policeman approaching on a horse; later he feels like a man being awarded a medal who is simultaneously told of a large win in the lottery.) The crowning, triumphant tautology—the limitless way in which nice things are nicer than nasty things—is no comfort to the afflicted. It is more of a stoic cliché, of the sort in which Larkin later specialized. Dixon also has a persistent, almost Chekhovian yearning to quit the provinces and move to the capital city, of which he has an idealized impression. Larkin stayed with the provinces: Leicester, Belfast, and eventually Hull, whereas Amis moved to London when he became a success. This partial estrangement between the two was what underlay their subsequent lifelong correspondence.

Both men thought of boredom as a form of tyranny and also (more important) as a symptom of it. To them, the bores of the world were not merely tedious. They were, by their dogma and repetition and righteousness, advertising an evil will to power. Dixon's eventual explosion of drunken defiance is something more than an enjoyable fiasco or—ancient Rome again—saturnalia. It gives expression to a term that seems incongruous when one first reads it: "active hatred." This is the only possible riposte to "orgiastic boredom." No one familiar with Larkin's caustic, understated poetic contempt can fail to recognize the kinship here.

Evelyn Waugh punished an Oxford don who had bored him—a Dr. Cruttwell—by using his name for purposes of ridicule in at least four novels. Amis took revenge against an editor named Caton by using his name for hateful or shifty parts in his first five books and then killing him off in *The Anti-Death League* (1966). It is Caton who plagiarizes the deadly essay—*The Economic Influence of the Developments of Shipbuilding Techniques, 1450 to 1485*—with which Dixon has been killing himself (with boredom). The self-hatred that can also arise from boredom is hilariously caught when Dixon mordantly reviews his own opening sentence.

> "In considering this strangely neglected topic," it began. This what neglected topic? This strangely what topic? This strangely neglected what? His thinking all this without having defiled and set fire to the typescript only made him appear to himself as more of a hypocrite and fool.

Hilarious but somewhat sobering. Dixon's later self-manumission needs to be seen in this light, as part of the declaration of Amis's protracted war against hypocrisy and phoniness of all kinds, a war in which Larkin was to be his long-term ally. The ensuing novels, at their best, all contain elements first tested in *Lucky Jim*. The brilliant indirect line about the mock-threatening letter ("There seemed no point in not posting it") recurs in *Girl, 20* (1971), in which another valuable rug is destroyed—this time to the narrator's displeasure. In that same novel the hero has to run hard for a bus, and discovers that a young woman is making sinister use of pills. He also has to go on a date in surroundings of musical chaos even more raucous than those Dixon endures at "the ball." Roger Micheldene, in *One Fat Englishman* (1963), is confronted with every type of pretentious academic tomfoolery; and he finds, as Dixon did with Christine, that girls threaten to leave when men start fighting over them. *One Fat Englishman,* Amis's only novel set in the United States, also begins in the middle of a dialogue. The asexual and ambitious woman is a recurrent theme for which Amis got himself accused of misogyny; but every objective person of either sex will admit to having met the terrifying Margaret in his or her time. Her "anterior bad luck of being sexually unattractive," a misfortune that is given full play in *Ending Up* (1974), is one of those facts of life from which Amis never spared his male characters either. (Actually, *Lucky Jim* is notable for the near complete absence of any explicit carnality—a considerable sacrifice for either a comic or a "serious" writer.)

It's not absolutely clear how the novel eventually came to be baptized, after its hideous first two tryout titles. But toward the end (and after he has nearly wrecked himself to catch the crucial bus) Jim does reflect on luck. As happens so often, fortune is coterminous with a lady.

> To write things down as luck wasn't the same as writing them off as non-existent or in some way beneath consideration. Christine was nicer and prettier than Margaret, and all the deductions that could be

drawn from that fact should be drawn: there was no end to the ways in which nice things are nicer than nasty ones. It had been luck, too, that had freed him from pity's adhesive plaster: if Catchpole had been a different sort of man, he, Dixon, would still be wrapped up as firmly as ever. And now he badly needed another dose of luck. *If it came, he might yet prove to be of use to somebody.*

The italics are mine. The statement, and the thought, are profoundly moral. Beware what you wish for, unless you have the grace to hope that your luck can be shared. *Lucky Jim* illustrates a crucial human difference between the little guy and the small man. And Dixon, like his creator, was no clown but a man of feeling after all.

THE ATLANTIC, MAY 2002

THE MISFORTUNE
OF POETRY

A review of *BYRON: LIFE AND LEGEND*
by Fiona MacCarthy

In Jane Austen's *Persuasion*, Anne Elliot has a surprising discussion with a shy naval officer about the relative merits of Sir Walter Scott and Lord Byron, and finds Captain Benwick to be "so intimately acquainted with all the tenderest songs of the one poet, and all the impassioned descriptions of hopeless agony of the other; he repeated, with such tremulous feeling, the various lines which imaged a broken heart, or a mind destroyed by wretchedness, and looked so entirely as if he meant to be understood, that she ventured to hope he did not always read only poetry; and to say, that she thought it was the misfortune of poetry, to be seldom safely enjoyed by those who enjoyed it completely; and that the strong feelings which alone could estimate it truly, were the very feelings which ought to taste it but sparingly."

It is notorious that the Napoleonic Wars seldom achieve even the level of offstage noise in Austen's work, but in *Persuasion*, which was finished not long after the Battle of Waterloo, there are repeated references to Byron—a figure who in his lifetime was often compared to Bonaparte himself, and who excited similar feelings of fear and loathing, as well as admiration, among his countrymen. Nobody would describe the virgin genius of Hampshire as a romantic, but when she considered the aspect of romance, she found it hard to keep Byron's unwholesome but fascinating visage out of her mind.

By a nice coincidence, when W. H. Auden came to write his "Letter to Lord Byron," he explained that he had originally thought of writing to Jane Austen instead.

There is one other author in my pack:
For some time I debated which to write to.
Which would least likely send my letter back?
But I decided that I'd give a fright to
Jane Austen if I wrote when I'd ∿ right to,
And share in her contempt the dreadful fates
Of Crawford, Musgrave, and of Mr Yates . . .

You could not shock her more than she shocks me;
Beside her Joyce seems innocent as grass.
It makes me most uncomfortable to see
An English spinster of the middle class
Describe the amorous effects of 'brass',
Reveal so frankly and with such sobriety
The economic basis of society.

Written in 1936, as Auden was about to set off for the war in Spain, and cleverly imitating the rhyme of Byron's *Don Juan*, this poem offers a key with which to decode the relationship between the personal and the poetic in the Byron myth. Byron, as Auden was to say later, "was an egoist and, like all egoists, capable of falling in love with a succession of dream-figures, but incapable of genuine love or fidelity which accepts a person completely . . . he was also acutely conscious of guilt and sin." However, "when Byron had ceased to identify his moral sense with himself and had discovered how to extract the Byronic Satanism from his lonely hero and to turn it into the Byronic Irony which illuminated the whole setting, when he realized that he was a little ridiculous, but also not as odd as he had imagined, he became a great poet."

In this way, and employing his gentle style of self-mockery, Auden was able to draw upon Byron in making his own great refreshment of English poetry. What might serve as an apt illustration of "the Byronic Irony"? I propose my favorite example. Byron's "The Isles of Greece" has for years been included in school anthologies, as a hymn to the lost glory of Hellas and an appeal for the noble revival of its epic period. The poet speaks of dying for liberty, and we all know of Byron's "romantic" end at Missolonghi. But if one looks up those celebrated lines in the third canto of *Don Juan*, one finds them set apart, in a different scheme and meter, as a kind of spoof or knockoff. Juan meets a poet at an Oriental court, a creator of *vers d'occasion* who is all things to all men and who works on the principle of "when in Rome."

> In France, for instance, he would write a chanson;
> In England a six canto quarto tale;
> In Spain, he'd make a ballad or romance on
> The last war—much the same in Portugal;
> In Germany, the Pegasus he'd prance on
> Would be old Goethe's (see what says De Staâl);
> In Italy, he'd ape the 'Trecentisti;'
> In Greece, he'd sing some sort of hymn like this t'ye:

and off we gallop into the soaring notes of "The Isles of Greece," which can still start a patriotic tear on a manly cheek but which was originally composed and offered as a self-parody. This goes some way toward vindicating Auden's definition of the ironic.

However, Auden was startlingly mistaken when he opined that "Byron was not really odd like Wordsworth; his experiences were those of the ordinary man." And Lord Macaulay, in his famous defense of Byron against the moralists and the censors, was also wrong in believing that a moment would soon come when people would forget the scandals and dramas of the life and pay attention solely to the poetry. Byron's career is more like a comet than the meteor to which it is usually compared: it comes around again and again, to be reviewed and revisited. And his life has become indissoluble from his work.

This is partly because he was an actual aristocrat as well as a natural one. His example, and his leadership, met two of Max Weber's criteria for authority in being simultaneously traditional and charismatic. While he was still at Cambridge University, with a princely allowance and a servant and a horse, he wrote to his half-sister Augusta Leigh to say that he felt "as independent as a German Prince who coins his own Cash, or a Cherokee Chief who coins no Cash at all, but enjoys what is more precious, Liberty." This was having it both ways in a handsome style, and also stating a paradox that would continue to stamp his life. There can be no doubt that a large element in Byron's impact pertained to "the economic basis of society."

Another element has to do with matters that are not treated at all in the work of Jane Austen. John Murray, of Albemarle Street (who was also Austen's publisher), famously destroyed the manuscript of Byron's memoirs and strove, often successfully, to bowdlerize the more profane and obscene passages in the output of his most profitable author—a historical deficit for which Fiona MacCarthy s biography seeks to compensate. This book is awash not just in incest and sodomy but also in fairly graphic mentions of the ravages of the pox, of piles and rectal damage, and of male and female prostitution. She makes a persuasive case for considering Byron's heterosexual promiscuity as at least in part a losing struggle with homosexual pedophilia. And she delivers some strong whiffs of Swiftian disgust. Byron detested the sight of women eating, and was obsessed with what might politely be called bathroom arrangements. He was acutely aware of society's being balanced precariously over a brimming cloaca. His years of innocence were brief: at the age of nine he was subjected to much groping and fondling by his nurse, May Gray, who also used to whip him savagely and to terrorize him with hellfire religious rants. In other words, before he was ten, Byron had been made intimately aware of the relationship between sex and cruelty, and also the relationship between authority and superstition. I once proposed that a search be made for the gravesite of this sordid woman. It should be restored and preserved as a temple of the Romantic movement.

Invocation of the inevitable term "Romantic" engages us in another paradox. Byron may have compared himself to Bonaparte, and may have been so compared by, among others, Carlyle and Macaulay. (Bonaparte was a Corsican; Byron always felt Scottish in allegiance, and was at an angle to the prevailing "English" culture.) He may have thrown away his chance of a political career by making a deliberately incendiary speech on Irish freedom and Catholic emancipation in the House of Lords. He may have sought to lay bare the hypocrisy of the dominant social and sexual mores, tilting with spectacular success (and from some dearly bought experience) at the pretense that women were never the initiators in matters of the bedroom. But in poetic and literary matters he was rather conventional. Sir Walter Scott thought him sound, and Byron returned the compliment. In *English Bards and Scotch Reviewers* he stood up for Dryden and Pope and the great tradition, and reprobated what he viewed as mere novelty and rebellion. The conservative and anti-Jacobin critics were full of praise for his attachment to proper form. His supposedly fellow "Romantics," most especially Wordsworth and Southey (Byron was later partially reconciled to Shelley and Coleridge), were targets he never tired of ridiculing. Keats's writing he dismissed as "a sort of mental masturbation—he is always frigging his *Imagination*." Indeed, *Don Juan* opens with a laughing attack on the insipid nature-worshippers whom Byron called (after their attachment to certain scenery) "the Lakers."

> *You—Gentlemen! by dint of long seclusion*
> *From better company, have kept your own*
> *At Keswick, and, through still continued fusion*
> *Of one another's minds, at last have grown*
> *To deem as a most logical conclusion*
> *That Poesy has wreaths for you alone:*
> *There is a narrowness in such a notion,*
> *Which makes me wish you'd change your lakes for ocean.*

By deciding to live dangerously, however, Byron met some of the other, rather vague criteria of Romanticism. There were several moments in this fascinating book when I was put in mind of Nietzsche, and when the energetic dashes of Byron's punctuation drove home the point.

> The great object of life is Sensation—to feel that we exist—even though in pain—it is this "craving void" which drives us to Gaming—to Battle—to Travel—to intemperate but keenly felt pursuits of every description whose principal attraction is the agitation inseparable from their accomplishment.

To a critic, Francis Palgrave, who deplored the alternation between high and low in *Don Juan,* Byron riposted in effect that the man had water or milk in his veins:

> Did he never spill a dish of tea over his testicles in handing the cup to

his charmer to the great shame of his nankeen breeches?—and he never swim in the sea at Noonday with the Sun in his eyes and on his head—which all the foam of ocean could not cool? did he never draw his foot out of a tub of too hot Water damning his eyes & his valet's? did he never inject for a Gonorrhea?—or make water through an ulcerated Urethra?—was he ever in a Turkish bath—that marble paradise of sherbet and sodomy?—was he ever in a cauldron of boiling oil like St. John?

Allowance made for the boiling oil, Byron could have claimed in every case to know what he was talking about (and we also have here an oblique reference to his seldom mentioned clubfoot and lifelong lameness). Indeed, not only did he swim the Hellespont in emulation of Leander's pursuit of Hero—and take time to notice that few lovers would have been in any condition for venery after such exertion—but he also swam three miles in blazing heat on the day of Shelley's funeral and lost swatches of skin as a consequence. Those who have seen the pure white marble of Shelley's exquisite corpse at his Oxford memorial will perhaps benefit from reading the description of his actual obsequies on that beach: the body putrid and bloated and blue, the skull crumbling in the fire while the heart would not "take the flame." For this reason only, and for no Romantic one, was it preserved as a ghastly, oozing relic.

By then Byron had also met his own condition of "changing his lakes for ocean," becoming not a mere local rebel but an internationalist one. The comparison with Bonaparte may seem absurd or disproportionate in many ways: for one (I was oddly struck when I realized the obviousness of this), Byron never actually engaged directly in any battle. But if modern celebrity has nineteenth-century roots, they are certainly in his combination of the role of poet with that of man of action, and on a Europe-wide scale. I say "Europe-wide" because he never crossed the Atlantic, even though his two other heroes were George Washington and Simón Bolívar, his fame in America was considerable during his lifetime, and he often expressed a desire to emigrate to the land from which the Hanoverian monarchs had been evicted.

It's difficult to picture Byron as an American. True, one of the very few "modern" things about him was a life-long obsession with his weight and his silhouette, both of which tended to fluctuate alarmingly. He once wrote that he had two fears, of getting fat and of going mad, and there were times when he was both. So he could in a pinch be a recruit to the future republic of diet and therapy. Most of his inclinations, however, lay toward those lands that had a connection to antiquity and embraced the possibility of excess. He was in some ways a premature Orientalist, very much taken with scenes of the voluptuous and the barbaric; the painting of Delacroix can be viewed as a sort of pictorial Byronism. But he was more than just a voyeur in these exotic latitudes. He took a serious interest in the religions and customs and traditions, and also the political convulsions, of the places he visited or studied. Re-reading *Childe Harold's Pilgrimage* recently, I came across this verse in the second canto, where the contest between the Muslim and Christian worlds, in Constantinople and in Athens, is evoked.

> *The city won for Allah from the Giaour,*
> *The Giaour from Ottoman's race again may wrest;*
> *And the Serai's impenetrable tower*
> *Receive the fiery Frank, her former guest;*
> *Or Wahab's rebel brood, who dared divest*
> *The prophet's tomb of all its pious spoil,*
> *May wind their path of blood along the West . . .*

The takeover and desecration of Mecca by the ultra-purist Wahhabi sect was then just a decade old. Byron's registering of this event—and his identification of a faction that now troubles us all—is the first literary mention that I know of.

Everybody understands that there was another reason why Byron liked to voyage in torrid zones. He put it pretty bluntly himself when he wrote that in England "*Cant* is so much stronger than *Cunt*." Defending *Don Juan* from the disapproving and the censorious, he wrote to his friend Douglas Kinnaird that it was "the sublime of *that there* sort of writing—it may be bawdy—but is it not good English?—it may be profligate—but is it not *life* , is it not *the thing*?" He continued, "Could any man have written it—who has not lived in the world?—and tooled in a post-chaise? in a hackney coach? in a Gondola?

Against a wall? in a court carriage? in a vis-a-vis?—on a table?—and under it?"
MacCarthy is surely correct in discerning a slight unease beneath this
boasting. Byron must have been aware that his compulsive, exorbitant sex life
was the enemy of his grander ambitions as a radical. Not only did his
debauchery, alcoholic as well as carnal, consume an inordinate amount of
his time, but it exacted a tremendous toll on his health. His years in England,
and the ceaseless and costly confrontations with a wronged wife, a wronged
mistress, and a deeply wronged half-sister, were truly an expense of spirit in a
waste of shame. He evinced an unattractive contempt for the dowdier and
more worthy democratic revolutionaries, notably Leigh Hunt, who seemed
earthbound and respectable. He admired Milton as a poet and a dissident, but
was frankly snobbish about his humble political descendants. And his post-
Miltonic epic poem *Cain,* which is actually a very moving and despairing
assault on biblical literalism and servile human credulity, was compromised
by the stress he laid on Cain's love for his sister, and the inescapable analogy
to his own dissipations with Augusta Leigh.

The two great and contrasting episodes when his life and work functioned
in harmony, rather than in antagonism, were his experiences in Venice and
Greece. Byron had a prejudice in favor of amphibious locations, perhaps
because in the water his crippled leg was no disadvantage; but his feeling for
the Serenissima went well beyond that, and so much did he help to rekindle
aesthetic and poetic sympathy for the city that John Ruskin, decades later,
viewed it almost entirely through his eyes. As for Greece, Fiona MacCarthy is
again correct in stating that, at last, Byron found a cause that summoned
from him a mature commitment. His flirtation with the Carbonari rebels in
Italy had an operetta flavor of pseudo-daring and extravagant gesture; but
once he had sailed past Ithaca to Missolonghi, leaving his mistress behind and
living on rough rations, he took on the lineaments of an authentic hero. It's
true that the theatrical did not desert him even there. As if achieving his
youthful ambition to be both a German prince and a Cherokee chief, he
shared risks and hardships with gaunt Suliote guerrillas while expending
much of his fortune on personally designed (mainly tartan) uniforms and
emblems for his private army. Had he lived, he might actually have been proclaimed King of Greece; Sir Harold Nicolson once wrote a marvelous essay on
this "what if?" proposition. Still, Byron persisted and sacrificed like a democrat

in the face of appalling discouragements and privations, and those hooked on the Romantic mythos should (as with Shelley's funeral) attend to the details, full of bleeding and excrement, of his last illness.

Of course, it was not to be expected that Byron would change utterly. At the last he appears to have become infatuated with a boy named Lukas Chalandritsanos. The beautiful closing poems "Last Words on Greece" and "On This Day I Complete My Thirty-Sixth Year" are fairly obviously encoded with a hopeless man-boy love. Byron was acutely conscious of his own physical decline, and his last agonies of obsession made me think at once of Mann's Aschenbach and his death—in Venice.

The grace of early death is the seal on the Romantic pact; Byron did not live to become gross and farcical and reminiscent. Instead his gallant ending was the signal and the symbol for later European revolt. Mazzini was inspired by it, Victor Hugo and Heinrich Heine were consumed by it, Adam Mickiewicz fought and wrote for Poland in Byronic mode, and one of the young poets who led the Decembrist revolution against the Czar went to the scaffold with a volume of Byron in his hand. Men of somewhat different temper were still much affected: Matthew Arnold wrote of Byron as "that world-fam'd Son of Fire." Oscar Wilde, always fascinated by hubris, worshipped Byron and made a sly guess or two about his relationship with Shelley. There's no equivalent in our own time—though Byron's decision to name his ship the *Bolivar* does suggest a connection with the cult of Che Guevara. At any rate, if his life may illustrate Jane Austen's admonition that the intoxications of poetry are not conducive to proper stability and well-being, his work is the best-known refutation of Auden's judgment, on Yeats, that "poetry makes nothing happen."

THE ATLANTIC, OCTOBER 2002

THE ACUTEST EAR IN PARIS

A review of *SWANN'S WAY*
by Marcel Proust, translated by Lydia Davis

I have not been able to discover whether there exists a precise French equivalent for the common Anglo-American expression "killing time."[*] It's a very crass and breezy expression, when you ponder it for a moment, considering that time, after all, is killing us. Marcel Proust was the man who, by contemplating in a way that transcended the moment, attempted to interpenetrate these two forbidding alternatives.

When the Monty Python gang acted out its "Summarize Proust" competition, one of the contestant teams, a madrigal group, was cut off abruptly by the master of ceremonies before it had got beyond the opening stave of *Swann's Way*. One can readily appreciate the difficulty; yet if I were asked to "summarize" the achievement of Proust, I should reply as dauntlessly as I dared that his is the work par excellence that exposes and clarifies the springs of human motivation. Through his eyes we see what actuates the dandy and the lover and the grandee and the hypocrite and the poseur, with a transparency unexampled except in Shakespeare or George Eliot. And this ability, so piercing and at times even alarming, is not mere knowingness. It is not, in other words, the product of cynicism. To be so perceptive and yet so innocent—that, in a phrase, is the achievement of Proust. It is also why one does well to postpone a complete reading until one is in the middle of life, and has shared some of the disillusionments and fears, as well as the delights, that come with this mediocre actuarial accomplishment. Because plainly, along with being

[*]I should have looked further. Baudelaire employs the term in precisely that way in his prose poem *Le Galant Tireur*.

"about" social climate and fashion, and the countryside versus the city, and sexual inversion and also Jewishness, with *l'affaire* Dreyfus one of the binding and constitutive elements in its narrative, Proust's novel ("the novel form," he wrote in one letter, is the form from which "it departs least") is all about time. And one does not fully appreciate this aspect until one has learned something of how time is rationed, and of how this awful and apparently inexorable dole may conceivably be cheated. The foregoing is intended as a word of encouragement. Proust can be regained, even if—in the very long run—time itself cannot.

My introduction to *A la recherche du temps perdu* came by way of Terence Kilmartin, who died in 1991, roughly a decade after completing his retranslation of C. K. Scott Moncrieff's original English rendering. Kilmartin was, as well as a translator, an editor of considerable verve and decision. He made the book pages of the London *Observer* into a necessary weekly resource for the literate—an infinitely elastic "section" in which more seemed to get itself discussed than the allotted space could conceivably permit. To give you an idea of Kilmartin's panache: I was once told by Gore Vidal that after turning in his first review to the Kilmartin regime, he received a telephone call from Kilmartin informing him that the piece had had to be shortened by half a dozen lines. Exigency at the printer's had meant that this pruning had been executed by the editor himself. "Oh, no you don't, Mr. Kilmartin," said an irate Vidal, shortly before replacing the receiver with a bang. "Nobody cuts my stuff except me. I shall not be contributing to your pages again." When he later seized that Sunday's offending *Observer* in a foul frame of mind, Vidal found that he could not tell where (or how) the excisions had been made. After duly stopping off at Canossa, he gave Kilmartin full power of attorney.

Kilmartin wrote a highly amusing and illuminating account of his experience as a Proust revisionist, which appeared in the first issue of Ben Sonnenberg's quarterly *Grand Street* in the autumn of 1981. The essay opened with a kind of encouragement: "There used to be a story that discerning Frenchmen preferred to read Marcel Proust in English on the grounds that the prose of *A la recherche du temps perdu* was deeply un-French and heavily influenced by English writers such as Ruskin." I cling to this even though Kilmartin thought it to be ridiculous Parisian snobbery; I shall never be able to read Proust in French, and one's opportunities for outfacing Gallic self-regard are relatively scarce. It seems to be the case, at all events, that Scott Moncrieff aroused a possessive instinct in the French. He published his translation of *Swann's Way* just as Proust was dying, in 1922, and by the time of his own death, in 1930, had made the work into something like a vogue or a cult in the Anglophone universe. (He did not live to undertake *Le temps retrouvé,* which was Englished by other hands.) For decades Proust was eclipsed in France, first by surrealism, next by *la littérature engagée,* and then by the existentialists. Not until the 1950s, with the advent of André Maurois's *A la recherche de Marcel Proust,* did French literary opinion decide to reclaim Proust, and was the celebrated Pléiade edition published. This event in its turn began to generate concern among English-speaking Proustians that their treasured translation might not be quite up to standard, which meant that French precedence had been restored and that—in Cartesian terms, at least—reason had regained her Parisian throne.

When I was quite young, I often made the trip between suburban North Oxford and the wooded grounds of Blenheim Palace, in Woodstock. At some stage of my boyhood I was told that the Oxford-to-Woodstock distance was ten miles, and to this day, if at the end of any tiring journey I see a road sign indicating the remaining distance to be ten miles, I instantly feel that I am almost home. I am sure that everybody has a similar mnemonic prompting, and Marcel Proust wrote the book, so to speak, about mnemonic devices. But the distance to be traversed between, or as between, the Swann and the Meseglise and the Guermantes "ways" is measured also in metaphysics. Kilmartin thought a good deal about the responsibility this entailed. He didn't cite Hegel's famous observation about the Owl of Minerva taking wing only as its surroundings turn crepuscular, but he did realize that "the complexities of the opening pages of the novel are especially difficult to decipher without the hindsight provided by the later volumes."

> I myself noticed too late (after the new version had gone to press) that in the paragraph evoking the bedroom at Tansonville *la chambre ou je me serai endormi* had become in English "the bedroom in which I shall presently fall asleep" (instead of "in which I must have fallen asleep"), thus giving the reader the impression that the narrator is writing at Tansonville instead of in Paris some years after.

A similar *bêtise*—this time caught by Kilmartin—had altered the spatio-temporal significance of Swann's jealous questioning of Odette. He demands to be told, of her possible lesbian encounters, "*Il y a combien de temps?*" Perhaps to an extent giving away his own proclivities, Scott Moncrieff made this into "How many times?" instead of "How long ago?" Even my French would be equal to that, as it would have been on the occasions when Scott Moncrieff, astonishingly, gave *actuel* as "actual." If only the present and the actual were indeed the same. But what's the occasional *faux ami* between real friends?

I think I am not wrong about Scott Moncrieff's tendencies; he was well attuned to the gay vernacular, and his translation of "*ce 'chichi' voulu*" as "this deliberate camping" is held by experts to be the first use of the expression in print. However, his youthfulness relative to Proust might furnish a clue to a certain insouciance about time and its passage, of the sort that I mentioned previously. The very first sentence of the novel, "*Longtemps je me suis couché de bonne heure,*" may very well be, as Kilmartin suggested, "deliberately ambiguous; it leaves the reader in a state of uncertainty as to the narrator's position in time." The chosen tense is the *passé composé,* or past perfect, but the imperfect keeps obtruding as the paragraph lengthens, and Kilmartin expressed frustration with the manner in which Scott Moncrieff had "smoothly evade[d] the issue" by phrasing it simply: "For a long time I used to go to bed early." (In my Modern Library edition of Proust, which has Kilmartin updated and refurbished by the late D. J. Enright, the first words now read, "For a long time I would go to bed early.")

I have so far not improved much on the progress made by the Monty Python madrigal group; but surely there is some charm in the discrepancies and eccentricities that at least potentially give every reader his or her "own" Proust. Nancy Mitford wrote to Evelyn Waugh, "There is not one joke in all the sixteen of S. Moncrieff's volumes. In French one laughs from the stomach, as when reading you." E. M. Forster, in *Abinger Harvest*, wrote in a somewhat aggrieved manner that he was disappointed by Scott Moncrieff, "because I was hoping to find Proust easier in English than in French, and do not." Forster continued, "All the difficulties of the original are here faithfully reproduced." That's not quite the same thing as stating that the difficulties were Scott Moncrieff's fault. As for jokes, I sometimes think that it's better to let them mature in the cask. In the chapter "Swann in Love" the eponymous figure quits an assignation with Odette, who has poured him some outstanding tea, and reflects as follows:

> This tea had indeed seemed to Swann, just as it seemed to her, something precious, and love has such a need to find some justification for itself, some guarantee of duration, in pleasures which without it would have no existence and must cease with its passing, that when he left her at seven o'clock to go and dress for the evening, all the way home in his brougham, unable to repress the happiness with which the afternoon's adventure had filled him, he kept repeating to himself: "How nice it would be to have a little woman like that in whose house one could always be certain of finding, what one never can be certain of finding, a really good cup of tea."

I can well imagine Nancy Mitford's laughing at that, with its bathos as regards the fluctuation of male passion, and its allied tone of English-style *froideur*. It is left to Proust to allow the other shoe to fall—more swiftly than is his custom—when the succeeding paragraph dispels Swann's fatuous idyll.

> An hour or so later he received a note from Odette, and at once recognised that large handwriting in which an affectation of British stiffness imposed an apparent discipline upon ill-formed characters, suggestive, perhaps, to less biased eyes than his, of an untidiness of mind, a fragmentary education, a want of sincerity and will-power. Swann had left his cigarette-case at her house. "If only," she wrote, "you had also forgotten your heart! I should never have let you have that back."

That letter would stand high in any anthology of what Kingsley Amis once called "cock-crinkling" remarks, and is an unusually severe, if oblique, rebuke to a member of the educated bourgeoisie who had been congratulating himself only for a good *cinq-à-sept* lay and a decent cup of tea (and who has been patting his pockets and wondering where he left his damn smokes). It's easy to see how the Proustian manner became a fashion among the Brits. And that's before one catches the distant echo of yet another shoe, almost muffled in its modesty and reticence: the very cup of tea and frail piece of fragrant cake from which the whole mnemonic epic derives its *mise-en-scène.*

Kilmartin's work as both editor and interpreter has been a cause of great happiness to me, so I bristled somewhat when I read, in Lydia Davis's introduction to her new translation of *Swann's Way*, the following rather back-handed tribute:

A revision of Scott Moncrieff's translation by Terence Kilmartin, based on the corrected edition of the French, brought the translation closer to the original, cutting gratuitous additions and embellishments and correcting Scott Moncrieff's own misreadings, though it did not go as far as it could have in cutting redundancy and also introduced the occasional grammatical mistake and mixed metaphor; in addition, Kilmartin's ear for the language was not as sensitive as Scott Moncrieff's.

I can really measure redundancy only in English, and I had already noticed in Davis's introduction a reference to "the wistful closing coda in the Bois de Boulogne." A coda can only be a closure, so the sin of redundancy (or tautology, or pleonasm) is one that Davis might be careful about stricturing in others. She also repeats the word "cutting" in the brief passage above, when other terms of art and editing are available to her and when, surely, the most one can hope to achieve in the case of Proust is the reduction of repetition, not its elimination.

I thus commenced in a fault-finding frame of mind. The best plan seemed to be a straight comparison between versions of my favorite passages in *Swann's Way*. One of these is the description of the loyal but venomous cook Françoise, unacknowledged ruler of the house at Combray. Her vendetta against the hapless and pregnant kitchen maid is one of the minor splendors of the early chapters. Of the unknown and presumably taste-lacking seducer of this foolish, fallen girl Françoise says in the Kilmartin translation, which comes more or less straight from Scott Moncrieff:

"Dear, dear, it's just as they used to say in my poor mother's day:
'Frogs and snails and puppy-dogs' tails,
And dirty sluts in plenty,
Smell sweeter than roses in young men's noses
When the heart is one-and-twenty.' "

The Davis version puts it like this:

> *"Oh dear! It's just as they used to say in my poor mother's patois:*
> *'Fall in love with a dog's bum,*
> *And thou'll think it pretty as a plum.' "*

Now, the original French is even more pungent, and also (grant Proust this much, for once) more terse:

> *"Qui du cul d'un chien s'amourose,*
> *Il lui parait une rose."*

The whole point of downstairs peasant wisdom, as quoted with amusement by those upstairs, is that it be brisk, vulgar, and memorable. The Scott Moncrieff/ Kilmartin rendition fails to observe this rule. It also shields the reader from indecency, which Scott Moncrieff doesn't elsewhere do, and which I would have thought would be unthinkable for Kilmartin. Benjamin Ivry, an experienced translator, has preferred to fault Davis—for using the word "patois," which admittedly is not the term that Françoise herself would be likely to employ. And he quarrels with the rhyme of "bum" and "plum," partly because "bum" is too British. I would say, rather, that using "plum" for "rose" (the latter is, after all, the same word in both tongues) constitutes the mistake here. The necessary image is that of a young man so pussy-trapped, and indeed ass-struck, that he acts like a dog and is prompted by rank and exciting scent. "Puppy-dogs' tails" is a sorry prettification of that notion. If we exonerate Davis for dropping the perfectly serviceable and probable locution "my poor mother's day" and substituting what has become the near Franglais word "patois," the honor here—in point of pungency as well as fidelity—belongs to her.

Proust was more acutely aware of the imminence of death in life than almost any other author, and he took the death of love as his special premonition of the impending or the inevitable. So, even as Swann is sinking,

> From that evening onwards, Swann understood that the feeling which
> Odette had once had for him would never revive, that his hopes of

happiness would not be realised now. And on the days on which she happened to be once more kind and affectionate towards him, had shown him some thoughtful attention, he recorded these deceptive signs of a change of feeling on her part with the fond and sceptical solicitude, the desperate joy of people who, nursing a friend in the last days of an incurable illness, relate as facts of infinitely precious insignificance: "Yesterday he went through his accounts himself, and actually corrected a mistake we had made in adding them up; he ate an egg today and seemed quite to enjoy it, and if he digests it properly we shall try him with a cutlet tomorrow"—although they themselves know that these things are meaningless on the eve of an inevitable death. [Kilmartin/Enright]

From this evening on, Swann realized that the feeling Odette had had for him would never return, that his hopes of happiness would never be realized now. And on the days when she happened to be kind and affectionate with him again, if she showed him some thoughtful attention, he would note these ostensible and deceptive signs of a slight renewal of feeling, with the loving, skeptical solicitude, the despairing joy of those who, caring for a friend in the last days of an incurable illness, report certain precious accomplishments such as: "Yesterday, he did his accounts himself, and he was the one who spotted a mistake in addition that we had made; he ate an egg and enjoyed it—if he digests it without trouble we'll try a cutlet tomorrow," although they know them to be meaningless on the eve of an inevitable death. [Davis]

The differences here may seem very slight, until we recall that Proust is matching and contrasting the expiry of love with the slow extinction of a human body and personality. Thus in the first version the word "revive" seems much more apropos, and in the second version the alternative use of "realize" involves committing an easily avoidable repetition. "Renewal of feeling" is a clear advance on "change of feeling," though "ostensible," in the second version, is redundant in the context of what are clearly outward, even if deceptively intended, "signs." The error in the accounting—such a perfect bourgeois touch at death's very door—is unlikely to be in anything but addition. It is far more consistent with the period and the tone, and also with the affected portentousness of the scheme, to say "we shall try him with a cutlet" than "we'll try a cutlet." Here the advantage is plainly with the first attempt. This poignant passage closes with Kilmartin/Enright saying of Swann, "He would have been glad to learn that she was leaving Paris for ever; he would have had the heart to remain there; but he hadn't the heart to go." This is again superior to Davis's "He would have been glad if she had left Paris forever; he would have had the courage to remain; but he did not have the courage to leave." To be "glad to learn" is better in keeping with the strenuous but ever maintained distance between what Swann knows and what he chooses to know. The etymological connection between "*coeur*" and "*courage*" is clearer in French than it is in English, but our association of "heart" with fortitude is equally strong, and we have to consider both Swann's mangled emotions and the disease that is consuming him, so "heart" is obviously *le mot juste*. Lastly, and given the terminal nature of the whole paragraph, it is much more apt and final to say "to go" than "to leave."

I can't be the judge of whether Davis is right or wrong in saying that Kilmartin's ear for French is deficient. But as the passage above serves to demonstrate, the laurels may go in the end to the one who has the superior feeling for English. Vladimir Nabokov, no mean multilinguist, wrote in his *Strong Opinions* and elsewhere that a translator must be (a) fairly good in the "out of" language, (b) very good indeed in the "in to" language, and (c) a male. That might give Kilmartin two advantages where he need claim only one (I mean the second one). Nabokov quarreled with Scott Moncrieff in the matter of titles, saying that the latter had "inflicted" some "more or less fancy translations" in this area. Nabokov proposed *The Walk by Swann's Place* as a replacement, which certainly meets the test of accuracy, if at some cost in literal-mindedness. A similar directness, almost off-putting this time, is involved in his choice of *In the Shade of Blooming Young Girls*. Unquestionably, the creator of *Lolita* was being true to Proust's *A l'ombre des jeunes filles en fleurs,* and there is prettification, again, in Scott Moncrieff's *Within a Budding Grove;* but perhaps something should be reserved for the reader's imagination.

The Kilmartin translation, to the ire of Roger Shattuck and other specialists, retained Scott Moncrieff's overall title, taken from Shakespeare's Sonnet XXX and thus naturally euphonious: *Remembrance of Things Past*. Proust himself, when told of this, said simply, "*Cela détruit le titre*," and as Kilmartin states, "There is no doubt that the notion of 'summoning up' the past contradicts the basic theme of the novel, which is a celebration of *involuntary* memory." But Proust, despite his Anglophilia, was not always the most exquisite judge; he complained about *Swann's Way* as well, because he thought that "way" could only connote "manner." Kilmartin's preference was for *In Search of Lost Time,* which has in fact been the title since Enright's successor edition of 1992. But he had reservations even about that, because "the English phrase lacks the specific gravity of the French and misses the double meaning of *temps perdu*: time 'wasted' as well as 'lost.' " This Viking edition preserves the new overall name and rechristens the second volume *In the Shadow of Young Girls in Flower*—a choice slightly less enthusiastically inflammatory than Nabokov's.

How one pines, incidentally, for a translation of Proust by the hand of Nabokov. Here is Professor Adam Krug, in *Bend Sinister,* the first novel that Nabokov wrote in America, as he touches a stone on a bridge on the night his wife has died:

> I had never touched this particular knob before and shall never find it again. This moment of conscious contact holds a drop of solace. The emergency brake of time. Whatever the present moment is, I have stopped it. Too late. In the course of our, let me see, twelve, twelve and three months, years of life together, I ought to have immobilized by this simple method millions of moments; paying perhaps terrific fines, but stopping the train. Say, why did you do it? the popeyed conductor might ask. Because I liked the view. Because I wanted to stop those speeding trees and the path twisting between them. By stepping on its receding tail. What happened to her would perhaps not have happened, had I been in the habit of stopping this or that bit of our common life, prophylactically, prophetically, letting this or that moment rest and breathe in peace. Taming time. Giving her pulse respite. Pampering life, life—our patient.

I think it was perfectly brilliant of Scott Moncrieff to look to the Sonnets for a title. They anticipate Proust in almost every respect, with their deep and melancholy reflections on the sorrows of love, the tortures of jealousy, and—

this perhaps above all—the tyranny of time. "When forty winters shall besiege thy brow . . ." "Those hours that with gentle work did frame . . ." "When I do count the clock that tells the time . . ." "Weary with toil, I haste me to my bed . . ." "Being your slave, what should I do but tend / Upon the hours and times of your desire?" "Like as the waves make towards the pebbled shore / So do our minutes hasten to their end." "Against my love shall be as I am now / With Time's injurious hand crush'd and o'erworn." "When I have seen by Time's fell hand defaced . . ." "When in the chronicle of wasted time . . ." It is also notoriously the case that we cannot know whether these morose and smoldering yet lovely lines are intended as addresses to boy or girl or both, and this makes them doubly fitting as either source or analogue (speculation about the identity of Albertine is almost as fervent as that concerning "Mr. WH" or the dark lady).

It is somewhat easier to keep an edition of the Sonnets at hand while immersed in Proust than it is to be simultaneously consulting the collected works of James Joyce or Henry James. In fact, I doubt that even the most tenacious reader has ever attempted the latter expedient. But Jorge Luis Borges thought that the achievement of *Ulysses*—a decade of Homer condensed into an average Dublin day—was its "unrelenting examination of the tiniest details that constitute consciousness," an examination that "stops the flow of time." And James could be terse when he chose to be, laying on the aspirant reader of *The Art of Fiction* the injunction to "write from experience and experience only," adding, in his least forbidding manner, the nevertheless intimidating motto "Try to be one of the people on whom nothing is lost!"

Time, then, is of the essence, and Proust is interested in slowing it down, if not exactly holding it up, so as to enable himself to take longer sips from the precious but evaporating fluid. Here is another measured moment from *Swann's Way*—a tiny episode from a boyhood walk in the Meseglise direction, where the question is whether time can ever be speeded up:

> Not a footstep was to be heard on any of the paths. Quartering the top-most branches of one of the tall trees, an invisible bird was striving to make the day seem shorter, exploring with a long-drawn note the solitude that pressed it on every side, but it received at once so unanimous an answer, so powerful a repercussion of silence and of immobility, that

one felt it had arrested for all eternity the moment which it had been trying to make pass more quickly. [Kilmartin/Enright]

We heard no sound of steps on the avenues. Dividing the height of an unknown tree, an invisible bird, contriving to make the day seem short, explored the surrounding solitude with one prolonged note, but received from it a retort so unanimous, a repercussion so redoubled by silence and immobility, that one felt it had arrested forever that moment which it had been trying to make pass more quickly. [Davis]

Surely the first of these is very much more evocative in English. I mean "evocative" in the strict sense of making one hear or apprehend the voice. To be "striving" to make the day seem shorter by holding one note is much closer to the original sense than to be "contriving" to do so. By means of a simple anthropomorphism Proust invests his own feelings in the lone, plaintive effort of the bird and shares in its failure to accelerate matters, noticing that instead it has appeared to make time stand still. Not unlike Berkeley's tree in the forest, since there is apparently no one (save the narrator) to hear it, the bird has been beautifully squandering its time. The necessarily preceding and succeeding dead silence is far better established by saying "not a footstep was to be heard."

Proust very seldom fails to provide a plangent echo or reverberation, and about forty pages later on we find (in the vicinity of the Rue de l'Oiseau, happily enough) the contrastingly inanimate steeple of Saint-Hilaire, where

when an hour struck, you would have said not that it broke in upon the calm of the day, but that it relieved the day of its superfluity, and that the steeple, with the indolent, painstaking exactitude of a person who has nothing else to do, had simply—in order to squeeze out and let fall the few golden drops which had slowly and naturally accumulated in the hot sunlight—pressed, at a given moment, the distended surface of the silence. [Kilmartin/Enright]

when the hour rang, you would have said not that it broke the calm of the day, but that it relieved the day of what it contained and that the steeple, with the indolent, painstaking precision of a person who has nothing else to do, had merely—in order to squeeze out and let fall the few golden drops slowly and naturally amassed there by the heat—pressed at the proper moment the fullness of the silence. [Davis]

Here the laurels seem equally distributable. Relieving "the day of its super-fluity" is altogether more languorous and telling, but it is by way of "the proper moment" rather than "a given moment" that one fully appreciates the subdued metaphor of winemaking, with its appropriate tribute paid to patience and the seasons.

Birdsong and bells are grace notes to the Proustian fascination with music as the means of unsealing the fount of memory. Swann's hesitant fascination at Mme. Verdurin's musical soiree, as he tries to net and identify the phrase of Vinteuil's sonata (and has his gratitude at the eventual recognition so eagerly and idiotically misconstrued by Mme. Verdurin), takes a full five pages to unfold, and can be read with delight and identification by anyone who has ever had a recollection teased or tortured by a secret harmony.

This rather solemn and touching interlude is succeeded, in a way that Nancy Mitford must have admired, by a first-rate set piece involving the gushing hostess and the crashing bore. Mme. Verdurin and Dr. Cottard are made for each other, like a sort of reverse of Mrs. Malaprop and Sir Anthony Absolute, and one has no choice but to laugh (*pace* Mitford) when the latter gazes at the former "with open-mouthed admiration and studious zeal as she skipped lightly from one stepping-stone to another of her stock of ready-made phrases." Thus Kilmartin/Enright with quite sufficient wit; Davis shows some verve in awarding the literal and platitudinous doctor a look of "speech-less admiration and zealous studiousness as she frolicked in this billow of stock expressions." Here it hardly matters whose English or French ear is the better; the acutest ear in Paris was Marcel Proust's, and there's no dulling it.

I have dwelt on micro-effects because in *Swann's Way* the slow movement (Edmund Wilson likened its first, deceptively soporific line to the opening chord of a grand symphony) is predominant. It is not until the later volumes that we sense Proust's excited awareness of modernity, in the form of newly arrived aeroplanes and motorcars. When he talks about soldiers in *Swann*, he is thinking about the prior war and not the next one—a pace and rhythm that does not alter until, in subsequent volumes, we feel the Great War coming on.

In *Swann* we glimpse the anatomy of pure snobbery; later comes the recognition of the viciousness of the forces of reaction. In something like the same way, *Swann* highlights love and intrigue, and sex is mostly reserved for the ensuing books. In an almost invisible manner Proust donned his innocence once again to write this, the better to shed it by degrees as he advanced. This is a work of memory like no other: it is conscious of itself even as it relies on the subliminal, the associative, and the contingent. We know from Proust's haggard original editors, as we do from the memoirs of his naive and devoted housekeeper, that the first manuscript might have come from someone more than half insane, including as it did interpolations, marginal additions, excisions, scrawls, and—the worst sign of all—strips of fresh paper stuck at odd angles onto exhausted pages. Part of the function of memory is to forget; the omni-retentive mind will break down and produce at best an idiot savant who can recite a telephone book, and at worst a person to whom every grudge and slight is as yesterday's. Yet Proust is reliably lucid and almost invariably kind. "The struggle of man against power," said Milan Kundera, reprobating amnesia, "is the struggle of memory against forgetting." Ernest Renan earlier took a different view, saying that in order for a nation to exist, it had to agree to remember a certain number of things and also to forget a certain number of things. The almost hypnotic effect of Proust is to make this into a distinction without a difference, and to demonstrate that an apparently self-absorbed individual may yet draw his strength and his insight from a passionate engagement with the interior and exterior lives of others, as well as his own. On him not much was lost.

THE ATLANTIC, JANUARY/FEBRUARY 2004

JOYCE IN BLOOM

A surly English overseer is standing at the entrance to a construction site in London. It's a filthy, wet day. He sees approaching him a shabby figure, with clay pipe clenched in mouth and a battered raincoat, and scowlingly thinks, Another effing Mick on the scrounge. The Irishman shambles up to him and asks if there's any casual job going. "You don't look to me," says the supervisor, "as if you know the difference between a girder and a joist." "I do, too," says the Irishman indignantly. "The first of them wrote *Faust* and the second one wrote *Ulysses.*"

This is my favorite "Irish" joke, not just because it revenges itself on generations of nasty English caricature—to have represented the Irish, the people of Swift and Wilde and Shaw and Yeats, as *stupid,* of all things—but because it is itself Joycean. His universe of words was a torrent of puns, palindromes, parallels, parodies, and plagiarisms (with a good deal of Parnell stirred into the alliteration). Every now and then I will see a word as if for the first time, and suddenly appreciate that Evian is "naive" spelled backward, or that Bosnia is an anagram of "bonsai." Preparing some salad the other day, I murmured, "I knew Olive Oyl before she was an extra virgin." Joyce could do this, at an infinitely higher standard of multiple entendre, drawing on several languages, for pages on end, so that—depending on your level of awareness, and your capacity to spot new allusions and analogies—you never reopen the same book of his, or even the same chapter, without realizing that you are holding a new text in your hands and haven't really read it before.

Word games and word jokes are the special province of growing children who are coming into language for the first time (lucky them). And, lucky for us, Joyce was a startling case of infantilism and arrested development. Why, just for a start, did he pick June 16, 1904, as the day on which Mr. Leopold Bloom of Dublin, at first alone and then in the company of Stephen Dedalus, mimics the several stages of Homer's Odyssey before dropping anchor with his blowsy Penelope, the dirty-minded Molly Bloom? On that day the newspapers reported on a terrible ferry accident at New York's Hell Gate and a war—between Russia and Japan—that would curtain-raise the Great War of 1914. These events are mulled over in the city, along with a spectacular reversal of fortune at the horse races, as Bloom goes on his way. But this wasn't what had fixed the date forever in the mind of James Joyce. On that day, he had made a rendezvous with a chambermaid, by the marvelous name of Nora Barnacle, who had newly arrived from Galway. She had failed to keep their first appointment (after he had initially picked her up in the street) and by a nice coincidence kept him standing outside the house of Oscar Wilde's father, on Merrion Square. But the second date exceeded his expectations. The couple took a walk out to Ringsend, beyond the city's docks, where, as Joyce later told her in a molten letter, it was not he who made a move but "you who slid your hand down inside my trousers and pulled my shirt softly aside and touched my prick with your long tickling fingers and gradually took it all, fat and stiff as it was, into your hand and frigged me slowly until I came off through your fingers, all the time bending over me and gazing at me out of your quiet saintlike eyes."

A century later, the literary world will celebrate the hundredth "Bloomsday," in honor of the very first time the great James Joyce received a handjob from a woman who was not a prostitute.

Many fine writers have sought to handle this delicate yet simple subject. One thinks of Mark Twain's "Some Thoughts on the Science of Onanism," or of Martin Amis, who did a good deal of hard and valuable reflection about handjobs in *Money,* and naturally of Philip Roth's Portnoy ("I am the Raskolnikov of jerking off!"). But, all too often, the subject matter here is the humble, unassuming, solitary version, sometimes adopted for reasons of economy ("Overheads are generally low," as Amis's John Self ruefully reflects) as well as for reasons of, well, solitude. Though it may be possible to take pride in one's work in this department, also. Joyce certainly did. When a stranger in a café in Zurich seized him by the mitt and exclaimed, "May I kiss the hand that wrote *Ulysses*?" Joyce responded, "No—it did lots of other things too." But the greatest effusion ever unleashed by a single, properly managed, and expertly administered (and how often can you say that?) female-to-male handjob is beyond doubt the 735-page mastur-piece that was first published by Shakespeare and Company in Paris, in just 1,000 numbered editions, in February of 1922—since which date, our concept of the novel has revolutionized itself.

I shall be returning to self-abuse as a theme (trust me), but I want to give just a slight indication of the influence the book has had. I knew that George Orwell, in his second novel, *A Clergyman's Daughter,* published in 1935, had borrowed from Joyce for his nighttime scene in Trafalgar Square, where Deafie and Charlie and Snouter and Mr. Tallboys and The Kike and Mrs. Bendigo and the rest of the bums and losers keep up a barrage of song snatches, fractured prayers, curses, and crackpot reminiscences. But only on my most recent reading of *Ulysses* did I discover, in the middle of the long and intricate mock-Shakespeare scene at the National Library, the line "Go to! You spent most of it in Georgina Johnson's bed, clergyman's daughter." So now I think Orwell quarried his title from there, too.

Then take the vast, continuing controversy over the bigotry of T. S. Eliot. In a notorious lecture entitled "After Strange Gods," delivered at the University of Virginia in 1933, Eliot had said that the presence of "too many free-thinking Jews" was "undesirable" in a well-ordered society. Seeking to define what was meant by a traditional community, he proposed that we call it "the same people, living in the same place." And this deceptively simple formulation is taken word for word from Leopold Bloom, who offers it in Barney Kiernan's pub when challenged, and then challenged again, by a violently anti-Jewish Irish nationalist. Nobody knows why Eliot chose to quote Bloom, without attribution, in a public address designed to attack Jewish influence. All we know is that he admired Joyce extravagantly, and that a novel mined by Orwell and Eliot within a year or so of each other, when *Ulysses* was still a banned book, is a considerable literary force.

In some intuitive manner, Joyce seems to have had the premonition that the Jewish question would be crucial to the twentieth century. (He was to die in 1941 while fleeing the German advance in Europe.) When not with Nora, or when not writing her frenziedly masturbatory letters, far, far fiercer than the mild incitements that Bloom sends to and receives from his mystery lady, he sought out Jewish girls (perhaps to be certain that they were not Catholics). One of Bloom's first actions is to stop at a pork butcher's and, in this improbable setting, to pick up a Zionist leaflet from an organization based in Berlin. Joyce admired the Jews because, like the Greeks, they lived in a diaspora and because, like Odysseus, they were wanderers. Furthermore, the Jews and Greeks proved that it was possible to worship higher goals without surrendering to the especial horror of Holy Mother Church—Joyce's lifelong enemy. He unceasingly blamed the priesthood for, among other things, the betrayal and abandonment of Charles Stewart Parnell, the heroic Protestant nationalist leader who was taken in adultery.

Indeed, largely because of that church, Joyce himself was forced to live in exile from Ireland most of his life, and much of *Ulysses* is an attempt to reconstruct, from memory, the sight and sound and feel of his beloved Dublin. "Nostalgia" means literally a yearning for home, and Joyce pined for the banks and bridges of the River Liffey as Odysseus had for Ithaca. Furthermore—and like Homer himself—he suffered from blindness. Those with poor vision are often compensated with extra sensation in other faculties, and Joyce's language pays minute attention to the sound and smell of everything, from food to horses to women. He loved strong color for the same reason, and insisted that the first edition of Ulysses be bound in a very specific shade of blue—the color of the Greek sea on which Odysseus had first sailed to recapture Helen, and then sailed again to escape from Troy. (Ask yourself, by the way, what part of Helen it was that Odysseus had failed to win. Her hand . . .)

Bloom is Ulysses/Odysseus himself in Joyce's highly individual version of the story, and if you love the original there is delight to be had in guessing which adventure is which. The Dublin "nighttown" brothel run by Bella Cohen is Circe's cave. The restaurant full of nauseating food and disgusting eaters is the encounter with the Laestrygonian cannibals. The enraged Jew-baiting Sinn Feiner is the Cyclops Polyphemus. And Bloom, whose son died in infancy, needs a Telemachus for his Ulysses and finds him, or fancies that he does, in Stephen Dedalus. Daedalus was the genius of antiquity who designed the impenetrable labyrinth that held the Minotaur, and the man who first learned to fly (losing his own son, Icarus, in the experiment). Together, in the second half of the voyage, Bloom and Dedalus negotiate the warrens and back alleys of Dublin's labyrinth, while Dedalus soars like Icarus with flights of poetry and quotation. At the end, with Jew and Greek united in one synthesis, Joyce gives us a long call-and-response section ("Of what did the duumvirate deliberate during their itinerary?" "Was there one point on which their views were equal and negative?") with most answers many, many times longer than the questions. In my opinion, while this is fairly obviously an echo of Plato's Symposium, it also evokes the question-and-answer part of the Passover Seder, with its emphasis on the education of the young. Wine is involved in both Symposium and Seder, and Ulysses is nothing if not well lubricated with gallons of booze.

Talking of lubrication . . . for all its soaring, Ulysses repeatedly comes back to earth in the earthiest sense, and reminds us that natural functions and decay and sexual frustration are part of the common lot. Here, Joyce's child-ishness about potty humor and playing with yourself was an enormous help to him. We are familiar now with the idea of "interior monologue" and "stream of consciousness," but nobody before Joyce had shown us a man—Bloom—partly planning his day around his handjobs. He at first thinks that he'll jerk off at the steam baths, but changes his mind and is glad he did because, encountering Gerty MacDowell and her girlfriends frolicking on the beach (Odysseus on Nausicaa's island), he is able to whack off to greater effect at a safe distance (as does, if I'm not mistaken, frisky Gerty herself). Joyce wrote to a friend about this passage, describing it as a "namby-pamby jammy marmalady drawersy (alto la!) style with effects of incense, mario-latry, masturbation, stewed cockles, painters palette, chitchat, circumlocutions, etc. etc."

Bloom's fantasies are mood swings of insecurity. At times, he is grandly imagined as a future Jewish lord mayor of Dublin. (In 1956, a Jew named Robert Briscoe actually was elected mayor of Dublin. When this news was brought to Yogi Berra he commented, "Only in America.") At other moments, Bloom is pictured with his own soft and vulnerable figure igno-miniously on trial, with all his dirty secrets exposed. The expert medical wit-ness in one such scene, Dr. Malachi Mulligan, pronounces him "prematurely bald from selfabuse." The doctor's namesake, the "plump Buck Mulligan" who opens the narrative, cannot stay off the subject, either. (He proposes a play called "Everyman His own Wife or A Honeymoon in the Hand.") And all the time, as he negotiates this jizz-flecked environment, Bloom is queasily aware that his Molly—his Penelope—has been giving herself to another man, or men. In the vast, rambling, lubricious, and unpunctuated soliloquy that closes the novel, Molly Bloom herself reviews some of her better bedroom moments and may well be having the longest solitary climax, or series of climaxes, ever set down on a page. The Victorians were evidently dead wrong when they said that wanking made you listless and unproductive (though Joyce might have wondered furtively and occasionally, and with good apparent reason, about the cause of his own blindness).

That great Victorian Matthew Arnold thought that the true cultural balance was between Hellenism and Hebraism, or between the polytheistic, the philosophical, and the aesthetic and the spare, stern monotheism of the Old Testament. He also believed that poetry should replace religion as the source of ethics and morality. Joyce, who liked the idea of Hellenizing and Hebraizing Ireland, and who refused—like his Stephen Dedalus—to kneel in prayer even at his mother's deathbed, employed literature to stave off guilt and to ward off faith. It was for this reason, as much as for any "indecency," that his *Ulysses* was for so long seized and burned by the police and customs. The book was held to be blasphemous and profane, as well as obscene. Nonetheless, when it first came to a trial, in New York City in December 1933, Judge John M. Woolsey had only to decide on the question of whether it was, or was not, pornographic. Which he did in the following unintentionally hilarious manner:

> I am quite aware that owing to some of its scenes *Ulysses* is a rather strong draught to ask some sensitive, though normal, persons to take. But my considered opinion, after long reflection, is that whilst in many places the effect of *Ulysses* on the reader undoubtedly is somewhat emetic, nowhere does it tend to be an aphrodisiac. *Ulysses* may, therefore, be admitted into the United States.

There, in all its rotund and brainless condescension, you have the censorship mentality, which is no less contemptible in its "liberal" mode. Joyce had managed to do something that few writers have even dared to attempt: the ventriloquizing of Shakespeare in such a manner that the reader may be unsure where the genuine leaves off and the parody begins. You try it. In fact, try reading the Hamlet passage in *Ulysses* aloud, which is a good scheme anyway since, like Homer, Joyce was hearing the music of language in his head and writing almost for recitation. And the censor will just about allow this, because, although it may make you sick, at least you won't get sexually aroused! Puke, yes. Orgasms, no. Though James Joyce himself may have written—to Nora—with his pen in one hand and his thing in another, I, too, very much doubt that anyone has ever employed Ulysses as a "manual" of that kind. Which makes it magnificently sobering to reflect that, without the many and various thrills of gratification *per mano,* it might never have been composed at all.

VANITY FAIR, JUNE 2004

THE IMMORTAL

A review of *BORGES: A LIFE*
by Edwin Williamson

I n early 1925, in a literary magazine in Buenos Aires called *Proa* ("Prow"),
which he had helped to found, Jorge Luis Borges wrote an essay called
"El *Ulises* de Joyce." He would then have been just twenty-five years old,
and was anxious to boast of being "the first Hispanic adventurer to have
arrived at Joyce's book." Far from content with this *avant-garde* claim, he
evolved the further ambition to do for his native Buenos Aires what Joyce had
done for Dublin, and to weave from its slums and boulevards the elements of
a universal city. On the centennial of Leopold Bloom's epic meanderings, this
is a delightful coincidence to come upon if you believe—but cannot perhaps
quite prove—that there is something universal about literature, too, and that
unforgiving Time, as Auden said in farewell to Yeats, nonetheless "Worships
language and forgives/ Everyone by whom it lives."

In this altogether marvelous biography, Edwin Williamson identifies
another element in Joyce that kindled an answering spark in Borges. The
Irish, Borges wrote, "have always been famous agitators of the literature of
England." Might it not be possible, then, that a young writer in Spanish, in a
Spanish ex-colony at the other end of the world, could also raise a body of
work which would resonate in the wider tongue, as well as bring the local
practice of letters one step beyond the national, the folkloric and the epic?

Had he cared to do so, Williamson could have pressed this analogy a
little further. Like Joyce, Borges was never quite at ease with his fellow-
countrymen, and was permanently at odds with the Roman Catholic
Church. Like Joyce, he was immured within an increasingly untreatable

blindness. He was fascinated by Old Norse and Anglo-Saxon philology. He is buried in Switzerland, which he loved and where he died. He even had a tempestuous girlfriend named Norah. But with the ostensibly negligible difference made by that single, redundant, non-aspirate "h"—a Borgesian micro-element of distinction between his own adored object and Nora Barnacle—the parallels would begin to diverge. Borges did not have even a hundredth of Joyce's libido. And he had been cursed with the opposite of Joyce's family problem: he had a somewhat weak and futile father and a mother who just would not quit. The father made the decision to send him, on or around his nineteenth birthday, to a brothel in Geneva. This was a course of action that we can be sure that Joyce could and would have decided for himself: the reverse effect upon a sensitive boy who could not quite rise to the occasion appears to have been lifelong and disabling. (It put me in mind of a narrator in Robertson Davies's *Deptford Trilogy,* a much less tender figure who is quite as thoroughly nauseated by the same paternal notion of what constitutes *un rite de passage.*)

Joyce had to struggle for his cosmopolitanism, and indeed for his philo-Semitism, which were in the case of Borges innate. As well as Spanish/Argentine lineage, he had a grandmother called Fanny Haslam, than which I suppose there could be no more English name outside the pages of Jane Austen, and she made sure to rear him, as I remember he once told me, so that he spoke both tongues before he could become aware of any distinction between them. His first immersion was in the literature of Anglophilia, from Stevenson to Shakespeare. The names Borges is originally Portuguese, and this Lusitanian-Brazilian blood was commingled through another branch of the family tree with an Italian Jew named Suarez. Buenos Aires has always had ethnic neighborhoods, principally Italian and German and Jewish, on which the grandeur of Spanish conquest and the aloofness of a British merchant and rancher colonial class are superimpositions. Someone had to be born to whom this was a natural and also appealing state of affairs; someone to whom the Babel of discrepant languages and cultures was not a chaos, but rather the design for an eventually imposing but also microscopically intricate tower.

Willamson lays an important stress on the keyword *criollo,* which in Argentina is cognate with "creole" without having at all the same meaning. It signifies an Argentine of inarguably Spanish descent, and it mixes this definition of ethno-linguistic security with the more uncertain pursuit of a distinctly "Argentine" identity. Taking up this cultural ambiguity, for Borges, meant trying for a specific national literature that could nonetheless be valuable and intelligible to non-Argentines. Taking up the same ambiguity in its political form involved a belief in democracy and in local vernaculars and idioms. Yet, as Joyce himself found when the Irish repudiated his beloved Parnell, a democrat and republican can sometimes find himself nauseated by public opinion. A version of this irony was to break Borges's heart.

Given the somewhat conservative demeanor that he had adopted by the time he became globally celebrated, it is fascinating to find just how much Borges, in his earlier years, was prepared to stake upon radical and modernist positions. He came onto the stage almost like an extra in Tom Stoppard's *Travesties*, where James Joyce converges with Lenin, and with the Dadaist Tristan Zara, in a Zurich setting. He welcomed the Russian revolution, made lifelong friendships with Swiss Marxist Jews, took part in surrealist and Expressionist masquerades and shuttled between Europe and Latin America. In 1928 he gave a public address in Buenos Aires in which he told his fellow *criollos* to integrate:

> In this house which is America, my friends, men from various nations of the world have conspired together in order to disappear in a new man, who is not yet embodied in any one of us and whom we shall already call an "Argentine" so as to begin to raise our hopes. This is a confederacy without precedent: a generous adventure by men of different bloodlines whose aim is not to persevere in their lineages but to forget those lineages in the end; these are bloodlines that seek the night. The *criollo* is one of the confederates. The *criollo*, who was responsible for creating the nation as such, has now chosen to be one among many.

As far as was possible, he remained true to this loftily expressed ambition. He argued earnestly about the national epic *The Gaucho Martin Fierro*, which is to Argentina—though it boasts a far more "accessible" demotic appeal—what the sagas are to Iceland or *Beowulf* is to Anglo-Saxon. That the lone gaucho might be the nation's emblematic figure—a Robin Hood or a Daniel Boone—

Borges was happy to concede. But that such a person—unscrupulous, untied by any social obligation, and thirsty for murder and spoil—should be the model citizen was a bit more debatable.

This may be the moment to say that Borges's own repeated fascination with tigers, knife-fighters, daredevils and solitary horsemen, some of it passed on from his stiff-necked *criollo* mother, has a tinge of the vicarious about it, and strikes the only faintly inauthentic note in his fiction. It corresponds, probably not all that obliquely, to his oft-manifested wince of fascinated disgust at sexual relations. In his intense story *The Cult of the Phoenix*, for example, the initiates are wedded to lubricity and indeed "slime" (*legamo*) and the penny will drop for most readers long before Borges closes by saying:

> On three continents I have merited the friendship of many worshipers of the Phoenix; I know that the Secret at first struck them as banal, shameful, vulgar and (stranger still) unbelievable. They could not bear to admit that their parents had ever stooped to such acts . . . Someone has even dared to claim that by now it is instinctive.

Williamson permits himself a rare lapse into the dead-literal by noting with solemnity that "Years later Borges would tell Ronald Christ that he meant the Secret to refer to sexual intercourse." Perhaps the name of this interlocutor was irresistible . . . ? Incidentally, I have taken the quotation above, as also the title of the story, from Andrew Hurley's translation. Some may prefer Norman Thomas de Giovanni's version of *The Sect of the Phoenix*. It sometimes amazes me that Borges, with his immaculate English, felt he needed a *dragoman* at all. But who would not have desired the job?

Keeping up his cultural optimism about Argentina in public, and spending ever more of his private and literary life in codexes and codicils, Babels and Babylons, lotteries and labyrinths, Borges postponed for some time the disagreeable realization that his country and his culture were turning against him. In the 1930s he took a bold position against the local version of fascism, while simultaneously distrusting and even disliking the great cats of the Hispanic literary "left," Pablo Neruda and Federico Garcia Lorca, both of whom paid notable visits to Buenos Aires. Williamson suggests persuasively that there was an element of sexual envy involved in this, too. But such considerations would not have influenced Borges in the detestation he felt for Juan Peron, and the fear that he experienced as he witnessed the birth of a raw, localist populism. The foul genius of Peronism lay in its demagogic dexterity: it was at once anti-oligarchical, anti-Jewish and anti-English. By persecutions large and small—he lost his job at a library; his mother and sister were briefly imprisoned; "elitist" magazines and clubs were peremptorily closed down—Borges became persuaded that the masses who applauded this kind of thing were not to be trusted. Every time Peron fell, or was exiled, the crowd yelled for him to come back. And in the sordid figure of his whorish wife Eva (or "Evita") all the brothels and tango-bars, all the popular culture of the city, allied to all the suspect *machismo* of the *Martin Fierro* ballad tradition, underwent a horrid mutation into the Philistine and the greedy and the cruel. Borges' story *Ragnarok*, about false gods and the need to destroy them, is very probably derived from this contempt for the votaries of such idols.

Peron, like Franco and Salazar, survived the supposed defeat of fascism in the Second World War, and kept on torturing Argentina with his revenant third and fourth acts, ultimately dying and then ruling by posthumous proxy through the cult of his first widow and the actual agency of his second one, the charmless Isabel. At a point in the mid-1970s, the armed forces decided to put a stop to all this, and to much else besides, by an employment of the mailed fist. So, when I called on Jorge Luis Borges in his upstairs apartment 6B at Calle Maipu 994, just off the Plaza San Martin, in December 1977, the streets of the city were being prowled by death-squads.

The inscription on Edgar Allen Poe's room-door at the University of Virginia—*"Domus parva magni poetae"* ("Small home of a great poet")—would have been almost perfectly apt for the tiny quarters in which Borges, and his tireless mother, had for so long resided. But, no less aptly, the place was lined and piled with volumes and the blind old man seemed to know the location of every one of them. He liked my English voice and asked me if I would do him the courtesy of reading aloud (I later found, without chagrin, that he did this to a lot of visitors). Pointing to where the Kipling anthology could be pinpointed, he asked me to begin with *The Harp Song of the Dane Women*. "And please, read it *slowly*. I like to take long, long sips."

This lovely and stirring poem is made up almost entirely of Anglo-Norse words (and, incidentally, there is no way to read it fast). He told me that he'd taken up the study of Old English "when I went blind in 1955. It helped me to write *The Library of Babel.*" Language in any permutation was a subject on which he showed immediate enthusiasm. "Do you know that in Mexico they say 'I am seeing you' when they mean 'I will see you'? I find the translation of the present into the future very ingenious." Without the smallest appearance of affectation, he said that reverse and obverse were always the same to him "which is why I find infinity almost banal." And that in his dreams he was always "lost—hence perhaps my interest in labyrinths."

His shy invitation to me to return on the morrow and read further from his library was at once the mildest and the most imperative request I have ever received. Later leading him slowly downstairs, and across the perilous traffic to "La Ciudad" for lunch, I felt as if I had been entrusted with a unique coin, or ancient palimpsest or precious astrolabe. (What if I tripped and took him down with me? It would be scant consolation to reflect that such a calamitous narrative would contain all other potential narratives: I was Anglo-Saxon enough to see myself being stuck with the *ur*–one.) Whatever I read, he commented upon. "Kipling was not really appreciated in his own time because all his peers were socialists." "Chesterton—such a pity he became a Catholic!" When I queried his rather stilted praise for Neruda, he admitted that he preferred Gabriel Garcia Marquez. (It was in 1926 that he had written an essay, "Tales of Turkestan," in which he praised stories in which "the marvelous and the everyday are entwined . . . .there are angels as there are trees." In 1931, in *The Postulation of Reality,* he declared that fiction was "an autonomous sphere of corroborations, omens and monuments" as demonstrated by the "predestined *Ulysses* of Joyce." As well as so-called "magic realism," this prefigures the realistic magic of his own "Tlön, Uqbar, Orbis Tertius"—another work that it is highly inadvisable to read in a hurry.)

The enduring enraptness in magic and fable has always struck me as latently childish and somehow sexless (and thus also related to childlessness). But *Orbis Tertius*—or "Third World"—had another, less innocent and more concrete meaning in those days, symbolizing the grainy and harsh battles of urban guerrillas against the empire. Buenos Aires was the scene of such a combat as we spoke: it was impossible to avoid asking the question. Borges placidly replied with a couplet from Edmund Blunden:

This was my country and it might be yet,
But something came between us and the sun.

That something, he left me in no doubt, had been Peronism. As for the generals and admirals who had seized power, he sounded like an Evelyn Waugh impersonator—"the sword of honor" was a frequent reference—when he announced that it was better to have a government "of gentlemen rather than pimps." Seizing the occasion to elucidate the specific Buenos Aires dockland slang for "pimp," which is *canfinflero:* a term of almost untranslatable—or do I mean too-easily translatable?—obscenity, he discoursed with some warmth about his enthusiasm for dictatorship. (Reading back my notes of our conversation today, and knowing now about that shriveling moment in the Geneva brothel, I wonder if the flesh trade had a special horror for him.)When he invited me back for the following day, I had to decline with real regret because I was taking an early plane to Chile. At this, he asked me with perfect gravity whether I would be calling on General Pinochet and, hearing my answer in the negative, expressed regret in his turn. "A true gentleman. He was kind enough to present me with a literary award when I last visited his country."

Edwin Williamson's biography passes what I consider to be a small but by no means paltry test. It is absolutely solid wherever it can be checked against the reviewer's knowledge. In particular, it brought back to me with extraordinary force and vividness the dizzying shifts in feeling that I experienced during those two Borgesian days of languorous conversation, careful reading, and sheer alarm. Moreover, the book shows with great care and fairness what had brought Borges to this latter pass. The world now knows, and some of us even knew then, that the regime of General Videla was also depraved by violence and corruption, as well as being viciously anti-English and pathologically anti-Semitic. As for the *canfinflero* question: Henry Kissinger's old confrere General Videla is now in prison for his part in selling the babies of the rape victims he held in secret prisons: something a little more raw than mere "pimping."

At our lunch, Borges joked a bit about his failure to win the Nobel Prize for Literature. ("Though when you see who *has* had it . . . .Shaw! Faulkner! Still, I would grab it. I feel greedy.") In another context, he described the sport of denying him the prize as "a minor Swedish industry." Williamson shows that, by his defense of Videla and especially Pinochet, and his public attack on the memory of Lorca during a visit to post-Franco Spain, Borges was almost wilfully denying himself the laureateship. That was a measure of how distraught he felt about chaos and subversion in Argentina. Thus, it speaks doubly well of him that, before the dictatorship fell, he had signed a statement of concern about the *desaparecidos,* or "disappeared," and written a sardonic poem lampooning the mad war of grandiose and futile aggression launched by the generals against the Falkland Islands.

If there is a key-story in Borges, as Williamson seems to imply there is it may be contained in or near *The Aleph.* Much of his work led up to this collection, and much depends upon it. In one of the tales within—*The Immortal*—we come upon this:

> There is nothing very remarkable about being immortal; with the exception of mankind, all creatures are immortal, for they know nothing of death. What is divine, terrible, and incomprehensible is *to know* oneself immortal. I have noticed that in spite of religion, the conviction as to one's own immortality is extraordinarily rare. Jews, Christians, and Muslims all *profess* belief in immortality, but the veneration paid to the first century of life is proof that they truly believe only in those hundred years, for they destine all the rest, throughout eternity, to rewarding or punishing what one did *when alive.*

It is this capacity, I believe, that promotes Borges so highly above the level of the exotic antiquarian, the obsessed bibliophile, the claustrated map-maker, the crazed pedant and the unreliable editor: diverting roles at which he excelled and that he vastly enjoyed playing. So often, one comes across a passage as perfectly-cut and honed as that one, uttered with a certain diffidence and yet—as frequently with perfectionists—the product of much silent labor, reflection and, I might add, stoicism.

When his yearning heart and brain were not engaged with the Vikings and the gauchos, or the equally heroic explorers and cartographers of the New World, he would turn again and again to the cool, shaded stone arbors of Cordoba and Baghdad and ancient Persia. He was evidently magnetized by the great scholars and reasoners of the Andalusian renaissance, as they sought to peer beyond the veils of clerical dogma. (His love for Fitzgerald and Old

Khayyam makes the same point in a different fashion: how marvelous that he praised Fitzgerald's "indolence and tenacity.") Other fascinations—with the Jewish Prague of Kafka and also of the *golem*—manifest the same commitment to cities that are at once authentic and imaginary. If Borges could have drawn at all, he would have wanted to fuse Piranesi with Escher. It was not by chance that one of his absolutely favorite critics was F. H. Bradley, the author of *Appearance and Reality*.

Borges may have secretly wanted a happy ending, and certainly appears to have secretly planned for one. Having survived a number of inconclusive courtships and a null marriage, all under the vulture-like surveillance of his mother, he managed at the end to form some kind of alliance with Maria Kodama, a devoted young half-Japanese student of his work who was, like him, a "seeker"; albeit a more amateur one. His subsequent interest in Shintoism and in Buddhism lacks the mordancy and introspection (the "agenbite of inwit," as Joyce liked to put it) of his earlier hermeneutic investigations. At a certain point, talk about "essence" and "oneness" and the universal becomes more tautological than inquisitive. But Borges did eventually live to be honored by a democratic Argentina, did finally get some time to himself with a girl of his own choosing, and did ultimately elect to arrive in Geneva and to surprise Kodama by telling her with decision that he wasn't leaving again. Thus, he managed to cancel—I should probably say "exorcize"—his adolescent humiliation in that city, and some of the disappointments of his maturity as well. The long self-examination of his life, one undevoutly hopes, had proved it to be worth living. Long before, F. H. Bradley had provided Borges with a reflection that is exactly right, in that it promises more than it delivers:

For love unsatisfied the world is a mystery, a mystery which satisfied love appears to understand.

THE ATLANTIC, SEPTEMBER 2004

AMERICANA

Nobody knows how it came by its name. Most probably, some city booster or real-estate hopeful of the 1890s wanted a beckoning title for some borderline property. And the whole cosmology of America tends towards the West, the Occident, the quenching of the sun in the sea. But the other quasi-magical street names of the United States are, when you unpack them, even more trite.

They say the neon lights are bright on Broadway . . . so let them.

The avenue I'm taking you to—*Forty-Second Street*? Park is banal, Madison was a politician, Fifth is a digit, Pennsylvania is a state, Bourbon is a drink. Only the alchemy of layered association invests these addresses with any patina. But Sunset, no matter how vulgar and obvious its origin, is quite something. I'll meet you on Sunset . . . It started on Sunset . . . Make a left on Sunset. You can't say that doesn't sound exotic.

Sunset runs from the newest hardscrabble immigrants at one end to the oldest and richest immigrants at the other. It traverses twenty-five miles of megalopolis, and where it ends, the United States of America comes to a stop. As it curves like a graph, you can read off much handy information about the condition of the national libido, the national economy, the national cuisine, the national composition, and the national dreams, to say nothing of some local cultural gossip that has become the costly thread from which international legend is made. If you can fake it here, you can fake it anywhere.

* * *

All things considered, I'm glad that I took my cruise along the strip—in the company of the great Billy Wilder—in torrential rain. One can forget that Wilder's imperishable *Sunset Boulevard,* which opens with a stencil of the title on the edge of a dingy pavement, is shot partly in a downpour: "a great big package of rain," as the deceased narrator puts it, "oversized—like everything else in California." Mr. Wilder consented to give me the tour on day one of what became the great Los Angeles flood of 1995. The few heroic sluts on this great working-girl turf looked as if they might offer to wash our windshield instead, and through the deluge I swear I glimpsed a sodden hustler clutching a soggy sign reading: WILL DIRECT FOR FOOD.

The torrents were a reminder that you never step into the same stream twice, and no observant person has ever seen identical Sunsets. Its nature is protean. Mr. Wilder is one of its archaeologists and historians. He sees it clearly, but he can see it as it once was. "When I came here in 1934—stayed at the Chateau Marmont for seventy bucks a month—half of this wasn't even paved. There was a bridle path from Hollywood to Holmby Hills. Douglas Fairbanks and Mary Pickford bought their place in Beverly Hills as a hunting lodge."

Everything that Wilder sees reminds him of something else. "That was Ciro's," he says, pointing at what is now the Comedy Store. "There was a big scandal there when it was reported that Paulette Goddard was doing it on the table and on the dance floor with Anatole Litvak: I never asked her—she was married to Charlie Chaplin and Erich Maria Remarque—but I asked him on his oath and he swore that her shoulder strap just slipped and all he did was kiss her on the breast."

We approach the Virgin Megastore, former site of Schwab's drugstore (known in *Sunset Boulevard* as "headquarters"). "Mervyn LeRoy told me that he didn't discover Lana Turner there, no matter what you read. He found her in another drugstore, just across from Hollywood High School."

Here are, and were, the clubs that defined what was hot for those who liked it that way. "There was a lot of illegal gambling and drinking at the Clover Club in the 1930s," says Wilder semi-fondly. "I saw David Selznick boozing it up in there before he made *Gone with the Wind.*"

At Le Dôme, the power-lunch parlor where Barry Diller created panic in 1992 by snacking with David Geffen right after he left Fox, Wilder talks about pictures. "Expensive as they are now, studios try and keep 'em popular.

They're either very broad or very cautious—they like it best if it's a picture they've already seen. That was always true, but we made *hundreds* of pictures. Even then, they liked to do test-marketing, only they did it with preview cards. One card for *The Lost Weekend* told me it was a great movie but I should take out all the stuff about drinking and alcoholism. Another time I went to Long Beach with Ernst Lubitsch for a preview of *Ninotchka* and he was reading the cards in the car on the way home. Started laughing and wouldn't tell me why, but finally passed me the card that said, 'Great movie. I laughed so hard I peed in my girlfriend's hand.' "

Wilder was a part of "the emigration of genius," the exodus of gifted anti-Nazi Germans and Austrians that brought Thomas Mann and Theodor Adorno and Bertolt Brecht to the California coast. Had he met these heroes? "I was introduced to Mann at a Kaffeeklatsch for exiles run by Salka Viertel, who was married to the director. I was so impressed—he'd won the Nobel Prize in the twenties—that I don't remember what he said or if I said anything."

He reminisces briefly about Will Rogers, who made the transition from vaudeville and silent pictures to talkies, and about Howard Hughes, who shared the Rogers passion for the new fad of aviation and once crashed a plane within earshot of Sunset. And then it's time for him to go back out into the rain.

Returning to the bar to relish the memory of lunch for a few moments, I am hailed from a good table by a very handsome black man who looks familiar. "I love your work, man," he says, leaving me quite undone. I ask a waiter discreetly. "That's Billy Dee *Williams,*" he whispers hoarsely. "He was in *Lady Sings the Blues* and . . ." The whole screen career and credits follow. Sunset—where every waiter is a producer/director. And you should see the signed star pix by the till at Gil Turner's liquor store on the corner of Doheny.

I reflect, after the great Wilder has left me, that at least in his day there must have been less talk about how great it all *used* to be. You couldn't hold forth about how everybody should have been here thirty or forty years earlier, because nobody really had been. Yet, on further reflection, all of *Sunset Boulevard* is about glory days departed. "I *am* big," responds Norma Desmond when Joseph Gillis tells her she used to be big. "It's the pictures that got small." Sunset may have been a great developer's idea for a name, but it does have the infallible connotation of the blazing hours just before darkness falls. Between the blaze and the *noir* falls the lengthening shadow. You can catch it in conversation: What if the Japanese wise up? What if the Japanese go *broke?* Hurry it up, buster. The strip is changing faster than you are.

Lost Angeles. That's it in a phrase. Some of the sites are easy to spot. Down the road is that health-nut hangout the Source, where Woody Allen was so hilariously discomfited in *Annie Hall,* vindicating his suspicion that L.A.'s only cultural advantage was the permission to make a right on red. There's the Chateau Marmont, where John Belushi OD'd, just after Michael Eisner's wife had seen him watching one of his reruns and found herself thinking . . . *Sunset Boulevard.*

There's the St. James's Club, so English and Anglophile that it's even on the corner of Kings Road where Tim Robbins went to keep his faithful appointment in *The Player* (with a stalker who used the name Joe Gillis, as it happens) and ended up hearing one of the funniest pitches ever delivered. But even the St. James's has opened under new management and become the Argyle, having already been the Sunset Towers apartment building and the home of Marilyn Monroe, Jean Harlow, and Clark Gable. It used to be said that the St. James's had been a skyscraper before it got "fucked flat."

Other corners and sites can be unearthed or recovered with just a few strokes of the archaeologist's brush. In *The White Album,* Joan Didion recounts being told, "You turn left at the old Mocambo," as she sought directions to Sammy Davis's place in the hills above Sunset. She didn't know where "the old Mocambo" was, but didn't have much trouble finding out. Yet listen to the old-timers talk about the fabled Garden of Allah, which used in Wilder's day to be just opposite the Marmont, and you need a trowel or a shovel, not a brush.

"The Garden of Allah was created by a fizzling silent-movie star called Alla Nazimova," says Marc Wanamaker, nephew of Sam and a meticulous local historian and archivist. "She was just like Gloria Swanson in *Sunset Boulevard,* only more savvy. She had a Spanish Mediterranean–style house and she added an *h* and turned it into an apartment complex which saw her through her slump. Scott Fitzgerald stayed there. Charles Laughton and Elsa Lanchester were there. The Errol Flynn and John Barrymore rat pack partied there."

Now there's a bank and a McDonald's enclosed in mini-mall architecture on the site. (When you've seen one cluster of generic stores grouped under one management or one roof, you've seen a mall.) The only tenuous connection remaining from the industry is Jay Ward's animation studio, home of Dudley

Do-Right and Rocky and Bullwinkle. A tacky and tattered statue of the goofy moose and the stupid squirrel still bestrides the sidewalk, one of those glimpses that one gets from the car as Sunset unspools itself.

The most frequent and sonorous commonplace about the City of Angels, and about its inhabitants, is that no sense of history adheres. Wrong. Hang out with Marc Wanamaker, or with Mike Davis, author of the amazing *City of Quartz: Excavating the Future in Los Angeles,* and you elicit an intense feeling for the ways in which the immediate past has fired the mold of the present. Sunset did not uncurl itself toward the ocean like some blind tendril seeking the light. It fought its way as part of a process of ambition and acquisition that still shows at every bend. One consequence is the way in which Sunset crosses the borders of three municipalities: Los Angeles, West Hollywood, and Beverly Hills.

Until 1984, West Hollywood was an autonomous, unincorporated district. As a result, the area between Doheny and Marmont known as "the strip"— the area lovingly photographed building by building by Ed Ruscha in 1966— was a law unto itself, a border town with frontier values. In the 1930s and 1940s it was a magnet for gambling, bootlegging, clublandism, and the informal or commercial carnal-knowledge industry, and some of this ethos still hangs about it like tattered finery.

"It was known as the Las Vegas of L.A.," says Wanamaker, "with its own sheriffs on one side of the line and the L.A.P.D. on the other."

The irony, of course, was that *Las Vegas* soon became the Las Vegas of L.A. "The big billboard in front of the Marmont was taken over by the Sahara Hotel in Vegas," Wanamaker says. "Putting that on the strip was a sign that the strip was on the way out. Behind the sign, incidentally, is the site of Preston Sturges's original Players Club, now called Roxbury."

The big Marmont billboard (Joan Didion says that she used to sit at Spago and tell what was new by the Sunset billboards) has been occupied for some years by the Marlboro cowboy. He looks even more rugged now that you can't light up anywhere on the strip. Asking diffidently at Dan Aykroyd's House of Blues if I could smoke, I was told by a stunning African-American hostess, "Honey, didn't we *have* this very conversation last year? You promised you'd stay healthy so I could bear your child." Just like that. Behind her, a large notice read, THIS JOINT IS DEDICATED TO THE MEMORY OF OUR DEAR BROTHER RIVER. Did Mr. Phoenix die in here? "No, honey, but he was an *investor*." Oh, O.K. I'll go and smoke outside, then.

Despite this attempt to impose a herbivorous style on all of California, there are still points of resistance along the strip. And the strip, after all, is where Humphrey Bogart was filmed outside the Trocadero in *Stand-in* (1937), and Robert Cummings exited the same club in *Hollywood Boulevard* (1936). *Hollywood Story* (1951) was shot at LaRue. There is a tradition of louche life to live up to. And so Bret Easton Ellis's affectless bastards cluster in Carney's railcar diner on the strip, and his narrator in *Less than Zero* is knocked back by a Sunset billboard that reads, cryptically, DISAPPEAR HERE. If you have some time and money on Saturday night, you can still get into trouble at the Viper Room or, if you want to feel more traditional about it, at the Whisky or the Roxy.

But if you want unauthorized excitement these days, it's eastward you should turn your horse's head. As Sunset dips downtown toward its terminus at Union Station, which is now the hub of a metro system that, in somebody's dreams, Angelenos will one day use, the street names mark the transition. The old Brooklyn Avenue, once home to the immigrant Jewish community, has been renamed after a struggle. It is now called Cesar Chavez.

In this district, new Chinese expansion meets the Hispanic underclass, and if you get up early enough you can see the day laborers waiting on the sidewalk for drive-by employers. Good-luck stores, some of them selling the mystique of Santeria, cater to the needs of those who most need a break. It's in this rather incongruous setting, by the crumbling walls of the old Mother Cabrini orphanage, that you can see the almost unvisited Fort Moore monument, just off Sunset at Hill Street. Cracked and faded, its waterfall no longer tumbling, it celebrates the conquest of California by the United States and the founding of Los Angeles by Anglos.

You would not guess, from these white stone reliefs of heroic Mormons and Yankees, how John Charles Frémont, "the Pathfinder" in California history, described his 1843 expedition as it moved south: "Our cavalcade made a strange and grotesque appearance . . . guided by a civilized Indian, attended by two wild ones from the Sierra; a Chinook from the Columbia; and our own mixture of American, French, German—all armed; four or five languages heard at once; above a hundred horses and mules, half-wild, American, Spanish, and Indian dresses and equipments intermingled."

As you move west along Sunset to Echo Park, it's worth a slight detour to see the Neutra and Schindler architecture up the hill (in an area now noted cheifly for clubs and dives consecrated to the polymorphous perverse). Hereabouts, too, is the Short Stop Bar, watering hole of the street cops, where you used to be able to see Joseph Wambaugh. As he phrases it so delicately in *The Choirboys*, "Spermwhale had persuaded Baxter to take him to the Sunset Strip once after work to meet Foxy and the two policemen were taken backstage by a burly assistant manager. Foxy was standing nude in her dressing room combing her pubic hair and pushing the vaginal lips back inside before the second show." Wambaugh was a Cal State English student when Christopher Isherwood was a professor, and admires his *Goodbye to Berlin*. Nice to feel the air of Weimar seeping onto Sunset.

At Sunset and Hillhurst, as you work your way back toward the strip from downtown, there once stood the colossal set of D. W. Griffith's *Intolerance*, which for two years was the most striking edifice in the city. (Griffith's *In Old California* was the first movie ever shot in Hollywood.)

The first comedy club, showing up on the right, brings one back onto the strip from the eastern approach. My guide this time, George Schlatter, used to be a nightclub booker for MCA until his lovely wife, Jolene, made an honest man of him, and set him on the stony upward path that led him to conceive *Rowan & Martin's Laugh-In*.

"There was a real café society in those days," says George, referring to the period in the early fifties when Sophie Tucker, Mae West, Nat Cole, and Sammy Davis were the aristos. "People did dress and dine a little." Listening to George, you can hear Bobby Troup doing "Route 66" (another magical American road name), and picture Sammy Davis tap-dancing at Ciro's before grabbing—and *playing*—every instrument in the band. "After Sammy came back from his eye injury, the whole town came out to see his first gig. Cooper was there. Gable and Bogart were there. Frank and Dean were playing cards at the stageside."

In contrast to Wilder, George was in Ciro's on the night of the Paulette Goddard-Anatole Litvak *scandale*. "If you believe the thousands of people who say they saw it, she sank beneath the table and he stayed upright and grinning." In 1954, Darryl Zanuck gave a huge party with a circus theme at Ciro's, and climaxed the bash by doing a trapeze act himself. "Can you imagine a studio head doing that today?"

On this world and its doings, Hedda Hopper and Louella Parsons were able to feed nightly and create the whole business of celebrity and showbiz journalism. Army Archerd, who was columnar legman for the gossip writer Harrison Carroll, still writes for *Variety*, but otherwise we're talking about a lost world. And some of it, as I listen to George, turns out not to have been so romantic. "When I got the account for the Crescendo club, Billy Eckstine was rumored to be a silent partner because blacks couldn't get a license on the strip. A couple of us had to get together and buy Judy Garland's old house for Sammy Davis, putting it in my name because of the 'no blacks' rule."

Schlatter and others were able to bust the color bar using showbiz success as a lever. "The time came when we could say to people, here or in Vegas, 'You want to book Sammy, you have to let him and his guests stay in your hotel.' And they had no choice." He talks fondly of the night Marlene Dietrich walked down the street to Bugsy Siegel's place with Lena Horne and Pearl Bailey for company and the doors fell open and the Jim Crow era was over.

And here's the Bullwinkle statue again. It used to face a twirling cowgirl statue, and in the opening scene of *Myra Breckinridge*, Myra/Myron looks out at it from the penthouse terrace of the Chateau Marmont, which had once had a view of the splendors of the Garden of Allah. "Ah yes, the Garden of Allah," says Gore Vidal today. "I used to stay there because of Sam Zimbalist, my MGM producer, who was Alla Nazimova's pet even though she was absolutely queen of the dykes. We worked on *Ben-Hur* there. But my cabin was next to Errol Flynn's, and his day began at midnight, so that I had to move out because of all the shrieks and splashes from the pool."

It's touching to summon the ghost of the young Vidal wishing that Flynn would pipe down and let him get on with recreating Roman decadence for the silver screen. There are all sorts of glamorous ghosts and phantoms in this *quartier*. Marc Wanamaker, for one, remembers how Ciro's outlived café society and metamorphosed into a rock club in the 1960s. Here the blissed-out young came to gaze upon the Doors, whose blissed-out name was borrowed from *The Doors of Perception,* one of Aldous Huxley's California meditations from the days when he was scheming pre-Leary voyages of the imagination from a bit further along the boulevard into West Hollywood.

By now we have left the wok and the burrito behind, and the joys of nouvelle are about to unfold themselves. Sunset Plaza, a ritzy stretch of restaurants, luxury stores, and hairdressers, begins to presage the more gorgeous and formal tones of Beverly Hills. Since this area is still privately held, by the old, established Montgomery family, it has been able to avoid the sorts of tawdry development that elsewhere make the boulevard feel, in Ed Ruscha's usefull phrase, "all malled out."

Joan Didion describes the intersection of Sunset and La Brea as "the dead center of nothing," but along the strip the heart still lifts a bit, and it becomes possible to believe that the odd dream might actually come true. Dyan Cannon really was pedaling along it on her bike when she was hailed from a smart car and asked if she was in movies. On replying in the negative, she was told that she ought to be, and would be.

You can only guess at the change by looking at Ruscha's Warholian set of 1966 foldout photographs, and it may become clearer when he presents his three-dimensional, three-decade work-in-progress of the entire boulevard, but the difference is made by the fact that for these blocks you get a north–south perspective as well as an east–west one. As if on a generous step cut out of some exotic hillside, you can look down and look over in one direction, and look up yearningly in the other (toward the plush European-style homes and mansions known to some as "the Swish Alps").

The very word "strip" has something snappy, urbane, and Runyonesque about it: a stretch of big shoulders, big wads, and wised-up, street-smart elements—an air of optimism, or at least of euphoria. Perhaps this is why, even as Sunset begins to shade into the manicured gentility of Beverly Hills people like to stress its gamy and risky side. Arguments occur about the precise location of "Dead Man's Curve," a fated corner just by the Beverly Hills city limits, where Jan of Jan & Dean survived a triple-fatality smashup in April 1966, only two years after pushing the road-accident hit "Dead Man's Curve" to No. 8 on the charts. Jon Wiener, biographer of John Lennon, who teaches at U.C. Irvine, directed me to the entry in *The Penguin Encyclopedia of Popular Music* which said that "it was years before [Jan] could remember an entire song lyric."

I think the likeliest spot for Dead Man's Curve is on the corner of Sunset and Carolwood (Barbra Streisand's street), where there appears to be a sort of wayside shrine. But that could be to Barbra. We are entering the neighborhood where casual laborers run roadside stands with big signs saying, STAR MAPS HERE. Within bull's roar of the shrine, you can pinpoint the homes of Englebert Humperdinck and Jayne Mansfield (the mapmakers provide a tasteful asterisk for the deceased). Marilyn Monroe and Walt Disney lived on Carolwood, I was intrigued to learn, and Tony Curtis and Burt Reynolds also.

Even in the drenching rain of the worst floods in memory, it is possible to visualize the lushness and grace of the area, the amazing combination of seclusion and ostentation that gives character to the equally seductive combination of wealth and fame, "Around here," says George Schlatter, who is from around here, "you don't ask if people have a tennis court. You ask do they have a north–south tennis court, to keep the sun out of their eyes. You don't ask if they have a pool; you ask what heating system their pool has."

Voyage up Rodeo to Sunset and imagine you are giving a tour to a starstruck newcomer. Swing by Jackie Collins's new place on Beverly Drive, go over four blocks to Lucille Ball's house on Roxbury, with Gene Kelly just down the street and the Kirk Douglas home on Rexford. Then, just above Sunset, you might get a glimpse of the Knoll, where Marvin and Barbara Davis find it amusing to entertain.

Mrs. Davis is the force behind the Carousel of Hope, a charity for children with diabetes, and at her last fund-raising gala managed to get Hillary and Barbra and the Duchess of York and Steven Spielberg and Tom Hanks and Governor Pete Wilson all at one table. In case they got bored with one another, they were entertained by Placido, by Kenny G., by Jay Leno and Neil Diamond and Phil Collins (whose home, now his wife's, was then at Sunset and Hillcrest). Not too shabby and, at ten grand a couple, not too bad from the diabetes-research point of view.

It's true that there's the odd mud slide and earthquake. (Local gag: "I've bought a place on Mulholland. My agent says it'll be beachfront one day.") But nowhere else in the world puts you so neatly in reach of skiing in one direction and surfing in another, positioned beautifully for the yachts of Catalina and the dune buggies of the pristine desert, with night-blooming jasmine thrown in. After working on *Lolita* with Stanley Kubrick, Nabokov went butterfly hunting in Mandeville Canyon.

But I'm straying from the free association with lawlessness, chance, and life in the raw. Down the road from the Beverly Hills Hotel—still closed while it is redone to the taste of the new owner, the Sultan of Brunei—is a vast empty lot. It marks the spot of the neighborhood's most famous arson. A Saudi princeling, tiring of austere desert morality, decreed himself a pleasure dome here and placed a row of pornographic caryatids with their pudenda fronting the street. The resultant fire-setting shows that there is a final arbiter of taste in this neck of the woods, and that its judgment is swift and sure.

Through Bel-Air we bowl, tipping our hats to the Ron and Nancy Reagan home on St. Cloud Road, which not long ago changed its street number. This was not to throw star-map rubberneckers off the trail, but resulted from the fact that the Reagan address was 666. On learning that this number was the mark of the beast in the Book of Revelation, they did what anybody would have done and altered it to 668. You can't be too careful.

These gentle hills and undulant canyons conceal a lot more coiled superstition, diabolism, and violence than they disclose at first review. The Sharon Tate house on Cielo Drive; the old Houdini house of tricks; some whispered-about houses that cater to rather specialized tastes. And don't forget that, as Mike Davis reminds me, the whole effort of sculpting these hospitable slopes was undertaken first with high-pressure water-blasting and, when that failed, by the discharge of many tons of TNT.

But it was in escaping violence and disorder that Thomas Mann came to stay at the Beverly Hills Hotel for a few days in April 1939. "We are charmed once more by this landscape," he wrote. "Its slight absurdity is outweighed by the manifold charms of nature and life. Perhaps we shall someday build a hut here." And build quite a decent hut he did. Having stayed for a time in Brentwood on North Rockingham, and then on Amalfi Drive, he settled just off Sunset on San Remo Drive: "Where the house is to be built, numerous lemon trees have been felled, and the foundation of the little house appears in, the form of a trellis on the ground. Thus at my visit yesterday, I saw the space for my future study, in which my books and my desk from Munich will stand."

Here he wrote *Doctor Faustus*. The family that now occupies the house is friendly and gracious about receiving pilgrims, as Mann himself was when the fourteen-year-old Susan Sontag came over shyly to crave a meeting almost half a century ago. From this address he kept in touch with neighbors like Arnold Schoenberg, caught a dangerous flu after making a pro Roosevelt speech in a foggy garden in Bel-Air, and, at the home of the composer Hanns Eisler, met Charlie Chaplin: "I laughed for three hours long at his imitations, scenes, and clownings and was still wiping my eyes as we got into the car." At this period, Mann was composing the foreword to a newspaper for German P.O.W.'s, so the laughs were not numerous. Hollywood ought to be more boastful than it is about this period of generosity and genius in its past.

Leaving Holmby Hills, the boulevard opens out a bit and becomes almost countrified.

"There are tributaries from every direction," says John Gregory Dunne, "but Sunset is the string that binds it all together." Up this canyon or that road, as he can tell you from his elaborate knowledge, lived Kenneth and Kathleen Tynan, and Christopher Isherwood and Don Bachardy. L.A. mayor Richard Riordan is OJ Simpson's current neighbor. Sunset serves to connect them to the amorphous idea of "El Ay" and the California dream.

(I did seriously consider leaving Mr. Simpson out of this account, just to be able to say I had done it. But there was no avoiding the police sawhorses that marked off the end of Rockingham, where Michelle Pfeiffer has put her house on the market and where Michael Ovitz and Stanley Sheinbaum—liberal fund-raiser *extraordinaire*—are still clinging on.)

Unlike most good things, Sunset doesn't really come to an end. It just peters out, amid a tacky modernist welter of junk-food stops and unsightly commerce. It almost literally dribbles away into the sand. Perhaps that is as it should be. It can be more satisfying to look back than to look forward. When I asked Billy Wilder what he made of Andrew Lloyd Webber's musical version of *Sunset Boulevard* he paused, not entirely for effect, before saying, "I thought to myself, This thing could make a great movie someday."

VANITY FAIR, APRIL 1995

The Ballad
of Route 66

J oseph Heller's masterpiece, originally entitled *Catch-18*, was renamed—or should that be renumbered?—by its editor, Robert Gottlieb. Comes the question. Would the novel have had the same pervading influence under its first digits? I can think of at least some reasons to doubt it. First, certain numbers have hieroglyphic power, and repetition has something to do with this quality. Just take the figure six. Consider the mark of the beast and its three sixes. Then, not every number can be made to rhyme with "kicks." Get your jive on Route 55? Not really. Get to heaven on Route 77? Feel free on Route 33? Too insipid. No hint of sexty-sex . . .

Whereas when Bobby Troup's wife leaned over and whispered in his ear as they were speeding toward California in the heady days of postwar liberty in 1946, murmuring, "Get your kicks on Route 66," he knew at once that he had a song right there. (Bob Dylan had to do "Highway 61" twice, or "revisit" it, and still didn't get the same effect.) Sixty-six is three times Heller's twenty-two. Two sixes is a good throw at dice, and always gets a cheer—"Clickety-click, all the sixes, *66*"—at bingo. Nat "King" Cole took the song off Bobby Troup's hands at once, and he sang the refrain as "Route Six Six" with no damage to the lyric. Since then it's been rerecorded or reworked by Dr. Feelgood, Buddy Greco, Depeche Mode, Chuck Berry, Bing Crosby, the Andrews Sisters, Rosemary Clooney, and the Sharks. Mythology says that Jack Kerouac heard the song on a jukebox in 1947 and decided on the spot to take a westward road trip. I first heard it in the great year of '66 itself, when it was belted out by the Rolling Stones. Here are the words, which have become the song lines of America's western destiny:

> *If you ever plan to motor west, travel my way,*
> *Take the highway that is best*
> *Get your kicks on Route 66!*
> *It winds from Chicago to LA,*
> *More than two thousand miles all the way.*
> *Get your kicks on Route 66!*
> *Now you go through St Looey, Joplin, Missouri*
> *And Oklahoma City is mighty pretty,*
> *You'll see Amarillo, Gallup, New Mexico,*
> *Flagstaff, Arizona. Don't forget Winona,*
> *Kingman, Barstow, San Bernardino.*
> *Won't you get hip to this timely tip:*
> *When you make that California trip,*
> *Get your kicks on Route 66!*

When I first bounced to Mick Jagger doing this, I initially heard the fifth line to say, "Forty-two thousand miles all the way," and thought, Jesus, the United States is *big*. And when I lowered myself behind the wheel of a blazing-red Corvette in Chicago in August and pointed myself at the Pacific, the country ahead didn't seem too small, either. From Grant Park on the shore of Lake Michigan—scene of riots at the 1968 Democratic convention—over to the junction of Santa Monica and Ocean.

Just to answer any questions you might have before I roar away: much local politics is highway politics. After the passage of the Federal Highway Act in 1921, which mandated interstate roads, it was determined that east–west highways would have even numerals, and north–south highways would have odd ones. Roads that cut state lines would be designated by shields, intrastate roads with circular signs. Major highways would carry numbers ending in zero. The Chicago–Los Angeles one was to be called Route 60. Or so the Illinois and Missouri authorities decided. But 60 meant so much to the state officials of Kentucky and Virginia that they were prepared to fight over it. The number 66 was still free when the Illinois, Missouri, and now Oklahoma bureaucrats caved in. So the famous "66" shield was born, and in 1926 marked

800 miles of paved road. It took until 1937 to pave the remaining 1,648 miles of gravel, dirt, and asphalt. In 1977 the route was decommissioned and replaced with a new interstate, which, as if in numerical mimicry of the year '77 and the number 66, leaves Chicago as Interstate 55, becoming 44 in Missouri before evolving into a banal 40 and an indifferent 15 before hitting L.A, where it peters out in Interstate 10 to the Pacific.

Yet the attachment to the music and mythology of the old road was and is very great, and for long and short and very broken-up stretches you can still leave the main "drag" of interstate-land, with its homogenized gas stations and chain restaurants and franchise motels, and take a spin into a time warp or a parallel universe, where you might have swerved suddenly into *The Last Picture Show* or *Bonnie and Clyde*, or even *The Twilight Zone*. It's all going, and going fast, but then, in my Corvette, so could I.

Perhaps, here, a word about the car. There was a TV series in the early 1960s called *Route 66,* where a couple of lads played by George Maharis and Martin Milner acted as knights of the road on a generic highway, backed by a theme tune from Nelson Riddle and employing a Corvette as a talisman and prop. The ladies among you will not (I hope and trust) be familiar with the sensation of strapping on a huge and empurpled projectile protuberance at about the midsection. But any man who has sat in the driver's seat of a fiery-red Corvette and seen the sweeping and rising hood twanging away in front of him may, as he looks along the barrel, want to make a wild surmise. The song by the artist who was then known as Prince, "Little Red Corvette," just doesn't cover it. Stephen King's mad-car-disease novel, *Christine,* is based on the huge number of songs from the fifties and sixties that personalized automobiles by giving them names, invariably female. My Corvette was too slim and graceful to be a boy, but it wasn't exactly a chick either. I soon got bored with forcing Winnebagos and U-Hauls to dine on my dust, and began to humble ever faster machines, including that of an Illinois state trooper who was fortunately engaged with someone else. The shimmer of Lake Shore Drive and the grime of Al Capone's Cicero fell away behind, and I was even thinking irresponsibly of giving downstate Illinois a miss until conscience pricked me to visit Springfield, home and resting-place of Abraham Lincoln.

At once I fell victim to three of the many banes that afflict the modern road warrior in America. Towns that have multiple exits don't tell you which exit will take you to, say, where you want to go. There is never anybody on the sidewalk to ask. People in cars, if you can catch them as every red light suddenly goes green, usually aren't from here. And when you do find a local, he or she doesn't know the way. It was a Hooters bar that finally helped me to get a fix on Honest Abe; the waitress knew several of the key sites and scrawled them daintily on a napkin and gave me a terrific quesadilla into the bargain. Thus I discovered, following the old brown "66" shields through a shaded part of downtown, that Lincoln may have been reared in a log cabin but it wasn't in Springfield. I also came to the painful realization that was to recur to me times without number. A shiny red Corvette can be a boy magnet, all right. When parked, it drew to my side many garage mechanics and hotel doormen and learned young black men and polite old roadside coots who would inquire after the finer points and details. When in motion it would summon cops from deserted streets and vacant landscapes. But it appeared to leave the female sex quite unmoved. Could it be a fault in the design? Perhaps the silhouette? I began to brood, and in fine brooding country.

Southern Illinois is flat. There is the punctuation of grain silos and elevators (and the elevators now have their own museum, just like every other "66" feature and artifact). This is "the prairie state" and signs along the road announce the restoration of prairie grass, to forestall complaints about unmown roadsides. Some of the 66 byways are explorable, but they are flat, also, and their surfaces are often too rugged for a low-to-the-ground beauty such as I am driving. Then, to the right, there's a sudden sign for the MOTHER JONES MEMORIAL, and I swing to it on impulse as the sky makes a long and leisurely turn from robin's-egg blue to glaring red. Here, just outside the little town of Mount Olive, is the incongruous sight of a cemetery devoted entirely to the union martyrs of the coal industry. And Mary "Mother" Jones, queen of the labor hell-raisers, has her shrine in its precincts. She was born on May 1, 1830, before there even was a May Day, and lived to be a hundred. This region, now so rural in appearance, was once a heartland of King Coal and the proving ground for the great John L. Lewis and his United Mine Workers. The rows—better say the ranks and files—of tombstones almost all bear German and Hungarian and Croatian names, and the dates of half-forgotten massacres on bloody picket lines. It was the coming of the highways that helped break the railroad monopolies in this and other states: another way in which the open road is associated with liberation. I bowed my head at the gate, where it said, THE RESTING PLACE FOR GOOD UNION PEOPLE, and was given a honk and a wave and many high signs by a carload of (entirely) boys as I drove away. Perhaps not many Corvettes are seen making this particular stop. At this stage, I reflected irrelevantly, I was about seven hours from Tulsa.

I crossed the big Mississippi into St. Louis—forever to be mispronounced as a result of Bobby Troup's lyric—as the darkness thickened and the lights picked out the huge arch, gateway to the West, that when finished in 1965 presumably did not make every tourist think consciously or unconsciously of McDonald's and wonder where the twin arch had gone. St. Louis is the city of Charles Lindbergh, pioneer of the aviation industry, which was to supplant both rail and road. It used to be the hub of Trans World Airlines, now deceased, and the TWA symbol was being replaced with the logo of a brokerage on the stadium where the Rams play. ("Flying across the desert on a TWA," as Buddy Holly sang in "Brown-Eyed Handsome Man," "saw a woman walking 'cross the sand." Who will get that line a decade from now?) This is an odd combination of frontier town and respectable town: the birthplace of T. S. Eliot and of Martha Gellhorn, the first of whom fled it because it was too provincial and uncouth and the second because it was too straitlaced. In the heart of music history it occupies a soft spot, as the birthplace of Chuck Berry, the home of the Scott Joplin museum, and the home, if not the native one, of Miles Davis and Tina Turner.

The most striking thing, to me, however, was the constant reminder of Middle America's German past. It's not just the prevalence of the Anheuser-Busch and Budweiser ambience. There was a big *Strassenfest,* or street fair, in progress, and in Memorial Park were playing the Dingolfingen Stadtmusikanten Brass Band, Die Spitzbaum, and the Waterloo German Band. Some fifty-eight million Americans tell the census that they are of German origin, even more than say English, and you would never really notice this, perhaps the most effective assimilation in history, any more than you "notice" that the minority leader in the House and the majority leader in the Senate are named Gephardt and Daschle.

In the morning, on an open-air platform of the St. Louis transit system, I fall into conversation with another visitor, named Kevin Honeywood. He wears a nice hat and works for IBM, and he is also looking for a decent place to eat down by the river, so we hunt as a pair. Mr. Honeywood is a boyhood veteran of black South Side Chicago, and as the Big Muddy runs past our equally long and meandering lunch he tells me many things about the old days of "66" as it ran through his neighborhood, things I could never have learned from driving through it. People knew which stretches they weren't allowed to use along Cicero and Cermak and McCormick, but on July 4 they liked to block a section of Ogden Avenue for drag racing. Driving is much easier now for black folks; the rhythm of the road starts to hit me more and more as a variation of upbeat and downbeat, as well as a rapid fluctuation of American geography and history.

In the evening I pay a call on Blueberry Hill, a bar out in the city's "Loop," where Chuck Berry still stops in to play one Wednesday each month. There's a Hollywood-style "walk of fame" on the adjoining sidewalk, with stars and short canned biographies for Tina Turner and the others. The joint itself is a bit tame—ID cards mandatory at the door and that sort of thing—but it has a terrific jukebox and girls playing darts in daring couples and an Elvis Room for events. There's no way to check out the urban-legend rumor that Chuck Berry once had this ladies' room wired for video. I'm beginning to weary of hamburgers already, but the signature version here is highly toothsome and comes with a cheese peculiar to St. Louis which I failed to write down but mean to check out. Still, the evening needs a round-off and so I favor BB's Jazz, Blues, and Soups, nearer the river, with a drop-by. A convincing rainbow-coalition band with a very strong sax is doing its stuff, and the tourist hour seems to have safely passed, until a terrifying skull-faced blonde detaches herself from a gaggle and whacks me in the features with a star wand. "How ya doin'?" I always think, What kind of a question is that?, and I always reply, "A bit early to tell." She gives me another smack with the wand and holds it up so I can see the number "50" emblazoned at the center. "It's mah *birthday!*" Christ. Does she know about the Corvette?

The next morning I roar past the Mississippi, scattering lesser cars like chickens, and nod to the Gateway Arch while noticing for the first time that gateway is an anagram of "getaway." Then it's down through Missouri and toward the Ozarks. Long ago, when there was an Ozark Airlines, I noticed at airports that that name was "krazo" spelled backassward. The hillbillies have taken enough sneers in their time, and you can tell they don't care, because the landscape is clichéd with revival chapels of obscure denominations, gun shops and gun shows, and liquor stores that say "whisky" or "whiskey" and mean bourbon. This is John Ashcroft country, or was until he lost the Senate race to a deceased person. On the radio, people who are very obviously products of evolution quarrel at the top of their leathery lungs with the verdict. My radio can't shake them for miles, but eventually finds a station that plays Chuck Berry singing the first of his songs that I remember—"No Particular Place to Go." This man's music, remember, is on the twin Voyager space probes, in case there is intelligent life anywhere else.

There are shimmering lakes and grand old steel and iron bridges on the side roads, and the wooded hills make it easy to amble, but I'm sorry I did because by the time I got to Springfield, Missouri, at evening the whole place was shut. It was a Sunday, and most restaurants just don't bother. I finally ran down a steak house, where the automatic raunchiness of the barmaids and waitresses, as they lobbed back-chat with the guys, was some consolation for the surrounding Sabbath gloom. Only some consolation, though, because it put me in mind of John Steinbeck's line in *The Grapes of Wrath,* about "the smart listless language of the roadsides." Reduced to the TV in my motel, I lucked into a rerun of *Thelma & Louise,* which, while it may not be the best buddy and road movie in history, surely features the best blue jeans. Susan Sarandon and Geena Davis pick up Brad Pitt on the way to Oklahoma City, which I was hoping to hit myself by the next nightfall. Among the soundtrack songs are "Badlands" and "Ballad of Lucy Jordan," which showcases Marianne Faithfull's nineteenth nervous comeback and tells of a girl who never had a ride in a car like mine.

The name Joplin seems to necessitate a stop, like the Bobby Troup line says, and on the way there's a good side stretch of the old Route. On its two-lane pavement, the mirages seem shinier and deeper, and there isn't the eternal nuisance of great swatches of black tire tread, or tire shed, flapping like crows or writhing like snakes under your wheels. For miles I saw no cars in either direction. The town of Albatross was to all outward appearances fast asleep. In Avilla, almost nothing broke the stillness. I tried Bernie's Route 66 bar, with its shanty look and old Pabst Blue Ribbon symbol, but a rail-thin man wearing only jeans and a cowboy hat (and guarding a sign on the fridge that read, free beer tomorrow) told me they didn't open until late. Following a road of unattended lawn and garage sales, I came to the comparative metropolis of Carthage, where in a slumberous old square there is a marker claiming the town as the site of the first major land battle of the Civil War. On July 5, 1861, it seems, local gallantry fought off "federal dominance" of Missouri in a series of what the polished granite calls "running engagments" (sic). That was enough to muse upon until I hit Joplin, which is a wilderness of strip malls and traffic stoplights. "Anything to see or do round here?," I asked the young man in the music store, determined as I was to purchase some independence from the radio stations. "Jack," he replied briefly, knowing from my credit card that this was not my name. Sad to think so of a town that has the same name as Scott and indeed Janis.

There are about a dozen miles of Kansas on Route 66, and if you blink, then, well, you aren't in Kansas anymore. A few of those burgs where, when the wind drops, all the chickens fall over. Kansas City, home of those "hungry little women," is back in Missouri. Best floor it and get to Oklahoma. In Missouri, a distinctive feature is the pull-over pay phone that has been downsized to allow you to call while sitting in your car. In Oklahoma, the keynote is roadside exhortation. Not only is Oklahoma ready to proclaim itself "Native America," but it is also "Cherokee Nation." Regular signs instruct you to KEEP OUR LAND GRAND. It's the boostering and the upbeat that force the downbeat into mind, and not just because of the luckless Cherokee and their "trail of tears."

One of the many breezy names for Route 66 is "the mother road," but this phrase was first deployed by Steinbeck (whose centennial is this year) in the following tremendous passage from *The Grapes of Wrath*:

Highway 66 is the main migrant road. 66—the long concrete path across the country, waving gently up and down on the map, from

Mississippi to Bakersfield—over the red lands and the gray lands, twisting up into the mountains, crossing the Divide and down into the bright and terrible desert, and across the desert to the mountains again, and into the rich California valleys.

Sixty-six is the path of a people in flight, refugees from dust and shrinking land, from the thunder of tractors and shrinking ownership, from the desert's slow northward invasion, from the twisting winds that howl up out of Texas, from the floods that bring no richness to the land and steal what little richness is there. From all of these the people are in flight, and they come into 66 from the tributary side roads, from the wagon tracks and the rutted country roads. Sixty-six is the mother road, *the road of flight*. [My italics.]

The title of his 1939 classic—and just try imagining *that* novel under a different name—comes from the nation's best-loved Civil War anthem. (It was Steinbeck's wife Carol who came up with the refulgent idea.) When first published it carried both the verses of Julia Ward Howe *and* the sheet music on the endpapers in order to fend off accusations of unpatriotic Marxism. But really it succeeded because it contrived to pick up the strain of what Wordsworth called "the still, sad music of humanity." Another subversive, Woody Guthrie, effectively set the novel to music with *Dust Bowl Ballads*: combine these with the photographs of Dorothea Lange and you have a historic triptych. A song of Guthrie's—"The Will Rogers Highway," another folksy name for 66—manages to rhyme Los Angeles with both "Cherokees" and "refugees." (Guthrie sounds a bit folksy, too, when you replay him today. But without Woody, never forget, we would have no Bob Dylan and perhaps no Bruce Springsteen.) I remind myself again that this superficially cheery and touristic route was a road of heartbreak for hundreds of thousands of the poor white underclass, who were despised foreigners in their own country.

But black Oklahoma was visited by tribulation far worse and somewhat earlier. (You can revisit part of it in Toni Morrison's Oklahoma novel, *Paradise*, which is the perfect antidote to Rodgers and Hammerstein.) In Tulsa, I made a stop to see the Greenwood memorial, which ought to be better known than it is. The Greenwood quarter of town included in 1921 a thriving business district, known as "the Negro Wall Street." On June 1, 1921, it was torched from end to end in a vicious and jealous pogrom, which burned out most of 35 city blocks, incinerating more than 1,200 homes and businesses as well as at least a half-dozen churches. The forces of law and order either pitched in or stood aside while as many as 300 citizens were murdered (and planned exhumations may raise that figure). Planes from neighboring airstrips reportedly even dropped explosives into the conflagration. As a symptom of bad conscience, part of the front page of the *Tulsa Tribune* and part of the editorial page were later ripped from the files, and it took a long while before acknowledgment was made, let alone reparations.

It's not an easy part of town to find, and I felt awkward asking directions, but a white receptionist in a motel near the Broken Arrow exit went out of her way to give me slightly too much guidance (and a clip from the local press about the monument), and when I got lost again I was told "follow me and I'll take you there" by a white female motorist. The neighborhood is still surrounded by vacant lots, and somebody has smashed one panel of the memorial, but as I pulled away, Tulsa's nearby Art Deco district seemed friendlier, and I even managed a bleak smile at the signposts to Oral Roberts University, former employer of Anita Hill.

Oklahoma City, miles on through more red-soil country, is not so pretty. (Oh, the sacrifices that songwriters will make for a rhyme.) And some of its inhabitants are a tad bored by its piety. In the joint that I find as evening descends, the bony young barman tells me that locals head for Texas for three things (it's always three things): "Booze, porn, and tattoos." His plump gay colleague, when I ask if there is anything else to look forward to on the road, exhales histrionically and breathes the magical name *"California . . ."* The thin one is an ex-soldier who gives directions by reference to army and air-force bases, and I notice again how much Route 66 has evolved according to military imperatives. It was pulled out of the Depression by the huge traffic of armaments and trainees between the coasts after 1941—Oklahoma! itself was the big musical Broadway hit of the wartime years—then hymned after 1945 by ex-G.I.'s spreading their wings, and finally doomed by President Eisenhower, whose cold war push for an interstate system had been influenced by the imposing straights and curves of the German autobahns.

A resentful ex-soldier, indeed, was the prompting for my pilgrimage the following morning. On the ruins of the Alfred P. Murrah Federal Building in Oklahoma City is another shrine to the murder of Americans by Americans. A reflecting pool borders a garden with the same number of upright symbols as there were victims of Timothy McVeigh. From a distance these symbols could be anything, but on close inspection they prove to be statuary chairs: rows and rows of stone-and-bronze chairs with straight backs to represent the bureaucratic pursuits of the innocent dead. There are 168 of them; 19 are slightly off-puttingly half-size to mark the murder of the children at the day-care center and elsewhere. The figures 9.01 and 9.03, which confusingly could be dates, are incised in stone to indicate the unforgiving minute that it took for the huge building to slide chaotically into the street. A new whitish concrete statue of Jesus stands with its back to the scene. It's all slightly bland, and the inscription puts the blame on generic "violence" rather than native American Fascism. When this memorial was unveiled, the United States wasn't yet a country that honored the frontline nature of office work. It's clearly a style of commemoration in which we are fated to improve, as the upward curve steepens.

Caring little for booze, porn, or tattoos, I noticed as I dressed to leave Oklahoma City that my white socks, washed together with my red ones, had produced a furtive but somehow flagrant pink. Secure in my own masculinity, and bodyguarded by the sleek Corvette, I decided to make nothing of it and turned the proud prow of the car toward Texas, the resulting unit one potent and seamless weld of man and machine. I stopped on 66 at the town of Clinton, which has the best of the "66" museums, featuring an antique T-Bird and an overloaded Okie truck, and paid a call on the Tradewinds Motor Hotel, now a Best Western, where Elvis Presley used to stop over and sleep on his way to and from Las Vegas. Room 215 is the one his manager always reserved, and the lady at reception, responsive to the name of *Vanity Fair* as well as to my own charisma ("Seen ya on that Fox tee-vee"), gave me and my pink socks a key. The same love seat is still there, with added photographs but—I thought—a bathroom too small for the King's heartbreaking needs. He never showed his face in the daytime, but was once spotted by a room-service maid who went on a Paul Revere ride to alert the whole town. After that, he signed a few autographs, checked out, and, according to at least some accounts, has never been seen in this area again.

* * *

To rejoin the main drag, one takes old 66 through Erick, a dying dump which used to be home to Roger Miller. I tipped my hat to the singer of "King of the Road," which I consider the best bum-and-hobo ditty since "Big Rock Candy Mountain," and passed on. As I thundered past Elk City, I was listening to Elton John—who, oddly, seemed to be imploring someone, "Don't let your son go down on me"—when I heard and felt an impressive *whomp* somewhere in the rear. The thoroughbred car seemed to shake it off with abandon until, a mile or so later, it nearly threw me by wrenching the steering wheel from my grasp and lurching like a stallion on amyl nitrite. Managing to gain the roadside, I was informed by the screen on the dashboard that the left rear tire had blown and I had experienced "reduced handling." The Corvette has tires which can drive flat for a while, so I limped on, man and machine a single, soggy weld of sagging flesh and soft rubber. Finding a turnoff, I entered the other, parallel world of those who live by vehicular misfortune. Larry's Transmission Shop was mercifully near the exit, and there I whimpered in, with the car (which is able to get in touch with its feminine side) looking suddenly like a brilliantly colored but wounded bird. Larry and Charolett Posey succored me, let me use their phone and their front parlor, refused all money, and summoned another Larry. Indeed, they activated a network—a whole underground railroad—of Larrys. A guy came swiftly with his truck, looked at the tire, briefly pronounced, "She's history," and gave me a ride, with the round and ruined object, back into Elk City. Here, at Larry Belcher's truck and tire center, I was allowed to hang out while strong men frowned at the rare catch. There were no eighteen-inch tires to be had anywhere in Elk City, and the Larrys built me a patch which they wouldn't guarantee would last as far as Amarillo, 140 miles over the horizon. It was, one of the men said, the worst puncture he had seen since he left his army unit in Korea twelve years ago. The damn hole looked as if it had been made by a bullet. (His National Guard unit was being recalled to the colors, and he wasn't that thrilled about it.) It was perhaps at this point, in a world of gruff and tough men who do nothing all day but wrestle with grease and machinery, that it occurred to me that my pink socks were a mistake. Arguably a big mistake. I think I may have sounded unconvincing and even a bit fluting as I bid farewell and decided not to miss my one chance of saying "Is This the Way to Amarillo?" Tony Christie's simpering seventies hit (he dared to rhyme "pillow" with "willow" while crooning and weeping) plainly hadn't registered with my rescuers, and so I drove on with a fragile tire: man and machine now an uneasy meld of psychological and mechanical anxiety.

However, I had promised myself to risk the byway that reaches the ghost town of Texola, and there was still enough daylight to chance it like a real man. In this part of southwestern Oklahoma, past the rock cuts and bridge spans of the undulant Ozarks, the horizons recede to the utmost, and the red soil shows itself only when there are roadworks. The land flattens out toward the Texas Panhandle, and there Texola lies, desolate down a deserted track. Its position right at the border has meant that it's also been named Texokla and Texoma in its day, before a prewar vote settled the matter. But the 100th meridian has been surveyed seven times, so that the locals had at various periods lived in both Texas and Oklahoma without knowing it, or at any rate without having to move, or care. The point is moot now, because Texola is dead, its barns and shacks boarded up and occasionally adorned with a NO TRESPASSING sign. This is one of the stretches where 66 is still made up of the original white portland-cement concrete squares, which are quaint enough but too quaint for a bulging and patched tire, let alone a bulging and patched driver. I tooled slowly back to the modern world and whispered softly to the Corvette all the way to Amarillo, which with Larry's fine work we reached without incident. On the way, outside the town of Groom, was advertised the largest cross in North America, forcing itself on everybody for miles around, but I deliberately stopped whispering at that point in case anyone thought I was beseeching not just one inanimate object but two.

Why a town should be named "Yellow" I don't know, unless it's after the famous rose of Texas or some long-demolished adobe, but the tones of Amarillo are identical to those of any other town. At this point the society and the landscape begin to vary a bit: you see more horses than cattle—and some noble palominos at that—and begin to hear Spanish on the streets and on the radio, and I was asked to check my unlicensed gun at the door of a restaurant. (I wasn't packing one, so I disobeyed.) But Texas still wasn't as different as it likes to think. You hear a lot about the standardization of America, the sameness and the drabness of the brand names and the roadside clutter, but you have to be exposed to thousands of miles of it to see how obliterating the process really is. The food! The coffee! The newspapers! The radio! These would all disgrace a mediocre one-party state, or a much less prosperous country. Even if you carry Jane and Michael Stern's *Roadfood* guide, you can't always time your stops to it, and if you can't, why, you are at the mercy of the plastic industry and its tasteless junk. The coffee is a mystery as well as an insult: how can it be at once so bitter and so weak? (In "Talking Dust Bowl Blues," Woody Guthrie sings of a stew so thin that you could read a magazine through it, today's percolators contain the ditchwater equivalent. It tastes as if it were sucked up through a thin and soured tube from a central underground lake of stagnant bile.) And talking of reading, what can one say about the local press? It looks like indifferently recycled agency copy from the day before yesterday, relentlessly trivial and illiterate. Happening upon a stray copy of *USA Today* seems like finding Proust in your nightstand drawer instead of a Gideons Bible. And as for the radio—it was a dismal day when the Federal Communications Commission parceled out the airwaves to a rat pack of indistinguishable cheapskates, whose "product" is disseminated with only the tiniest regional variations.

I hear the first curtain-raising show about the twenty-fifth anniversary of Elvis's death as I enter Amarillo, and something in me causes me to lift the phone and send some flowers to my rescuers, Larry and Charolett, back in Elk City. A posy for Ms. Posey. I make it anonymous, except for "the guy in the Corvette." No doubt this will resolve any remaining doubt in her mind about having aided a limp-wristed Brit, but so much the better for the next pink-socked straggler on that road.

The great Dr. Samuel Johnson had his answer ready when he was asked whether it was worth visiting some piece of scenery. "Worth seeing," he replied, "but not worth going to see." One has to make this snap decision often along Route 66. The Meramec Caverns, supposedly a hideout of Jesse James's and perhaps the site where the first bumper sticker was handed out? No. The Cadillac Ranch outside Amarillo? Yes, all right. In the dirt on the western edge of town ten Caddies, ranging in model from a 1948 Club Coupe to a 1963 Sedan DeVille, have been driven into the ground at what local freaks say is the same angle as the Great Pyramid of Cheops. First rammed home in 1974 by Stanley Marsh, the cars were moved away from the city in 1997 as the sprawl increased, and are now right next to a handy snake farm.

As I trudge across the field toward the half-buried vehicles I am treading where Bruce Springsteen once trod. He later wrote "Cadillac Ranch":

James Dean in that Mercury '49
Junior Johnson running through the woods of Caroline
Even Burt Reynolds in that black Trans Am
All gonna meet down on the Cadillac Ranch.

Sounds improbable. Spray paint—the very essence of Pop art—had been layered thickly over the exhibits, giving them the look of New York subway cars in pre-Giuliani days. Nobody had written a single thing of interest. I was at first their only visitor, but as I traipsed back across the field I met a man wearing a "Chicago Law Enforcement" jacket who said brightly, "Definitely not something you see every day!" No, sir, but if I did see it every day I'd very soon stop noticing it. Nothing goes out of date faster than the ultra-modernistic. Exiting, I see a sign that reads: BATES MOTEL. SHOWERS IN ALL ROOMS. TAXIDERMY. KNIVES SHARPENED. Like a sap, I follow the arrows until I hit a dead end. American kitsch combined with a cheesy false alarm.

Trying to shake a bad mood, I meander over to the ghost town that marks the other frontier of the Texas Panhandle. Here is Glenrio, killed off by the opening of the interstate. Old 66, a pavement which is punctuated in town by a vestigial slab divider, simply peters out into red dirt and potholes. A cemetery for wrecked cars makes a nice counterpoint to a wooden water tower leaning at a drunken angle, downstreet from a wrecked coffee shop. This used to be the site of the celebrated "First and Last Motel in Texas," and some shards of the old sign can still be seen on the abandoned skeleton of the building, which is a dried-out mausoleum preserving the faint redolence of countless cross-border fornications. For additional Larry McMurtry-like eeriness, the spot is so negligible and dilapidated and done-in that my radio "seeker" can't pick up a signal in any direction. A deep calm descends upon me at this discovery, and I just sit listening to the insects until a nearby dog gets up the courage to break the silence. If I roused myself from the enveloping torpor and threw him a stick, it would fall into the next-door state.

This is the New Mexico border, which jauntily announces that I'm now on Mountain time and, as if to press home the point, gradually discloses a handsome mesa hoving into view on my left. At last, some landscape after the flatlands. The mesa also signals the old town of Tucumcari, which is a place of motels, a strip of motels, a grid of motels, a theme town of motels. You could stay in a motel while you looked for a motel room. A motel owners' convention would be a distinct possibility. Queen of the flops is the Blue Swallow Motel, which preserves the old and charming and discreet idea of an individual attached garage, placed like a pigeonhole next to each room. The buildings are pink. The garage doors are blue. Down by the wrong side of the railway tracks, I cheer up further by engulfing two bowls of cheap but gorgeous chili at Lena's Cafe, where Spanish is the tongue and where a flyswatter is placed wordlessly next to my plate. I am politely asked twice, "Are you sure?" The first time is when I ask for a second bowl. The second time is when I leave a three-dollar tip on an eight-dollar check. A large color poster of Jesus Christ is on the outside of the men's-room door: somehow it's a different Jesus from the one featured in the Protestant highlands and lowlands a few hundred miles back.

The road through Albuquerque mimics an 1849 gold-rush trail, cut in a hurry for those seeking to reach the California diggings from Arkansas and other Dixie territories. Extreme modernity imposes itself at the Kirtland Air Force Base, on the fringe of town, which houses the National Atomic Museum, the nation's principal destination for those who like collectible cards of weapons of mass destruction. I always strive to avoid writing about the "land of contrasts" when I travel, but here in the most ancient settled part of America— there is an Indian pueblo at Acoma which archaeologists theorize has been continuously inhabited since about A.D. 1150—the nuclear state was born, and its weaponry first designed and tested. Every effort has been made to leach both of these historic dramas out of the roadside scene: the wigwam-shaped tourist stops and gas stations are parodic and chirpy, and the main reminders of the military-industrial world are the long, anonymous trainloads over to the right, which according to local opinion are rumbling across their high desert from the huge bases in California. The motels and shops prefer to present this as a relic of the old Santa Fe Railroad days, when trains had cow-catchers on the front rather than hazardous materials in the boxcars. There's an extremely short strip of old 66 around here, perhaps the shortest of all, that preserves the old steel bridge across the Rio Puerco. The Puerco is a dry gulch, or is at this time of year.

A big rampart of red rock starts to dominate the same right-hand view, and also begins to look familiar, which, I suddenly realize, it would to any-body who had viewed an old Western movie. (You've seen it, probably just as a bristling rank of filmic feathered warriors appears at the summit.) This ridge also marks the Continental Divide, where rainfall—everything hereabouts is decided by water—makes its decision about whether to flow east or west. The elevation approaches 7,000 feet and the wind can be fierce. As I get near to Gallup, a sign on a bridge advises me that GUSTY WINDS MAY EXIST—a fasci-nating ontological proposition. Here, between the Navajo and Zuni lands, is the town that has some claim to be the capital of Native America. But it too is utterly buried in an avalanche of kitsch, with more bogus beads and belts and boots on sale than you can shake a lance at. I find that "folkloric" displays of the defeated and subjugated have a marked tendency to induce diarrhea at the best of times, but there is something especially degrading and depressing in the manner of all this: I prefer the United States of America to the idea of Bronze Age tribalism, yet surely a decent silence could be observed some-where, instead of this incessant, raucous, but sentimental battering of the cash register. On many stretches of road, you can barely see the primeval hills for billboards and pseudo-tepees. The El Rancho Hotel in Gallup is actually one of the more restrained evocations of the oldish days, with only a thin veneer of neon surmounting its basic structure of wooden fittings and weathered exterior. However, this is more like an outpost of old Hollywood, where the stars of those movies filmed in and around nearby Red Rock State Park could get a decent meal and some comfort. The brochure is the only one I've ever seen that claims both Ronald Reagan and his first wife, Jane Wyman, as guests (it doesn't state whether together or separately), and every room is "starred" with Alan Ladd, Paulette Goddard, and so forth. I'm billeted in the one named for Carl Kempton, whoever he was, right next door to Rita Hayworth. Cali-fornia, which has seemed so far away for so long, suddenly begins to feel attainable. The annual Inter-Tribal Indian Ceremonial, which sounds like the corporate or casino or cable version of a clan gathering, was soon to get under way in the town. One might have expected this to be an occasion for even more cashing in, but all I can tell you is that in Gallup, with its hard and acquisitive glitter and its resolute face to the future, I met with many trivial moments of hostility. Roadside America is always polite, even when the politeness is synthetic, and almost always friendly. But here—and I don't think it was the car—it was the monosyllable and the averted glance, even when I was only asking directions. I couldn't tell whether I was running into a superiority complex, or an inferiority one, but I was glad of a thick skin. I wasn't going to buy anything anyway.

Bleakness stayed with me until I traversed the Arizona border and turned off, near the absurdly named "Meteor City," to view this continent's most astonishing crater. Here, some 50,000 years ago, a huge piece of iron-and-nickel asteroid slammed into the desert with enough force to transform graphite into diamond. It displaced 175 million tons of limestone and sandstone, and left a beautifully rounded hole, 570 feet deep and 2.4 miles in circumference. We have a silly way of trying to make human scale out of these majestic things, so, O.K., if it were a football stadium, I am informed by the "Meteor Crater Enterprises Inc." brochure, it would seat two million spectators for twenty simultaneous games, and include the Washington Monument as a flagpole in the center. I saw, clustered around the telescopes on the rim, the largest concentration of that special tourist species—those who wear shorts and shouldn't—that I have ever witnessed outside Disneyland. The swaying, pachydermatous haunches of my fellow creatures seemed bizarrely transient and vulnerable in the context. Perhaps in reaction, I found it impossible to stand on the edge without looking up rather than down—though down is very impressive—and trying to picture what the last seconds before impact could conceivably have been like. It doesn't take long to give up on the endeavor: try imagining the apocalypse. NASA trained in this crater for a lunar dress rehearsal. And the moon itself was probably the result of a much more dynamic collision with our planet. The whole solar system is the outcome of similar smashes, as probably was the extirpation of the dinosaurs, whose jokey features are much exhibited locally to capture the kiddie market.

It all bears out what I've always said, which is that there can be no progress without head-on confrontation. However, an impact site of this magnitude lends a bit of perspective. Large meteorites or asteroids get through the atmosphere of Earth about every 6,000 years or so without burning up, so we are about due for another smack. Go and see Arizona while you can.

On the road into Flagstaff the Corvette gives a slight whinny as it senses a rival. Off to the left is what looks like an old Rolls-Royce, parked outside yet another wigwam-shaped souvenir store. On inspection, it proves to be a beautiful Austin Princess, still with its English license plates, standing aloof in the broiling sun. Inquiries within disclose that it's the property of the store owner, who proudly reveals that he bought it out of a garage in nearby Winslow, where it had been sitting undriven for years. He has no idea how such a vintage masterpiece, with its original ID, came to be hiding in the Arizona desert. Giving Flagstaff a bit of a miss—too metropolitan for my needs—I venture down the hairpin forest road to Sedona, which offers me the most slender and cathedral-like mesa columns as they are noosed in the rays of evening sun. Sedona has become the Aspen of the area, with resort hotels and golf courses and fancy restaurants in phony Spanish courtyards, but the air and light and verdancy are astoundingly refreshing after the high desert.

"Don't forget Winona," urges the song. Winona is put in, I can promise you, only because it rhymes with Arizona. But then, so does Sedona, and you can really find Sedona, whereas you drive straight through Winona without noticing it, and can't even identify it when you turn back. It's become a Flagstaff sub-burg, another featureless location. But the old 66 between Flagstaff and Kingman is one of the best and easiest stretches of the remaining pavement, and it's deliciously quiet and still and untraveled. On one fence post I see a beautiful motionless bird, which to my trained ornithological eye resembles either a very large hawk or a medium-size eagle. It waits imperturbably for a rodent or other small mammal to break cover and make the crossing. It returns my gaze without flinching. Turning away from feral nature, I find this is the only road on which the tradition of the Burma-Shave ad survives. In the interwar years, the makers of that amazingly successful brushless cream evolved the idea of putting a line from a jingle every half-mile or so, thus forcing motorists and their families to keep pace with the rhyme. So you would see, punctuated at intervals, lines such as "If you / Don't know / Whose signs / These are, / You can't have / Driven very far. *Burma-Shave*." Or "Shaving brushes / You'll soon see 'em / On the shelf / In some / Museum. *Burma-Shave*." Old-timer accounts of 66 never fail to cite this nostalgic feature. On the road into Seligman, the tradition has revived in the form of a public-service announcement. Over the course of a couple of miles without another car in view, I learn in sequence that: "Proper distance / To him was bunk / They pulled him out / Of some guy's trunk." Can't be too careful.

Seligman itself is one of the smallest and sweetest stops on the Route, and aptly enough its centerpiece is a one-chair barbershop, owned and operated for decades by Angel Delgadillo, a senior citizen with a huge, toothy smile who founded the original Historic Route 66 Association and probably stopped his hometown from going the way Texola and Glenrio did when the road passed them by. These days it's tourism or death, or both. Angel is cutting chunks from the mane of a Christ-bearded hippie type when I walk in, and has the practiced air of an unofficial mayor and ambassador, with a roomful of visitors, so I amble down to the Black Cat Bar and brown-bag store. Here, the friendly Tim tells me that he was moving his truck and his dogs from New Orleans to Washington State about a year ago when he broke down in Seligman and decided to stay. It's nice for the dogs, you can save money, and people are friendly enough, though in a town of fewer than 1,000 souls you have to watch out for "the Peyton Place side of things. Everything is everybody's business." All the time I am in Seligman, with its Marilyn Monroe posters and old-style gas pumps, there is a train longer than the town standing at the nearby station.

Kingman is the last major stop before the real desert begins, and here too the old Santa Fe system makes its point with a noble steam engine mounted—like a fish out of water? Like a train off the rails?—at the edge of a park. There was a random, decent full-service restaurant as well, named Calico's, where a hauntingly beautiful Spanish waitress had a good sense of the times and distances ahead, fueled me with a rich variety of calories for the ordeal to come, and warned me that the California Highway Patrol was a good deal more picky than the New Mexico and Arizona boys. (The speed limit varies from seventy-five to sixty-five as you cross state lines: the limit on the old 66 road is a euphonious fifty-five, and the optimum overall is seventy-seven unless you have a Corvette rearing and plunging under you.)

Steinbeck wrote of his desperate Okies as they left behind "the terrible ramparts of Arizona" and attempted to cross the desert at night because of the appalling glare and heat, and I try to make up time across the anvil of pain that stretches before me. A baby twister gets up outside Kingman and struggles to become menacing. But the turnoff sign to "London Bridge" proves too seductive, and I make the detour to Lake Havasu City, which regularly posts some of the highest temperatures in the continental U.S. I remember reading in my boyhood that some idiot had taken down a bridge over the Thames stone by stone and re-erected it in the desert, and here it all is. On the edge of a lake formed by the Colorado River, an artificial stream has been created, and the old gray span of London Bridge, which had survived fog and drizzle and German bombs between 1825 and 1968, is draped across it. This is the grand scheme of Robert P. McCulloch Sr., a chainsaw and oil and real-estate king who bid on the bridge and got it shipped across the Atlantic, shrapnel scars and all. Apparently he believed that he was getting the spires and draw-bridges of Tower Bridge and didn't discover his error until too late. (The one he got was a descendant of the star of the old song "London Bridge is falling down.") But it would be wrong to call this McCulloch's folly, as one is tempted to do. Last year more than one million people made the stop. The howling absurdities of desert-oasis Anglophilia dwarf the collector's item Austin Princess near Flagstaff as I pass the "Canterbury Estates Gated Community"—gated against what? the Navajos?—and view the Jet Skiers on "Windsor Beach" and the shoppers at "Wimbledon Goldsmiths." Union Jacks hang limply in the heat next to Old Glory. There's a "pub," of course, and some red telephone boxes and a red double-decker London bus. Yet the beer isn't warm enough to be authentic, and while the weathered old stone may last longer in this arid frazzle, it still sags a bit. The genuine fake is starting to become a bit of a theme along here.

Returning to the main road, I pass through Yucca, near Yucca Flat, where the open-air nuclear tests of the 1950s and 1960 had many glowing and electrifying effects, of which the best are captured in the movie *The Atomic Cafe*. Which would have been the more impressive and terrifying to see: the landing of the meteor that turned graphite into diamond, or the detonation of man-made devices that could fuse sand into glass? In 1955, John Wayne was playing Genghis Khan, possibly the very worst of his roles, downwind from Yucca Flat during the tests. Of those on the shoot, he was only the most famous one to get lung cancer later on: that location was a culling field. Susan Hayward, Agnes Moorehead, and Dick Powell were also to succumb. Can Wayne have been fatally poisoned by the military hero so adored? According to a recent biography it looks as if that was the way it was. This sinister worked-over sandscape has a weird antenna on every other hill, and the alien effect persists as the Colorado River cuts again across the wilderness, appearing rather shiny with false modesty after its epic work in designing and forging the Grand Canyon less than a hundred miles upstream. California! Here I come. But right away I am forced to pull in to a state "Inspection Station," as if meeting a frontier in Europe. The boredom and conceit of this—it's the only such barrier in all the eight states of Route 66—plays to the Californian narcissistic fantasy of being a semi-independent nation, with its own economy. But it also provides a reminder of the cruelty with which the state treated the migrants of the 1930s, tearing up their driver's licenses and turning them back as vagrants, until the courts finally put a stop to it. The gray-haired taxpayer-funded lady at the barrier waves me through after saying she preferred the color of my car to its make. Who the hell asked her?

The Mojave Desert is almost frightening. No—it *is* frightening. It's easy to see why the surviving Okies wanted to cross it at night, and not just because of the annihilating heat. In the dark, you wouldn't have to see the grim, dirty hues of the rock and the soil, and the endless, discouraging length of the road stretching ahead forever. There is something infinitely wearying about seeing one summit after another prove to be an illusion, range replacing range with ruthless monotony. The mile markers seem to slow down—*surely* I came farther than that? The sensation, of moving fast but never escaping, is dreamlike and hypnotic but not in a relaxing way, and the knowledge that this is home-stretch territory makes me superstitious about a last-minute mishap. Many of the turnoffs on the map are to vanished places that are only names, and the truth is that somewhere along this harsh and lifeless highway the old Route

66 just dies. It disappears into the trackless mess of suburban California as Los Angeles spreads out to embrace and claim it, and the last real stop is in Barstow, where the old road is blocked at the edge of town by a huge Marine base. Here at the El Rancho motel, built out of old railroad ties and festooned with 66 memorabilia, I mentally announced journey's end. The motel is indeed journey's end for a number of other people; in its rear court I was offered crystal meth and the services of a haggard and punctured whore before I could get out of the car. Snarling and shivering figures mingled with those to whom blank, inert amiability has become a signature. Down at the end of lonely street . . .

Bobby Troup's original ditty was better than perhaps he knew. He borrowed from the Homeric tradition by drawing a word-picture treasure map with memorable and rhyming place-names, an *Odyssey*-like mnemonic for the American Dream. And he and Cynthia, who suggested that crucial rhyme in the refrain, were able to buy a house in California within weeks of the release of the song. Postwar optimism drew on freedom of travel, extra dough, and sexual emancipation. Those words and that music touched such a nerve that I don't think I met anybody of any age last summer who, on hearing my plan, failed to respond with something like "Get your kicks, huh?" But try listening to the newer songs that mention the nation's most beloved road trip. On "Lost Causeway," Jason Eklund sings, "Get your kicks on what's left of 66," and says, "So follow state and homespun signs, leading on this historic route / Take a grab at the corporate crapola where history has been rubbed out." (Interestingly, he preserves the eastern pronunciation of "route.") Picking up on the cynicism of the commercialized Indian reservation with its tax-free cigarette bonanzas, he suggests "Get your *fix*."

The Red Dirt Rangers in their song "Used to Be," which has a tang of Springsteen's "My Home Town," speak of "holes in the roof and weeds by the door" of the trailer where the motor courts once stood, while the Mad Cat Trio intones the words "Get your kicks" with positive sarcasm. The Dusty Chaps, in "Don't Haul Bricks on 66," put their advice—"Route 66 ain't the way to go"—on the same level of obviousness as "Don't go pissing in the wind" and "You know the white hats always win." The music didn't quite die on this road, but it changed from celebration to melancholy and disappointment. Perhaps it all went when the last hitchhiker gave up, or was banned. Larry McMurtry was certainly right, in *Lonesome Dove,* to point out that once something is sold as "the Wild West" it means it's become domesticated. The luminous Robert Crumb registered a similar point in a twelve-frame cartoon, showing the evolution of a roadside scene from a setting with a road to a place where the road was the setting. The old 66 tried to be genuinely different from the new for a while, but it could survive only by selling itself as different, and those very sales tactics meant that it had to become the same. It's another coffee mug, another T-shirt, another line of cheap "Route 66" jeans from Kmart. The living bits of antique 66 are colonies of the new interstate, and the dead bits are, well, dead. I doubt that Texola or Glenrio will still be there if I travel that way again; outside Glenrio, I could already see and hear the earth-movers. In California the fifty-year-old Trails Restaurant, a 66 holdout in Duarte, was demolished almost as I drove by. You never step into the same river twice. All travel is saying farewell. Most voyaging in the United States has become either impossible (by rail) or a misery and a humiliation (by air) or a routine (by roads with no individuality). No poet has yet attempted to say what this defeat means for the American idea. But the melancholy is all around us, transmitted on frequencies that nobody can possess. After one last, brief, yearning sweep along Sunset, I did what I would once have bet I could never do, and roared down Rodeo Drive in a brash Corvette. The window-shoppers barely looked up. The drop-off point for my mettlesome steed was just at the corner of Wilshire. I tethered it, patted it, handed over the keys, and forgot to look back.

VANITY FAIR, NOVEMBER 2002

THE ADVENTURES
OF AUGIE MARCH

A ugie March stands on the Chicago lake-shore at dawn Year's Day in the 1930s:

> I drank coffee and looked out into the brilliant first morning of the year. There was a Greek church in the next street of which the onion dome stood in the snow-polished and purified blue, cross and crown together, the united powers of earth and heaven, snow in all the clefts, a snow like the sand of sugar. I passed over the church too, and rested only on the great profound blue. The days have not changed, though the times have. The sailors who first saw America, that sweet sight, where the belly of the ocean had brought them, didn't see more beautiful color than this.

Nick Carraway muses on the shoreline at the close of *The Great Gatsby*:

> And as the moon rose higher the inessential houses began to melt away until gradually I became aware of the old island here that flowered once for Dutch sailors' eyes—a fresh green breast of the new world . . . the trees that had made way for Gatsby's house had once pandered in whispers to the last and greatest of all human dreams; for a transitory enchanted moment man must have held his breath in the presence of this continent . . . face to face for the last time in history with something commensurate to his capacity for wonder.

One man is reflecting at day's end, and one at day's beginning. Both have just been put through it by flawed and wretched humanity—Carraway has been to several funerals and Augie has had a close shave while helping a girl who isn't his girlfriend to survive an illegal abortion. (I pause to note that one is a belly man, while the other favours the breast.) Both draw strength from the idea of America. But Carraway derives consolation, while it might be truer to say that Augie finds inspiration. Reflecting on Gatsby's futile quest—his "dream"—Carraway decides that: "He did not know that it was already behind him, somewhere back in that vast obscurity beyond the city, where the dark fields of the republic rolled on under the night." Augie doesn't take much stock in dreams, and he is about to venture on to those very fields.

I do not set myself up as a member of the jury in the Great American Novel contest, if only because I'd prefer to see the white whale evade capture for a while longer. It's more interesting that way. However, we do belong to a ranking species and there's no denying that this contest is a real one. The great advantage that *Augie March* possesses over *Gatsby* lies in its scope and its optimism and, I would venture, in its principles. Or its principle—in the opening pages Augie states it clearly and never loses sight of it:

> What did Danton lose his head for, or why was there a Napoleon, if it wasn't to make a nobility of us all? And this universal eligibility to be noble, taught everywhere, was what gave, Simon airs of honor . . .

Simon is Augie's older brother, but "the universal eligibility to be noble" (eligibility connotes being elected as well as being chosen) is as potent a statement of the American dream as has ever been uttered. Simon doesn't "make it"; that's not the point. Augie doesn't exactly make it either; well, it's an ideal not a promise. He decides to match himself against the continent, seeking no one's permission and deferring to no idea of limitation. His making, like his omnivorous education, will be his own.

This was the first time in American literature that an immigrant would act and think like a rightful Discoverer, or a pioneer. The paradox of the American immigrant experience had hitherto been exactly this: that so many of them came to the New World in order not to spread their wings but to adapt, to conform, to fit in. When we are first introduced to Augie he is in cramped conditions; a poor Jewish family semi-stifled by its own warmth and replete with dreads about the wider world. Our hero doesn't know any better than this, and yet he does know. "I am an American, Chicago born," he proclaims in the very first line of his narrative. It's important to understand what this assertion meant when it was made, both to Bellow himself and to the audiences he had in mind.

Barely a half-century before *The Adventures of Augie March* was published, Henry James had returned to New York and found its new character unsettling in the extreme. In *The American Scene,* published in 1905, he registered the revulsion he felt at having "to share the sanctity of his *American* consciousness, the intimacy of his *American* patriotism, with the inconceivable alien" [my italics]. On the Lower East Side he discerned "the hard glitter of Israel." In the Café Royale, a locus of Yiddish-speaking authors and performers, he found himself in one of "the torture rooms of the living idiom." And he asked himself: "Who can ever tell, in any conditions, what the genius of Israel may, or may not, really be 'up to'?" The Master was by no means alone in expressing sentiments and sensitivities of this kind. With *Augie March,* and its bold initial annexation of the brave name of "American," his descendants got the answer to the question about what the genius was "up to."

Saul Bellow was in point of fact born, and named Solomon, across the border in Lachine, Quebec. (Lachine itself was named by a Columbus-minded French officer who was sent to look for China and declared he'd found it.) His parents smuggled him across the Great Lakes as an infant and he didn't discover that he was an illegal immigrant until he signed up for the United States armed forces in the Second World War. The authorities sent him back to Canada and compelled him to reapply—kept him hanging about, in other words. Among other things, then, *Augie March* is an adieu to the Bellow of *Dangling Man* and *The Victim;* a farewell to the age of his own uncertainty.

Affirmatively, almost defiantly American, the novel is by no means a paean to assimilation and amnesia. As a youth, Bellow composed and performed a stand-up spoof of *The Love Song of J. Alfred Prufrock* in Yiddish, and has always remained acutely aware of his Russian roots. He helped Irving Howe and *Partisan Review* in the first translations of his future fellow-Nobelist Isaac Bashevis Singer. One triumph of *Augie March* is that it takes *Yiddishkeit* out of "the torture rooms," and out of the ghetto, and helps make it an indissoluble and inseparable element in the great American tongue. This linguistic faculty and facility is taken for granted by those of us who inherit Lenny Bruce and Walter Matthau and Woody Allen and Philip Roth and Joseph Heller as part of our vernacular birthright. But it wasn't so in 1953.

Only in the preceding year, for one thing, had Bellow's peers and co-thinkers and *kibitzers* got around to producing the famous *Partisan Review* symposium *Our Country And Our Culture.* In these pages, the veterans of the cultural combat of the 1930s—most but not all of them Jewish—had asked if perhaps the time had not come to rewrite their project of permanent opposition. There were demurrals and reservations, but on the whole the formerly "alienated" began to speak as lawfully adopted sons and daughters of the United States. The exceptions, those who distrusted what they saw as a coming age of conformism, included Irving Howe and Delmore Schwartz. But when *Augie* astonished the critics by showing that an egghead novel could be a literary and a commercial success, Schwartz was won over. His review of it opened with the simple declaration that "Saul Bellow's new novel is a new kind of book." He compared it favourably with the grandest efforts of Mark Twain and John Dos Passos. And he was struck at once by the essential matter, which is the language and the style:

> Augie March rises from the streets of the modern city to encounter the reality of experience with an attitude of satirical acceptance, ironic affirmation, the comic transcendence of affirmation and rejection.

Indeed, he made the immigrant vengeance on the old guard quite explicit:

> For the first time in fiction America's social mobility has been transformed into a spiritual energy which is not doomed to flight, renunciation, exile, denunciation, the agonised hyper-intelligence of Henry James, or the hysterical cheering of Walter Whitman.

The future protagonist of *Humboldt's Gift* ("Let me in! I'm a poet! I have a big cock!") admired Augie the character for the very quality that some reviewers distrusted: his unreadiness to be committed or, as he puts it, "recruited." Among the hostile reviewers was Norman Podhoretz who as recently as the year 2000 revisited the squabble and—almost incredibly but probably unconsciously—again echoed Henry James in accusing Bellow of "twisting and torturing the language"!

If I've succeeded at all in establishing this context, I hope I've helped explain why it is that *Augie March* still constitutes a template for modern American literature. Just as it formed and altered the Jewish and the Anglo-Saxon attitudes of its time—which is what I meant when I alluded earlier to Bellow's "audiences"—so it still waits for readers and critics and helps them to measure their own perspective on America. (This pilot-light effect can be seen in the work of Martin Amis, who in 1987 wrote that "for all its marvels, *Augie March,* like *Henderson the Rain King,* often resembles a lecture on destiny fed through a thesaurus of low-life patois." In 1995 he began an essay with the words: "*The Adventures of Augie March* is the Great American Novel. Search no further. All the trails went cold forty-two years ago. The quest did what quests very rarely do; it ended.' Not unrelatedly, perhaps, but in sharp reverse, Kingsley Amis greeted the original publication by telling the readers of the *Spectator* of Bellow's "gaiety and good humour, his fizzing dialogue, his vitality." Two decades later he wrote: "Bellow is a Ukrainian-Canadian, I believe. It is painful to watch him trying to pick his way between the unidiomatic on the one hand and the affected on the other." Twenty years further on he had sunk into the belief that everyone in America was "either a Jew or a hick.")

Augie himself is little better than "the by-blow of a travelling man." He informs us early that the expression "various jobs" is the "Rosetta Stone" of his life. But the awareness of eligibility is in him, and he'll fight his corner for it and never be a hick. "What I guess about you," says one of his pals— guessing correctly—"is that you have a nobility syndrome. You can't adjust to the reality situation . . . you want to accept. But how do you know what you're accepting? You have to be nuts to take it come one come all. . . . You should accept the data of experience." To which Augie replies more confidently than perhaps he feels: "It can never be right to offer to die, and if that's what the data of experience tell you, then you must get along without them."

Even while he is still stranded at home, knowing somehow that there must be more to life and America, Augie invests his banal surroundings with a halo of the numinous and the heroic. He transfigures the cliché of the Jewish mother, for a start:

[Mama] occupied a place, I suppose, among women conquered by a superior force of love, like those women whom Zeus got the better of in animal form and who next had to take cover from his furious wife. Not that I can see my big, gentle, dilapidated, scrubbing and lugging mother as a fugitive of immense beauty from such classy wrath . . .

And then there is old Einhorn, the lamed and misshapen local organizer and fixer and memoirist, who Augie ("I'm not kidding when I enter Einhorn in this eminent list") ranks with Caesar, Machiavelli, Ulysses and Croesus. It is Einhorn who so memorably lectures Augie after he has a narrow squeak with a two-bit, no-account piece of larceny that could have turned nasty.

"That was what you let yourself in for. Yes, that's right, Augie, a dead cop or two. You know what cop-killers get, from the station onward— their faces beaten off, their hands smashed, and worse; and that would be your start in life . . . But wait. All of a sudden I catch on to something about you. You've got *opposition* in you. You don't slide through everything. You just make it look so."

Einhorn then takes the role of Augie's missing father; releasing in his listener a spurt of love that he's too wised-up to acknowledge at the time.

"Don't be a sap, Augie, and fall into the first trap life digs for you. Young fellows brought up in bad luck, like you, are naturals to keep the jails filled—the reformatories, all the institutions. What the state orders bread and beans long in advance for. It knows there's an element that can be depended on to come behind bars and eat it . . . It's practically determined. And if you're going to let it be determined for you too, you're a sucker.

"Just what's predicted. Those sad and tragic things are waiting to take you in—the clinks and clinics and soup lines know who's the natural to be beat up and squashed, made old, pooped, farted away, no-purposed away. If it should happen to you, who'd be surprised? You're a setup for it."

Then he added, "But I think I'd be surprised."

Before Einhorn is through with his homily, he adds one more thing. "I'm not a lowlife when I think, and *really* think," says the poolroom king and genius swindler. "In the end you can't save your soul and life by thought. But if you *think,* the least of the consolation prizes is the world."

I judge this as a hinge moment in a novel that sometimes has difficulty with its dramatic unities. Einhorn summons the shades of the prison house for the growing boy, and evokes for us the omnipresence of violence, injustice and stupidity. He senses the lower depths of the underclass while we sense, in him, what we feel in reading Thomas Gray's *Elegy*: the unrealized potential of a great man who might have been. He, too, has felt the eligibility. And he has an untrained instinct for the examined life. Whatever this is—and it's demotic American English all right—it's not low-life patois.

So when Augie breaks free and sets out, he is no Candide or Copperfield. And this novel is no Horatio Alger tale. Many of Augie's ground-down relatives do end up in institutions, all of them achingly well-drawn and one—the "home" for Augie's retarded baby brother—poignantly so. Bellow's Chicago is not vastly different from *The Jungle* of Upton Sinclair. Even in the peace and prosperity of the 1950s he was able to recall the bitterness of want and exploitation, the reek of the hobos met on stolen train-rides, the sharpness of class warfare, the acuteness of ethnic differences among poor whites in the days before all non-blacks were absurdly classified as "Caucasian." (One of Simon's coal-yard drivers has a dread of running over a kid in a "Bohunk" neighborhood; exactly the sort of confrontation-nightmare that is now reserved for the black South Side.)

Of all the odd jobs that Augie takes (and these include being a butler as well as a shoe salesman; a paint-seller as well as a literary looker-upper) the three best-described are those that obliquely or directly involve his oppositionism. As a dog-groomer for the upper classes he feels a sense of wasteful absurdity in the work; as a contract book-stealer he increases his knowledge of the classics and also his acquaintance with Marxist intellectuals; as a union-organizer for the CIO he is brushed by the grandeur of the American labor movement, which briefly did unite all trades and ethnicities in a collective demand for justice. This episode of mobilization of the *jacquerie* calls on all of Bellow's power of taxonomy and onomatopoeia:

There were Greek and Negro chambermaids from all the hotels, porters, door-men, checkroom attendants, waitresses . . . All kinds were coming. The humanity of the under-galleries of pipes, storage and coal made an appearance, maintenance men, short-order grovelers . . . And then old snowbirds and white hound-looking faces, guys with Wobbly cards from an earlier time, old Bohunk women with letters explaining what was wanted, and all varieties of assaulted kissers, infirmity, drunkenness, dazedness, innocence, limping, crawling, insanity, prejudice, and from downright leprosy the whole way again to the most vigorous straight-backed beauty. So if this collection of people had nothing in common with what would have brought up the back of a Xerxes' army or a Constantine's, new things have been formed; but what struck me in them was a feeling of antiquity and thick crust.

Later when, adrift in Mexico, he meets that incarnation of opposition Leon Trotsky himself:

I was excited by this famous figure, and I believe what it was about him that stirred me up was the instant impression he gave—no matter about the old heap he road in or the peculiarity of his retinue—of navigation by the great stars, of the highest considerations, of being fit to speak the most important human words and universal terms. When you are as reduced to a different kind of navigation from this high starry kind as I was and are only sculling on the shallow bay, crawling from one clam-rake to the next, it's stirring to have a glimpse of deep-water greatness.

(Bellow himself had been to Mexico in order to try and see Trotsky; he arrived the day after the old man's assassination and viewed the body with blood still in its white hair. In an early draft of the novel, Augie signs up to go and work for the exiled heretic.)

Opposition is, however, only one of Augie's internal compasses. The other, operating both more and less predictably, is love and sex. To be blunt, young Mr. March is led around by his cock. He prefers earthy and honest expressions for this preoccupation, mentioning at one point "stupendous quiff" and at another a girl whose virtue was that she "made no bones" about what they were together for. Occasionally he can be rhapsodic (the paramour of Guillaume the dog-trainer is "a great work of ripple-assed luxury with an immense mozzarella bust"). And he can also be tender; there are few sweeter girls in fiction than Sophie Geratis, the staunch little Greek union militant ("She had a set of hard-worked hands and she lived with her beauty on rough terms. I couldn't for even a minute pretend that I didn't go for her.") However, he doesn't get the thunderbolt until he meets Thea Fenchel.

Thea has an eagle named Caligula, and she wants Augie to help her "man" this eagle and train it to smash full-grown iguanas in Mexico. He falls in with the plan because he's fallen completely for the woman. He falls so completely for the woman because—this is his weakness—she is so utterly sold on him. The magnificence of the bird he can appreciate; the project of making it into a trained hunter gives him a chill. And the lordly avian Caligula turns out to be, of all things (and in Thea's contemptuous word) "chicken." It will not fight Stone Age lizards, and it will not obey. Once she sees that Augie doesn't mind this—indeed secretly approves it—Thea's respect for Augie is gone. Not all reviewers admire this long and necessary passage, and many have puzzled over the significance of the bird (Is an eagle symbolically *American?* Not if it's called Caligula it's not. Not if it's chicken it's not.) But I think it is essential, as it shows that Augie is compelled to admire anything, especially something so noble, that will not permit itself to be domesticated. The price is high. He suffers appalling torment at the loss of Thea; lovesickness and sexual jealousy have seldom been more flayingly depicted. But the wrench does get him back to Chicago, "that somber city," to take stock and begin again.

Love, Poverty and War are, they say, the essential elements in the shaping of a man, as of a *Bildungsroman*. And when war deposes the Depression as the great disciplinarian of the lower orders, Augie signs up for the navy right away, thinking the while "What use was war without also love?" (This, by the way, may be the most masculine sentence ever penned.) He lucks out with Stella. His brief and near-terminal combat experience gives him his best opportunity yet to release the *"animal ridens"* within himself; a man of "various jobs" is never going to be more at home than in the lower deck of a ship, and he makes comedy out of the confidences of his messmates. Here again, the ear is unerring. (" 'You think I maybe have an inferiority complex, do you think?'

one of them asked me. 'I passed out advice in moderate amounts; nobody is perfect. I advocated love, especially.' ")

After a harrowing experience in a post-torpedoing open boat ("they found one reason after another to detain me at the hospital" as he laconically phrases it) he hopes at war's end for a safe and tranquil harbour. But how true it is that: "Brother! You never are through, you just think you are!" For a very brief while he imagines being a sort of Catcher in the Rye, running a foster-home where his broken-up family could also shelter. But life isn't through with him yet and he has to live up to the great sentence on his opening page: "Everybody knows there is no fineness or accuracy of suppression; if you hold down one thing you hold down the adjoining." To hold down his own curiosity would be to betray his profoundest instinct. And thus we find him sardonically installed at a European café table at the novel's close, working as middleman for an Armenian entrepreneur and declaring "that I was an American, Chicago born, and all these other events and notions." (Bellow incidentally boasts that not one word of *Augie March* was written in Chicago; he took himself off to Positano, Rome, Paris and London; there is nothing provincial about his Americanism.)

If we reflect along with Augie, we look back at a host of brilliantly realized minor characters, warranting comparison with Dickens and with that remarkable boy on the Mississippi who also had "The Adventures of..." in his title. One shouldn't play favorites perhaps, but Guillaume the fancy dog-trainer, who relies too much on the hypodermic when dealing with recalci-trant pooches ("Thees jag-off is goin' to get it") will always be mine. And Jimmy, the Struldbrug-like cop in the bowels of that Detroit precinct, who has everyone's face and rap-sheet in his head ...

The two keywords that encapsulate the ambitions of the book are "demo-cratic" and "cosmopolitan." Not entirely by coincidence, these are the two great stand-or-fall hopes of America. The two qualities that carry Augie through are the capacities for love and for irony; these, together with reason, are the great stand-or-fall hopes of humanity. The Metaphysical poets used the evocative word "America" as their term for the new and the hopeful, even addressing lovers by that name. Augie March concludes, more cannily, by seeing the unfunny side of the funny side:

Or is the laugh at nature—including eternity—that it thinks it can win over us and the power of hope? Nah, nah! I think. It never will. But that probably is the joke, on one or the other, and laughing is an enigma that includes both. Look at me, going everywhere! Why, I am a sort of Columbus of those near-at-hand and believe you can come to them in this immediate *terra incognita* that spreads out in every gaze. I may well be a flop at this kind of endeavor. Columbus too thought he was a flop, probably, when they sent him back in chains. Which didn't prove there was no America.

INTRODUCTION TO
THE ADVENTURES OF AUGIE MARCH
BY SAUL BELLOW, 2001

illiam Faulkner's novel *Intruder in the Dust* is actually a twentieth-century detective story (that, in my opinion, leaves *To Kill a Mockingbird* eating dust of its own). But, toward its close, it reverts to the inescapable historic texture of the Old South, and the way in which that history can't relinquish its inheritors, or be relinquished by them. The white protagonist Chick Mallison recalls a soliloquy of his uncle's:

It's all *now* you see. Yesterday won't be over until tomorrow and tomorrow began ten thousand years ago. For every Southern boy four-teen years old, not once but whenever he wants it, there is the instant when it's still not yet two o'clock on that July afternoon in 1863, the brigades are in position behind the rail fence, the guns are laid and ready in the woods and the furled flags are already loosened to break out and Pickett himself with his long oiled ringlets and his hat in one hand probably and his sword in the other looking up the hill waiting for Longstreet to give the word and it's all in the balance, it hasn't hap-pened yet, it hasn't even begun yet, it not only hasn't begun yet but there is still time for it not to begin against that position and those cir-cumstances which made more men than Garnett and Kemper and Armistead and Wilcox look grave yet it's going to begin, we all know that, we have come too far with too much at stake and that moment doesn't need even a fourteen-year-old boy to think *This time. Maybe this time* with all this much to lose and all this much to gain: Pennsylvania,

Maryland, the world, the golden dome of Washington itself to crown
with desperate and unbelievable victory the desperate gamble . . .

You may find this a touch overwrought, even romanticized. (Gore Vidal in his
haunting and superb *Lincoln* points out that in 1861 there was no dome on the
unfinished Capitol, and the Washington Monument itself was an ugly stump
that stood incomplete for lack of funds.) You may even think it a trifle ethnically incorrect. (It's only white southern boys aged fourteen years who can or
do have this reverie.) You may even say that it's sentimental. (Many boys of all
ages in the Old Confederacy were consecrated Unionists, and many since have
gotten over it and learned to deal with it.) But either you can feel a thrill and
a catch in the throat at the mention of Thermopylae and Agincourt, Culloden and Gallipoli, Jarama and El Alamein, or you cannot. And the great
martial epic at Gettysburg—which you notice Faulkner doesn't even name,
considering it to lie too deep for words—belongs in that roster of battles, both
because it was a deciding engagement and because it featured a culminating
moment of immolating, futile gallantry.

Which is why, on another hot July afternoon, in 1998, 135 years to the day
since the suicidal charge that still bears Pickett's name, I found myself
standing in the wondrously beautiful and unchanging scenery of southern
Pennsylvania. I was myself an intruder in the dust—the dust of perhaps
15,000 Civil War reenactors, and twice that number of spectators. Hoop-
skirted women moved in and out of the sutlers' stores, while brass bands
played "Dixie" and "Battle Cry of Freedom" at one another, and blue- and
gray-clad detachments kept a respectful mutual distance. The blue side was
more uniform in the strict sense, as befits a regular army, while the gray was
often self-equipped or barefoot or decked out in chaotic slouch hats and
overalls. Nevertheless, you got the strong feeling that this is a shade of gray
that still sees things in black and white.

Available were copies of *Civil War Times* and *Camp Chase Gazette* ("The Voice of
Civil War Reenacting"), from which it's possible to discover that there are
many people who do this more than just once a year. Indeed, I ran into a gentleman named Brian Talbert, accoutred for Battery E of the Third United
States Artillery, who reckoned that he turns out in full kit between twenty-
five and thirty weekends each year, mostly for the Civil War but occasionally

for the Indian Wars as well. (Union and Confederate officers, who had often been friends at West Point, agreed at least on how to deal with Mexicans and Indians.) The rest of the time he is an aerospace-facilities mechanic for Honeywell in Clearwater, Florida. And he is for Honest Abe, the rail-splitter and country lawyer from Illinois. Most of the serious, hard-core reenactors are worshipers of J. E. B. Stuart and Robert E. Lee. (They have, you might say, more to win.) Outside a souvenir tent I ran into Tony Horwitz, whose book *Confederates in the Attic: Dispatches from the Unfinished Civil War* is the finest account of this stubborn American subculture. He pointed to the Johnny Reb character on his dust jacket—a distinctly *farouche* individual named Robert Lee Hodge. "His special trick is a brilliant impersonation of a bloated battlefield corpse," Horwitz instructed me. "He might be round one of the bars this evening." Mr. Hodge, I later learned, has patented the term "wargasm" for those "super hardcore" enthusiasts who like their reenactments down and dirty. Some of these are in need of a life; others are genuine history students; still others tend to regard the movie *Deliverance* as an invasion of their personal privacy. But, for all those who chafe at the redneck jeer, the Stars and Bars is a title and connection to nobility.

Although nobody appreciated the fact at the time, the Battle of Gettysburg was won on the first of its three days, and was effectively over before it began. The Army of Northern Virginia crossed the Mason-Dixon Line into Union territory, in real strength for the first time, but without very much hard information. Its supposed "eyes"—the dashing cavalry of the aforementioned Stuart—preferred to go off on a raiding expedition. So when the Army of the Potomac, under General George Meade, met the advance guard of the foe, it was like two ships colliding in the fog. General John Buford's Union cavalry decided there and then to make a fight of it and to preserve the high ground. Once they had done that, it's no cliché to say, the rest was history. I watched this defining and fateful moment as it was reenacted under a broiling sun. The musketry rattled and volleyed, and the cannons boomed and gave off a satisfying smoke, and files and ranks and columns advanced and redeployed. Only one element of authenticity was missing. Nobody much wanted to mime the bit where you throw up your arms, or, more likely (given the regular instruction of those days to "aim low"), clutch them terribly and suddenly over your viscera and genitalia. Hardly anybody volunteered to fall. You can understand why in one way, because where's the fun in lying hot and still for the rest of the afternoon? You can see why in another too, because there are many people who truly, madly, deeply want to "be a part of it" and who, as Faulkner understood, half believe that it can still be made to come out differently.

It used to be said of the American Civil War, or "the War Between the States," or "the late unpleasantness," or "the war of Northern Aggression," that it was the last of the old wars and the first of the new. There was still cavalry and dash and individual initiative, in other words, but the long growling notes of mechanized warfare were to be heard under and over the canter of hooves and the drum taps and the noble call of the bugle. About 55,000 men were blown to shreds or died of appalling wounds or expired from thirst and neglect on the Gettysburg field, and it seemed to me somewhat profane to be strolling this nearby turf and buying kitsch souvenirs, or pamphlets with titles such as *Freemasons at Gettysburg*, or T-shirts emblazoned with the legend IT'S A SOUTHERN THING—YOU WOULDN'T UNDERSTAND. (Why is it, when I see a Confederate battle flag flapping from the rear of a pickup truck, that I don't axiomatically make the association with courtesy, gentility, chivalry, and hospitality? Perhaps that's the bit I don't understand.) Anyway, on these occasions there's usually a shortage of volunteers to play the Yankee part.

So it was a shock to see the first black face I'd seen all day. It belonged to a man wearing a Union blue cap with an otherwise denim outfit. He proved to be not a teen reenactor but a history buff from Baltimore who had put on the cap only as a badge of solidarity. He spoke very knowledgeably of Charles Francis Adams, Lincoln's envoy to London, and of his son Henry, author of *The Education of Henry Adams,* and of contemporary British politicians such as Gladstone and Russell, before he was abruptly drowned out by a band striking up "Dixie." It turned out that we were standing within a few yards of General Lee's tent, and that the Confederate leadership was about to give a "press conference." My new acquaintance declined my suggestion that we walk over together and see what was up. (One of the first acts of the Army of Northern Virginia, on entering Pennsylvania and thus re-entering the Union, was to round up freed slaves and send them south to be reincorporated into the unpaid workforce. Talk about forced integration.) But on presenting myself to Lee's staff I met the one reenactor I decided to stay with.

He was easy to spot, in his red coat and smart black cap. "Colonel Fremantle, I think?" He bowed politely in response. Lieutenant Colonel Sir Arthur James Lyon Fremantle of Her Britannic Majesty's Coldstream Guards is a noticeable figure in Michael Shaara's tremendous novel, *The Killer Angels,* and in the made-for-TV movie *Gettysburg,* which is based upon it. Fremantle attached himself as an observer to the Confederate forces and wrote one of the most vivid, if least intelligent, Civil War diaries. (He believed to the last that the South was unvanquishable.) Had Lee carried the day in Pennsylvania, he could next have moved against Philadelphia or Washington or both, and in that event the British Empire might well have abandoned its rather pro-southern neutrality and intervened on the side of Jefferson Davis. The man who played Fremantle turned out to be Roger Hughes, a jovial Brit from Nottingham who now lives in Orlando and works as a marketing consultant. He's been doing the part for seven years. We repaired to his nearby and well-appointed tent. Almost every passerby recognized him. "Of course, it's partly the scarlet tunic. All the fault of that film. Fremantle never wore his uniform on the battlefield; insisted on a gentleman's shooting suit. But now people expect it of me."

Having been recruited as a bit of a joke to what he ironically termed "the reenactment community," Hughes has found the role subtly taking over his life. He has researched every detail of Fremantle's career, has written a novel entitled *Fremantle,* and had it privately published in leather bindings, has visited the spots where the great man served, and has dug forgotten photographs of him out of military archives in London. "I think," he said gravely, "I've got the best job in the Confederate army." He was free to wander the battlefield without taking part in hostilities. Fremantle had actually heard General Robert E. Lee, after the sanguinary fiasco of Pickett's charge, exclaim, "This has all been my fault." At the time, most southern partisans did not want to hear this. It was one thing for thousands of men to throw away their lives by marching up a slope under heavy fire and insane orders—that's glory for you—but quite another to think of it as a blunder committed by a vain and fallible old mortal. The 1854 charge of the Light Brigade was sound tactics by comparison. (A salient element in Charles Frazier's 1997 novel, *Cold Mountain,* is the way that the footsore Confederate deserter, Inman, comes to the realization that he has been duped, and treated as expendable: "At wide intervals in the valley stood big houses with white columns. They were ringed around with scattered hovels so that the valley land seemed cut up into fiefdoms. Inman looked at the lights in the big houses at night and knew he had been fighting battles for such men as lived in them, and it made him sick.")

Sitting with "Fremantle" under the awning of his tent was the bowler-hatted and suspender-wearing Francis Charles Lawley, correspondent of the London *Times* and a keen partisan for the Land of Cotton. He proved to be another jovial Brit, named John Bottoms, a systems analyst for Cincinnati Bell. The frantic diatribes of the *Times* against Lincoln and the Union, and in favor of the slavocracy, were the despair of Charles Francis and Henry Adams. But this propaganda was regularly answered by Britain's leading pro-Union journalist. In his articles for Horace Greeley's *New York Daily Tribune*, this columnist, Karl Marx by name, who helped lead the pro-Lincoln agitation in England, foresaw the era of ironclad ships, the sacking of the incompetent Union general George McClellan, and the adoption of the Emancipation Proclamation, which declared free those slaves in Confederate hands. He was much admired by Adams *père et fils*. I have often wondered why the Dixiecrat right doesn't make more of this historical fact, which is certainly among those things that they don't teach you in school.

In the main tent at midday, there was an attraction billed as "Civil War Past Lives: A Regression Talk by Barbara Lane." I attended. Ms. Lane, in crinoline and parasol and with a bottle of sarsaparilla no doubt nearby, expounded to a big audience about her belief in the reincarnation of veterans as reenactors. An understudy of the moderately disastrous Confederate general Henry Heth was produced to share his hallucinations with us. So were some other dubious revenants. Only one man broke the usual rule of the reincarnated, most of whom (you must have noticed) claim to have been kings or demigods in past lives. "I was just a drunken private," this chap announced. His state at the time certainly lent plausibility to the claim. I found myself growing irritated, not merely by the silliness of the business but by its modernism. If I visit blood-soaked and therefore supposedly hallowed ground, I want at least to hear bombastic rhetoric, not subtherapeutic babble.

* * *

The very reason for the imperishability of Lincoln's Gettysburg Address, delivered four months later on the same hallowed ground, is that it departed from conventional bombast and oratory, while managing both to honor the past and to summon a common democratic future. (This, in under 300 words.) I went straight from the faux event to the real national monument down the road and tried to decide what it is that makes Gettysburg so enduring and intense.

- It could have gone the other way, with the future republic partitioned and partly enslaved.
- The dead don't have a say. I would prefer to hear from Pickett's squandered foot soldiers than from those who conscript them for later speeches and who take their names. Since we can't hear from them, we shouldn't in all decency presume to speak for them. (This goes for most such rhetoric on all sides.)
- Gettysburg lasted only three days, and ended on the eve of the Fourth of July. Before the Civil War, people of all classes and professions would say "The United States are . . ." After 1865, it was "The United States is . . ."
- The Confederate army was the last white Anglo-Saxon Protestant (if not exactly Wasp) army to take the field on American soil, or from American soil. (Its battle flag was the Saint Andrew's cross. Faulkner always considered himself Scottish, and thought yearningly back to the analogous defeat of the gallant clans of the Highlands at Culloden in 1746.) In the Union ranks were numerous polyglot refugees from Europe, many of them veterans of the 1848 revolution. The great melting pot started to bubble only after Gettysburg had been decided.
- The British Empire never again tried to intervene militarily in American affairs, and acknowledged that a continental Union was inevitable, so Gettysburg was a hinge event in the gradual eclipse of Britain by the United States. (In the famous essay collection *If It Had Happened Otherwise*, edited by J. C. Squire in 1931, Winston Churchill gave this as his main reason for wishing that Lee had won.)

- The southern forces were defeated by the very qualities—J. E. B. Stuart's reckless and charming indiscipline, Lee's steadfast faith in God's guidance, General James Longstreet's dogged and unswerving loyalty—that they admired in themselves and had imagined would give them victory. As Bertolt Brecht says in "A Worker Reads History": "And even in Atlantis of the legend / The night the sea rushed in / The drowning men still bellowed for their slaves."

- An unheeded warning—about the superiority of artillery over infantry seems in retrospect to make Gettysburg the premonition of the Western Front, and of the superannuated and stubborn generals who presided over it and surpassed their predecessors in folly.

- Glorious defeats often have a greater emotional effect than muddy victories. The Confederacy continued to make a human sacrifice of its best sons, in the name of General George Pickett, for nearly two years after the lesson of Gettysburg had been ruthlessly driven home. Dunkirk was a glorious and inspiring defeat, but on that occasion the big effort was expended in saving the British army from Hitler rather than throwing it heroically away. And one of the flashiest officers on the Union side was George Armstrong Custer . . .

- This was the first war to be chronicled by photographers. Mathew Brady's stark, chiaroscuro studies of the unburied dead at Gettysburg meant that civilians could see what warfare really looked like, instead of relying on propaganda sheets, instant ballads, and secondhand dispatches.

These were broken thoughts on a stricken field, yet they seemed to connect to one another. (The unexploited and uncluttered landscape helps one's thoughts to jell, even if Three Mile Island is only a day's march away.) Above all, there is the masculinity of the thing. Warfare, they say, is to men what childbirth is to women: the essential and formative and bonding experience. It makes you part of it all, and enlists you in the unimpeachable company of combatants, and defines you as an individual. Here is Michael Shaara's description of the critical scene at Little Round Top—the desperately fought turning point in the Gettysburg struggle—where the men from Maine were told that on no account could they give up the high ground seized by General Buford, because they were the end of the line:

The men were digging in, piling rocks to make a stone wall. The position was more than a hundred yards long, Chamberlain could see the end of it, saw the 83rd Pennsylvania forming on his right. On his left there was nothing, nothing at all . . . Chamberlain took a short walk. Hold to the last. To the last what? Exercise in rhetoric. Last man? Last shell? Last foot of ground? Last Reb? . . . He felt the emptiness to his left like a pressure, a coolness.

And here is Ernest Hemingway in *For Whom the Bell Tolls*:

If both flanks ever held I suppose it would be too much to take, he thought. I don't know who is prepared to stand that. And if you extend along a flank, any flank, it eventually becomes one man. Yes, one man . . . You are going to be the left flank when we have the battle, he thought . . . Well, I always wanted to fight one on my own. I always had an opinion on what was wrong with everybody else's, from Agincourt down. I will have to make this a good one.

Robert Jordan and the other American volunteers in the Spanish Civil War were fighting, of course, in the Abraham Lincoln Battalion. I believe that Hemingway must have had Gettysburg in mind when he was writing (and perhaps he was also thinking of Stephen Crane, who described the May 1863 battle at Chancellorsville in *The Red Badge of Courage* to such electrifying effect that people thought he had "been there," when he hadn't been born at the time).

American letters and literature became less flowery, more terse, more ironic, and in a way more modest and understated after Gettysburg and the pungent, economical address that bears its name. Walt Whitman's *Drum-Taps* is nearly prosaic, while Robert Lowell's elegy "For the Union Dead" borrows from the almost Puritan scene that it describes: "On a thousand small town New England greens, / the old white churches hold their air / of sparse, sincere rebellion; frayed flags / quilt the graveyards of the Grand Army of the Republic." Yet, still, more people north and south would recognize the name of Pickett than would know of Joshua Lawrence Chamberlain. A skeptical professor of religion and rhetoric at Bowdoin College and a friend of Harriet Beecher

Stowe's, Chamberlain commanded the 20th Maine at the extreme end of Little Round Top. He did not hurl his Maine troops into senseless or theatrical engagements. He did not commit lethal flourishes. He was frugal with the ammunition. He stoically held the left flank for the Union, and only as a last and meditated resort led a charge downhill rather than up, thus clinching matters in a memorable way. If he'd been more of a bloodbath-artist and war-lover, he'd probably be the toast of innumerable men who have never seen a bloated corpse or smelled a chest wound, and who use such episodes for brag-gartry and beer chasers. But, as it happens, it was the thoughtful Chamberlain who won the day, while those who can't forgive the past are condemned, not without pathos, to reenact it.

AMERICA'S POET?
BOB DYLAN'S ACHIEVEMENT

A review of *Dylan's Visions of Sin*
by Christopher Ricks

Not all great poets—like Wallace Stevens—are great singers," Bob Dylan once suggested. "But a great singer—like Billie Holiday—is always a great poet."

It would be an enterprise in itself to disentangle the many ways in which this brief statement is dead wrong. The antithesis, if it is meant as an antithesis, between poet and singer, is false to begin with. The "not all" is based on a non-expectation: How many poets have been singers at all? Certainly not Dylan Thomas, the Welsh boozer and bawler from whom Bob Dylan—a Jewish loner from Hibbing, Minnesota, who was born as Robert Zimmerman—annexed his *nom de chanteur*.

Other cryptic or pretentious observations, made by Bob Dylan down the years, have licensed the suspicion that he's been putting people on and starting wild-goose chases for arcane or esoteric readings that aren't there. There are also those who maintain that Dylan can't really sing. (This latter group has recently been reluctantly increasing.) Of his ability as a poet, how-ever, there can be no reasonable doubt. I used to play two subliterary games with Salman Rushdie. The first, not that you asked, was to re-title Shake-speare plays as if they had been written by Robert Ludlum. (Rushdie, who invented the game, came up with *The Elsinore Vacillation*, *The Dunsinane Reforestation*, *The Kerchief Implication*, and *The Rialto Sanction*.) The second was to recite Bob Dylan songs in a deadpan voice as though they were blank verse. In addition to the risk of the ridiculous, it can become quite hypnotic. Try it yourself with "Mr. Tambourine Man": It works so well, you hardly care that a tambourine man can't really be playing a song. "Lily, Rosemary and The Jack of Hearts," "Chimes of Freedom," and "Desolation Row" all have the same elasticity.

But as a guide to Dylan's poetic moments, do we really need help from Christopher Ricks, author of *Keats and Embarrassment*, editor of T.S. Eliot's juvenilia, instructor on the funny side of *Tristram Shandy*, and all-around literary mandarin? Need him or not, we now have Ricks—who, in *Dylan's Visions of Sin*, performs over five-hundred pages of literary criticism on the lyrics. Reading Dylan as the bard of guilt and redemption, Ricks takes his stand on the recurrence in the songs of the seven deadly sins, only just balanced as they are by the four cardinal virtues and the three theological virtues (or heavenly graces: faith, hope, and charity).

It's Ricks's own potentially deadly virtues that bother me. What temptation should one avoid above all, if one is a former professor of English at Cambridge? The temptation to be matey, or hip, or cool—especially if one is essaying the medium of popular music. But Ricks begins his book like this: "All I really want to do is—what, exactly? Be friends with you? Assuredly I don't want to do you in, or select you or dissect you or inspect you or reject you."

The toe-curling embarrassment of this is intensified when one appreciates that Ricks is addressing his subject, not his reader. Why did he leave out other verbs Dylan had in that song: *simplify you, classify you, deny, defy, or crucify you?* And surely, he's already at least "selected" him?

Then, accused by one of his usually admiring rivals in Dylanology, Alex Ross of the *New Yorker*, of "fetishizing the details of a recording," the prof resorts to unbearable archness. ("What me? All the world knows that it is women's shoes that I am into.") Some of Ricks's jokey attempts at making puns work ("cut to the chaste"), but "interluckitor" is a representative failure. This last is coined to deal with a claim by Dylan, made in 1965, that every song of his "tails off with: 'Good Luck—I hope you make it.' " Such a claim, if taken seriously, would in any case vitiate most of Dylan's claims to profundity.

Having said that distinguished academics ought not to try and be ingratiating with the young, I pull myself up a bit and realize that true Dylan fans are probably well into their fifties by now. It must have been in 1965 that I first heard what Philip Larkin called, in a quasi-respectful review of *Highway 61 Revisited*, his "cawing, derisive voice." And it will be with me until my last hour. Some of this is context. The "sixties" didn't really begin until after the Kennedy assassination (or "Nineteen Sixty-Three," as Larkin had it in another reference), and Bob Dylan was as good a handbook for what was supposedly happening as Joseph Heller. Much of it of course also had to do with the sappiness, in both "sap" senses, of adolescence. Yet even at the time, I was somehow aware that Dylan wasn't all that young, and didn't take "youth" at its face value. A good number of his best songs were actually urging you to grow up, or at any rate to get real. Dylan respected his elders, most notably Woody Guthrie. And he was braced for disillusionment. *How does it feel? Don't think twice, it's all right. It's all over now, baby blue. I was so much older then, I'm younger than that now.*

Ricks essentially wants to argue that Dylan has always been swayed by the elders and that his verses consistently defer to the authorities. How else to explain, for example, the many latent affinities between "Sad-Eyed Lady of the Lowlands" and the Book of Ezekiel? The kings of Tyre, the dying music, the futility of earthly possessions. . . . That's Covetousness taken care of, with Pride (or at any rate hubris) given a passing whack into the bargain. Six sins to go.

Ricks has no success with Greed (as he admits) and not much with Sloth, either. There is a good deal of anomie and fatalism in Dylan; a fair amount of shrugging and dismissal and an abiding sense of waste and, equally often, of loss. It's pervasive but nonspecific in "Time Passes Slowly," which Ricks interrogates without any great profit. So I pushed on to "Lust," and was taken aback.

"Lay, Lady, Lay" is one of the great sexual entreaties, and it has in common with "I Want You" and "If You Gotta Go, Go Now" a highly ethical reliance on the force of gentle persuasion. There is no blackmail, moral or otherwise, and no hint of a threat or even a scene in the event of nonconsummation. But nor is there any doubt of what the minstrel wants: *His clothes are dirty but his hands are clean. | And you're the best thing that he's ever seen.* Of this false modesty and abject flattery, Ricks astonishingly says that "his hands are clean because he is innocent, free of sin: no lust, for all the honest desire, and no guile." Had Dylan written "his clothes are dirty but his mind is clean," this might have been believable. And is there no guile in the succeeding stanza?

> *Stay, lady, stay, stay with your man awhile*
> *Why wait any longer for the world to begin?*
> *You can have your cake and eat it too.*
> *Why wait any longer for the one you love*
> *When he's standing in front of you?*

Ricks then moves to a laborious comparison with Donne's "On His Mistress Going To Bed," at which point I thought, well, as soon as I turn the page he'll stop clearing his throat and make the obvious metaphysical connection to Andrew Marvell and "To His Coy Mistress." But no. And here's the clue to Ricks's method. The words "bed," "show," "see," "man," "hands," "world," he says, all appear in both Donne and Dylan, while the words "unclothed" and "lighteth" appear in Donne, balanced by "clothes" and "light" in Dylan.

Shall we agree that all the words just specified are in somewhat common use today, and were in equally ordinary employment in the seventeenth century? Whereas, if you care to glance again at the Dylan lines I just cited, not only do you think at once of Marvell's *Had we but world enough and time | This coyness, Lady, were no crime* (which gets "lady" in there, right enough, and in delicious apposition to "world" at that), but you also find yourself grappling with Marvell's gentle but urgent sense of delay and frustration. Dylan further beseeches the lady to stay *while the night is still ahead* and *to have [her] cake and eat it too*: Metaphysically speaking this is not so remote from Marvell's reminder that the darkness of death will last an awfully long time, while in the grave the worms may dine long and well. This is something different from Donne's poem, which swiftly becomes a near-raunchy celebration of achieved carnal knowledge of someone familiar to him. Finally, Marvell speaks beautifully and seductively about keeping the sun in motion since there's no chance of making it stand still, and Dylan longs to see his beloved "in the morning light," having banished the night in the only way that lies open to him. I hope I don't boast about my own poor exegesis, but Ricks's procedure is more like that of the people who pore over Bible codes or kabbalistic crossword puzzles.

Dylan's version of anger is sardonic and bitter: an exemplary match for the "cawing, derisive" tones noted by Larkin. In "Masters of War," "Only a Pawn

In Their Game," and "The Lonesome Death of Hattie Carroll," he said to the military-industrial complex and the racists, in effect, "You win. For now. But for now you also have to live with your shame. And judgment will follow, and is coming." (I have always hoped, for this reason, that Joan Baez was wrong in claiming that Dylan wrote "When The Ship Comes In"—his most Jeremiad and vengeful poem—in response to bad service at some hotel.)

"The Lonesome Death of Hattie Carroll" was based on a real event in 1963: the lethal beating of Hattie Carroll by William Zanzinger in a Baltimore hotel. Zanzinger's lenient treatment by the courts fired Dylan into a hot rage, yet producing his most glacial and most measured poem of fury and contempt. He simply relates the story, with deadly counterpoint as between the rich and careless white man and the dispensable black servitor. The song never uses the words "black" or "white," as Ricks points out, but just: He *owns a tobacco farm of six hundred acres*, while she *emptied the ashtrays on a whole other level*. Thus is the plantation relationship re-cast and, as Ricks rightly says, "it's a terrible thing that you know this [their respective colors] from the story." But then again, as Ricks also emphasizes, Dylan's affecting line *And she never done nothing to William Zanzinger* is a sort of clue. I have always thought that this was Dylan ventriloquizing, without condescension, the "Black English" demotic comment on the affair. Ricks improves on my intuition by giving the example of James Baldwin in *The Amen Corner*: "He hadn't never done nothing to nobody."

Doomed and determined to destroy all the gentle, in Dylan's haunting phrase, Zanzinger slew Hattie Carroll *with a cane that he twirled around his diamond-ring finger*, and who would pass up the chance to recall the first murderer, Cain, in this context? Not Ricks, who also calls attention to the words *lay slain by a cane* and to the triple repetition of the word "table," which closes three consecutive lines. "Does this—*able"* he inquires, "prepare for the word that soon follows, 'cane'? Cain and Abel, masculine and feminine endings?" Well, no, I shouldn't think so. Whatever the song is about, it most decidedly isn't about fratricide. And Cain and Abel—scarcely unique metaphors where murder is concerned—appear in other Dylan songs under their own names. Ricksian hermeneutics has its limits.

I could, nonetheless, have used some more counsel from Ricks about the title. In what way was Hattie Carroll's death "lonesome"? There is an unmistakable sentimentality in this word; a tear-jerking note that is wondrously absent from the song itself. Insufficient guidance is forthcoming: Ricks proposes without much brio that Dylan "perhaps" wanted the word to evoke a contrast between Hattie's death and the crowded hotel. But with or without that "perhaps," ultimately, everybody dies alone.

Ricks's closing thought is superior. He argues that T. S. Eliot understood the difference between writing religious poetry and writing poetry religiously, and that Dylan with "The Lonesome Death of Hattie Carroll" has written politically rather than merely writing a political song. That seems to be a distinction well worth observing, most especially at a time like the present with its ephemeral garbage of pseudo-protest. ("We've suffered for our music— now it's your turn.") The finest fury is the most controlled. One still feels a generous anger when listening to the song—incidentally, William Zanzinger turned up again a few years ago in the Baltimore courts, for leasing black people squalid, waterless cabins that he didn't even own—and the pairing of generosity with anger (annexed from Orwell out of Dickens) might license some interpenetration of sin and virtue, or even sin with grace.

It's back to hermeneutics in Ricks's study of "Love Minus Zero / No Limit," which occurs in the chapter on "Temperance." As you will recall, the song begins *My love she speaks like silence / Without ideals or violence*, while in a succeeding verse:

> *In the dime stores and bus stations*
> *People talk of situations*
> *Read books, repeat quotations*
> *Draw conclusions on the wall.*

For Ricks, this is Belshazzar's feast in the fifth chapter of Daniel: "In the same hour came forth fingers of a man's hand, and wrote over against the candlestick upon the plaster of the wall of the king's palace. And this is the writing that was written: MENE, MENE, TEKEL, UPHARSIN. This is the interpretation of the thing: MENE; God hath numbered thy kingdom and finished it."

Building upon this, Ricks insists that the biblical "candlestick" furnishes Dylan not only with his song's reference to candles and matchsticks, but that the biblical word "numbered" may have a relation to the "Minus Zero" in Dylan's title. This same chapter of Daniel has the words "people," "tremble," "wise men," and "gifts"—and also "spake," "said," and "that night." What more could one want as proof of the direct influence of the prophet Daniel upon the song?

Something more, as it happens. The words of the prophets are written on the subway wall, as Paul Simon and Art Garfunkel were to say in "The Sounds of Silence," and it was as obvious to me the first time I heard "Love Minus Zero / No Limit" as it is today that Dylan was alluding to graffiti: a special emphasis in that time and place. If you really want to connect Babylon to Dylan, you might have better luck with "Lily, Rosemary and the Jack of Hearts": "The cabaret was silent—except for the drilling in the wall."

At the same time I was digesting all this in *Dylan's Visions of Sin,* I noticed that Ricks deals with an obvious contradiction in his account (the king being "reduced" to the pawn) in the following evasive manner: " 'Even the pawn must hold a grudge.' Even the king? Even Dylan, whom I ungrudgingly admire?" This is ingratiation raised to the level of unction. I remember the first time that I ever felt a qualm about Dylan's claims. It was early on as well: He said that he had written "A Hard Rain's Gonna Fall" at the time of the Cuban missile crisis—and he had been in such an apocalyptic hurry that every line could be the first line of another song. Even in my early teens, I knew that that was bravado.

Oddly, perhaps, Ricks spends almost no time on the influences that Dylan actually does affirm or the influences that we know about. "Blowin' In the Wind" borrows from an old slave spiritual called "No More Auction Block," with its haunting words about "many thousands gone." Dylan was actually sued by Dominic Behan, brother of Brendan, for plagiarizing not only the tune but the concept of "The Patriot Game" for his "With God on Our Side." More recently, his song about a Japanese yakuza was tracked down to an obscure but identifiable source, while the deft Daniel Radosh has blogged a near-perfect match between Dylan's "Cross the Green Mountain" (written for Ron Maxwell's movie *Gods and Generals*) and Walt Whitman's "Come up from the Fields, Father." If I had to surmise another influence, it would be William Blake, not just for the speculative reasons given by Ricks but because, as Blake phrased it: "A Last Judgment is Necessary because Fools flourish."

Even secularists often find themselves thinking things like that, and there is a store of words in the Bible that springs ready-made, as it were. Thus, Ricks could well be correct in thinking that Dylan's "how many times" is an echo both of "How long, oh Lord, how long?" and of Christ's injunction in Matthew on the number of times that it might be needful to turn the other cheek. (He may also be right, though coming down-market more than he likes, in discerning a vague sacred/profane overlap between "I Believe in You" and "Smoke Gets In Your Eyes.")

But Christianity as a religion of peace and tolerance and forgiveness is not, superficially at least, compatible with ringing phrases about judgment and the sword: In order to believe in the apparently kindly and reassuring verses about taking no thought for the morrow, one had better have a lively sense of the second coming. This was the line that Dylan actually did take in his born-again period, where he spoke of "spiritual warfare" as well as his "precious angel," and warned that there would be no hiding place on The Day. But this, which produced some of his most beautiful writing (and singing) would appear to have been as lightly affected as the gritty dustbowl socialism which the Old Left was already denouncing him for abandoning as far back as 1964. Dylan dropped it and kept moving on.

Indeed, I am sure I remember Ricks welcoming him "back," as it were, when he came up with "Most of the Time" about fifteen years ago. But here, and in his discussion of this superbly apt and lovely and troubling song, I began to write heavy notes in the book's margin: "Most of the time," Ricks writes, " 'Most of the Time' consists of repeating the words, 'most of the time.' " [Marginal note: Oh no it doesn't .] Unbelievably, Ricks manages to go on for a half-dozen pages about this song, without ever achieving the realization that it is one of the most vertiginous, knife-edge accounts of a post-love trauma ever penned. You should only listen to the song if you are not currently trying to persuade yourself that "it" is all over and that you are all over "it."

Ricks wraps up blandly: "It is only most of the time that the man in this long black song succeeds in being not disturbed. But he is halfways there. On the other hand, 'She's that far behind.' One too many mornings and a thousand miles behind, to be exact." [In the margin: To be inexact, you mean, you fool. She's right behind him and in front of him and all around him, all of the time. His attempted banishment of her is a hopeless failure! What have you got in your veins—tapwater?]

There follows a lengthy Ricksian contrast between the words of Dylan's song "Not Dark Yet" and Keats's "Ode to a Nightingale." Not, you understand, that our author wants to be taken too seriously. "I don't believe that Keats's poem is alluded to in Dylan's song. That is, called into play, so that you'd be failing to respond to something crucial to the song unless you were familiar with, and could call up, Keats's poem." [In the margin: Oh no, of course, not that.] After all, the deep connection between Keats's "My heart aches, and a drowsy numbness pains" and Dylan's "Well, my sense of humanity has gone down the drain" is transparent neither in sense nor rhythm.

It is true that the words "dark," "shadow," and "day"—together with "sleep" and "time," or their cognates—are to be found in both sets of verses. I am quite ready to believe that Dylan had a subliminal memory of being taught the poem in school. But Renata Adler did much better than this, during the 1968 Republican convention that nominated Nixon in Miami. Surveying the sea of placards with their jaunty slogan "Now More Than Ever," she suddenly recognized that it came from verse six of the "Nightingale" ode: "Now more than ever seems it rich to die, / To cease upon the midnight with no pain."

I think that might have afforded Dylan a smile, and possibly Ricks too. But only one of them has an attitude to sin that is in any sense original.

THE WEEKLY STANDARD,
JULY 5, 2004

I Fought the Law
in Bloomberg's New York

M any and various are the New York tales that are told of professor Sidney Morgenbesser. During a conference of linguistic philosophers at Columbia University, he interrupted the pompous J. L. Austin, who was saying that while many double negatives express a positive—as in "not unattractive"—there is no example in English of a double positive expressing a negative. Morgenbesser's interjection took the form of the two words "Yeah, yeah." Or it could have been "Yeah, right." On another occasion, he put his pipe in his mouth as he was ascending the subway steps. A policeman approached and told him that there was no smoking on the subway. Morgenbesser explained—pointed out might be a better term—that he was leaving the subway, not entering it, and had not yet lit up. The cop repeated his injunction. Morgenbesser reiterated his observation. After a few such exchanges, the cop saw he was beaten and fell back on the oldest standby of enfeebled authority: "If I let you do it, I'd have to let everyone do it." To this the old philosopher replied, "Who do you think you are—Kant?" His last word was misconstrued, and the whole question of the categorical imperative had to be hashed out down at the precinct house. Morgenbesser walked.

That, in my opinion, is the way that New York is supposed to be. Irony and a bit of sass, combined with a pugnacious independence, should always stand a chance against bovine officials who have barely learned to memorize such demanding mantras as "zero tolerance" and "no exceptions." Today, the professor would be stopped, insulted, ticketed, and told that if he didn't like it he could waste a day in court, or several days dealing with the bureaucracy, or both.

Take the case of Brian Bui, who owns the Mekong restaurant in SoHo. Like everyone else, he has been deprived of the choice of allowing his customers to smoke. He lives under a city government that knows better about what's good for him and his clients. So smokers have to step outside. But is that the end of it? By no means. You see, there is no smoking allowed under an awning. So Mr. Bui was fined $200 for allowing one of his guests to smoke in that space. But the awning was, at the time, retracted. Never mind that, said the inspector who wrote the ticket. There was a canopy involved. Thus, a hardworking Vietnamese was penalized for, in effect, having an awning in the first place. He was also told by the judge that he hadn't made "a good-faith effort" to police his guests or to draw their attention to this anomaly. Upon the second occasion that he was cited, again at a time when the awning was retracted, Mr. Bui went to court and won. But it cost him $3,000 in legal fees to prove that the health department and the city's judges are unclear on the law.

In fact, the law these days is very clear. It states that New York City is now the domain of the mediocre bureaucrat, of the inspector with too much time on his hands, of the anal-retentive cop with his nose in a rule book, of the snitch willing to drop a dime on a harmless fellow citizen, and of a mayor who is that most pathetic and annoying figure—the micro-megalomaniac.

The lawbreaking itch is not always an anarchic one. In the first place, the human personality has (or ought to have) a natural resistance to coercion. We don't like to be pushed and shoved, even if it's in a direction we might choose to go. In the second place, the human personality has (or ought to have) a natural sense of the preposterous. Thus, just behind my apartment building in Washington there is an official sign saying, Drug-Free Zone. I think this comic inscription may be because it's close to a schoolyard. And a few years back, one of our suburbs announced by a municipal ordinance that it was a "nuclear-free zone." I don't wish to break the first law, though if I did wish to do so it would take me, or any other local resident, no more than one phone call and a ten-minute wait. I did, at least for a while, pine to break the "nuclear-free" regulation, on grounds of absurdity alone, but eventually decided that it would be too much trouble.

So there are laws that are defensible but unenforceable, and there are laws impossible to infringe. But in the New York of Mayor Bloomberg, there are laws that are not possible to obey, and that nobody can respect, and that are enforced by arbitrary power. The essence of tyranny is not iron law. It is capricious law. Tyranny can be petty. And "petty" is not just Bloomberg's middle name. It is his name.

In the space of a few hours late in November, I managed to break a whole slew of New York laws. That is to say, I sat on an upended milk crate, put my bag next to me on a subway seat, paused to adjust my shoe on a subway step, fed some birds in Central Park, had a cigarette in a town car, attempted to put a plastic frame around a vehicle license plate, and rode a bicycle without keeping my feet on the pedals at all times. I also had a smoke in a bar and at a table in a restaurant. Only in the latter two cases would I hitherto have been knowingly violating a city ordinance.

I decided that, partly to protect those who were with me or hosting me, I would not do anything to directly taunt the forces of law and order. I would be the Zelig of the scofflaws. So I took a bike to Central Park and, starting near the boathouse, rode it uphill until blood started to rush to my head and blackness to descend—i.e., for about a quarter of a mile. I then turned and coasted down, allowing the brisk air of a crisp fall day to whoosh disturbingly up my trouser legs as I lifted my feet in the air. I compounded the offense by having no bell on my handlebars. This was midmorning on a weekday, with almost no traffic, but that was just the luck of the draw. Policemen interviewed recently have confirmed that they are under orders to spot riders who take their feet off the pedals, or who have no bell. (Try getting attention in New York by pinging a bike bell, by the way.) It's all part of the ticket harvest that they are expected to reap. The mayor denies that there is a quota, which would be unlawful, but he looks and sounds even more like a weasel than unkind nature intended when he admits that there are "performance measurements" that his Police Department might be observing.

Flinging the bike into my town-car trunk, I proceeded to Bethesda Fountain on foot. The park was wearing its fiery autumnal best, but there wasn't a goddamn pigeon in the sky, or on any neighboring branch or twig. So I took a loaf and crumbled it for the swans and ducks on the lake, who flocked and gobbled gratefully. Chucking a few crusts and fragments onto the shore, I did finally manage to attract a small swirl of pigeons, as I might well have done by accident. Pedro Nazario, an eighty-six-year-old man in Morningside Heights, was whacked with a summons for doing it on purpose. The citation specified pigeons, but I would like to know how anyone scattering crumbs can be responsible for the avian species he or she manages to nourish. Old people and children are often fond of feeding birds, but Bloombergism wants them to understand that they'd better stick to sparrows, thrushes, or starlings if they know what's good for them.

Deciding on a downtown lunch after this orgy of lawlessness, I asked my town-car driver if I could have a cigarette. He was a smoker himself, but he told me that we'd both be breaking the law if we lit up. The said law defines these cars as enterprises or some such—in any case as mobile containers of atmosphere that can fall under fatherly and authoritarian regulation. For some reason almost all the drivers of these vehicles were born in Russia or the Ukraine and live in Brighton Beach. I have gotten used by now to hearing them say that Bloomberg's attitude reminds them of precisely the mentality that they left home to escape. In an agreeable fug of Chernobyl proportions (his car, his rules—gotta problem with that?), we made decent progress through the insane Midtown traffic that was attempting to negotiate the mayor's brilliant new "no turning" restrictions.

Resolving to work up an appetite by breaking a few more laws before lunchtime, I quit the car and descended into the subway. It didn't take me long to pick a seat, to put my bag next to me, to prop my leg up and ease the pins and needles, to pause on the steps and adjust my shoe, and in general to undermine civilization as we know it. An Israeli tourist named Yoav Kashdia was recently fined fifty dollars for nodding off between stations and implicitly occupying two seats by virtue of his slumping. ("Shalom! Welcome to New York!") This is just as illegal if you are in an empty subway car as it is impossible during rush hour, and the joyless and literal mind now ruling City Hall is content to ignore the distinction. No, I wouldn't put my bag or stretch my leg on the next seat when there were fellow riders standing up, but, yes, I would if I were all alone, and it's only in the second case that I'd get a ticket. Here we approach the shriveled core of the tiny Bloombergian mind. At rush hour, my fellow passengers and my innate sense of right and wrong would discipline me (and there'd be no room for some ticket-happy inspector to see what was going on, let alone correct it). At a time when foot traffic was heavy, moreover, I wouldn't try to sit on the subway steps. Ms. Crystal Rosario, a pregnant woman from Brooklyn who was overcome by exhaustion, made herself conspicuous and received a fine for doing just that. There was no evidence that she had actually obstructed anyone. She sat because she felt she had to, and the cop issued the ticket because . . . well, let's say for the same reason a dog licks his thing. Because he could. That's why the Morgenbesser moment keeps coming back to me.

The previous night I had been to the movies and had been annoyed, as one often is, by people chatting and commenting in the back row. This is the height of antisocial behavior, because it ruins the pleasure of others while bringing no benefit to the offender. I normally deal with it as I do when people in cinemas fail to turn off their cell phones. I turn round and tell them that I know where they live, and I know where their children go to school. Others are usually on hand with similar suggestions, especially in New York. It's all part of the fun. Ask yourself: what if uniformed cops were standing at the back of the theater enforcing the no-talking rule? It wouldn't be quite the same, would it? But in Bloombergville, where the citizen is treated like a backward child, I wouldn't be surprised to learn that this was the next bright idea.

Decency forbids me from mentioning where I ate lunch, because the proprietor is an old friend and a beautiful and conscientious restaurateur and I can't risk having him treated like a fractious juvenile. On September 11, 2001, he turned his place into a casualty-treatment station and general refuge, and he does everything he can think of to make his guests welcome and well fed. It was a fairly slow lunchtime, and I was able to ask all diners present if they minded my lighting a cigarette for the purposes of a *Vanity Fair* photo shoot. All of them said go right ahead and good luck to you. So that's all I need say about that, except that New Yorkers are no longer trusted with such discretion or good manners. It is government alone that knows what's "appropriate." There cannot be a single exception. One size must fit all. This casual destruction of Bohemia, in one of its oldest and most famous redoubts, is an unquantifiable loss. It misses the point of New York—in fact, it negates it. The backward child in this case—also the spiteful and bullying and smug and spoiled child—is His Honor the Mayor. May he one day be cornered in the schoolyard at recess, and without his team of hired toadies and informers, and taught the lesson of a lifetime.

My next challenge was to tempt the same fate that overtook Jesse Taveras, who sat on a milk crate outside the hair salon in the Bronx which is his place of employment and was fined $105 for "unauthorized use" of said crate. If you look closely at a milk crate, you will see an inscription confining its use to the crating of milk bottles and cartons by its owner, so don't go using a crate as a safety razor, say, or a contraceptive. If you see a fleeing thief, don't push a milk crate into his path, to lend a hand to the pursuing cop. (Thieves are exhausting to pursue, whereas men sitting on milk crates tell a lazy cop that he's added another collar to his day's "performance measurement." And it's the lazy cops who thrive under this dispensation, which has been protested loudly by the Patrolmen's Benevolent Association. Indeed, the cop who cited Mr. Nazario for feeding those pigeons later came by his apartment and voided the ticket.)

I took my crate to the sidewalk outside the Strand bookstore on Broadway, where there are bookshelves. This attracts all kinds of untidiness, such as browsers, but it seems to be tolerated for the moment. I like to browse but don't like to stand up, so I seized a book and sat down. As I did so, I noticed quite a few unoccupied and empty milk crates already on the scene.

Just for good measure, I had another cigarette, outside a barbershop. Kim Phann and Bruce Rosado were doing just this not long ago, again in the Bronx, when a police car stopped and disgorged an officer who cited them for "loitering in front of a business." It made no difference that they worked there and had stepped outside only so as to obey the New York City Smoke-Free Air Act (Chapter 5 of Title 17 of the New York City Administrative Code). You notice that tonsorial establishments in the Bronx have now been mentioned twice? Perhaps the local station house does them on Tuesdays and, say, pet stores on Wednesdays. But note the extension of policing to unintended consequences of earlier policing. Go into the "fresh" air to smoke, say, late at night outside a restaurant, and soon there will be complaints that you are too noisy for local residents. This kicks in "Operation Silent Night," a doomed attempt to use police power to bring blissful silence to the city—The City That Never Sleeps, if you can stand such a corny reference to the town's great days. (Bloomberg does not support the measure to silence the useless and maddening car alarm: he would rather impose himself on people than on mechanical devices.)

When I worked at the old *New Statesman* magazine in London, we had an annual competition for advice to tourists visiting the city for the first time. "Try the famous echo in the British Museum Reading Room" was, I remember, one of the winners. We also advised people that prostitutes could be easily recognized by their habit of rattling collection tins, that it was considered ill-mannered not to shake hands with all other passengers before taking your seat on the London subway, and that readers doing the *Times* crossword on trains were always glad if you offered to help. When I first arrived in New York, some thirty-three years ago, I swiftly came to appreciate that no such competition would "resonate" here. The place was a round-the-clock carnival of eccentricities and idiosyncrasies, with an attitude to match, and you could make yourself conspicuous in almost any way you chose, as long as you didn't mess with anyone else. I never expected to see a day when it would become a plastic-imitation Disneyland, with the mirthless smirk of the uniformed attendant making sure that everyone had a boring and wholesome time and was tucked up in bed before two in the morning.

To resume: there were some laws I was in no position to break, like the one that limits the number—and the size!—of words I can have on my shop awning, or the requirement to have an "employees must wash hands" sign over the bathroom sink. (A bit like the old "no spitting" signs of my boyhood, these latter exhortations obviously won't work on the very people who are likely to ignore them—the people, say, who bypass the soap and water on their way from the bathroom stall to the restaurant.) And New York has had no anti-sodomy laws since the year 2000, so I didn't have to prove anything on that front. My last attempt to live free or die was too exhausting and annoying to complete: I don't have the manual dexterity to fit a dealer-issued frame around the license plate of a car. But something about this clear-plastic or glass protector, sometimes used to shield a customized plate, brings out the micro-megalo tendencies of the mayor and his underlings, who can fine you up to $200 for each "offense."

I have only ever heard one defense of this reign of error, which is that it mimics the "broken window" street-level campaign that began to tackle crime under Bill Bratton and Rudy Giuliani about a decade ago. But, excuse me, that was directed at people making a nuisance of themselves by wielding squeegees at intersections, or panhandling with an attitude, or offering their bodies for sale at unwanted moments and locations, or jumping over turnstiles. This current Niagara of pettiness and random victimization may well be Bloomberg's attempt at a wannabe reputation as heroic crime-fighter and disciplinarian. Who knows what goes on in the tiny, constipated chambers of his mind? All we know for certain is that one of the world's most broad-minded and open cities is now in the hands of a picknose control freak.

VANITY FAIR, FEBRUARY 2004

FOR PATRIOT DREAMS

O, what a fall was there, my countrymen!
Then I, and you, and all of us fell down.

—*JULIUS CAESAR*, ACT III, SCENE II.

I commenced to dream about the Manhattan skyline when I was in my early teens and an ocean away. It remains the only fantasy-dream that I have ever had that's come true or, perhaps, the only one that hasn't been some kind of a disappointment. (And I am going to stay with "I" for now, because I haven't yet earned the right to say "we," and "we" is what I want to come to.)

The World Trade Center wasn't yet finished when I first got my wish and disembarked in New York. In the summer of 1970, you could see two *Titanic*-size hulls and keels being constructed, at the southern extremity of the island, but you could not yet imagine what the great vessels would resemble when they were triumphantly launched. Some locals bitched and moaned about how the towers were too grandiose in design, and about the nice little neighborhood that had been doomed by development. Even then I understood that no New York argument would be complete without this refrain.

Once I had found the magnetic compass point of my life, which is a piece of good fortune that doesn't occur for everyone, it was an easy matter to follow it. That skyline had pull. And so did the southern part of the island. I know people who never go above Fourteenth Street, and I know people who seldom venture below it, and while I was never that dogmatic, I became a southerner from the start. It was the East and West "villages" that drew me, and the idea of a skyscraper-free zone is essential to their charm. Still, it would have seemed provincial and lowly to ignore the big shiny twins. I conducted a tempestuous romance in the Windows on the World restaurant, with its oddly erotic view of New Jersey. I once got engaged there, in a moment of folly and euphoria for which I have since been forgiven. When I decided to become an immigrant, it was to the Social Security office in the south tower that I went, to get in line for the first digits of my American identity.

The place I stayed first, before I got my own address, was with patient friends on Bank Street—the green thoroughfare of that lovely fretwork of little streets around Greenwich and Bleecker. Later, over on Tompkins Square in the early 1980s, the W.T.C. was my city view at sundown as I sat writing. I wasn't exactly bewitched by it, as I was by the Chrysler Building, but it was a good part of my sky. With the light refracting through the twins, I would pause and have a cocktail break and play some music. Then I'd generally go out to St. Marks Place and eat in the neighborhood where W. H. Auden had become, if not the first Englishman to become an American, the first Englishman to become an accepted New Yorker. He was actually uptown, in a bar on Fifty-Second Street, when he wrote one of the most reproachful and haunting poems of the twentieth century. It consists of ninety-nine perfectly incised lines. Its title is a date. The date is "September 1, 1939." It shudders with premonitions of a coming cataclysm, and it contains the early-warning couplet "The unmentionable odour of death / Offends the September night."

Now I'm just back from walking through my old neighborhoods. As with every scene of calamity, it is the stench that makes the difference between seeing it on TV and seeing it for yourself. The unmentionable odor this September was a compound of a refugee camp and a blitzed town. So I'm confronting the inescapable fact that others, too, dreamed from far away about the Manhattan skyscape. But dreamed yearningly of bringing it down, didn't see it from Ellis Island or the Statue of Liberty, thought only of maiming and disfiguring and poisoning it. "Let it come down," says Banquo's murderer in *Macbeth*, expressing so much, and in so few thuggish words, by this brutish fatalism. There's a cadence for you: "Let it come down." What am I to do with a thought like this?

> *Into this neutral air* [wrote Auden]
> *Where blind skyscrapers use*
> *Their full height to proclaim*
> *The strength of Collective Man,*

Each language pours its vain
Competitive excuse . . .

There are no excuses. Many people missed this evident point when they began, in their aching search for an appropriate poetry, to circulate that same Auden poem via E-mail. What is the poet saying? He is saying that the great towers of New York may be "capitalist" (the lines come from the end of his Marxist phase) but that they also represent the combined labor and skill and hope of untold numbers of tough and dignified workers. Much the same applies to the lines on languages. The coded suggestion is that of Babel, but the Twin Towers actually looked down quite benignly on a neighborhood, a district, a quarter, where each language had a chance. My Palestinian tobacconist, my cheap all-you-can-eat Ukrainian joint, my Italian grocery . . . everybody knows the mosaic. The college where I teach, the New School for Social Research, became the lighthouse for the anti-Nazi scholars of the 1930s. (Our downtown dorm had to be closed and evacuated "that week.") The numberless cafés and bars and chess hangouts where the fugitive spirit of bohemia found a home, and where there were bookstores to spare. The offices of the indispensable "little magazines," which helped keep the culture going on a shoestring. The Cedar Tavern, the White Horse, the old Lion's Head, where exiles could be safe to curse their own governments and locals could excel at cursing the American one. What can I say? I was happy there. The work and the conversation were worthwhile. And there was something more: the crucial four words in the greatest of all documents. The pursuit of happiness. Just to name that is to summarize and encapsulate all that is detested by the glacial malice of fundamentalism and tribalism. That's what they can't stand. They confuse it with hedonism and selfishness and profanity, and they have no idea. No idea at all.

The word "village" sounds provincial in its way, and no less so if you put "East" or "West" in front of it. The time came when, having been mugged in New York (a rite of passage in those days) and married in New York, and otherwise infected with its multifarious fevers, I had to move away. I went to live in Washington, D.C., the nation's capital. As it happens, I took the train on the day I left and twisted round in my seat, like a child leaving a seaside holiday, until I could see the Twin Towers no more. But I couldn't have lived in D.C. without an umbilical cord to New York, and every time I came back on a train or plane or by car, it was the big friendly commercial twins that signaled my return. Now each of them has met its own evil twin. As you know, my new hometown was also gravely injured that week. But Washington has always seemed to me more parochial than New York. You may feel patriotic about the United States, but you can't quite feel patriotic about Washington, D.C. (Not even the blitzing of the Pentagon could accomplish this transformation: it's a sad subject for another time, but it's true. New York and Pennsylvania are the only shrines of the national heart in this extremity.)

Mark Antony, speaking to the movable crowd in the lines with which I began, was addressing his fellow Romans as his "countrymen." And Mr. Bush and the networks, for the first few days addressed their fellow Americans. But it didn't take very long before that rhetoric was being qualified and modified. For a moment, indeed, it looked as if there were too many nationalities to be mentioned in any one speech: Turks, Filipinos, Yemenis, Pakistanis, Icelanders. At a certain point, I was asked if I wanted to attend the midtown memorial service for the hundreds of my immolated fellow Englishmen. I can't say that it was exactly at this moment that my thoughts crystallized, but it was at about that time. No, I don't want to go to anybody's gender-specific or national or ethnic-identity ceremony. I have found the patch of soil on which I will take my own stand, and the people with whom I'll stand, and it's the only place in history where patriotism can be divorced from its evil twins of chauvinism and xenophobia. Patriotism is not local; it's universal. (Now, finally—and what a relief!—all together: All politics are *not* local.) I checked carefully every day with my friend Hussein Ibish, a Lebanese Kurd who speaks for the American Arab Anti Discrimination Committee, and who had a lot of monitoring to do. There were not all that many nuts and dolts that week who were so shameless and idiotic as to bully or insult a Sikh or a Sri Lankan. But of the incidents of vandalism and barbarity reported and recorded, barely a one took place in the epicenter of Manhattan. If patriotism can be democratic and internationalist—and this remains to be fought for—then that's good enough for me; perhaps there's a better chance now than anyone could have envisioned. In this microcosm, there was the code for a macrocosm. Call it a rooted cosmopolitanism.

I told newly enrolled New School students, some of whose parents wanted them back in the heartland, that they'd be sorry forever if they abandoned the city at such a time. I told the same to some nervous students who had arrived from countries with far more gruesome problems. I went at night to Union Square and Washington Square Park, and though the herbivorous ethos was a bit too much "Strawberry Fields" and even "Candle in the Wind" for my taste, I recognized that the atmosphere was serious and reflective. Auden, whose emotions lay in the direction of religious pacifism, would have felt at home. But he would also have registered some feeling, I think (and I don't mean to be flippant about his famous tastes), for the burly, uncomplaining, stoic proletarian defenders, busting their sinews in the intractable and nameless wreckage and carnage of downtown. I took the groaning subway underneath Chambers Street, as it slowed to the pace of a funeral cortege (whether out of respect for the dead or out of respect to the mountain of hell above, I don't know). I got out at the Broadway-Nassau station and paced the streets until my clothes reeked and until another evacuation was called because of the toxic material in the hideous core. And I swore a small oath. One has to be capable of knowing when something is worth fighting for. One has to be capable of knowing an enemy when one sees one.

That enemy, let us never forget, had hoped to do far, far worse. Limited only by the schedules and booking of civilian aviation, the airborne death squads could have counted on packed planes and, with a slight flight delay, on much more densely crowded towers. They could also have hoped to bring the towers down sideways—each of them a quarter of a mile high—across the streets. A toll of more than 50,000 was possible, and—as was doubtless fantasized at many a sniggering and giggling secret meeting—a body count of 100,000 could have been seriously aimed at. This would not have been—in the stalest phrase of the crisis—a "Pearl Harbor." It would have been the Dresden of the Taliban.

In the fall of 1940 (and the once beautifully combined words "New York" and "the fall" will never again have quite the same sound to me), George Orwell wrote of a certain human quality that attaches itself to particular horrors. He was looking back to his boyhood, through the prisms of a frightful war that had just begun and a frightful war that had clouded his youth. As he put it:

I must admit that nothing in the whole war moved me so deeply as the loss of the *Titanic* had done a few years earlier. This comparatively petty disaster shocked the whole world, and the shock has not quite died away even yet. I remember the terrible, detailed accounts read out at the breakfast table (in those days it was a common habit to read the newspaper aloud) and I remember that in all the long list of horrors the one that most impressed me was that at the last the *Titanic* suddenly up-ended and sank bow foremost, so that the people clinging to the stern were lifted no less than three hundred feet into the air before they plunged into the abyss. It gave me a sinking sensation in the belly which I can still all but feel. Nothing in the war ever gave me quite that sensation.

"Look, teacher," a child cried during a school evacuation as the towers were becoming pyres. "The birds are on fire." The infant was rationalizing the sight of human beings making a public choice between incineration and suicide, and often suffering the most extreme pangs of both fates. Yes, we will look. And yes, we will remember it long after other miseries have intervened. The title of Orwell's 1940 essay, incidentally, was "My Country Right or Left." Confronted in this manner, and affronted too, one has to be able to say, My country after all.

And one may have to say it without waving or displaying any flag. My reservations about this are not just the usual ones. More than I worry about flag-waving I worry about what will happen when flag-waving has to stop. All these ceremonies of emotion, from children's drawings to fund drives, are prone to diminishing returns. A time will come when fewer taxis fly the Stars and Stripes, and it could be just at that point that another awful wound is inflicted by covert and nefarious enemies. What then? What encore? One should probably start now to practice the virtues of stoicism and solidarity—and also of silence. No more brave and vague military briefings; no more bluff boosterism by local politicians. Just a set, private determination, as the French once resolved when they lost Alsace and Lorraine to foreign conquest: "Always think of it. Never speak of it."

As Auden too pessimistically phrased it in the closing lines of the greatest poem ever written in the city:

Defenceless under the night
Our world in stupor lies;
Yet, dotted everywhere,
Ironic points of light
Flash out . . .

I don't know so much about "defenseless." Some of us will vow to defend it, or help the defenders. As for the flashes of light, imagine the nuance of genius that made Auden term them "ironic." It would be a holy fool who mistook this for weakness or sentimentality. Shall I take out the papers of citizenship? Wrong question. In every essential way, I already have.

VANITY FAIR, DECEMBER 2001

II. POVERTY

MARTHA INC.

American life depends on every one of us doing his or her duty. Just as that butterfly, lazily flapping its gossamer wings in faraway Japan, can inaugurate a tiny zephyr that will one day become a mighty typhoon, so every credit-card holder in these United States, by splurging that bit extra at the store, can strike the keynote of a vast, soon-to-be, consumer-led recovery (which will in time teach every butterfly in Japan who is boss in the world market).

American babies know this as they learn to recognize Gerber products with a toothless beam of contentment. American rug rats and yard apes elaborate on the same essential knowledge as they reach hungrily for the brass ring of aerated shoes and simulated-reality helmets (many of them, alas, manufactured by M. and Mme. Butterfly in faraway Japan). The heroic consumer is our last uncomplicated, authentic American hero. Who was so base as not to experience a surging thrill of pride last Christmas as Yuletide cash registers pinged and beeped a collective "Yes, *yes*" to the optimism and brio of a dauntless Clinton transition team? *Confidence.* That's the ticket. Always has been. Get out there and spend.

But do we ever stop to think of our role models? As we strip the mall and patrol the shelves, do we honor the pioneers? What of those whose waking and sleeping lives are sacrificed that we may learn to live and consume, and cram the landfills and dumps in order to consume again? Where is their temple, their shrine? How can we hallow those who went before, and who bear the torch still? Ladies and gentlemen, I give you Martha Stewart.

Martha Stewart is a force of nature before which a million flailing fritil-
laries are as nothing. She is a possible answer to the question "What do
women want?" She is the artiste of the deal. She is a balm to all those who fret
themselves about the unsayable word "class." She is a reproach to the laggard
American corporations which have been fatally postponing the essential
business of vertical and horizontal integration.

It's a treat to watch her doing her NBC *Today* segment, with either Katie
Couric or Bryant Gumbel mugging for the camera as Stewart explains a
recipe, plans a festivity, or gives a social hint from one of her three homes-in-
progress. Couric faithfully plays the "How *do* you do it?" career woman, full
of feigned envy and forever marveling at Martha's sheer, brazen *competence*.
Gumbel has the easier task of playing the man lost in the kitchen, pinafore
likably worn, with a stock of wry expressions to pull as our Martha displays
another culinary coup or confides a feminine wile or two in the hostessing
line. My favorite moment is when Gumbel, with an air of "Well, all good
things must come to an end sometime," turns to us and announces that there
will now be a commercial break. What does NBC suppose the *previous* segment
has been?

By "vertical and horizontal integration" I mean that Martha Stewart has
got the market wired and trussed, like a *poussin* awaiting the herbal stuffing
and the feathery baste of olive oil. Each TV segment furnished by the network—not that she doesn't have her own on-screen syndication—is a piece
of plugola for a Martha Stewart book (published by Crown), the *Martha Stewart
Living* magazine (published by Time Warner), a Martha Stewart video (tie-in to
the books), a Martha Stewart classical-music dining CD with fold-in menu
accompaniment (handled by Sony Masterworks), or a Martha Stewart brand-
name line of products (distributed nationally through Kmart). This is
emphatically not Betty Crocker about whom we are talking here.

Joyce Cary once coined the term "tumbril remark" to describe those offhand sayings by members of the nobility that were liable to incite thoughts of
revolution. (A classic was that of a certain English duke, who, urged to econ-
omize by letting go one of his three pastry cooks, grumbled, "Can't a chap
have a bit of biscuit when the fancy takes him?" Another came from a lady of
the aristocracy confronted by a mendicant who claimed not to have eaten for
three days. "Silly man," she trilled, "you must try. If necessary you must *force*

yourself.") Powerful reminiscences of the tumbril surged through me as I viewed the Martha Stewart oeuvre. Talking about the new frugality of the '90s, she instructed one TV audience that "we're going to spend much less time in restaurants and country clubs and more time at home." This was a somewhat less than recession-proof remark (Stewart was an admirer of the Ross Perot campaign, which also sought to treat the United States as one vast business), but it was surpassed, I thought, by her observation to Paula Zahn on her new magazine during a segment about Christmas preparation. "This is something that everyone in the country can enjoy," she averred breathily, before gliding straight to an everyday discussion on the finer points of the serving of champagne, the care of crystal, and the maintenance of silver. Another TV segment featured a hot tip on the hollowing out and throwing away of the interior of a large and costly loaf of bread—the perfect Marie Antoinette sandwich surprise for all the family.

Actually it's all *what* family, since while she was off promoting *Weddings,* a how-to guide for that blushing bride with a trunkful of time and a trust fund, she found herself husbandless as Andy Stewart, her lawyer-and-publisher spouse, left the matrimonial home. It is speculated that he found it tough sledding being wed to a one-woman deficit-reduction industry.

The phrase "domestic economy" takes on a new resonance when you consider the estimates and projections of the Stewart business. As the too perfectly named Faith Popcorn (she of the trend-tracking outfit Brain-Reserve) has put it, "Mass wants class and can recognize it, Martha's leveraged that beautifully." Mass wants class. I like it.

It's not normally considered kosher to speak either of "the masses" or of "class," but as long as you're not considered a troublemaker, then it's only another taboo waiting to be broken. And Kmart doesn't consider Martha Stewart a troublemaker, paying her about $5 million for a seven-year contract, in addition to royalties on her signature lines. At the other end of the social scale—Stewart says rightly but defensively that her output appeals "to people of all economic classes"—there have been seminars that could run you $300 a day or $1,000 for a three-day immersion. Topics in this design for living included: "What Is Gold Leaf?," with the enticing subtitle "Edible and Decorative Uses," as well as the more homely "Entertaining with Your Collectibles" and the downright practical "How to Dispose of Your Valuables."

This all suggests, incidentally, that "mass" and "class" are more uneasy with each other than they like to let on. There's a great deal of status insecurity out there, and it vibrates powerfully to the influence of someone who can assure you that you are doing the right, the tasteful, the *elegant* thing. Stewart herself confides the ambition to create a garden "like Sissinghurst," the bower and boscage and arbor that sheltered the weird Vita Sackville-West and the no less fey Harold Nicolson. Some things never change, as they say in the attemptedly tonier ads for scotch whisky, and snobbery about the great houses of England is certainly one of them, as Faith Popcorn can well attest from her trend studies.

Great fortunes, Balzac once said, are often conceived in sin. Fortune did not come easily to Martha Stewart, who began life as Martha Kostyra in a large Polish family in New Jersey. And it would be truer to say peccadillo than sin. But before success started really cascading over her, when things were still a struggle and before she managed her vertical and horizontal integrations, Martha was much haunted by charges of inspired borrowing. They began with the publication of *Entertaining*, her first book, which featured recipes with a familiar ring. The orange-almond cake and the raisin-cherry pound cake in *Entertaining* certainly looked familiar to Julia Child, who had lovingly included them in her own volume *Mastering the Art of French Cooking*. Child had also instructed people in the mysteries of the crusty mustard chicken, another formula which appeared later in a Martha Stewart book, *Quick Cook*.

The foodie world is a bitter and competitive one, roiled by great, passionate gusts which it is given to few to understand. What was the harvest when Martha's Chinese feast, laid out in gorgeous detail in the pages of *Entertaining*, turned out to have originated in Barbara Tropp's rival and predecessor volume, *The Modern Art of Chinese Cooking*? After a fair bit of hissing and whispering, everybody faced the cameras with faultless smiles and acted like friends again; later editions of *Entertaining* concede that Barbara's book "inspired" the Oriental banquet, and Barbara sportingly wished Martha all the best with her future efforts. Still, even after that there was a certain Martha Stewart seminar spoken of in shocked murmurs, where recipes for a chaudfroid sauce and for a chocolate jelly roll were handed out on Martha's letterhead. The chaudfroid sauce was from Julia Child, I regret to say, and the jelly roll from *The Joy of Cooking*. In a way, of course, to be a culinary plagiarist is to be no more than an omnivore. The world of decorating, cooking, and embellishing might seem tender and feminine, but the laws of cutthroat capitalism are not suspended for allegedly "soft" subjects like bridal veils, menus, sconces, and flower arrangements. If anything, since these represent consumption at its purest, those laws intensify.

I'm not a great cook or flower arranger or country-house refurbisher, so I wasn't sure if I was able to give some of the books and magazines a fair test. (The videos I found useful mainly as a language course; Martha likes to point out that *spiedini* is Italian for "skewers," and at one point instructed Bryant Gumbel that on this dessert he could spread whipped crème fraîche or, if he chose, whipped fresh cream.) But I have been married on occasion, so I looked up the Martha Stewart *Wedding Planner*. After only a few pages I was gripped by a stark terror. The tone is one of inflexible, pitiless correctitude. "It takes at least six months to plan a formal wedding (often longer) and at least three to four months to plan an informal wedding."

I'd only just gotten over that when I learned from Martha (everyone in her world calls her Martha, by the way) the concept of leaving nothing to chance. "Remember daylight savings time—you may find that your wedding is taking place in the dark when you had expected gentle twilight." Then, because facts must be looked squarely in the face, came an injunction to the bride to "keep your own monthly calendar in mind when scheduling the wedding date and honeymoon."

But all this, which I perused with mounting horror as it ran from "Budget" (with several pages for estimated as opposed to actual costs of boutonnieres and musicians—"check attire of musicians"—and videos) through tasteful hymnal selections, paled to nothing when I came to the honeymoon trousseau. All those gags about WASP weddings ("How can you tell the bride?" "She's the one kissing the golden retriever") vanished before Martha's stern admonitions. "Accomplish as much as possible in the weeks before the wedding: shop, exchange money, buy travelers' checks, pack, etc." Then the travel-and-trousseau checklist: "First aid kit, medications, contraceptives, tampons"— oh, Martha, not in that order, *surely?* Worse still: "Sewing kit, scissors, tweezers, Swiss-army knife"—let me out of here.

It occurred to me, as I read this alarming taxonomy, that Martha Stewart might think people were stupid. How dumb do you have to be in order to be reminded to "buy or borrow any luggage you need"? But then I reflected that this is really a stroke of genius. All over the United States there are millions of people petrified at the idea they might be doing the wrong thing. Many of them are also what Alan Clark, son of the great art critic Lord Clark, disdainfully refers to as "nouves." In other words, they have acquired a bit of capital but are mortally afraid of being thought vulgar. Books bought by the yard used to be a solution, but these days the pressure is more intense. How can I tell if this is a real antique? Will the boss laugh if we have him to a candlelit dinner and put Bartók on in the background? ("I don't think," said Martha's old friend Janet Horowitz, "I've ever been to a dinner party at Martha's that wasn't photographed.") What does one wear to the races? Are fish knives the sign of the phony?

Down all the ages, those who aspire to bourgeois status have been tormented by these worries. Tell us, O all-knowing Martha, how to avoid making fools of ourselves. Tell us what is *appropriate*. Martha Stewart's etiquette and entertaining guides may look like illustrated Filofaxes from hell, but they are the tools and building blocks by which all of us, one day, will do our duty and become middle-class.

VANITY FAIR, OCTOBER 1993

SCENES FROM AN EXECUTION

Last May 22, Larry Wayne White was executed by lethal injection in Huntsville, Texas. As a celebrated double murderer, he attracted few mourners and only a thinly attended vigil of death-penalty opponents. I've been spending a fair amount of time in and around death row in the past few years, and two aspects of White's terminal experience caught my attention. First, he was turned off at six P.M. so that the event was more within the manageable compass of business and working hours. No midnight dramas. Strictly routine. Second, he asked for a last cigarette and was refused it by the prison authorities. (This, sir, is a nonsmoking facility. Our policy is one of zero tolerance.)

They call it gallows humor for a reason. You may laugh at death all you like, but only on the recognized condition that you allow death the concluding cackle. Kingsley Amis, a man of a deep, awed respect for the Grim Reaper, once wrote:

> *Death has got something to be said for it:*
> *There's no need to get out of bed for it;*
> *Wherever you may be,*
> *They bring it to you, free!*

And, passing from the absurd to the near sublime, Yeats wrote of an Irish airman who "foresaw" his own death: "I know that I shall meet my fate / Somewhere among the clouds above."

The two verses share an ineluctable element of the random and the uncertain. "*Wherever* you happen to be," "*Somewhere* among the clouds above." Our whole existence as a species is made unique by our absolute foreknowledge of death combined with our complete ignorance of its timing.

So here is our paradox. Nothing is more predictable and more certain than death, and nothing is less predictable and less certain. Two classes of people are exempt from this rule: those who plan their own deaths, and those who are sentenced to be "put to death."

Most "advanced" countries in the world have abolished capital punishment. In order to be a fully signatory nation of the Council of Europe, for example, you have to show that you have wiped it from your book of statutes. The very first act of the Constitutional Court of liberated South Africa was to abolish the penalty of death. Russia, which is applying to join the Council of Europe, has pledged the abolition of capital punishment. And in the diminishing group of countries which claims, with the United States, the right of life and death over the citizen, the Japanese practice a peculiar protocol. They don't notify either the family or the condemned of the time or the date. If you are the leading actor in this little drama, your cue comes without warning. A cell door opens all of a sudden, and a group of strangers is standing there. And then you jump—to a conclusion.

This policy strikes many people as barbarous, which it most certainly is. But, like other similar barbarities, it may have its origin in a vague humanitarianism. Dostoyevsky wrote that if, in the last moment before a man's execution, he were given the alternative of passing the rest of his life on the summit of a bare rock he would choose the rock with gratitude. Some methods of punishment were so ghastly and so elaborate that even the clearly worded U.S. Constitution could only prohibit them with a shudder as "cruel and unusual." The guillotine, a symbol of horror to Albert Camus, was originally installed by the French Republic as a swift and tender alternative to the wheel and the fire. In keeping a man uncertain of the time of his own death, the Japanese are bizarrely and ironically preserving his status as a human being—ignorant of the biggest date he's ever scheduled to make.

This is a country rather short on irony and long on euphemism, so here I am in Potosi, Missouri, in a brightly lit barracks in the Ozark Mountains, to keep a bureaucratic appointment with death. Somewhere in the bowels of this building is a man who knows the very hour of his own terminus, and who has known it for a while.

Samuel Lee McDonald, a burly, balding black man a few months older than I, is tonight in the ticklish position of being the retiring dean of Missouri's death row. On May 16, 1981, in the parking lot of a convenience store, he shot an off-duty policeman. Officer Robert Jordan had no idea that this evening was to be the one booked for his death. So far from that, he had taken his eleven-year-old daughter to buy "treats" for the weekend, and she was the one who had to watch while McDonald shot her father down. And then, as he lay on the ground, blasted him again. Jordan got off several shots himself, two of which hit McDonald. The assailant had to be nursed back to life so that the process of putting him to death could get properly under way.

Every feasible appeal has now been exhausted—this is all happening on the night and morning of September 23–24, 1997—and McDonald has had a "date certain" since July. The American execution drama used to make a special feature of the last-minute reprieve, the phone call from the governor to the death cell and all the rest of it. (At Parchman prison farm in Mississippi, where I once went to talk to someone who was about to be gassed, they still wait a ritual extra few minutes after midnight because, according to unshakable death-house folklore, Chief Justice Earl Warren actually did once call and was told he was just a tad too late.) But in these increasingly unsentimental times, the cry is all for taking the uncertainty out of the procedure. The U.S. Supreme Court, in a number of recent rulings, has effectively allowed states to lower a boom after which not even the production of fresh evidence can save you. "Get on with it" is the slogan. Are the clotted and clogged death rows a national embarrassment? Well, then, let's expedite the business!

As a consequence, it's really quite easy to book an appointment with death, and see for yourself your tax dollars at work. Missouri calls itself the "Show

Me State." The jaunty motto appears on the license plates, which, it just occurs to me, are manufactured in the prison system. The Missouri Department of Corrections sent me a form, which asked me my Social Security number and arrest record and all that, and also inquired in a friendly way why I had asked to see an execution in Missouri. I did not reply, "Because Missouri is executing somebody almost every week this month, so I won't have to hang about." I replied, "Because this is a major policy debate and because Missouri is in Middle America and because it's the 'Show Me State.' " They said, Come right on down.

As a designated "state's witness" I was was instructed to appear no later than a certain hour on a cold and rainy night. Buzzed in to the interior, I was placed in a room with coffee and doughnuts and overfriendly officials. They did everything they were supposed to do, like giving me the full menu of the condemned man's traditional last meal ("Rib-eye steak, fried shrimp, catfish fillet, Texas toast, French fries, two eggs over easy, and a Coke"). Too *physical* somehow. Too gross and fleshly. Also, I couldn't help recalling Rickey Ray Rector, the man executed by Governor Clinton during the 1992 New Hampshire primary. So gravely impaired and lobotomized was he that, when they came to take him away, he explained that he was leaving a wedge of pecan pie "for later." Laid upon the gurney, he helped them find a vein for the IV because he thought they were doctors come at last to cure him.

Like a majority of capital-punishment states these days, and like the new federal execution "facility" in Terre Haute, Indiana, which I have toured (and which might have the honor and distinction of killing Timothy McVeigh), Missouri now employs the lethal-injection method, first used in the Lone Star State in 1982. This is supposed to be more tranquil and predictable and benign than the various forms of burning, shooting, strangling, and gassing that in the past have squeezed themselves through the "cruel and unusual" rubric. It looks and feels—to the outsider at least—more like a banal medical "procedure." Here's what's supposed to happen, as the supervisors gently and patiently explain. A few hours before the appointment, the "inmate"—as he is still called—is offered a sedative shot. This is seldom refused. At the midnight hour, once attached to a gurney or medical trestle, he is given a dose of sodium pentothal, which induces unconsciousness. This is swiftly rammed home, as it were, by a shot of pancuronium bromide, which causes cessation of respiration. A final chaser of potassium chloride immobilizes the heart.

As with the increased practice of "doing" the condemned in batches, in remote prisons and in working hours, this medicalized "putting down" is designed to leach the drama and agony out of the business: to transform it into a form of therapy for society and "closure" for the perp. In Arkansas last January, three men were executed by clinical injection in one night. State corrections officials explained unironically that this (a) was cheaper and (b) made for a great saving in wear and tear on staff emotions. "By doing these together," said spokeswoman Dina Tyler, "you only have to make that climb once to get mentally prepared to do this. I think everybody gets a little tense." I think so, too. But I also think that efforts to smooth or remove all that tension are unlikely to be crowned with success. Why, even that night in Arkansas there was a glitch. Kirt Wainwright, one of the three men in the execution queue—they choose the order by prison number—did get himself a brief last-minute stay. Clarence Thomas's clerk called from the Supreme Court. The justices deliberated for an hour. Mr. Wainwright lay strapped to a gurney for this period, with a needle in his arm. Sixty minutes of that and then Justice Thomas called to say they could press the plunger after all. Talk about your stress factor!

There have been some extraordinary scenes in these lethal-injection parlors. Tubes and needles have come adrift. In the execution of former heavy intravenous "users," agonizing periods of time have elapsed in the search for a usable blood vessel. (Rickey Ray Rector underwent what the authorities brusquely termed a "cutdown" as his arm was laid open to find a vein.) The American Medical Association considers it unethical for its members to take part, so the work is often farmed out to the inadequately trained correctional officers. As a result, thicker and heavier layers of denial and obfuscation have already begun to encrust this new, pristine, hygienic, pain-free system. Let me tell you what I saw when Samuel Lee McDonald, No. CP 17 in the Potosi correctional facility, was kicked off the planet in your name this past fall.

* * *

The time came when the smiling officials and amiable spokespersons could do no more for the state-witness contingent, and we were delivered into the domain of the mirthless ones with the big keys on the big belts. Escorted through various blindingly lit yards and along massively secure corridors (the other inmates still get to enjoy the traditional "lockdown" on execution nights), we were ultimately led into the lethal chamber itself. Here, a most grotesque and unexpected proscenium had been erected. Mr. McDonald was concealed on the far side of a thick glass window, which was covered first by a rather frail and delicate venetian blind and second by an ordinary curtain. On either flank of the peep-show-size window stood two amazingly butch guards, almost absurdly motionless and impassive in their heavy equipment, each holding the end of a tiny cord in a hamlike fist. As they waited for the order to tug on the dainty strings and unveil the set, I was assailed by a powerful sensation of voyeuristic indecency. There was something camp and wrong and over-rehearsed about it—the result of an ill-considered attempt to impose primness and decorum on something obscene. There was something else, too. It took me a little while to "get" it. It was the moment in *Great Expectations* when Magwitch is put back in the prison hulk:

> No one seemed surprised to see him, or interested in seeing him, or glad to see him, or sorry to see him, or spoke a word. . . . Then, the ends of the torches were flung hissing into the water, and went out, as if it were all over with him.

Snuffed, in fact. That was the word for what I then witnessed. Radiating the most professional indifference imaginable, the huge warders pulled the small strings, and the blinds opened and rose. Through the narrow window we could discern Samuel McDonald, already lying on the gurney, covered to his chin by a sheet, as if all "prepped" and ready for the physician. He was looking urgently at the opposite window, behind which stood his friends and family and lawyer to the number of about six. A third window shielded the family of Officer Robert Jordan. McDonald was speaking hurriedly but inaudibly, yet was perhaps lip-readable by his own team. At 12:02 A.M., he stopped talking. It was as if he'd suddenly gagged or hiccuped, and given a slight arch of his back, as the pentothal—delivered by remote control from offstage—hit him. The one thing this hopeless, helpless splutter didn't resemble, even with the greatest permissible metaphorical strain, was "a moment of truth." A robotic voice from somewhere announced that we had duly witnessed the first injection. The next two were counted out loud, but there was no visible impact. So when the robot voice assured us that the McDonald-shaped form was now "deceased," we had to take the statement on trust. That was it. From gurney to slab in three moves. Hustled out quickly, I heard someone say, "Sam McDonald bought the farm. E-I-E-I-O." Even the most spotless scaffold must have its jester.

Back in the coffee-and-doughnut section, we were introduced to some of Officer Jordan's male relatives. They were black also, which made them as conspicuous in this part of Missouri (if not in this jail) as Sam McDonald had been. They spoke beautifully and with gravity and bearing, though with that slight constriction and constraint that you sometimes notice when people are employing a script that is not quite their own. Neologistic words like "closure" did not, I could easily see, form part of their daily vernacular. Nonetheless, when they said they had been praying for McDonald and his family and knew what they were going through and bewailed the appalling length of time that everything had taken, they were genuine and—it seemed to me— rather baffled. It's the done thing to feature the victim's family at trials and at executions these days; this after all is a populist and "feeling" epoch. But I had the slight suspicion that, for this family, revenge was sour or perhaps even tasteless.

That of course is presumptuous of me. Otherwise, though, I can be confident in stating that the entire enactment involves a series of unintended consequences. As a state's witness, I was supposed to sign a book saying that everything had been kosher. It was, by definition, too late for that. What if I didn't think so and wouldn't sign? The shrug I got in response only proved that we were, all of us, spending an off night in Absurdistan. For example, who *was* that announcing the chemical hits? Was it a doctor? And why the curtain and the blind before the first injection? "The curtains are to preserve staff anonymity. The EKG is monitored by a physician." Make what you will of that. As in "A Hard Rain's A-Gonna Fall" so in the United States of Therapy: "The executioner's face is always well hidden."

Did McDonald have any last words, and if so, what were they, please? Official face consults official cue card. "The inmate's last words were: 'Tell my brothers to be strong.'" Oh, come *on*. I was there, He was talking for very much longer than that, and more animatedly. And why were we not permitted to hear what he said? A final address was the privilege of the condemned even in the Dark Ages. Every attempt, in other words, to make this "procedure" more rational, more orderly, and more hygienic succeeded only in calling attention to something that I'm now firmly convinced is inescapable—namely, that it's irrational, random, and befouled and bemerded with the residues of ancient cruelty and superstition. They can deny it's cruel, they can certainly make it less unusual, but they are still stuck with the task of running a premeditated state killing: Big Government at its worst. (When the French finally abolished the guillotine in 1981 they did so on the noble grounds that "It expresses a totalitarian relationship between the citizen and the state.")

CP 17 was in effect Samuel McDonald's lottery number. I had myself (I am rather disgusted to admit it now) drawn him out of a hat, feeling that I could no longer ride the long train of argument about the death penalty if I kept on getting off before the last stop. I had deliberately not interested myself in his case. I was just surfing the capital-punishment Web, soliciting an invitation to a beheading in a country that seeks the solace of execution almost daily. But if you have seen someone snuffed, choked off and put down, you are almost bound to feel a certain curiosity. It seemed only polite to inquire what had brought us together.

Five days after his seventeenth birthday, McDonald had enlisted in the United States Army and been promptly sent off to Vietnam. There he earned a Good Conduct Medal, a Vietnam Service Medal, a Vietnam Combat Service Medal, a Combat Infantryman Badge, and two Overseas Service Bars. But he also lost his nerve and his moral center of gravity. At one point during the Tet offensive, he was cut off behind Vietcong lines for five panic-stricken days. On another occasion, he saw almost three-quarters of his company become casualties of war in a single engagement. In his own opinion, he became a killer, if not a murderer. In the course of sweeping a village for "unfriendlies," he heard a sound he didn't care for and machine-gunned an old woman and an infant. Narcotics were his means of escape.

I spoke to his attorney, Richard Sindel, who is your typical overworked and under-recognized capital-punishment pro bono local hero. There's one of these in every state of the union, which isn't anything like enough in these days of photo-op executions on election eve. He showed me the court transcript, where McDonald's former platoon commander, Douglas Falek, had turned up to testify on his behalf and had indeed eloquently done so—but in the absence of the jury. An impressive stable of medical men and psychiatrists, including the reigning experts in the field of Post-Vietnam Stress Disorder, had him down as a classic case. In deciding for death, judges and juries are supposed to consider elements such as premeditation, mental condition, and depraved indifference to human life. In this instance, the jury was denied the information with which to do so. A small break, said Sindel, and his client would have gone to long-term confinement but not to death row. Is it impossible to imagine an arrangement whereby he'd have gone to rehab *before* being turned loose, howling and neurotic and war-torn, onto the streets? Don't be such a bleeding heart. Get with the program.

"The program" is that lottery I mentioned. In spite of a well-publicized decline in the murder rate in New York City, the number of murders and murderers in the United States continues to be many, many times greater per capita than for any comparable country. (And certainly, by the way, for any comparable country that has abolished the death penalty.) There are approximately *one hundred thousand* convicted murderers stockpiled in the American prison system. If they were all to be executed, the country would become a charnel house; a saturnalia of eye for eye and tooth for tooth. So, instead, a certain number are selected for the ultimate vengeance and the severest sanction. You can make the procedure as ponderous and pedantic as is humanly possible. You can build in so many "safeguards" and "reviews" that the process will be lengthened until it's tantamount to torture. But this will only emphasize what you most desire to conceal—the fact that you are running a game of chance with a crooked wheel.

In effect, nobody who is not from the losing classes has ever been thrust into a death cell in these United States. Clinton Duffy, the warden of San Quentin who supervised ninety executions, once tersely described the penalty as "a privilege of the poor." You could say, without much of a stretch, that Samuel Lee McDonald drew a fairly low lottery number on the day his mother bore him. That is not to relieve him of his responsibility. But it is not to forget our own either. There are many strong arguments against the very principle of capital punishment, which any intelligent person can deploy, and which I like to think I could deploy conclusively in another article. But it is the *practice,* not the principle, that has been making the most converts lately, and making these converts among the very people who are supposed to administer the business.

"From this day forward," wrote former Supreme Court justice Harry Blackmun in 1994:

> I no longer shall tinker with the machinery of death. For more than twenty years I have endeavored—indeed I have struggled—along with a majority of this Court, to develop procedural and substantive rules that would lend more than the mere appearance of fairness to the death penalty endeavor. Rather than continue to coddle the Court's delusion that the desired level of fairness has been achieved and the need for regulation eviscerated, I feel morally and intellectually obligated to concede that the death penalty experiment has failed.

When I went to Parchman prison farm in Mississippi that time, to see the last hours of Edward Earl Johnson, I asked to meet the warden. Parchman is the most feared prison in the whole of the former Confederacy, and did not earn its reputation by accident, so I wasn't expecting to run into any fancy liberals. But it did seem to me that the warden, Donald Cabana, was undergoing some distress of mind. Now he has resigned from the prison service and written an extraordinary book entitled *Death at Midnight: The Confession of an Executioner,* in which he "comes out" as a convinced foe of the penalty. I tracked him down at the University of Southern Mississippi, where abolitionists don't grow on trees, even if some people wish they dangled from them. "Christopher," he said, "it's bingo personified. Except that the odds change drastically with your geographical location, your jury pool, your . . ." He didn't need to add race or class or education level.

All right then, what about the victims and what about society's right to be firm? The family members I met at Potosi were concerned above all else with how long it had taken to get justice, if that's what they had indeed ended up getting. Fifteen years is certainly a long time to wait. Speed it up? Be aware of what you may be asking for: an increase in the velocity of the lottery wheel. But between 1973 and the present, we know of *seventy-three* documented cases where innocent people were found on death row and released. Before me is a brilliant and haunting article from the 1995 *Boston University Law Review,* written by Stephen Bright and Patrick Keenan. Its title, "Judges and the Politics of Death: Deciding Between the Bill of Rights and the Next Election in Capital Cases," is a fair guide to its contents. In most states of the union which employ the death penalty, judges are subject to re-election. The effect upon the judicial process is the same as upon the electoral and political processes. There are, as Clinton proved in the Rickey Ray Rector case, poll-driven executions in this country. The contrast between the vulgarity and populism of that and the supposed clinical detachment of the lethal injection is a repellent one. (It's the supporters of capital punishment, in other words, and not its opponents, who rely upon emotion.) Norman Mailer and Phil Donahue have both proposed that executions be either public or televised, so that the voters can be faced with what they are demanding. They, too, are trying to be ironic. The fact is that the crowd already plays more of a role than anyone cares to admit. The lottery affects, and is affected by, even the people who don't play in it.

In my time, I have seen people die and be killed, in sickness and in warfare. I have watched children being born, and I'm morally certain that I once even watched a child being conceived. I would, in principle and in very different degrees, be prepared to see any of that again. It's all, in a manner of speaking, part of life. But I feel permanently degraded and somewhat unmanned by the small part I played, as a complicit spectator, in the dank and dingy little ritual that was enacted in that prison cellar in Missouri. The medical butchery of a helpless and demented loser, the descendant of slaves and a discarded former legionary of the Empire, made neither society nor any individual safer. It canceled no moral debt. It was a creepy, furtive, and shameful affair, in which the participants could not decently show their faces or quite meet one another's eye. I don't know that I shall ever quite excuse myself, even as a reporter and writer who's supposed to scrutinize everything, for my share in the proceedings. But I am clear on one thing. Death requires no advocates. It is superfluous to volunteer for its service. Those who argue "for" it are missing the point. Edna St. Vincent Millay hit on the truth long before Justice Blackmun and Donald Cabana. "I shall die," she wrote in her poem *Conscientious Objector*, "but that is all that I shall do for Death." Me, too.

VANITY FAIR, JANUARY 1998

IN SICKNESS
AND BY STEALTH

A review of *AN UNFINISHED LIFE: JOHN F. KENNEDY, 1917–1963*
by Robert Dallek

E ven as I was grazing on the easy slopes of this book, in June and July, the quotidian press brought me fairly regular updates on the doings and undoings of the "fabled Kennedy dynasty." A new volume by Ed Klein, portentously titled *The Kennedy Curse*, revealed the brief marriage of John Kennedy Jr. and Carolyn Bessette to have been a cauldron of low-level misery, infidelity and addiction. The political-matrimonial alliance between Andrew Cuomo and Kerry Kennedy was discovered to be in the process of acrimonious dissolution. Representative Patrick Kennedy of Rhode Island, whose ability to find his way to the House unaided has long been a source of intermittent wonder, became inflamed while making a speech at a liberal fund-raising event and yelled: "I don't need Bush's tax cut! I have never worked a ****ing day in my life." The electoral career of Kathleen Kennedy Townsend, which had never achieved escape velocity from local Maryland politics, seemed to undergo a final eclipse in the last mid-term vote. Robert F. Kennedy Jr. failed to convince anyone of the innocence of his cousin Michael Skakel, convicted of beating a teenage girlfriend to death with a golf club.

Senator Edward Kennedy of Massachusetts still retains a certain grandeur, on the grounds of longevity and persistence alone, but his solidity on the landscape derives in part from his resemblance, pitilessly identified by his distant kinsman Gore Vidal, to "three hundred pounds of condemned veal." And even Vidal, who first broke a lance against the Kennedy clan with his 1967 essay "The Holy Family," might be open-mouthed at the possibility of Arnold Schwarzenegger winning the upcoming race for the governorship of

California and thereby making Maria Shriver, a collateral Kennedy descendant, the first lady of the nation's richest and most populous state. Such a macho Republican triumph would be a bizarre way for the family charisma to mutate. Or would it? Not if you bear in mind Vidal's phrase about the tribe's "coldblooded jauntiness." The calculated combination of sex, showbiz, money and bravado was—as Robert Dallek unwittingly demonstrates in *An Unfinished Life*—the successful, if volatile, mixture all along.

Otherwise, one can reasonably look forward to a future where the entire meretricious Kennedy cult has staled. It is already more or less meaningless to younger Americans. And even those like myself, who are near-contemporary with all the verbiage and imagery of the "New Frontier" or—even worse— "Camelot," have had the opportunity to become bored, sated and better informed. Pierre Salinger and Oliver Stone, votaries of the cult, have spun off into the bliss that comforts and shields the paranoid. Arthur Schlesinger Jr. and Theodore Sorenson, the officially consecrated historians, are, one feels, at last reaching an actuarial point of diminishing returns. Meanwhile, the colossal images of September 11, 2001 have easily deposed the squalid scenes in Dallas, of the murders of Kennedy and Oswald, which once supplied the bond of a common televised melodramatic "experience."

This is not to say that hair and nails do not continue to sprout on the corpse. Professor Dallek's title, itself portentous and platitudinous at the same time, is part of the late growth. Since President Kennedy was shot dead at the age of forty-six, it is self-evidently true in one way to describe his life as "unfinished." But anyone scanning this or several other similar accounts would have to be astonished, not that the man's career was cut short, but rather that it lasted so long. In addition to being a moral defective and a political disaster, John Kennedy was a physical and probably mental also-ran for most of his presidency. Even someone impervious to his supposed charm has to feel a piercing pang of pity when reading passages such as this one:

Despite the steroids he was apparently taking, he continued to have abdominal pain and problems gaining weight. Backaches were a constant problem . . . . He also had occasional burning when urinating, which was the result of a nonspecific urethritis dating from 1940 and a possible sexual encounter in college, which left untreated became a chronic condition. He was later diagnosed as having "a mild, chronic, non-specific prostatitis" that sulfa drugs temporarily suppressed.

Moreover, a strenuous daily routine intensified the symptoms— fatigue, nausea and vomiting—of the Addison's disease that would not be diagnosed until 1947.

This was the state of affairs when the young "Jack," pressed and driven by his gruesome tyrant of a father, first ran for a seat in Congress in 1946.

Obviously, a good deal of "spin" is required to make an Achilles out of such a poxed and suppurating Philoctetes. The difference was supplied by family money in heaping measure, by the canny emphasis on a war record, and by serious attention to the flattery and suborning of the media. (As Dallek is the latest to concede, the boy-wonder later had a Pulitzer Prize procured for him, for a superficial book he had hardly read, let alone written.) One doesn't want to overstress the medical dimension, but it is the truly macabre extent of disclosure on that front that constitutes this book's only claim to originality. At the very time of the Bay of Pigs disaster, Kennedy "struggled with 'constant,' 'acute diarrhea' and a urinary tract infection. His doctors treated him with increased amounts of antispasmodics, a puree diet, and penicillin, and scheduled him for a sigmoidoscopy."

During the next crisis over Cuba—the nuclear confrontation in the autumn of 1962—

we learn that the president took his usual doses of antispasmodics to control his colitis; antibiotics for a flareup of his urinary tract problem and a bout of sinusitis; and increased amounts of hydrocortisone and testosterone as well as salt tablets to control his Addison's Disease. . . . On November 2, he took ten additional grams of hydrocortisone and ten grams of salt to boost him before giving a brief report to the American people on the dismantling of the Soviet missile bases in Cuba. In December, Jackie asked the president's gastroenterologist, Dr. Russell Boles, to eliminate antihistamines for food allergies. She described them as having a "depressing action" on the president and asked Boles to prescribe something that would ensure "mood elevation without irritation to the gastrointestinal tract." Boles prescribed one milligram twice a day of Stelazine, an antipsychotic that was also used as an antianxiety medication.

Further mind-boggling revelations are given, and it becomes clearer and clearer that Dallek wants the credit for the disclosures without allowing any suggestion that they might qualify his hero-worship for the subject. Thus, and again in lacerating detail from the "previously secret medical records" of another of his numerous physicians, Dr. Janet Travell:

During the first six months of his presidency, stomach/colon and prostate problems, high fevers, occasional dehydration, abscesses, sleeplessness and high cholesterol accompanied Kennedy's back and adrenal ailments. Medical attention was a fixed part of his routine. His physicians administered large doses of so many drugs that they kept an ongoing "Medicine Administration Record" (MAR) cataloguing injected and oral corticosteroids for his adrenal insufficiency; procaine shots to painful "trigger points," ultrasound treatments, and hot packs for his back; Lomotil, Metamucil, paregoric, Phenobarbital, testosterone, and Transentine to control his diarrhea, abdominal discomfort, and weight loss; penicillin and other antibiotics for his urinary infections and abscesses; and Tuinal to help him sleep.

To this pharmacopoeia, Dallek somewhat fatuously adds that "Though the treatments occasionally made him feel groggy and tired, Kennedy did not see them as a problem." He thus perpetuates the fealty required by and of the "JFK" school, which insists that we judge Kennedy more or less as he judged himself. Plain evidence is available on neighboring pages that this would be simplistic or foolish in the extreme. Dr. Travell and her colleagues did not know that their famous patient had a secret relationship with yet another doctor, who flew on another plane. As early as the election campaign of 1960—this revelation is not original to Dallek—Kennedy had begun seeing Dr. Max Jacobson, the New York physician who had made a reputation for treating celebrities with "pep pills," or amphetamines, that helped combat depression and fatigue.

Jacobson, whom patients termed "Dr Feelgood," administered back injections of painkillers and amphetamines that allowed Kennedy to stay off crutches, which he believed essential to project a picture of robust good health.

The clumsy phrasing here makes it slightly obscure whether Kennedy or Jacobson was nurturing the image, but it was clearly the candidate himself.

Even on the day of his celebrated inaugural speech, he worried that his steroid-inflated face would be too fat and puffy for the cameras, and was saved by a swift Palm Beach suntan. This false projection of youthful vigor was more than narcissism. It was the essence of the presentation, and had been the backdrop to his wild accusation of a "missile gap" between the Soviet Union and the USA, neglected by the wrinkly and tired Eisenhower regime. Also, and unlike, say, Franklin Roosevelt's polio, the concealment was of a serious condition, or set of conditions, that might really affect performance in office. If Kennedy had not succumbed to his actual ill health, he might as easily have flamed out like Jimi Hendrix or Janis Joplin from the avalanche of competing uppers and downers that he was swallowing.

But the furthest that Dallek will go here is to admit—following Seymour Hersh's earlier book *The Dark Side of Camelot*—that Kennedy's back-brace held him upright in the open car in Dallas, unable to duck the second and devastating bullet from Lee Harvey Oswald. This is almost the only connection between the president's health and his fitness that is allowable in these pages, and I presume that it is its relative blamelessness which allows the concession. On other pages, Dallek flatly if unconsciously contradicts his own soothing analysis. "Judging from tape recordings of conversations made during the crisis, the medications were no impediment to long days and lucid thought; to the contrary, Kennedy would have been significantly less effective without them and might not have been able to function."

Consider for yourself: how reassuring is that? Elsewhere we learn that, during the disastrous summit with Khrushchev in Vienna:

A long day under much tension certainly accounts for most of Kennedy's weariness by the early evening, but we cannot discount the impact of the Jacobson chemicals on him as well. As the day wore on and an injection Jacobson had given him just before he met Khrushchev wore off, Kennedy may have lost the emotional and physical edge initially provided by the shot.

This is no small matter, because the sense that Kennedy retained—of having been outdone by Khrushchev in their first man-to-man confrontation—decided him to show "resolve" in the worst of all possible locations, which was Vietnam.

A mere sixty-three pages later, Dallek simply states without qualification that "Personal problems added to the strains of office, testing Kennedy's physical and emotional endurance. His health troubles were a constant strain on his ability to meet presidential responsibilities."

The other "personal problems," which Dallek also approaches with a combination of fawning and concession, are at least suggested by the injections of testosterone mentioned above. This was notoriously a department in which Kennedy did not require any extra boost. We learn again from this book about the way in which he regularly humiliated his wife, abused his staffers and Secret Servicemen by suborning them as procurers, and endangered the security of his administration by fornicating with a gun-moll—the property of the Mafia boss Sam Giancana—in the White House. But Dallek almost outpoints Schlesinger himself in the deployment of euphemism here:

Did Kennedy's compulsive womanizing distract him from public business? Some historians think so, especially when it comes to Vietnam. Kennedy's reluctance, however, to focus the sort of attention on Vietnam he gave to Berlin or other foreign and domestic concerns is not evidence of a distracted president, but of a determination to keep Vietnam from becoming more important to his administration than he wished it to be.

Certainly, when one reviews Kennedy's White House schedules, he does not seem to have been derelict about anything he considered a major problem. . . . But the supposition that he was too busy chasing women or satisfying his sexual passions to attend to important presidential business is not borne out by the record of his daily activities.

> And, according to Richard Reeves, another Kennedy historian, the womanizing generally "took less time than tennis."

One is forced into a bark of mirth by the way that bathos succeeds banality here. (Forget the fact, already admitted, that some of Kennedy's health problems originated with a clinging and neglected case of VD.) A solemn review of the official appointment book is supposed to show no trace of strenuous venery and thus to rule it out as a problem, while this non-evidence is allegedly buttressed by the assertion that the tennis court was as much of an arena as the boudoir. We are not, here, really comparing like with like. And if record-keeping is to count as evidence, then what of the numerous holes and gaps in the White House taping system that Kennedy secretly installed? Dallek does his best to explain these away, admitting in the process that the excisions probably involve assassination plots against Castro, as well as involvement with Marilyn Monroe and with Judith Campbell Exner (Giancana's girlfriend). The Kennedy Library remains as hermetic as ever, withholding the transcripts of four missing tapes "which may contain embarrassing revelations or national security secrets." Wrong-footing himself at almost every step, Dallek lamely concludes that "By and large, however, the tapes seem to provide a faithful record of some of the most important events in Kennedy's presidency. . . ." "By and large," the same could be said of the Nixon tapes too.

Like many of his fellow devotees, Dallek rests a tentative defence on what might have been: the speech at American University about ultimate disarmament, or the possibility that reason might have prevailed in Indo-China— always given the chance of a second term. Why is it not recognized, with Kennedy, that the job of the historian is to record and evaluate what actually did happen? And why is it forgotten that, had he lived, Kennedy would necessarily have been even more distressingly ill than he was already? The usual compromise is to invest with a retrospective numinousness the relative banality of what did occur. Thus Dallek relates the set-piece events with the customary awe: the brinkmanship over Cuba, the "ich bin ein Berliner" speech, the confrontations with revolution in Vietnam and the Congo. Tougher scholarship has dimmed the phoney glamor of most of these recovered memories. Michael Beschloss's *Crisis Years* demonstrated, in 1991, that Kennedy was for most practical purposes complicit in the erection of the Berlin Wall, played it down as an issue wherever possible, and only made his defiant public speech when he was quite sure that it could make no difference. As in the case of Cuba, he first created the conditions for a crisis by using inflamed rhetoric and tactics, then just managed to extricate himself from catastrophe, and finally agreed to a consolidation of Communist power that was much more "locked in" than it had been before.

Whether you approach matters from the standpoint of those concerned with nuclear holocaust and superpower promiscuity, or of those desiring a long-term strategy to outlast the Stalinist monolith, this record is a dismal one. It was further punctuated by episodes of more or less gangsterish conduct, most conspicuously in the coup that murdered Kennedy's South Vietnamese client Ngo Dinh Diem, but also in such vignettes as Robert Kennedy's serious proposal to blow up the American consulate in the Dominican Republic, in order to supply a pretext for a U.S. invasion. Dallek allows this latter moment all of two sentences.

Their hysterical and profitless hyperactivity on one front is in the boldest contrast to the millimetrical trudging and grudging with which the Kennedy brothers approached their genuinely urgent, and constitutionally mandated, responsibility for civil rights. Confronted with an inescapable matter, they abandoned the flamboyance of their overseas melodramas and confined themselves to the most minimal Fabian tactics. Since Robert Kennedy was at least physically robust, it may not be fair to attribute this mood-swing regime too intimately to the influence of stimulants and analgesics. But as Robert Dallek inadvertently shows, it would be highly imprudent to discard the hypothesis altogether. The reputation of the Kennedy racket is now dependent on a sobbing effort of will: an applauding chorus demanding that the flickering Tinkerbell not be allowed to expire. It is pardonable for children to yell that they believe in fairies, but it is somehow sinister when the piping note shifts from the puerile to the senile.

TIMES LITERARY SUPPLEMENT,
AUGUST 22, 2003

THE STRANGE CASE
OF DAVID IRVING

A review of *The Holocaust on Trial*
by D. D. Guttenplan
and *Lying About Hitler*
by Richard J. Evans

hen the first news of the Nazi camps was published in 1945, there were those who thought the facts might be exaggerated either by Allied war propaganda or by the human tendency to relish "atrocity stories." In his column in the London magazine *Tribune,* George Orwell wrote that though this might be so, the speculation was not exactly occurring in a vacuum. If you remember what the Nazis did to the Jews before the war, he said, it isn't that difficult to imagine what they might do to them during one.

In one sense, the argument over "Holocaust denial" ends right there. The National Socialist Party seized power in 1933, proclaiming as its theoretical and organizing principle the proposition that the Jews were responsible for all the world's ills, from capitalist profiteering to subversive Bolshevism. By means of oppressive legislation, they began to make all of Germany *Judenrein,* or "Jew-free." Jewish businesses were first boycotted and then confiscated. Jewish places of worship were first vandalized and then closed. Wherever Nazi power could be extended—to the Rhineland, to Austria and to Sudeten Czechoslovakia—this pattern of cruelty and bigotry was repeated. (And, noticed by few, the state killing of the mentally and physically "unfit," whether Jewish or "Aryan," was tentatively inaugurated.) After the war broke out, Hitler was able to install puppet governments or occupation regimes in numerous countries, each of which was compelled to pass its own version of the anti-Semitic "Nuremberg Laws." Most ominous of all—and this in plain sight and on camera, and in full view of the neighbors—Jewish populations as distant as Salonika were rounded up and put on trains, to be deported to the eastern provinces of conquered Poland.

None of this is, even in the remotest sense of the word, "deniable." Nor is the fact that, once the war was over, surviving Jews found that they had very few family members left. The argument only begins here, and it takes two forms. First, what exactly happened to the missing ones? Second, why did it occur? The first argument is chiefly forensic and concerns numbers and methods: the physical engineering of shooting, gassing, burial and cremation. The second argument is a debate among historians and is known as the "intentionalist versus functionalist" dispute. The "intentionalists" say that Hitler and his gang were determined from the start to extirpate all Jews and that everything from 1933 to 1945 is a vindication of certain passages in "Mein Kampf." The "functionalists" point out (correctly) that the Nazis actually *killed* almost no Jews until after 1941 and that the *Endlosung,* or "Final Solution," was a semi-secret plan evolved after Germany began to lose the war on the Eastern front. On this continuum, Daniel Jonah Goldhagen, with his view that Germans had a cultural gene of anti-Semitism, is an extreme "intentionalist"; Yehudah Bauer, of the Yad Vashem museum in Jerusalem, is a moderate "functionalist."

Differences of opinion between these two schools, and discrepancies in the evidence, have recently permitted the emergence of something that is more of a phenomenon than a "school," by which I mean the movement of "Holocaust denial" or (because it consists of two contrasting tendencies) "Holocaust revisionism." This movement contains some Nazi revivalists in Germany and elsewhere, some crackpots and conspiracy theorists and one practicing historian, an Englishman named David Irving. Among revisionist forces there is even more confusion; they either argue that nothing much happened at all and that the whole thing is a fabrication or they maintain that the unforgettable piles of corpses were the result of epidemics, to be blamed on the disruption of food and medical supplies by Allied bombing. (It will be seen at once that this latter faction has no good explanation for why the Jews of Europe were packed into remote camps in the first place.)

The toxicity of the argument is increased by four other factors. First, there are those who maintain that the German people have been blamed enough and that endless suggestions of collective guilt—accompanied by incessant demands for compensation—are an insult and possibly a provocation. Second, there are those who resent the exploitation of the Holocaust, or Shoah, by extreme Israeli nationalists. Third, there is a collective awareness that neither the international community nor organized Jewry did much to help the victims when it could have made a difference. Finally, in many countries, including Germany and France, it is actually a crime to dispute the established version of events, which means that the "revisionist" movement now has its free-speech martyrs. While in the United States, protected as it is by the 1st Amendment, the Holocaust has become a secular religion, with state support in the form of a national museum. Accusations of ill will or bad faith are often made against anyone with reservations about the elevation of this project into something combining a cult, an entertainment resource and an industry, each claiming to represent the unvoiced dead. Indeed, I myself feel constrained to state here that my mother's family is of German and Polish Jewish provenance and that on my wife's side we have not just an Auschwitz "survivor" in our lineage but a man—David Szmulewski—who was one of the leaders of the communist resistance in the camps as well as one of those who smuggled evidence out of it and later testified against the war criminals in court. I look forward to a time when I won't feel any need to mention this.

I was raised in two other traditions as well, however. The first was to believe, with the late Karl Popper, that a case has not been refuted until it has been stated at its strongest. The second was to take it for granted that historians have prejudices. To manifest the first point, then, let us summarize the best case that the revisionists can make. Would it surprise you to know that:

1) there were no gas chambers or extermination camps on German soil, in other words, at Belsen or Dachau or Buchenwald;

2) there were no Jews made into soap;

3) the "confession" of Rudolf Hoess, commandant of Auschwitz, was extracted by force and contains his claim to have killed more Jews than was "humanly" possible?

These are, however, the now-undisputed findings of all historians and experts on the subject. And if they are sound, then it means that much "eyewitness" testimony is wrong. It necessarily changes our attitude toward the everyday complicity of average Germans. It also means that much of the evidence presented and accepted at Nuremburg was spurious. Of course, we knew some of this already—the Nazis were charged by Soviet and Allied judges with the massacres at Katyn in Poland, which had obviously been ordered by Stalin and are now admitted to have been. And every now and then, a bogus Holocaust merchant makes an appearance. The most recent was the fantasist "Binjamin Wilkomirski," whose book, *Fragments,* was a whole-cloth fabrication by someone who had spent the entire war in Switzerland. This did not prevent him from receiving several awards and the warm endorsement of Goldhagen. Earlier, a high Israeli court found the evidence of witnesses useless, ruling that John Demjanjuk had not been at Treblinka in the mythical shape of "Ivan the Terrible."

The confrontation between Irving and the consensus was therefore long overdue. He forced the confrontation himself, by putting his own work on trial in attempting to sue the work of another. But it was high time to have this out in public, in the relatively objective context of an English courtroom. And so to my second observation, about bias and historians.

History, especially as written by historians in the English tradition, is a literary and idiosyncratic form. Men such as Gibbon and Macaulay and Marx were essayists and polemicists in the grand manner, and when I was at school, one was simply not supposed to be prissy about the fact. We knew that Macaulay wrote to vindicate the Whig school, just as we knew of the prejudices of Carlyle (though there were limits: Nobody ever let us read his *Occasional Discourse on the Nigger Question,* a robustly obscene defense of slavery). Handing me a copy of *What Is History?* by E. H. Carr, my Tory headmaster loftily told me that it was required reading in spite of its "rather obvious Marxist bias." The master of my Oxford college was Christopher Hill, the great chronicler of Cromwell and Milton and Winstanley and the Puritan Revolution. Preeminent in his field, Hill had been a member of the Communist Party and could still be slightly embarrassed by mention of his early book, *Lenin and the Russian Revolution,* in which the name of Leon Trotsky was conspicuous by its absence. Moving closer to our own time, we had Sir Arthur

Bryant, whose concept of history as a pageant culminated in extreme roy-
alism and a strong sympathy for Franco and Mussolini and Hitler. Then there
was A. J. P. Taylor, one of the most invigorating lecturers of all time, who
believed that the Nazis had more or less been tricked into the war. And how
can one forget Hugh Trevor-Roper, author of the definitive narrative of
Hitler's final days, who had close connections to British intelligence, who
might be overheard making faintly anti-Jewish remarks and who later pronounced the forged Hitler diaries genuine? These were men who had been
witnesses and participants as well as archivists and chroniclers. Their accounts
were essential reading; the allowance for prejudice and inflection was part of
the fun of one's bookkeeping.

This of course doesn't license absolute promiscuity. Eric Hobsbawm, a
member of the Communist Party (much later than Hill), may have advertised
his allegiances but retained the respect of most critics because he had a strong
sense of objectivity in his historical work. In other words, no dirty tricks were
to be allowed.

So, what I mean to say for now is that when I first became aware of Irving,
I did not feel it necessary to react like a virgin who is suddenly confronted by
a man in a filthy raincoat.

That he had a sneaking sympathy for fascism was obvious enough. But his
work on the bombing of Dresden, on the inner functioning of the Churchill
government and on the mentality of the Nazi generals was invaluable. He
changed sides on the issue of the Hitler diaries, but his intervention was crucial to their exposure as a pro-Nazi fabrication. His knowledge of the German
language was the envy of his rivals. His notorious flaunting of bad taste and
his gallows humor were not likely to induce cardiac arrest in anyone like
myself, who had seen many Oxford and Cambridge history dons when they
were fighting drunk.

While helping to edit the *New Statesman* in 1981, I encouraged the American
historian Kai Bird, now a distinguished student of the cold war, to analyze
Irving's work. Bird turned in a meticulous essay, which exposed Irving's
obvious prejudice and incidentally trashed his least-known and worst book—
a history of the 1956 Hungarian uprising that characterized the revolt as a
rebellion of sturdy Magyar patriots against shifty Jewish Communists. Irving
briefly threatened to sue and then thought better of it. In the early 1990s, he

took part in a public debate with the extreme denier Robert Faurisson, at which he maintained that there was definite evidence of mass extermination at least by shooting (and gratuitously added that he thought the original Nazi plan to isolate all Jews in Madagascar was probably a good scheme). I noted this with interest—there's nothing like a good faction fight between extremists—but had no contact with him, direct or indirect, until he self-published in England his biography of Josef Goebbels in 1996.

This book is still on my shelf. I read it initially because St. Martin's Press in New York decided not to publish it, or rather, decided to breach its contract to do so. This action on its part was decisive, in that it convinced Irving that his enemies were succeeding in denying him a livelihood, and it determined him to sue someone as soon as he could. It was also important in that St. Martin's gave no reason of historical accuracy for its about-face. For the publisher, it was a simple question of avoiding unpleasantness ("Profiles in Prudence," as its senior editor Thomas Dunne put it to me ruefully).

Well, as I say, I'm a big boy and can bear the thought of being offended. The biography, based largely on extracts from Goebbels' diaries, told me a great deal I hadn't known. I'll instance a small but suggestive example. Irving had in the past been associated with the British fascist movement led by Sir Oswald Mosley. In my hot youth, I'd protested at some of the meetings of this outfit and had circulated the charge that, before the war, it had been directly financed by the Nazis. This charge was always hotly disputed by the Mosleyites themselves, but here was Goebbels, in cold print, discussing the transfer of funds from Berlin to the British Black Shirts. On the old principle famously adumbrated by Bertrand Russell—of "evidence against interest"—it seemed that Irving was capable of publishing information that undermined his own position. He also, in his editorial notes, gave direct testimony about the mass killing of Jews in the East (by shooting) and of the use of an "experimental" gas chamber in the Polish town of Chelmno. The "deniers" don't like this book; on the strength of it you could prove that the Nazis tried to do away with the Jews. There was some odd stuff about Hitler's lack of responsibility for Kristallnacht but, as I say, I allowed for Irving's obsessions. I wrote a column criticizing St. Martin's for its cowardice and described Irving himself as not just a fascist historian but a great historian of fascism. One should be allowed to read *Mein Kampf* as well as Heidegger. Allowed? One should be able to do so without permission from anybody.

As a result of this, Irving contacted me when he was next in Washington, and I invited him to my home for a cocktail. He got off to a shaky start by refusing any alcohol or tobacco and by presenting me with two large blue-and-white stickers. Exactly the size of a German street sign, they were designed to be pasted over the originals at dead of night. "Rudolf Hess Platz," they said; a practical-joke accessory for German extremists with that especial sense of humor. Because they were intended to shock, I tried to look as unshocked as I could. Irving then revealed, rather fascinatingly, that some new documents from the Eichmann family might force him to reconsider his view that there had been no direct order for the annihilation of the Jews. It was a rather vertiginous atmosphere all around. When it came time for him to leave, my wife and daughter went down in the elevator with him on their own way out. Later, my wife rather gravely asked me if I would mind never inviting him again. This was highly unlike her; we have all sorts at our place. However, it transpired that, while in the elevator, Irving had looked with approval at my fair-haired, blue-eyed daughter, then five years old, and declaimed the following doggerel about his own little girl, Jessica, who was the same age:

I am a Baby Aryan
Not Jewish or Sectarian;
I have no plans to marry an
Ape or Rastafarian.

The thought of Carol and Antonia in a small space with this large beetle-browed man as he spouted that was, well, distinctly creepy. (He has since posted the lines on his Web site, and they came back to haunt him at the trial.)

The next time Irving got in touch with me was after his utter humiliation in court, and I thought I'd give him one last chance—though I arranged to meet him in a neutral restaurant this time. I wanted to know if it was true, as I had read in the press, that he had abruptly addressed the judge in the case as "Mein Fuhrer." With some plausibility, he explained to me that this was a misunderstanding; he had been quoting from the slogans shouted at a rally he was addressing in Germany and had glanced up at the bench at the wrong moment. The transcript of the trial seemed to make this interpretation possible. So when telephoned by my friend Ian Buruma, who was writing on the case for *The New Yorker,* I suggested that he might check it out. He called me back with the information that, when he had asked Irving directly about the incident, Irving had taken him into confidence and said, "Actually, I did say it." At this point I finally decided that anyone joining a Fair Play for Irving Committee was up against a man with some kind of death wish.

The Holocaust on Trial and *Lying About Hitler* make that very point in widely differing ways. Like me, D. D. Guttenplan is full of contempt for the censorship of Irving and quite prepared to consider the idea that the Holocaust has been exploited and even distorted. However, Guttenplan became disgusted by Irving's alternately bullying and ingratiating style and by his repeated failure to make good on his historical claims. His account of the courtroom confrontation, most vividly the confrontation between Irving and the Dutch expert on the mechanics of Auschwitz, Robert Jan van Pelt, could hardly be bettered. He also provides a masterly guide to the byways of English law, especially the grossly biased and oppressive law of libel that Irving hoped to enlist on his side.

This in itself has led to an intriguing subplot, with Richard J. Evans' London publishers abandoning his book, *Lying About Hitler,* because of their own pusillanimous fear of a libel suit and with Evans giving Guttenplan a rather dismissive review in a London newspaper. The issue before the court, says Evans, was not whether the Holocaust occurred but whether Irving is a fabricator. Of course that is formally true, but to my mind, Guttenplan rather beautifully shows it to be a distinction without a difference. Justice Gray, presiding, expressed the repeated hope that the case would not involve revisiting Auschwitz, but he had to "go there" all the same before the case was fully heard. It could not have been otherwise. As Raul Hilberg once phrased it, at Auschwitz history was destroyed at the same time that history was made. The question cannot be approached from the standpoint of truth without accepting this contradiction.

As an expert witness at the trial, however, Evans was quite devastating. *Lying About Hitler* is essentially an expanded version of his affidavit, and it redraws the whole terrain of the argument. No longer are we faced merely with the question of Irving's elementary right to speak or be published. We are invited to see if he deserves the title of historian at all. Evans' method is quite a simple one. He shows, first, that there are a number of errors, omissions and unsupported assertions in Irving's work. Now, this might be true of any historian, and there were indeed some distinguished academic practitioners in the witness box who maintained that no narrative is or can be free from error. However, what if, as Evans said under cross-examination:

> There is a difference between, as it were, negligence, which is random in its effects, i.e. if you are a sloppy or bad historian, the mistakes you make will be all over the place. They will not actually support any particular point of view. . . . On the other hand, if all the mistakes are in the same direction in the support of a particular thesis, then I do not think that is mere negligence. I think that is a deliberate manipulation and deception.

Evans' knowledge, both of the period and of the German language, are of an order to rival Irving's. He has little difficulty in showing that there are suspicious mistranslations, suggestive ellipses and, worst of all, some tampering with figures: in other words, that Irving knowingly inflates the death toll in the Allied bombing of Dresden while deflating it in the camps and pits to the East. And, yes, all the "mistakes" have the same tendency. In a crucial moment, Irving "forgot" what he had said about the Nazi general Walter Bruns, who had confessed to witnessing mass killing of Jews and had been taped by British intelligence while doing so. When it suited Irving to claim that Bruns didn't know he was being recorded, he claimed as much. When it didn't, he suggested that Bruns was trying to please his hearers. Having listened myself to Irving discuss this fascinating episode, I mentally closed the book when I reached this stage in it. It was a QED.

Irving has long been notorious for his view that Hitler never gave any order for the Final Solution and that there is no irrefutable document authorizing it. In court, he was unpardonably flippant on this point, saying airily that perhaps, like some of Richard Nixon's subordinates, a few of the rougher types imagined they knew what would please the boss. This argument has always struck me as absurd on its face in both cases, but Evans simply reduces it to powder. It's not too much to say that by the end of the trial, the core evidence for the Holocaust had been tested and found to be solid. The matter of Irving's reputation as scholar and researcher—which was the ostensible subject of the hearing—was so much "collateral damage."

It would be tempting to summarize this as a neat morality tale, in which the truth emerges as the stainless winner over bigotry and falsification. However, the conflict is not conducted in quite such hygienic conditions. Irving did not publish a series of books on the Nazi era that were exposed as propaganda by a magisterial review from Evans. That's the way things are supposed to happen but rarely do. Instead, the efforts of a few obsessive outsiders have sharpened the orthodox debate between intentionalists and functionalists and also provoked a grand crisis in the "Holocaust denial" milieu, which now subdivides yet again between those who see Irving as a martyr and those who see him as a conscious, dedicated agent of Zionism who let down the team.

I myself learned a good deal, about both the subject and the author, by becoming involved on the periphery of this debate. I still regard it as ridiculous that Irving's books are almost impossible to obtain in the homeland of the 1st Amendment. This culture has assumed several great responsibilities. It sponsored the Nuremberg trials, with all their peaks and troughs of evidence. It has elevated the Holocaust into a universal moral example. It is the chief international guarantor of the state of Israel, at whatever proper size of territory or jurisdiction over others that that state turns out to possess. And it is the home—on the basis of equality—of the most flourishing Jewish community in history. Given this quadrilateral of historical commitments, there can be no prohibition of any voice whatever. One asks only, as one must ask with all morally serious arguments, that those entering the arena be transparent as regards motive and scrupulous as regards evidence. Irving's contribution to this very outcome is an amazing instance of the workings of unintended consequence.

LOS ANGELES TIMES,
MAY 20, 2001

WHY AMERICANS
ARE NOT TAUGHT HISTORY

W e dwell in a present-tense culture that somehow, significantly, decided to employ the telling expression "You're history" as a choice reprobation or insult, and thus elected to speak forgotten volumes about itself. By that standard, the forbidding dystopia of George Orwell's *Nineteen Eighty-Four* already belongs, both as text and as date, with Ur and Mycenae, while the hedonistic nihilism of Huxley still beckons toward a painless, amusement-sodden, and stress-free consensus. Orwell's was a house of horrors. He often seemed to strain credulity because he posited a regime that would go to any lengths to own and possess history, to rewrite and reconstruct it, and to inculcate it by means of coercion. Whereas Huxley, writing of a California-style utopia of 1932, rightly foresaw that any such regime could break but could not bend. In 1988, four years after 1984, the Soviet Union scrapped its official history curriculum and announced that a newly authorized version was somewhere in the works. That was the precise moment at which the regime conceded its own extinction. For true blissed-out and vacant servitude, though, you need an otherwise sophisticated society where no serious history is taught at all.

And yet there is still an unmet need, an unanswered yearning, for an intelligible past. It finds its expression in surrogate forms, like the "referred pain" of a complex ailment, but it may still be registered. A few years back, just as many major university departments of English were sidelining Shakespeare or dropping him altogether, the Hollywood sensibility "kicked in" to bring us Ian McKellen as a Weimar-like Richard III, or Kenneth Branagh as Hamlet, or

Laurence Fishburne as the first black man to take the part of Othello on-screen. In somewhat the same way, the departure of the historical muse from the standard curriculum has been revenged or requited by a torrent of retrospectives. Some locate this moment in the vast popular response to Ken Burns's television series on the Civil War; in any event, the "history" and "biography" menu on A&E and the History Channel, and on PBS, is not furnished by those who are quixotically determined to lose money for integrity's sake. Nor do the lords of celluloid believe that they are acting pro bono when they revisit the beaches and cliffs of Normandy, the fouled hulls of the Middle Passage, the suggestive outlines of Dealey Plaza or the Watergate building. Nor is their product received as mere entertainment: Mel Gibson's *Braveheart* is credited with fueling a revival of Scottish nationalism that even now discomfits Tony Blair and the monarch whose bacon he saved last September.

Consider, too, the question of memorials. Is there a major city in the United States that is not currently arguing over some statue or plaque, or disputing the name given to some school or public building? These tussles are often sorry enough to make one reel and clutch the brow (Washington National Airport was already named for a president before some bright sparks thought to dub it again, in honor of the nation's leading amnesiac), but even in their paltriness they disclose a readiness to take history seriously.

Yet this fluttering cultural pulse has no attending physician. According to the last "National Assessment of Educational Progress in U.S. History," which was undertaken in 1994, we can no longer call upon the traditional schoolmarm concept of history as a pageant, or even as one damn thing after another. In order to argue against this caricature, you would need to know at least the official reason why Pilgrims and Puritans first voyaged to America, which 59 percent of fourth graders were unable to do. You would certainly need to be able to name one of the original thirteen colonies, which was beyond the capacity of 68 percent of that grade. By the eighth grade, matters have got worse, as they are bound to do. Ninety percent of eighth graders could recount nothing of the debates at the Constitutional Convention. Even when prompted by mentions of Yalta, Lend-Lease, and Hiroshima, 59 percent of the eighth grade were unprepared to say which conflict these references brought to mind. In the twelfth grade, 53 percent looked blank when invited to specify "the goal that was most important in shaping United States foreign policy between 1945 and 1990."

It isn't as if today's twelfth-grade students are giving the "wrong" reply to that last question, and scrawling ironic references to "imperialism" or "folie de grandeur" or even "Globocop" on their tests, let alone some variant like "Stalinism" or "Kulturkampf." They just don't know, and very probably don't care. Their immediate past has been airbrushed, or whisked, as surely as antiquity. When Henry James was writing *The American Scene* at the very opening of this century, he fretted about what Leon Edel, James's biographer, termed "America's cult of impermanence" or what James himself called "the perpetual repudiation of the past, so far as there has been a past to repudiate." So there is perhaps an innate cultural bias against "dwelling on the past," unless it is for the sanctified purposes of good citizenship. Sheer ignorance generally stems from plain ignorance, and surveys have been turning up results like this for generations. An amazing 54 percent of eleventh graders "knew," at least by dint of multiple choice, that Joseph Stalin was the leader of the Soviet Union during World War II, according to the determinedly pessimistic 1987 work of Diane Ravitch and Chester E. Finn Jr. (*What Do Our 17 Year-Olds Know?*). Yet a poll published by the *New York Times* in 1995 discovered that only 49 percent of American adults could say with confidence that the Soviet Union had been on the same side as the United States for that period, with the rest either having no opinion or identifying "Russia" as an enemy or, most remarkably of all, as a noncombatant. And even this is salutary, by comparison with a *New York Times* survey of fifty-five years ago, which found that a quarter of entering college freshmen in 1943 could not name the man who had been president of the United States during the Civil War. In the contemporary "debate" on the inculcation of history, the United States has even managed to forget its own amnesia.

The measure of an education is that you acquire some idea of the extent of your ignorance. And it seems at least thinkable that today's history students don't quite know what subject they are not being taught. At the time when alarm first (or last) began to be registered on this score, which was around the middle of the present decade, the good people at the National Council on History Education did some homework. They found that most states required high-school students to "take" a maximum of one year each of American and "world" history, and that several states had no history "requirement" of any kind. You might be startled to find that among the no-history-curriculum states was numbered the Commonwealth of Pennsylvania. So would I have been, if I had not been a visiting professor of English at the University of Pittsburgh in 1997. Since you can't teach the American literary canon (indeed, you can't even teach people to deconstruct it) without some reference to historical context, I began every class with an abbreviated introduction about the period in which the author was writing. I still have the notes and papers sent me by my students, asking why they had to get all the way to college before anyone bothered to fill in this nagging blank. Michigan and Alaska also let history slide altogether, while much-derided West Virginia wanted two years of U.S. history (combined with world history) and three years of world history (combined with U.S. history). Between these two poles, Nevada stipulated three years of U.S. history, while mandating that this should include "state history and government" and omitting world history altogether. Ohio opted for a judicious and restrained 0.5 years of American history and left it at that. Numerous other states, few of them asking for more than a year's reflection on the American past, folded history, national or global, into a package that included "world geography or world cultures," "global studies," "psychology/sociology" (the Montana solution), or the babble of "outcomes-based" or "core-competency" requirements. Every classroom a hive of inactivity; every flag-draped school a factory for the mass-production of a little learning.

About four years ago I began to ask the teachers of my own children how it came to be that they could not tell Thomas Jefferson from Thomas the Tank Engine. In the preceding sentence, it is unclear whether I mean that the children didn't know unless I told them, or that the teachers didn't know unless I told *them*. The confusion is intentional. One instructor, at a rather costly District of Columbia day school, cheerfully avowed that she herself "had never been that much of a reader." Others, more candid, announced that history was a bit of a minefield subject and that "good examples" (like Pocahontas and, on a good day, Frederick Douglass) were the thing. Parson Weems himself could hardly have bettered the modern method whereby children get good reports in a subject that they have never studied in order that a tiny pump be applied to the valves of their fledgling self-esteem.

According to statistics compiled by the National Center for Education Standards, fewer than 19 percent of high-school and middle-school social studies teachers in 1994 had majored (or minored) in history. That same year, when Alan Bennett's wonderful play *The Madness of George III* was released as a motion picture, its title was given as *The Madness of King George*. Hollywood's publicity people worried that audiences might think they had missed parts I and II.

It was time for one of those full-dress cultural sham-fights, like the earlier one about core values and "Western Civ," that animate the op-ed pages every decade or so. We need new standards! Alas, with no galvanizing Sputnik to unlock real money and talent, and with no encircling foe to spark another rewrite of the Pledge of Allegiance, federal monies went to subsidize a rather pallid and prolix set of "guidelines" that might as well have been marketed as "American History—Making a Difference Since 1776" or "Our Past—Serving the Community with Pride." As with many such trite labelings, however, the small print should have carried the dire admonition "Contents Under Pressure" or "Some Assembly Required."

Batteries were included. The tempestuous Lynne V. Cheney, spouse of George Bush's one-time secretary of defense, found herself temporarily at a giddying and pivotal point. Not only did she chair the National Endowment for the Humanities, which the zealots in her own party desired to abolish, but this same endowment had funded, to the tune of $2 million, the new "standards," which she found she wanted to abolish also. An article, catchily titled "The End of History," written either by or for Cheney, appeared in the *Wall Street Journal* in October 1994. You know the sort of thing—too many Native Americans and slaves in the new standards, too few pioneers, too much *political correctness*. In a matter of months, on the motion of Senator Slade Gorton, Republican of Washington, the full Senate had repudiated the "standards" in a vote of 99–1. It is safe to say that few if any of the legislators and deliberators had cleared their own passage through the offending volumes.

Thus began the current dialogue of the deaf, still raging at a school near you. Working toward his master's in tautology, John Fonte of the conservative Committee to Review National Standards said that "if you have a ninety-nine to one vote in the Senate against it, obviously it was not consensual enough." He and his co-thinkers believe that consensus is best achieved by letting "states and local school districts" decide on the tenor of history teaching, which would certainly help insulate children from the news about

McCarthyism and the Ku Klux Klan that Cheney found so depressingly salient in the original "guidelines."

Ever since the tussle between Cheney and the forces of P.C., history classes and textbooks have been oscillating between demands for a patriotic and intelligible narrative and cries for a story that is more "userfriendly" to minorities and new arrivals. School bureaucracies everywhere have responded by looking for safe and tepid waters, and educational publishers have been keen to abet the process in order to sell their bland and uncontroversial series. Combine this with lobbying from disparate confessional, regional, and ethnic groups, and each tributary blends imperceptibly to produce a uniform flow of drool:

TIME, CONTINUITY AND CHANGE

CONTENT STANDARD A:

Students in Wisconsin will learn about history through the concepts of time, continuity and change in order to develop historical perspective and answer questions about our contemporary world and future.

RATIONALE:

Human beings want to understand their historical roots and to locate themselves in time. In developing these insights the students must know what things were like in the past and how things change and develop. Knowing how to reconstruct and interpret historic events provides a needed perspective in addressing where we have been, what we have become, and where we might be going. In Wisconsin schools, this teaching focus typically appears in units and courses in history and the humanities.

The above is the preamble to a "standards" blueprint of mid-1996. It seems to have been written by some kind of poorly engineered machine. It violates a principle that holds good for education as well as for medicine: "First Do No Harm." And it is the sort of prose in which "history" is increasingly packaged by state authorities.

The ensuing Wisconsin paragraphs are headed with the minatory words "Performance Standards" and assure us with more assertion than conviction that:

By grade twelve, students will:

learn how to use a variety of sources and to check their credibility in order to interpret the past and to better understand current issues

apply theories and historical inquiry to decision making about the future, such as citizenship responsibilities in the 21st century, the long term possibility for peace in Eastern Europe and the evolving role of China in a world economy.

It's all there—the slovenly grammar, the weary obeisance to the millennium and to "globalization," the inept repetitions: all of it boiled into a mush wherein history is offered cajolingly and apologetically as a sort of "Old News You Can Use."

Let no one doubt the extent of the damage done by comfort teaching or therapeutic education, which has reversed the idea that educators should be educated (a decent teacher will teach in order to learn) and which has made the relationship of instructor to student into an exercise in the mutual, restful softening of the cortex. Here is how the state of Illinois, long renowned for toughness and direct speech, proposed to illuminate the past to its future citizens as recently as 1996. Students were ostensibly required to:

Assess the long-term consequences of major decisions by leaders in various nations of the world, drawing information from a variety of traditional, electronic and on-line sources.

Explain the effects of urbanization, industrialization and technology on society and institutions throughout history.

These and other fatuities—or impossibilities, if you try and guess the real weight of the second stipulation above—were the result of a history "curriculum" that had been collapsed into the social-science department and that furthermore had to be "clear and meaningful to students, parents, educators, business representatives and the community at large." The capacious "inclusiveness" of that last gorgeous mosaic demands that the whole project be preintelligible to those who haven't studied it yet, those who missed it last time, those who need it most, and those whose business it isn't! The exhausted phraseology melds with the upward-and-onward automatic rhetoric to produce nullity. In a gesture to aspiration, the compilers of the standards quoted George Santayana to the effect that those who did not learn from the past would be condemned to repeat it. By Santayana's absurd standard, the grade-schoolers of Illinois should be entering their Babylonian epoch just about now.

In December 1950, in the course of his presidential address to the American Historical Association, Samuel Eliot Morison expressed the view that it was time to abandon the "Jefferson-Jackson-F. D. Roosevelt line" and to have at last an American history "written from a sanely conservative point of view." This was the midpoint in a reaction against "progressive" history teaching, which reaction ran almost unchecked (especially in the states of the old Confederacy) from about 1939 until the high noon of the cold war. There was then an opposite but not equal reaction from certain revisionists, many of them excellent, such as Barton Bernstein and Christopher Lasch, but some of them callow and annoying. In due time, this collision expressed itself in a fight over history textbooks, in one of the few advanced nations that does not establish a nationally mandated curriculum where all students learn, so to speak, from the same page. The result is a version of *News from Nowhere*, written from nobody's point of view and deferential to the largest book-buying market or the most loquacious lobby.

The Greek verb *historein* means "to ask questions" and was employed by Herodotus, who, often credited with being the first or founding historian, described his work as "inquiries" or *historiai*. In 1950, Henry Steele Commager and Samuel Eliot Morison jointly produced a textbook entitled *The Growth of the American Republic*. Describing the antebellum state of affairs below the Mason-Dixon line, they wrote:

> As for Sambo, whose wrongs moved the abolitionists to wrath and tears, there is some reason to believe that he suffered less than any other class in the South from its "peculiar institution."

272

I would not, personally, wish to be deprived of this excerpt when teaching American history. Essay questions and classroom discussions might inquire: (1) What "reason to believe"? (2) Why were abolitionists so moved? (3) What gave rise to the notable coinage "peculiar institution"? (4) Why did both camps believe they had biblical authority? and (5) What has changed in America since 1950 to stop distinguished Yankee historians from employing the term "Sambo"? I think any competent teacher would and should have been able to cope with any "hurt feelings" that might arise in or out of the classroom. (If there were no such feelings, then something other than history would be the subject being taught.) But as matters stand, we have Southern textbooks that euphemize the Confederacy, Northern ones that scant the whole unpleasant subject, and a recent national debate on a possible presidential "apology" for slavery so etiolated that hardly anyone thought to ask whether President Lincoln's Second Inaugural had not in fact contained a rather finely worded section on the subject, dealing not just with apology for slavery but with real-time revenge for it. One can phrase the "First Do No Harm" injunction, as it applies to teaching, in another way: You must not bore young students, and you must not—may not—condescend to them. Who would dare argue, in the inculcation of geography or mathematics or French, that there are volatile elements to which the tender, rising generation ought not to be exposed? Who would dare insist that instruction in physics, for example, ought to be "clear and meaningful" to ignorant parents or to local "business representatives"?

Young Americans are at home with the concept of black holes and the imminence of cloning. The idea that human life may be a cosmic joke is well known to them. They understand that viruses and other microorganisms can be more powerful actors than dictators. The youngest of them share the wised-up humor of *The Simpsons* ("Springfield Youth Center: Building Unrealistic Hopes Since 1966"). But can they be allowed to consider their own history as anything other than a story of uplift, or, at worst, a chronicle of obstacles overcome? Not really, says David McCullough, whose *Why History?* is widely circulated by those hoping for a revival of the subject: "History shows us how to behave. History teaches, reinforces what we believe in, what we stand for, and what we ought to be willing to stand up for. History is—or should be— the bedrock of patriotism, not the chest-pounding kind of patriotism but the

real thing, love of country." And no, also, says Joy Hakim, a self-starting amateur historian who decided to write her own textbooks (marketed as *A History
of US*) and ignited a brief spark of hope by breaking the monopoly of so-called
educational publishing. Her introduction states:

> Learning about our country's history will make you understand what
> it means to be an American. And being American is a privilege. People
> all over the world wish that they, too, could be American. Why?
> Because we are a nation that is trying to be fair to all our citizens. . . .
> The more you study history, the more you will realize that all nations
> are not the same. Some are better than others. Does that seem like an
> unfair thing to say? Maybe, but we believe it.

The third sentence does express a factual truth. But the reason given in the
fifth sentence is mere propaganda, at least insofar as it distinguishes the
United States from Italy, say, or Iceland or Chile. In what other discipline may
a teacher so readily assume what has to be proved? Many critics have hailed
Hakim for contesting the relativists and the guilt-trip historians head-on. But
how different is her approach from the standard textbooks of the last generation, entitled as they were: *The American Pageant*, *The American Way*, *Land of Promise*,
American Adventures, *Life and Liberty*, *The Challenge of Freedom*, *Triumph of the American
Nation*? It was under this benign rule that the current crop of unlettered
teachers and distracted pupils was sown.

In many ways, the low-level argument between the safe traditionalists and
the ingratiating multiculturalists mirrors the dispute over the teaching of literature. And since history is literature, among other things, and since most
historians have been literary authors, the comparison may be an illuminating
one. In which class should students be asked to read Charles Dickens's *American
Notes*, for example (not that they are given this opportunity in either English
or history)? The chapter on slavery in that short book contains a list of small
ads from the contemporary Southern press in which masters would identify
runaway serfs: "Clog of iron on his right foot"; "several marks of lashing." It
electrifies every student to whom I have shown it, partly because Dickens is a
recognized "canonical" author and partly because of the stark immediacy of
the reportage.

Or consider the great Samuel Clemens. *Huckleberry Finn* is one of the few books that all American children are mandated to read: Jonathan Arac, in his brilliant new study of the teaching of Huck, is quite right to term it "hyper-canonical." And Twain is a figure in American history as well as in American letters. The only objectors to his presence in the schoolroom are mediocre or fanatical racial nationalists or "inclusivists," like Julius Lester or the Chicago-based Dr. John Wallace, who object to Twain's use—in or out of "context"—of the expression "nigger." An empty and formal "debate" on this has dragged on for decades and flares up every now and again to bore us. But what if Twain were taught as a whole? He served briefly as a Confederate soldier and wrote a hilarious and melancholy account, *The Private History of a Campaign That Failed.* He went on to make a fortune by publishing the memoirs of Ulysses Grant. He composed a caustic and brilliant report on the treatment of the Congolese by King Leopold of the Belgians. With William Dean Howells he led the Anti-Imperialist League, to oppose McKinley's and Roosevelt's pious and sanguinary war in the Philippines. Some of the pamphlets he wrote for the League can be set alongside those of Swift and Defoe for their sheer polemical artistry. In 1900 he had a public exchange with Winston Churchill in New York City, in which he attacked American support for the British war in South Africa and British support for the American war in Cuba. Does this count as history? Just try and find any reference to it, not just in textbooks but in more general histories and biographies. The Anti-Imperialist League has gone down the Orwellian memory hole, taking with it a great swirl of truly American passion and intellect, and the grand figure of Twain has become reduced—in part because he upended the vials of ridicule over the national tendency to religious and spiritual quackery, where he discerned what Tocqueville has missed and far anticipated Mencken—to that of a drawling, avuncular fabulist.

Ours is a society wedded to the idea that "Western" and "civilization" are cognate terms, ready to do battle for the heritage of fifth-century Athens as our ancestor, consecrated in its state architecture and statuary to the Graeco-Roman ideal—and there is not a whiff, not a hint, not a suspicion of the Socratic method in the way it instructs and elevates its young. *What Is History?* inquired E. H. Carr in a short book, published in 1961 and written well within the grasp of anyone with a reading age of sixteen, that appears on no reading list anywhere in the fifty states. Well, whatever it is (and Professor Carr had his own freely stated dogma), we know that it proceeds by means of irony, contradiction, and unintended consequence. Theodore Draper's entirely engrossing book *A Struggle for Power*, about the origins of the American Revolution, finds its locus in a "pamphlet war" in London in 1759. Anticipating the victorious outcome of the Seven Years' War, the British disputed about which French colony they should annex. The choice narrowed to Guadeloupe, rich in spices, and Canada, rich in space. The acquisition of Guadeloupe would complete British control of the Caribbean basin, while Canada would offer a great potential market for future British manufactures. Mercantile factions and lobbies formed on both sides of the question, and you can look up their exchanges and read them in plain English. The pro-Canada forces were better organized and financed. But the pro-Guadeloupe lobby made a telling point on the eve of its defeat. If we take Canada, it argued in a finely written polemic, then the ambitious American colonists will no longer require our protection from France. Indeed, they already manifest the stirrings of an independence movement . . . Within two decades of this debate, the Tory loyalists of His Majesty King George (Part III) were scuttling to sanctuary over the Canadian border. I have taught Draper's book in several classrooms and have had the pleasure of watching even the most indifferent students undergo the kindling of an interest: "What if the British had plumped for Guadeloupe? Would that have meant no Declaration of Independence?" "Not necessarily, but the context and conditions would have been different. Next week I want someone to tell us why the word 'czar' is an odd one to employ in today's American social engineering."

The idea of trying to teach the whole story, not just "warts and all" but as an *inquiry* or an argument, has been well advocated by Dr. James Loewen, a veteran lecturer in history at university level and the author of *Lies My Teacher Told Me: Everything Your American History Textbook Got Wrong*. Testifying to the thirst for honest and well-written discussion of history, this 1995 book has a quarter-million copies currently in print. In Loewen's opinion, the present teaching of history by rote is neither a science nor an art and has manifestly and confessedly, and for all reasonable purposes also completely, failed. There is no chance of amassing, as Bishop Stubbs once fondly hoped, a true bill of facts to be memorized. Von Ranke's famous dictum just to show "how it really was" represents a noble but impossible aspiration.

Loewen once won a benchmark case, beautifully entitled Loewen et al. v. Turnipseed et al., against the crass censorship of schoolbooks in Mississippi. But unlike Joy Hakim, whose verve he admires, he does not recommend the teaching of history as any kind of inspiration. Instead, he proposes that students be given two contrasting texts: Howard Zinn's *A People's History of the United States*, for instance, as against Clarence B. Carson's *A Basic History of the United States*, published by the conservative American Textbook Committee in Alabama in 1986. When there is a basic grasp of narrative and evolution, and a corresponding grasp of the idea of differing views of the same story, it will become apt to consider theories and interpretations.

This is how the Greeks, more honored by invocation than by emulation, conceived the theory and practice of teaching by dialectics. What was the influence of Pericles' funeral oration on the Gettysburg Address? This engrossing question, open to any mind of average ability, cannot even be asked if, as was recently discovered, the majority of America's schoolchildren don't know in which century the Civil War was fought. But if an appreciation of history as a continuous argument, and not a dull Whiggish series of "problems resolved," can be instilled, then a student entering college might be ready to attempt the pleasurable exercises of a reasonably trained mind. False and emptily moralistic trails, such as "Are We Too Eurocentric?" or "Was Columbus Ecologically Friendly?" can be abandoned in favor of the real thing. Why did Basil Davidson have to refute Hegel in order to show that Africa had a history? Was Bertrand Russell right in saying that the disappearance of North American Indians was no tragedy? And why was he banned from teaching in the United States? Had Russell read Bartolomé de Las Casas, first historian of the Americas, who doubted that the "discovery" had been a good thing? Why did the first historian of the Americas have a Spanish name? Why do New Yorkers no longer speak Dutch, and who proposed that the official language of the United States be German? Was the Civil War really fought to free the slaves? Why are Woodrow Wilson's "Fourteen Points" unthinkable without Lenin's dissolution of the Constituent Assembly? Was the Great Depression caused by too little government intervention or too much? Why is the largest military base in Cuba an American one? Why is it possible to swim from America to Russia?

Each of these questions admits of several answers, many of them equally "valid." In such cases, what matters is how you think and not what you think. E. D. Hirsch Jr. and other scholars of cultural literacy have already been solidly vindicated in their view that fresh knowledge builds on existing knowledge. It remains to apply this realization to the most despoiled and neglected subject in the curriculum. The task cannot be left to the "community of scholars"—and what an antique ring that phrase has now acquired— because they have mostly elected to desert the field or to clutter it with the wrappers of comfort food.

Those who care about cultural literacy are chiefly volunteers, and they are already hard-pressed on numerous fronts. But the potential "pool" of volunteers for a struggle to reinstate historical discourse is quite substantial. What needs to be combated is the idea, so often and so worthily expressed—and so stultifying—that "light" is to be preferred to "heat." Heat, as can be learned in other classrooms, is the only possible source of light. History must become a field of ardent contestation and not another arid patch of middle ground. If properly joined, this battle would also and of itself lead to more confident and thoughtful citizens, whose formation requires more than a mixture of Crispus Attucks, Betsy Ross, and Emma Lazarus. Pluralism is a means as well as an end. "Such a lot of things seem to me such rot," says a young girl in one of Agatha Christie's mysteries. "History, for instance. Why, it's quite different out of different books!" To this her mentor, wise in the ways of the world, replies: "That is its real interest." Confronted by the philistine verdicts of "bunk" and "rot," and the wasteland created by the attempts at an authorized version, we can, in the time where Hawking and Heisenberg are commonplaces, at least borrow the last phrase of Professor E. H. Carr's Trevelyan Lecture: "I shall look out on a world in tumult and a world in travail, and shall answer in the well-worn words of a great scientist: 'And yet—it moves.' "

HARPER'S MAGAZINE,
JUNE 1999

A HUNDRED YEARS OF MUGGERY

A review of *MALCOLM MUGGERIDGE: A BIOGRAPHY*
by Gregory Wolfe

T here are numberless ways in which the faithful may taunt, or perhaps I should better say tease, the unbeliever. One such tactic—and for my money the most irritating—is to say that God believes in you, even if you can't return the compliment. Another is to contrast the modest simplicity of belief with the contortions of the malcontent intellectual. "Don't mind me," says the humble friar or devoted nun, brushing past on some modest errand of altruism. "I'm just doing the Lord's work."

Those of us who experience difficulty in recognizing this as genuine humility always used to have a fine old time at the expense of Malcolm Muggeridge, the centennial of whose birth in 1903 has caused a small flurry of notice this year, thirteen years after his death in 1990. Here was a man ever-ready to uncork a sermon about the fallen state of the species and the pathetic vanity of our earthly desires—all while he was notorious as an apostle of carnality and a ringmaster at the circus of his own self-promotion. Every personality type in the eternal argument over divinity is to be discerned in John Bunyan's *Pilgrim's Progress,* that founding text of Protestant fundamentalism. And it was there in *Pilgrim's Progress*—winding between Vanity Fair and Doubting Castle, encountering the likes of "Great-Heart," "Mr. Standfast," and "Little-Faith"—that one seemed to have the best chance to capture the lineaments of Muggeridge. He was Mr. Worldly Wiseman.

A difference between American and British audiences is that Americans tend to know Muggeridge by his writing, while the British associate him with the early days of television celebrity. When I was young in the 1960s, Muggeridge seemed to be ubiquitous, on game shows and quiz-marathons no less than on brow-furrowing panels about serious matters. The man appeared to have no unaired thoughts.

An excellent mimic would be required to do an impression of his face, which resembled that of a vain old turtle. But almost anyone could have a shot at imitating his voice, with its commingled bray and bleat. My own first appearance on the tube was to debate apartheid as a guest on his Sunday-evening chat-show, portentously called *The Question Why.* (I forget if it had a question mark or not. Perhaps it was like the title of Sidney and Beatrice Webb's apologia for Stalinism: *Soviet Communism—A New Civilization,* which had a question mark for its first edition and none for the second.)

Muggeridge was married to Beatrice Webb's niece, Kitty, and had been brought up in that area of the British Left that was bounded by the Fabian Society, the *New Statesman,* the London School of Economics, and Bloomsbury more generally. The tone-setters of this melioristic and high-minded environment placed a lot of faith in social action for the improvement of health, housing, and the rights of labor. But they also stressed the improveability of human nature, this last to be attained by more sexual and educational freedom. In those days, the word "crusade" was still acceptable, and the great anthem of the movement was William Blake's "Jerusalem": "I will not cease from Mental Fight, / Nor shall my Sword sleep in my hand / Till we have built Jerusalem / In England's green & pleasant Land."

It's easy to mock this tradition, though it has some great achievements still standing to its credit. But one would not wish to sneer at a man like Henry Thomas Muggeridge, Malcolm's father, who devoted a good life to the socialist cause. One of the several merits of the recently reprinted biography *Malcolm Muggeridge* is that its author understands the duality of motive. He shows us a young Muggeridge who became impatient with his father's do-good schemes and with the heresy of the perfectibility of man. Yet Wolfe also describes a rather selfish and unappealing figure, embarrassed by his family's dowdiness and desiring to be more dashing and fashionable and renowned.

No serious person is without contradictions. The test lies in the willingness or ability to recognize and confront them. Wolfe's biography suggests that

Muggeridge was sometimes opaque to himself and sometimes not. But the book is clear on one thing. Those of us who had thought that the man came to religion only late in life, after years of exhausting debauchery, were quite mistaken. I once contributed some doggerel to the *New Statesman,* expressing the received opinion about Muggeridge: "In my youth, quoth the sage, as he tossed his grey locks, / I behaved just as any young pup. / But now I am old I appear on the box— / And tell others to give it all up."

The time has come to take back those lines. Wolfe establishes that Muggeridge had a sort of epiphany as a very young man, being overwhelmed by a rural sunset which "in its all-embracing beauty conveyed a oneness" and deciding "that to identify oneself with the spirit animating it and giving it meaning, contained the promise of ecstasy." This trope recurs in an undergraduate study that Muggeridge did at Cambridge, based on the "Evidences of Christianity" by the early-nineteenth-century natural philosopher William Paley. The result may be no more than the Argument from Design writ large, but there's no reason to doubt Muggeridge's sincerity about it.

Continuing this rather soft-centered, impressionable attitude to the Numinous, Muggeridge made the voyage to India that so many progressive-minded young Englishmen undertook in those days, and he was duly impressed with the saintliness and simplicity of Gandhi. But paradox intrudes itself here at once. When Muggeridge was not being awed by spiritual simplicity, he was being attracted by religious complexity. He wrote about his "love" for "the inconsistencies of Christianity" and his belief that "faith must be based on doubt." He was still a long way from Roman Catholicism, but his quest for the "inclusive"—for a reconciliation between the sacred and the profane, as well as between the simple and the difficult—already involved catholicity.

Perhaps, like St. Augustine, he didn't want full acceptance quite yet or, knowing himself pursued by the Hound of Heaven, was prepared to give it time to catch him. Meanwhile he had a certain toughness and curiosity to keep him going. He saw plainly that the British day in India was waning (he was ahead of his time in this respect), and he was soon to see through communism, the grand illusion of the twentieth century. Enlisting at the *Manchester Guardian,* another flagship of the English bien-pensant class, he was quick to realize that its lofty policies masked an institutional hypocrisy about, among other things, the true source of the newspaper's income. Satirizing this in his first novel, *Picture Palace,* he made the valuable discovery that there is no intolerance like liberal intolerance. (The paper's owners took harsh legal steps to ensure that the novel was suppressed.) Thus, when he became the *Guardian*'s correspondent in Moscow in 1932, he was riper than perhaps he understood for a crisis of belief.

A. J. P. Taylor told him as he was embarking, "If the Russians do not come up to your expectations, don't take it out on them." Muggeridge's reply is worth quoting: "No, no. It will be Utopia. I must see the Ideal even if I am unworthy of it." This Mosaic echo is evidence that Muggeridge already had a religious cast of mind. Of course, it was not only the Left in those days that believed in the virtues of a planned economy and hungered for an alternative to post-Versailles chaos and misery. But the disillusionment in Muggeridge's case was on a scale commensurate to the original fantasy. Stalin's Russia hadn't just fallen short of the ideal; it had become a plain Hell for the body and the mind. His reports from the Ukraine in the year of the famine stand comparison with Andre Gidé's *Retour de l'URSS* and Eugene Lyons's *Assignment in Utopia* as irrefutable evidence of a new barbarism. The ancillary lesson he drew, about the gullibility and credulity of Western intellectuals, was to last Muggeridge the rest of his life.

Muggeridge's sheet isn't as snow-white, however, as some of his admirers like to believe. A previous and more hagiographic biography, written by Richard Ingrams, mentions that in his dotage Muggeridge became prey to anti-Semitic outbursts and paranoid suspicions. I had thought that this late lapse was the extent of it, but Wolfe bluntly points out Muggeridge's lifelong susceptibility to this most toxic of all prejudices. And in *Winter in Moscow,* a 1934 novel that dwells on the most lurid aspects of Judeo-Bolshevism, he gave full vent to his dislike. Some subsequent exposure to Nazi ideology and practice qualified, but did not entirely dispel, this disfiguring element.

While he was thus engaged in becoming a failed novelist and a brilliant journalist (his book *The Thirties* remains a classic snapshot of what his friend Claud Cockburn called "The Devil's Decade") and managing to turn up always in the right place at the right time, his private life was a cauldron of adultery, misery, and penury. He fought incessantly with Kitty, whom he may not have forgiven for his repeated betrayals of her, and she requited this by openly bearing another man's son. (The boy was to become in some ways Muggeridge's favorite child.)

All the while, Muggeridge could not shed the fear that he was a phony and a failure. Enlisting in British Intelligence in World War II was a near-faultless decision on his part, because it gave him the excuse to leave home and it caught him up in a world where things were deceptive and dishonest by definition. From this came his long friendship with Graham Greene. From this, also, came the moment of despair in which he attempted suicide.

Muggeridge had actually been rather a good British agent in the Portuguese African port of Lourenço Marques, hampering the German spies at every turn and even helping to trap and capture a U-boat. But he felt himself a hollow poseur and one night swam out to sea with the intention of drowning. He changed his mind only at the very last minute. Even on this grave matter, he could not quite achieve authenticity. At the time, he passed off the fiasco as an attempt to baffle the local Nazis, and he stuck to this version for many years before confessing in his autobiography that he had sincerely meant to take his own life but had undergone yet another epiphany when he saw the lights of the shore. (I cannot resist adding that he was challenged to come up with a true account only because David Irving had unearthed the cover story while making one of his dark trawls through the German archives.)

All this invites the question: Was Muggeridge a "fool for God," or just a fool? For the first four or even five decades of his life, he could scarcely tell his alienation from his anomie. Despite the steadying influence of his old Cambridge companion Alec Vidler, an unassuming priest who really did have a vocation, Muggeridge rolled and pitched from job to job, home to home, and mistress to mistress. Claud Cockburn, who despite their vast quarrel over communism really admired Muggeridge for his qualities as a friend, made an excellent diagnosis when he told him, "With you, the tendency to become bored has the quality of a vice." Kingsley Amis once told me of a night of impossible squalor and depression, when a drunken Muggeridge proposed that both men try and take advantage, seriatim, of an equally sozzled Sonia

Orwell. This joyless, wretched orgy was proposed merely in order that an already dispirited evening should not end.

It seemed at one stage that his appointment to the editorial chair at *Punch* would give Muggeridge something solid to do. The venerable Victorian weekly had a big circulation but a flickering pulse; it urgently required what P. G. Wodehouse would have called snap and vim. The appointment of Anthony Powell as literary editor and Claud Cockburn as roving scribbler at the magazine resulted in two excellent pen-portraits of Muggeridge, who might have become the English Harold Ross.

Cockburn wrote, "I began to have the feeling that with this fiercely gentle, chivalrously ungentlemanly man on the far side of the grandiose editorial desk, jerking and flashing his eyes, from time to time cackling out a cacophony of furiously raucous expressions like a sailor's parrot loose in the Mission Hall, something new and special in the way of clowning and satire might yet be made of this ancient publication."

Powell, not atypically somewhat more circuitous, added:

In the beginning . . . was the sceptical wit mocking all, and the wit was with Muggeridge and the wit was Muggeridge. This first Muggeridge— never wholly exorcised but undergoing long terms of banishment from the Celestial City of his personality—would sometimes support, some- times obstruct, what then seemed his sole fellow, Second Muggeridge.

Second Muggeridge, serious, ambitious, domestic, . . . with a strain of Lawrentian mysticism, . . . had a spell-weaving strain and violent political or moral animosities (animosity rather than allegiance being essential expression of Second Muggeridge's teachings), both forms of vituperation in the main aimed at winning a preponderant influence in public affairs. . . .

In due course, . . . Third Muggeridge became manifest at full strength, hot-gospelling, near-messianic, promulgating an ineluctable choice between Salvation and Perdition. He who was not with Third Muggeridge was against him, including First and Second Muggeridge. In this conflict without quarter First Muggeridge, who treated life as a jest—now so to speak a thief crucified between two Christs—came off worst.

That last arresting image, of a uniquely Muggeridgian Golgotha, illuminates the way in which Cockburn and Powell both naturally employed the image of the clown or the jester. As it happens, this was Muggeridge's own favorite point of comparison between religion and Shakespeare—for both afforded special roles to the "rough and tumble acrobat, horseplay jester for God": religion with St. Francis of Assisi and Shakespeare with King Lear's only sincere and simple friend. Occasionally, and despite his reputation for hard-headedness about totalitarianism, Muggeridge would enact the role of the näif without apparently volunteering for it. He described the KGB's most ruthless agent, his former acquaintance Kim Philby, as "a boy scout who had lost his way." And, during much of World War II, he preferred to think of the Nazis as absurd and pitiable rather than wicked.

Having briefly been banned by the BBC for a 1955 *New Statesman* attack he wrote on the soap-opera culture of the British royal family—a polemic that now seems astonishingly mild—and having drifted morosely away from the *Punch* editorial chair as if to vindicate Cockburn's judgment, Muggeridge was at last to find his milieu.

Again, he was drawn compulsively to that which he found loathsome. Television, he could plainly see, would be the death of literacy and the handmaid of instant gratification. It would instill cheap and commercial values and incite the nastiest forms of populism. He fell for it like a ton of bricks. He wallowed exuberantly in its corruption. He was a natural. He was perfectly well aware, as his diaries show, that he was expending his spirit in a waste of shame. But he enjoyed it and excelled at it, and he may have hoped to turn the greatest weapon of crass modernity against itself.

Sex was the selling point, overtly and subliminally, of the television "mass-cult." (Did Muggeridge ever read or encounter Dwight Macdonald?) Very well, then, a guru would appear on the seductive screen and warn that sex was ultimately a disappointment. Ridicule was the predictable harvest for this, of course, and Muggeridge reaped it in heaping measure. I think it's clear that he enjoyed the obloquy and felt that he was earning it, so to speak, vicariously. He plodded on with a series of well-made television documentaries, which I personally find intolerably mawkish but which gradually won him a sort of underdog's respect. Gnarled pilgrims at Lourdes, simple fisherfolk on the shores of Galilee, mitered bishops with the common touch. . . . And then the jewel in the crown. In a 1969 film entitled *Something Beautiful for God,* he launched the persona that we all came to know as Mother Teresa.

In a near-perfect return-serve to the hedonism of the day, he made a star out of a woman who scorned pelf and pleasure. Wolfe's book gives this chapter fairly straight. I have a minor quarrel to register with a biographer who is in general punctiliously honest. Wolfe has obviously read the testimony of Ken Macmillan, Muggeridge's ultra-professional cameraman, but he chooses to elide it, and thus lets stand the claim, directly rebutted by Macmillan, that the filming of the documentary involved a miracle, manifesting allegedly divine light around the figure of Mother Teresa. The simple explanation involves a Kodak film especially designed for crepuscular scenes. (Simplicity isn't always to be despised, as I may have hinted.)

Wolfe's *Malcolm Muggeridge* begins with a pledge. "The temptation," the biographer writes, "is to play Boswell to Malcolm's Johnson, concentrating on his innumerable witty retorts, bons mots, and other examples of his dazzling sense of humor. This is a temptation that I have resisted." He keeps that rather forbidding promise throughout, and I'd say that the world of the devastating riposte was not Wolfe's natural territory in any case. "Urbane and witty," he writes about the magazine *Night and Day,* which was brought low by a lawsuit from Shirley Temple against Graham Greene, "it could also be acerbic and satirical. Ironically, this satirical sharpness was to hasten its downfall." The contrasts here are non-contrasting, and the irony is no irony at all. Having met the Muggeridges in Canada, Wolfe records in a deadpan fashion that "after partaking of the simple dinner that was their regular fare . . . ," and one wants to say, yes, well, that's quite enough about that.

Wolfe makes some errors that may be simple clumsiness: George Orwell underwent no "disillusionment" with communism, in which he had never believed. But other errors are not stylistic. I'll eat my shoes if Claud Cockburn was ever even for a moment a religious "seeker." Still, the cumulative effect of Wolfe's narrative in *Malcolm Muggeridge* is so serious and so genuine that the biography ultimately forces a reconsideration of its subject.

Muggeridge was not the C. S. Lewis of his time, any more than he was the Samuel Johnson. Just as his actual witticisms were few (is there really a Muggeridge epigram or aphorism for the ages?), so his grasp of theology was slight. But he was the first to admit the latter deficiency, and not even Wolfe will defend his *Confessions of a Twentieth-Century Pilgrim.* One respects Muggeridge, rather, for his imperfections and contradictions and shortcomings, and for his readiness to be boring rather than fascinating on questions that he believed to be important.

In his later years, Muggeridge formed alliances with moralistic authoritarians like Mary Whitehouse of Moral Re-Armament, who were not so much foolish as plain sinister. (His other colleague, the late Lord Longford, was a fool for God, all right, and a tremendous fool in his own right, but would never have harmed so much as a fly.) And these alliances—together with his own behavior—left Muggeridge easy to make sport of, as long as you could be convinced that there was nothing meretricious about the various shallow theories of "liberation" that were near-regnant at the time.

Most impressive to me is the anti-climax of his reception into the Church of Rome very late in life. This did not give Muggeridge the peace that he had expected (Ingrams's biography is better on this than Wolfe's), and he may have vaguely understood that it wasn't really peace he had been desiring. He was a fair example of restlessness and unease—of what has been called divine discontent. There certainly remain moments when Muggeridge was entirely Mr. Worldly Wiseman. But to read his biography is to see there are other moments in his turbulent life when he was temporarily promoted in Bunyan's cast of characters and could stand in for Mr. Valiant-For-Truth.

THE WEEKLY STANDARD,
MAY 5, 2003

UNFAIRENHEIT 9/11:
THE LIES OF MICHAEL MOORE

O ne of the many problems with the American left, and indeed *of* the American left, has been its image and self-image as something rather too solemn, mirthless, herbivorous, dull, monochrome, righteous, and boring. How many times, in my old days at *The Nation* magazine, did I hear wistful and semienvious ruminations? Where was the radical *Firing Line* show? Who will be our Rush Limbaugh? I used privately to hope that the emphasis, if the comrades ever got around to it, would be on the first of those and not the second. But the meetings themselves were so mind-numbing and lugubrious that I thought the danger of success on either front was infinitely slight.

Nonetheless, it seems that an answer to this long-felt need is finally beginning to emerge. I exempt Al Franken's unintentionally funny Air America network, to which I gave a couple of interviews in its early days. There, one could hear the reassuring noise of collapsing scenery and tripped-over wires and be reminded once again that correct politics and smooth media presentation are not even distant cousins. With Michael Moore's *Fahrenheit 9/11*, however, an entirely new note has been struck. Here we glimpse a possible fusion between the turgid routines of MoveOn.org and the filmic standards, if not exactly the filmic skills, of Sergei Eisenstein or Leni Riefenstahl.

To describe this film as dishonest and demagogic would almost be to promote those terms to the level of respectability. To describe this film as a piece of crap would be to run the risk of a discourse that would never again rise above the excremental. To describe it as an exercise in facile crowd-pleasing would be too obvious. *Fahrenheit 9/11* is a sinister exercise in moral frivolity, crudely disguised as an exercise in seriousness. It is also a spectacle of abject political cowardice masking itself as a demonstration of "dissenting" bravery.

In late 2002, almost a year after the Al Qaeda assault on American society, I had an onstage debate with Michael Moore at the Telluride Film Festival. In the course of this exchange, he stated his view that Osama bin Laden should be considered innocent until proven guilty. This was, he said, the American way. The intervention in Afghanistan, he maintained, had been at least to that extent unjustified. Something—I cannot guess what, since we knew as much then as we do now—has since apparently persuaded Moore that Osama bin Laden is as guilty as hell. Indeed, Osama is suddenly so guilty and so all-powerful that any other discussion of any other topic is a dangerous "distraction" from the fight against him. I believe that I understand the convenience of this late conversion.

Fahrenheit 9/11 makes the following points about bin Laden and about Afghanistan, and makes them in this order:

1) The bin Laden family (if not *exactly* Osama himself) had a close if convoluted business relationship with the Bush family, through the Carlyle Group.

2) Saudi capital in general is a very large element of foreign investment in the United States.

3) The Unocal company in Texas had been willing to discuss a gas pipeline across Afghanistan with the Taliban, as had other vested interests.

4) The Bush administration sent far too *few* ground troops to Afghanistan and thus allowed far too many Taliban and Al Qaeda members to escape.

5) The Afghan government, in supporting the coalition in Iraq, was purely risible in that its non-army was purely American.

6) The American lives lost in Afghanistan have been wasted. (This I

divine from the fact that this supposedly "antiwar" film is dedicated ruefully to all those killed there, as well as in Iraq.)

It must be evident to anyone, despite the rapid-fire way in which Moore's direction eases the audience hastily past the contradictions, that these discrepant scatter shots do not cohere at any point. Either the Saudis run U.S. policy (through family ties or overwhelming economic interest), or they do not. As allies and patrons of the Taliban regime, they either opposed Bush's removal of it, or they did not. (They opposed the removal, all right: They wouldn't even let Tony Blair land his own plane on their soil at the time of the operation.) Either we sent too many troops, or were wrong to send any at all—the latter was Moore's view as late as 2002—or we sent too few. If we were going to make sure no Taliban or Al Qaeda forces survived or escaped, we would have had to be more ruthless than I suspect that Mr. Moore is really recommending. And these are simply observations on what is "in" the film. If we turn to the facts that are deliberately left out, we discover that there is an emerging Afghan army, that the country is now a joint NATO responsibility and thus under the protection of the broadest military alliance in history, that it has a new constitution and is preparing against hellish odds to hold a general election, and that more than three million of its former refugees have opted to return. I don't think a pipeline is being constructed yet, not that Afghanistan couldn't do with a pipeline. But a highway from Kabul to Kandahar—an insurance against warlordism and a condition of nation-building—is nearing completion with infinite labor and risk. We also discover that the parties of the Afghan secular left—like the parties of the Iraqi secular left—are strongly in favor of the regime change. But this is not the sort of irony in which Moore chooses to deal.

He prefers leaden sarcasm to irony and, indeed, may not appreciate the distinction. In a long and paranoid (and tedious) section at the opening of the film, he makes heavy innuendoes about the flights that took members of the bin Laden family out of the country after Sept. 11. I banged on about this myself at the time and wrote a *Nation* column drawing attention to the groveling Larry King interview with the insufferable Prince Bandar, which Moore excerpts. However, recent developments have not been kind to our Mike. In the interval between Moore's triumph at Cannes and the release of the film in the United States, the 9/11 commission has found nothing to complain of in the timing or arrangement of the flights. And Richard Clarke, Bush's former chief of counterterrorism, has come forward to say that he, and he alone, took the responsibility for authorizing those Saudi departures. This might not matter so much to the ethos of *Fahrenheit 9/11*, except that—as you might expect—Clarke is presented throughout as the brow-furrowed ethical hero of the entire post-9/11 moment. And it does not seem very likely that, in his open admission about the bin Laden family evacuation, Clarke is taking a fall, or a spear in the chest, for the Bush administration. So, that's another bust for this windy and bloated cinematic "key to all mythologies."

A film that bases itself on a big lie and a big misrepresentation can only sustain itself by a dizzying succession of smaller falsehoods, beefed up by wilder and (if possible) yet more contradictory claims. President Bush is accused of taking too many lazy vacations. (What *is* that about, by the way? Isn't he supposed to be an unceasing planner for future aggressive wars?) But the shot of him "relaxing at Camp David" shows him side by side with Tony Blair. I say "shows," even though this photograph is on-screen so briefly that if you sneeze or blink, you won't recognize the other figure. A meeting with the prime minister of the United Kingdom, or at least with this prime minister, is not a goof-off.

The president is also captured in a well-worn TV news clip, on a golf course, making a boilerplate response to a question on terrorism and then asking the reporters to watch his drive. Well, that's what you get if you catch the president on a golf course. If Eisenhower had done this, as he often did, it would have been presented as calm statesmanship. If Clinton had done it, as he often did, it would have shown his charm. More interesting is the moment where Bush is shown frozen on his chair at the infant school in Florida, looking stunned and useless for seven whole minutes after the news of the second plane on 9/11. Many are those who say that he should have leaped from his stool, adopted a Russell Crowe stance, and gone to work. I could even wish that myself. But if he had done any such thing then (as he did with his "Let's roll" and "dead or alive" remarks a month later), half the Michael Moore community would now be calling him a man who went to war on a hectic, crazed impulse. The other half would be saying what they already say—that he knew the attack was coming, was using it to cement himself in power, and couldn't wait to get on with his coup. This is the line taken by Gore Vidal and by a scandalous recent book that also revives the charge of FDR's collusion over Pearl Harbor. At least Moore's film should put the shameful purveyors of that last theory back in their paranoid box.

But it won't because it encourages their half-baked fantasies in so many other ways. We are introduced to Iraq, "a sovereign nation." (In fact, Iraq's "sovereignty" was heavily qualified by international sanctions, however questionable, which reflected its noncompliance with important UN resolutions.) In this peaceable kingdom, according to Moore's flabbergasting choice of film shots, children are flying little kites, shoppers are smiling in the sunshine, and the gentle rhythms of life are undisturbed. Then—wham! From the night sky come the terror weapons of American imperialism. Watching the clips Moore uses, and recalling them well, I can recognize various Saddam palaces and military and police centers getting the treatment. But these sites are not identified as such. In fact, I don't think Al Jazeera would, on a bad day, have transmitted anything so utterly propagandistic. You would also be led to think that the term "civilian casualty" had not even been in the Iraqi vocabulary until March 2003. I remember asking Moore at Telluride if he was or was not a pacifist. He would not give a straight answer then, and he doesn't now, either. I'll just say that the "insurgent" side is presented in this film as justifiably outraged, whereas the thirty-year record of Baathist war crimes and repression and aggression is not mentioned once. (Actually, that's not quite right. It is briefly mentioned but only, and smarmily, because of the bad period when Washington preferred Saddam to the likewise unmentioned Ayatollah Khomeini.)

That this—his pro-American moment—was the worst Moore could possibly say of Saddam's depravity is further suggested by some astonishing falsifications. Moore asserts that Iraq under Saddam had never attacked or killed or even threatened (his words) any American. I never quite know whether Moore is as ignorant as he looks, or even if that would be humanly possible. Baghdad was for years the official, undisguised home address of Abu Nidal, then the most-wanted gangster in the world, who had been sentenced to death even by the PLO and had blown up airports in Vienna and Rome. Baghdad was the safe house for the man whose "operation" murdered Leon Klinghoffer. Saddam boasted publicly of his financial sponsorship of suicide bombers in Israel. (Quite a few Americans of all denominations walk the streets of Jerusalem.) In 1991, a large number of Western hostages were taken by the hideous Iraqi invasion of Kuwait and held in terrible conditions for a long time. After that same invasion was repelled—Saddam having killed quite a few Americans and Egyptians and Syrians and Brits in the meantime and having threatened to kill many more—the Iraqi secret police were caught trying to murder former President Bush during his visit to Kuwait. Never mind whether his son should take that personally. (Though why should he not?) Should you and I not resent any foreign dictatorship that attempts to kill one of our retired chief executives? (President Clinton certainly took it that way: He ordered the destruction by cruise missiles of the Baathist "security" headquarters.) Iraqi forces fired, *every day, for ten years*, on the aircraft that patrolled the no-fly zones and staved off further genocide in the north and south of the country. In 1993, a certain Mr. Yasin helped mix the chemicals for the bomb at the World Trade Center and then skipped to Iraq, where he remained a guest of the state until the overthrow of Saddam. In 2001, Saddam's regime was the only one in the region that openly celebrated the attacks on New York and Washington and described them as just the beginning of a larger revenge. Its official media regularly spewed out a stream of anti-Semitic incitement. I think one might describe that as "threatening," even if one was narrow enough to think that anti-Semitism only menaces Jews. And it was *after*, and not before, the 9/11 attacks that Abu Mussab al-Zarqawi moved from Afghanistan to Baghdad and began to plan his now very open and lethal design for a holy and ethnic civil war. On Dec. 1, 2003, the *New York Times* reported—and the David Kay report had established—that Saddam had been secretly negotiating with the "Dear Leader" Kim Jong-il in a series of secret meetings in Syria, as late as the spring of 2003, to buy a North Korean missile system, and missile-production system, right off the shelf. (This attempt was not uncovered until after the fall of Baghdad, the coalition's presence having meanwhile put an end to the negotiations.)

Thus, in spite of the film's loaded bias against the work of the mind, you can grasp even while watching it that Michael Moore has just said, in so many words, the one thing that no reflective or informed person can possibly believe: that Saddam Hussein was no problem. No problem *at all*. Now look again at the facts I have cited above. If these things had been allowed to happen under any other administration, you can be sure that Moore and others would now glibly be accusing the president of ignoring, or of having ignored, some fairly unmistakable "warnings."

The same "let's have it both ways" opportunism infects his treatment of another very serious subject, namely domestic counterterrorist policy. From being accused of overlooking too many warnings—not exactly an original point—the administration is now lavishly taunted for issuing too many. (Would there not have been "fear" if the harbingers of 9/11 had been taken seriously?) We are shown some American civilians who have had absurd encounters with idiotic "security" staff. (Have you ever met anyone who can't tell such a story?) Then we are immediately shown underfunded police departments that don't have the means or the manpower to do any stop-and-search: a power suddenly demanded by Moore on their behalf that we know by definition would at least lead to some ridiculous interrogations. Finally, Moore complains that there isn't *enough* intrusion and confiscation at airports and says that it is appalling that every air traveler is not forcibly relieved of all matches and lighters. (Cue mood music for sinister influence of Big Tobacco.) So—he wants even more pocket-rummaging by airport officials? Uh, no, not exactly. But by this stage, who's counting? Moore is having it three ways and asserting everything and nothing. Again—simply not serious.

Circling back to where we began, why did Moore's evil Saudis not join "the Coalition of the Willing"? Why instead did they force the United States to switch its regional military headquarters to Qatar? If the Bush family and the al-Saud dynasty live in each other's pockets, as is alleged in a sort of vulgar sub-Brechtian scene with Arab headdresses replacing top hats, then how come the most reactionary regime in the region has been powerless to stop Bush from demolishing its clone in Kabul and its buffer regime in Baghdad? The Saudis hate, as they did in 1991, the idea that Iraq's recuperated oil industry might challenge their near-monopoly. They fear the liberation of the Shiite Muslims they so despise. To make these elementary points is to collapse the whole pathetic edifice of the film's "theory." Perhaps Moore prefers the pro-Saudi Kissinger/Scowcroft plan for the Middle East, where stability trumps every other consideration and where one dare not upset the local house of cards, or killing-field of Kurds? This would be a strange position for a purported radical. Then again, perhaps he does not take this conservative line because his real pitch is not to any audience member with a serious interest in foreign policy. It is to the provincial isolationist.

I have already said that Moore's film has the staunch courage to mock Bush for his verbal infelicity. Yet it's much, much braver than that. From *Fahrenheit 9/11* you can glean even more astounding and hidden disclosures, such as the capitalist nature of American society, the existence of Eisenhower's "military-industrial complex," and the use of "spin" in the presentation of our politicians. It's high time someone had the nerve to point this out. There's more. Poor people often volunteer to join the army, and some of them are duskier than others. Betcha didn't know that. Back in Flint, Mich., Moore feels on safe ground. There are no martyred rabbits this time. Instead, it's the poor and black who shoulder the packs and rifles and march away. I won't dwell on the fact that black Americans have fought for almost a century and a half, from insisting on their right to join the U.S. Army and fight in the Civil War to the right to have a desegregated Army that set the pace for post-1945 civil rights. I'll merely ask this: In the film, Moore says loudly and repeatedly *that not enough* troops were sent to garrison Afghanistan and Iraq. (This is now a favorite cleverness of those who were, in the first place, against sending any soldiers at all.) Well, where does he think those needful heroes and heroines would have come from? Does he favor a draft—the most statist and oppressive solution? Does he think that only hapless and gullible proles sign up for the Marines? Does he think—as he seems to suggest—that parents can "send" their children, as he stupidly asks elected members of Congress to do? Would he have abandoned Gettysburg because the Union allowed civilians to pay proxies to serve in their place? Would he have supported the antidraft (and very antiblack) riots against Lincoln in New York? After a point, one realizes that it's a waste of time asking him questions of this sort. It would be too much like taking him seriously. He'll just try anything once and see if it floats or flies or gets a cheer.

Indeed, Moore's affected and ostentatious concern for black America is one of the most suspect ingredients of his pitch package. In a recent interview, he yelled that if the hijacked civilians of 9/11 had been black, they would have fought back, unlike the stupid and presumably cowardly white men and women (and children). Never mind for now how many black passengers were on those planes—we happen to know what Moore does not care to mention:

that Todd Beamer and a few of his co-passengers, shouting "Let's roll," rammed the hijackers with a trolley, fought them tooth and nail, and helped bring down a United Airlines plane, in Pennsylvania, that was speeding toward either the White House or the Capitol. There are no words for real, impromptu bravery like that, which helped save our republic from worse than actually befell. The Pennsylvania drama also reminds one of the self-evident fact that this war is not fought only "overseas" or in uniform, but is being brought to our cities. Yet Moore is a silly and shady man who does not recognize courage of any sort even when he sees it because he cannot summon it in himself. To him, easy applause, in front of credulous audiences, is everything.

Moore has announced that he won't even appear on TV shows where he might face hostile questioning. I notice from the *New York Times* of June 20 that he has pompously established a rapid response team, and a fact-checking staff, and some tough lawyers, to bulwark himself against attack. He'll sue, Moore says, if anyone insults him or his pet. Some right-wing hack groups, I gather, are planning to bring pressure on their local movie theaters to drop the film. How dumb or thuggish do you have to be in order to counter one form of stupidity and cowardice with another? By all means go and see this terrible film, and take your friends, and if the fools in the audience strike up one cry, in favor of surrender or defeat, feel free to join in the conversation.

However, I think we can agree that the film is so flat-out phony that "fact-checking" is beside the point. And as for the scary lawyers—get a life, or maybe see me in court. But I offer this, to Moore and to his rapid response rabble. Any time, Michael my boy. Let's redo Telluride. Any show. Any place. Any platform. Let's see what you're made of.

Some people soothingly say that one should relax about all this. It's only a movie. No biggie. It's no worse than the tomfoolery of Oliver Stone. It's kick-ass entertainment. It might even help get out "the youth vote." Yeah, well, I have myself written and presented about a dozen low-budget made-for-TV documentaries, on subjects as various as Mother Teresa and Bill Clinton and the Cyprus crisis, and I also helped produce a slightly more polished one on Henry Kissinger that was shown in movie theaters. So I know, thanks, before you tell me, that a documentary must have a "POV" or point of view and that it must also impose a narrative line. But if you leave out absolutely everything that might give your "narrative" a problem and throw in any old rubbish that might support it, and you don't even care that one bit of that rubbish flatly contradicts the next bit, and you give no chance to those who might differ, then *you have betrayed your craft*. If you flatter and fawn upon your potential audience, I might add, you are patronizing them and insulting them. By the same token, if I write an article and I quote somebody and for space reasons put in an ellipsis like this (. . .), I swear on my children that I am not leaving out anything that, if quoted in full, would alter the original meaning or its significance. Those who violate this pact with readers or viewers are to be despised. At no point does Michael Moore make the smallest effort to be objective. At no moment does he pass up the chance of a cheap sneer or a jeer. He pitilessly focuses his camera, for minutes after he should have turned it off, on a distraught and bereaved mother whose grief we have already shared. (But then, this is the guy who thought it so clever and amusing to catch Charlton Heston, in *Bowling for Columbine*, at the onset of his senile dementia.) Such courage.

Perhaps vaguely aware that his movie so completely lacks gravitas, Moore concludes with a sonorous reading of some words from George Orwell. The words are taken from *1984* and consist of a third-person analysis of a hypothetical, endless, and contrived war between three superpowers. The clear intention, as clumsily excerpted like this (. . .) is to suggest that there is no moral distinction between the United States, the Taliban, and the Baath Party and that the war against jihad is about nothing. If Moore had studied a bit more, or at all, he could have read Orwell really saying, and in his own voice, the following:

> The majority of pacifists either belong to obscure religious sects or are simply humanitarians who object to taking life and prefer not to follow their thoughts beyond that point. But there is a minority of intellectual pacifists, whose real though unacknowledged motive appears to be hatred of western democracy and admiration for totalitarianism. Pacifist propaganda usually boils down to saying that one side is as bad as the other, but if one looks closely at the writing of the younger intellectual pacifists, one finds that they do not by any means express impartial disapproval but are directed almost entirely against Britain and the United States . . .

And that's just from Orwell's *Notes on Nationalism* in May 1945. A short word of advice: In general, it's highly unwise to quote Orwell if you are already way out of your depth on the question of moral equivalence. It's also incautious to remind people of Orwell if you are engaged in a sophomoric celluloid rewriting of recent history.

If Michael Moore had had his way, Slobodan Milosevic would still be the big man in a starved and tyrannical Serbia. Bosnia and Kosovo would have been cleansed and annexed. If Michael Moore had been listened to, Afghanistan would still be under Taliban rule, and Kuwait would have remained part of Iraq. And Iraq itself would still be the personal property of a psychopathic crime family, bargaining covertly with the slave state of North Korea for WMD. You might hope that a retrospective awareness of this kind would induce a little modesty. To the contrary, it is employed to pump air into one of the great sagging blimps of our sorry, mediocre, celeb-rotten culture. Rock the vote, indeed.

SLATE, JUNE 21, 2004

VIRGINITY REGAINED

Before you ask, I should say that it's pronounced med-u-GOR-y. This is worth stressing, because it's almost the only thing about the place that is in the least complicated. The nonfacts are these: On June 24, 1981, a fourteen-year-old peasant girl, unoriginally named Ivanka Ivankovic, unoriginally came across a light that she took to be the Virgin Mary. Not many hours later, three other girls and two boys claimed to have had the identical experience, or sense-impression. Within a matter of weeks, thousands of the credulous had started to appear at the site, and it has now been trampled by millions. Those who turn up have miraculously emanated a number of false claims, such as the ability to stare calmly and without harm at the sun (a pointless achievement even if verifiable) and the more acquisitive and medieval capacity to turn their rosary beads into pure gold. Every sort of foolishness is indulged, and every green acre of this once backward village has been transmuted into a knickknack mall.

Three things, however, distinguish Medjugorje from the average racketeering religious hub. First, the children claimed to go on seeing the Virgin Mary every day, and some of them keep up this claim to the present moment. Since she exists in their imaginations and is not a weeping or bleeding statue of the traditional sort—smeared with pig's fat or otherwise rigged—she is harder to expose than the more palpable frauds at, say, the shrine of San Gennaro. Second, the Vatican and the local hierarchy will not, as they have with similar hallucinations at Fatima or Lourdes or Knock, bestow recognition on the supposed miracle. Third, the element of politicization is so obvious as to do what no blue-cowled lady can do, and make you catch your breath in wonder.

There is a principle or saying in the world of Catholic scholasticism: *Quicquid recipitur per modem recipientis recipitur.* (Whatever is received is received in the manner of the receiver.) An alternative, or looser, rendering of the Latin would be "Garbage in, garbage out." The children were asked excitedly and often, and understandably, what the Virgin had said to them. They replied that she recommended prayer, Bible study, fasting and the rosary. The dullest Croatian parish priest could have said as much: It's worse than the pointless burblings from the beyond that are produced at spiritualist seances. A pretty young guide took me to see a statue of Our Lady outside an ugly new basilica in the center of town. "This one," she breathed reverently, "is the one that the children say looks most like the apparition." I gazed. The banal stone figure precisely resembled every wayside mass-produced Virgin I had ever seen. Perhaps this is why, from Guadalupe to Knock, she only ever manifests herself to people who have been trained to recognize her.

The hostility of the local church hierarchy and (thus far) even of an extremely Marian Pope is more difficult to explicate. But as with the Vatican's denunciation of the supposed apparition at Garabandal in Spain in the sixties— we can make a good guess. People "channeling" the Virgin of Medjugorje have interpreted her as preferring the Franciscans to the Jesuits. None of her purported "healings" have survived even the scrutiny of the clerics at Lourdes. Pagan conduct and superstitious ecstasy have been observed at the site, as has the grossest commercialism. And anyway, as Aaron's Old Testament competition with Pharaoh's sorcerers can attest, the ability to conjure is not in itself proof of a Christian or even monotheistic god, because otherwise the polytheistic sorcerers wouldn't have been able to do it. (The latter point is not made by the Pope, but it ought to be.) So Holy Mother Church has reached a compromise, whereby the faithful are neither enjoined to worship at Medjugorje nor discouraged from doing so. On the verge of the millennium, Rome does not need another embarrassing bogus revelation.

Part of the fraudulence of Medjugorje is manifested in its political opportunism. The site is on the territory of Bosnia and Herzegovina, but it also lies within the area claimed and occupied by Croatian irredentists. In the unbelievably awful souvenir shops that pollute the entire landscape, the accepted local currency is the Croatian kuna, declared by the Dayton accords to be illegal tender in these parts. Try using it in Mostar, only a few valleys away. Here, the wreckage of an entire city and the ruin of an entire society is still open to view. The bridges are down, the minarets are amputated; in many parts of town there is still not one stone piled on another. One pile of stones, on the riverbank, represents all that remains of the exquisite Stari Most, or "old bridge," erected by the Sultan in 1566. And all this was done, in plain view of NATO, by Croatian government forces who had pictures of the Virgin taped to their rifle butts. While the pilgrims chanted only a few miles away and gave out stupid and cupiditous yelps about their rosaries turning into gold, the soldiers of Christ were methodically leveling every sign of the existence of another monotheism. They were also killing, deporting and torturing those of their fellow citizens who professed the wrong faith or who didn't profess the right one or who professed no faith at all.

This episode of atrocity weighs still on the meditations of serious Catholics. It doesn't weigh quite enough, or His Holiness the Pope would not have beatified the late Cardinal Stepanic, who was the clerical face of the wartime Croat Nazi regime led by Ante Pavelic. (If Pat Buchanan was a mere "isolationist," rather than someone soft on fascism, he wouldn't be such a strong supporter and endorser of the Croatian extreme right, past and present.) Still, even on that dismal occasion the Holy Father was constrained to utter a few words against genocide and sectarianism. And I imagine that it is this—unstated yet inescapable—that moves the church to speak softly but skeptically to its overeager Medjugorje flock. Bad as things are, they are not so counterecumenical as to make us bow down before Our Lady of the Ustashe.

THE NATION,
OCTOBER 18, 1999

THE DIVINE ONE

T he Dalai Lama has come out in support of the thermonuclear tests recently conducted by the Indian state, and has done so in the very language of the chauvinist parties that now control that state's affairs. The "developed" countries, he says, must realize that India is a major contender and should not concern themselves with its internal affairs. This is a perfectly Realpolitik statement, so crass and banal and opportunist that it would not deserve any comment if it came from another source.

"Think different," says the ungrammatical Apple Computer advertisement that features the serene visage of His Holiness. Among the untested assumptions of this billboard campaign is the widely and lazily held belief that "Oriental" religion is different from other faiths: less dogmatic, more contemplative, more . . . transcendental. This blissful, thoughtless exceptionalism has been conveyed to the West through a succession of mediums and narratives, ranging from the middlebrow bestseller *Lost Horizon* by James Hilton (creator of Mr. Chips as well as Shangri-La), to the memoir *Seven Years in Tibet* by the SS veteran Heinrich Harrer, prettified for the screen by Brad Pitt. China's foul conduct in an occupied land, combined with a Hollywood cult that almost exceeds the power of Scientology itself, has fused with weightless Maharishi- and Bagwan-type babble to create an image of an idealized Tibet and of a saintly god-king. So perhaps the Apple injunction to think differently is worth heeding.

The greatest triumph modern PR can offer is the transcendent success of having your words and actions judged by your reputation, rather than the other way about. The "spiritual leader" of Tibet has enjoyed this unassailable status for some time now, becoming a byword and synonym for saintly and ethereal values. Why this doesn't put people on their guard I'll never know. But here are some other facts about the serene leader that, dwarfed as they are by his endorsement of nuclear weapons, are still worth knowing and still generally unknown.

Shoko Asahara, leader of the "Supreme Truth" cult in Japan and spreader of sarin nerve gas on the Tokyo subway, donated 45 million rupees, or about 170 million yen, to the Dalai Lama, and was rewarded for his efforts by several high-level meetings with the divine one.

Steven Seagal, the robotic and moronic "actor" who gave us *Hard to Kill* and *Under Siege*, has been proclaimed a reincarnated lama and a sacred vessel, or "tulku," of Tibetan Buddhism. This decision, ratified by Penor Rinpoche, supreme head of the Nyingma School of Tibetan Buddhism, was initially received with incredulity by Richard Gere, who had hitherto believed himself to be the superstar most favored. "If someone's a tulku, that's great," he was quoted as saying. "But no one knows if that's true." How insightful, if only accidentally. At a subsequent Los Angeles appearance by the Dalai Lama, Seagal was seated in the front row and Gere two rows back, thus giving the latter's humility and submissiveness a day at the races. Suggestions that Seagal's fortune helped elevate him to the Himalayan status of tulku are not completely discounted even by some adepts and initiates.

Supporters of the Dorge Shugden deity—a "Dharma protector" and an ancient object of worship and propitiation in Tibet—have been threatened with violence and ostracism and even death following the Dalai Lama's abrupt prohibition of this once-venerated godhead. A Swiss television documentary graphically intercuts footage of his Holiness, denying all knowledge of menace and intimidation, with scenes of his followers enthusiastically flaunting "Wanted" posters and other paraphernalia of excommunication and persecution.

While he denies being a Buddhist "pope," the Dalai Lama is never happier than when brooding in a celibate manner on the sex lives of people he has never met. "Sexual misconduct for men and women consists of oral and anal sex," he has repeatedly said in promoting his book on these matters. "Using one's hand, that is sexual misconduct." But, as ever with religious stipulations, there is a nutty escape clause. "To have sexual relations with a prostitute paid by you and not a third person does not constitute improper behavior." Not all of this can have been said just to placate Richard Gere, or to attract the royalties from *Pretty Woman*.

I have talked to a few Dorge Shugden adherents, who seem sincere enough and certainly seem frightened enough, but I can't go along with their insistence on the "irony" of all this. Buddhism can be as hysterical and sanguinary as any other system that relies on faith and tribe. Lon Nol's Cambodian Army was Buddhist at least in name. Solomon Bandaranaike, first elected leader of independent Sri Lanka, was assassinated by a Buddhist militant. It was Buddhist-led pogroms against the Tamils that opened the long and disastrous communal war that ruins Sri Lanka to this day. The gorgeously named SLORC, the military fascism that runs Burma, does so nominally as a Buddhist junta. I have even heard it whispered that in old Tibet, that pristine and contemplative land, the lamas were the allies of feudalism and unsmilingly inflicted medieval punishments such as blinding, and flogging unto death.

Yet the entire Western mass media is uncritically at the service of a mere mortal who, at the very least, proclaims the utter nonsense of reincarnation and who affirms the sinister if not indeed crazy belief that death is but a stage in a grand cycle of what appears to be futility and subjection. What need, then, to worry about nuclear weaponry, or sectarian frenzy, or the sale of indulgences to men of the stamp of Steven Seagal? "Harmony" will doubtless kick in. During his visit to Beijing, our sentimental Baptist hypocrite of a President turned to his dictator host, recommended that he meet with the Dalai Lama and assured him that the two of them would get on well. That might easily turn out to be the case. Both are very much creatures of the material world.

THE NATION,
JULY 27–AUGUST 3, 1998

THE DEVIL AND
MOTHER TERESA

You've said it at least once in your life. "Let me play devil's advocate for a moment." This is when you demonstrate your powers of contrary argument, prove to yourself and others that you can live dangerously on both sides of a question, play the ironic or amoral role. The exercise brings with it that vague and distant frisson that still occurs when you drop the name of the Prince of Darkness, talk of the Devil, utter or mutter some satanic verses.

Early last June, I had a once-in-a-lifetime chance to perform this Luciferian task for real. I spent a morning in a closed room with three priests, a Bible, and a tape recorder. And I gave my solemn evidence against the late Agnes Bojaxhiu of Skopje, Macedonia—the artist formerly known as Mother Teresa of Calcutta. Her beatification and canonization may yet take place, but somewhere in a vault in Rome my ten cents' worth of *inferno* will still sit, irritating and negating the pious invocations of *paradiso*. And who knows? It took Pope Paul VI to decanonize my namesake, Saint Christopher, whose supposed visage used to appear on countless medallions for faithful travelers. It turned out that he didn't belong in the calendar after all. He and other miracle-working role models were discovered to have been frauds or myths. My day of vindication may come, though it will be scant comfort to be joined in hell by an unsmiling nun who has undergone a reversal of fortune and who may—since she was, after all, only human—bear me a grudge.

It was Father David O'Connor of the Archdiocese of Washington, D.C., who gave me the call. "We've been asked by Rome," he told me, "to invite your testimony in the sainthood cause of Mother Teresa." This followed some E-mails and letters from the church authorities in Calcutta, who had sought to find out if I would be ready to do it. I replied that I would be more than happy to go to either Calcutta or Rome, but they said, No, we'll set up a hearing for you right where you live. So one morning I put on a suit, and very nearly a tie, and had a shave, and set off to be *advocatus diaboli*.

The actual job of "devil's advocate" as I very well knew, had been abolished by the present Pope in 1983. John Paul II has beatified or canonized more candidates for sainthood than his seventeen immediate predecessors combined, and one way in which he enabled this assembly line of sanctity was to remove ("More's the pity," sniffed Father O'Connor confidingly) the one officer of Holy Mother Church whom everybody, sacred and profane, actually believed in. In his book *Making Saints,* the devout *Newsweek* correspondent Kenneth Woodward describes this enormous doctrinal change thus: "No longer would the church look to the courtroom as its model for arriving at the truth of a saint's life; instead, it would employ the academic model of researching and writing a doctoral dissertation."

The room into which I was ushered at the archdiocese was indeed more like a professor's office than a court or a confessional. Around a polished table sat Monsignor Joseph Sadusky, Deacon Bernard Bernier, and the good Father O'Connor. All of them looked the part in their different ways: the monsignor somewhat thin and ascetic, the deacon rather round and worldly, the father a minor masterpiece of Brooklyn Irish sculpture, white hair and red cheeks contrasting happily. I thought it wasn't conceited of me to assume that they had read my short book *The Missionary Position: Mother Teresa in Theory and Practice* so when asked if I had any opening statement I said, in effect, that I thought it was very sporting of them to have invited such a conspicuously nonbelieving witness. I added that I realized it was none of my business what the church decided concerning its saints, but that the word "saintly" did have a secular meaning that was commonly understood, and that I was prepared to argue that their candidate was highly undeserving of this interpretation. Monsignor Sadusky then handed me the Testaments and asked for my preliminary oath. In a court I would have asked to affirm, but it seemed ridiculous to stick on this point in such a setting, so I duly swore by Almighty God.

It turned out that these three men of the cloth were long-distance ventriloquist's mediums for the Vatican. On the table lay an enormous questionnaire, designed to be put to all witnesses. The task was to get through it, with no deviations from the script. The tape recorder was switched on, there was the usual business of ensuring that it could indeed play back a human voice (which it miraculously could, on the first try), and we got going. Sticking to the text before him, Monsignor Sadusky asked if, in the matter of "the Servant of God, Mother Teresa," I could throw any light on the holiness and simplicity of her childhood years. Glancing at the questionnaire, I saw that there were pages of follow-up questions all couched in the same terms. I asked if I could keep a copy and was told that the request had been noted. At this stage I noted for myself that the monsignor had a slight but very noticeable speech impediment, and, foreseeing a longish dialogue of the deaf, requested permission to scroll down. (Even though I have been to Mother Teresa's birthplace, I can be of no use in illuminating her first girlish moments of revelation.) Permission was granted. We agreed to skip the sections about her inner grace and piety.

Reviewing Leopold von Ranke's famous *History of the Popes,* Lord Macaulay once said that the Catholic Church "thoroughly understands what no other church has ever understood, how to deal with enthusiasts." I had a chance to remind my invigilators of this when we came to the doctrinal section. Mother Teresa had been a great critic of Pope John XXIII and the reforms proposed at Vatican II. She disliked any reconsideration of orthodox teaching, always taking the most extreme version of all dogmas. For example, when awarded the Nobel Prize for Peace, she announced that the greatest threat to world peace was . . . abortion. And on other occasions she had proclaimed that abortion and contraception were morally equivalent. Logically, this would mean she believed that contraception was also a great—if not indeed the greatest—threat to world peace. Did the Vatican, I asked, really want to honor such a ludicrous application of its principled defense of the unborn? It may have been my imagination, but I thought I saw Deacon Bernier shoot me an interested glance from down the table.

When asked if I knew anything about her work among the poor, and whether I had ever met her, I replied that I had walked around Calcutta in her company and formed the conclusion that she was not so much a friend of the poor as a friend of poverty. She praised poverty and disease and suffering as gifts from on high, and told people to accept these gifts joyfully. She was adamantly opposed to the only policy that has ever alleviated poverty in any country—that is, the empowerment of women, and the extension of their control over their own fertility. Her famous Calcutta clinic was in fact nothing more than a primitive hospice—a place for people to die, and a place where medical treatment was vestigial or nonexistent. (When she became ill herself, she flew first-class to a private clinic in California.) The vast sums of money she raised were spent mainly on building convents in her own honor. And she had befriended a whole series of rich crooks and exploiters, ranging from Charles Keating of the Lincoln Savings & Loan to the hideous Duvalier dynasty in Haiti, having accepted from both large donations of money that had actually been stolen from the poor.

As it happens, I can prove all the above assertions to be true, and had brought the evidence with me. But I wasn't asked to produce it. The recorder turned silently and the men of the church sat still as I delivered these apparent profanities. It was a shock to me when I first discovered that none of the things commonly believed about Mother Teresa—such as her unworldliness and her modesty—are even in the least bit true. And I am an atheist. If it was a shock to the monsignor, the deacon, and the father to hear me, they did not betray the fact.

I thought I detected a slight stirring when I mentioned the fact that no audit of the Missionaries of Charity has ever been published, in spite of the vast sums of money that have been showered upon the order. The church is notoriously sensitive about money matters, and the various scandals at the Vatican bank can still make the faithful wince. I added that nobody accuses Mother Teresa of embezzling any of this for her own purposes, but if the cash was indeed spent on proselytizing for Catholic fundamentalism in impoverished countries—as she more than once seemed to claim—that was not the purpose for which most people thought they had parted with it. Meanwhile, a prosecutor in the district attorney's office for Los Angeles County was seeking the return of the ill-gotten money which Charles Keating (convicted of fraud, racketeering, and conspiracy in 1991) had given her. (She had written to the judge in the case—a certain Lance Ito—pleading that Keating was a good man. He'd been good to her all right, lending her a private jet and handing her $1.4 million.)

At a certain stage in the questionnaire, I was asked if I thought her guilty of the sin of hypocrisy. I said no to this. She had always advertised her extreme reactionary beliefs; it wasn't her fault if nobody took any notice and if the media herd had decided that she was a bleeding-heart compassionate type. There was just one thing, though. In 1995 the people of Ireland held a referendum on whether to allow divorce and remarriage. Mother Teresa intervened forcibly on the side of the "no" campaign. An Irishwoman, if married to an alcoholic, incestuous abuser, was supposed to put up with it, or offer it up. But in the same year, Mother Teresa gave an interview to *Ladies' Home Journal* saying she was glad to hear that her friend Princess Diana was getting divorced, since the royal marriage was so obviously an unhappy one. I said that I hoped this was hypocrisy, since otherwise it would look like the medieval church, preaching strict morals to the poor and offering indulgences to the rich.

A few more formalities and the hearing was complete. Father O'Connor took me to his own sanctum and allowed me a cigarette. "Rome really wanted this done," he said in rather blunt tones. "We've been instructed to get the tape transcribed and sent by the end of the week." (This was a Thursday morning.) He added, "The Pope takes a personal interest; it's a fast track for this one." He told me that I could review the transcript, and that he'd see about getting me a copy of the questionnaire—which hadn't been allowed to leave the room. I asked him what he'd made of my evidence. He was surprisingly candid. "Well, a lot of people in the church will tell you that she was indeed a very difficult woman. We had her here in Washington, to set up a little house for her order. A nice little place—but she wanted everything modern stripped out of it, right down to the Formica. Very difficult she was." I knew this was true of all her operations; nothing but absolute austerity for the poor and the sick. I must have interviewed a dozen former volunteers who left her for that reason alone. But, of course, extreme zeal of this kind often convinces impressionable people that they are in the presence of greatness.

It was only when I'd got home that I realized something. Miracles. They hadn't asked me about miracles. In order for a person to undergo the process of beatification—the prelude to full canonization—at least one miracle must be attributable to her or to him. (It used to be two miracles, but the Holy Father has eliminated that condition as well.) Archbishop Henry d'Souza of Calcutta, head of Mother Teresa's "sainthood commission," wrapped up his inquiries and forwarded all the relevant materials to the Pope in the middle of August. This represents yet another break with the traditional rules; hitherto, hearings on sainthood could not even start until five years after the candidate's death, and Mother Teresa died in 1997. But it is clear—Archbishop d'Souza has himself publicly used the vulgarism about the "fast track"—that Pope John Paul II wants personally to announce her beatification—if not her canonization before (to be frank about it) he himself hands on the keys.

This means, not to put it any more subtly, that d'Souza's people must have found and certified a miracle in a very considerable hurry. According to sources in the archbishop's camp, they have selected a young Hindu woman from the town of Raiganj in northern Bengal. In 2000, this unfortunate girl had apparently been suffering from a tumor, but after she prayed to Mother Teresa she suffered no longer. If that doesn't prove it, I'm sure I don't know what does.

Doctors must now decide on the case, but they are asked only to certify that a cure is "organic, immediate and irreversible." Since such inexplicable recoveries occur in large hospitals almost every day, the conclusion that there is "no natural explanation" can be arrived at by a rational person. The second step of argument—that there must therefore be a supernatural explanation—involves a leap of faith. Miracles by themselves prove nothing to a Christian, or are supposed to prove nothing. After all, the Bible is full of miraculous feats pulled off by devils, wizards, and pagan or Pharaonic sorcerers. The difference therefore insisted upon by the church is that a miracle occur *after* the death of a saint, but yet be directly attributable to him or her. By this means, the authorities ensure against hucksterism in one way—because there can be no personal conjuring or witchcraft—while proposing an impossible standard of proof and disproof.

* * *

Last September, the Missionaries of Charity in Calcutta were hugely embarrassed by a lawsuit against one of their nuns, Sister Francesca. This woman had taken the hand of a seven-year-old girl named Karabi Mandal and scorched it with a hot knife. The child's father, a local ragpicker, took the nun to court. I would never be so crass as to say that one such incident condemns a whole order. (The church would have to close down if that were true.) But if Sister Francesca had testified that Mother Teresa had spoken out of heaven saying, "Do not touch that child," I would be impressed. It just never seems to happen that way. And Sister Francesca herself, as court proceedings loomed, seemed miraculously to disappear.

I have already helped disprove one miracle attributed to Mother Teresa in her lifetime. The British journalist Malcolm Muggeridge, a propagandist for the divine, made a film about her life called *Something Beautiful for God*. (It was this documentary, broadcast on the BBC in 1969 and later adapted as a book, that launched Mother Teresa as a media star.) In the course of filming, the militant old lady was interviewed in a very dark room in one of her charitable homes. It was thought that the footage would be too poorly lit for transmission, yet when the crepuscular sequence was played in the editing suite, a strange and lovely light pervaded the scene. Muggeridge immediately contacted the press to announce "the first authentic photographic miracle," and the discovery by technology of what he termed Cardinal Newman's "kindly light." In an interview, the cameraman Ken MacMillan announced that this had in fact been the first test of a special new film made by Kodak that was designed for shooting in poor light. "Three cheers for Kodak," he said, was what it proved. But by the time he had given his evidence, the rumor was off and running like a UFO sighting, and Mother Teresa herself, modest as ever, did nothing to discourage it.

As I say, I didn't have the chance to go into any of this with my three men of the cloth. But I later discovered that the miracle part of the case is not their business. A whole separate commission is involved in deciding that Mother Teresa can posthumously cure the sorts of tumor that afflict believers. There are those, in Rome and elsewhere, who think that all this smacks of indecent haste. But they are too shrewd to argue with success. This is the fastest of fast tracks: who would want to try and derail it? To give you an idea, the previous record for speed in beatification is held by Blessed Monsignor Josemaría

Escrivá de Balaguer, the founder of the lay movement Opus Dei and a great favorite with Pope John Paul II. He achieved beatitude in 1992—only seventeen years after his death.

Not everybody in the church likes Opus Dei. It was involved in propping up the decaying Franco regime in Spain; it is secretive and cultish and reactionary. It also had in its ranks Mr. Robert P. Hanssen, the FBI. agent who sold out numerous colleagues to the KGB. and who has just plea-bargained himself down from a capital charge. According to his wife, Bonnie, he confessed to her in 1980 that he had started receiving a second salary from Moscow. She says that she persuaded him to see their priest, Father Robert Bucciarelli. Beyond confirming that he indeed knew Mr. Hanssen in 1980, Bucciarelli has declined to discuss the matter further. This in turn means that he doesn't deny advising Hanssen to give his first Soviet stipend—$20,000 at 1980 prices—to Mother Teresa. That is, at any rate, what Hanssen told his wife he had been told to do, and had done. The Missionaries of Charity can't confirm the donation, which Hanssen says he made in small installments, but then, the Missionaries of Charity don't provide financial records. They rely, in the words of Sister Mary Dominga of their Eastern United States region, "on divine providence." And if Father Bucciarelli had told Hanssen to give the money back and resolve to sin no more, I feel he would have found some way to communicate that fact without violating the seal of the confessional—if that is what it was, and not a "consultation." These disclosures occurred after my day at the archdiocese, so I have no way of knowing whether Rome thinks that guilty consciences can be expiated in this way by traitors who go on to take more money, and to send more colleagues before Stalinist firing squads. However, Mr. Hanssen remains a member in good standing of Opus Dei. (In order to be excommunicated, he would probably have had to employ a contraceptive or seek either an abortion or a divorce.)

Very much against my will, the network that broadcast my documentary *Mother Teresa* decided to entitle it *Hell's Angel,* a rather cheap and sophomoric name. And it's under that unfortunate title that it has since been screened at some film festivals and other locales. When I went to introduce it a few years ago at a showing on the campus of the University of Rochester, I was picketed furiously by a group called the New York Lambs of Christ, a distinctly sheep-like organization. But then the police arrived and told me that I'd require a full security escort because some very dangerous criminal elements had been spotted in the crowd. I didn't believe that the Lambs would resort to blood-shed, and declined the protection. So I was amazed to see, as I pushed toward the hall, a gang of hirsute, leather-jacketed roughnecks yelling at me. The penny didn't drop, so I approached them and asked what they wanted. With some awkwardness, they handed me a notarized "cease and desist" order, claiming that I had violated their trademark. This was the local chapter of the Hell's Angels. Their honor satisfied, they bestrode their bikes and roared away, leaving me clutching the writ and thinking, It's finally happened. Everybody in this country is a fucking lawyer. Yet I was mistaken. The Hell's Angels may have their own pricey advocate, but the Devil himself does not. The Pope has deprived him of his right to counsel. Now, I have a sneaking regard for the Holy Father. He may be very conservative in doctrinal matters, but he was a real man when it came to the struggle for his native Poland, and he has almost single-handedly changed the posture of the church on the filthy prac-tice of the death penalty. It's therefore slightly sad for even an unbeliever to see him end his days like some medieval seller of relics, bending the rules to allow special dispensation for a sly and worldly sinner. And that's why it was my pleasure and privilege to be the first ever to represent the Evil One pro bono.

VANITY FAIR, OCTOBER 2001

BLESSED ARE THE PHRASEMAKERS

A review of *GOD'S SECRETARIES: THE MAKING OF THE KING JAMES BIBLE*
by Adam Nicolson

I t has been said that a camel is a horse designed by a committee, but not all the works of collective or bureaucratic imagination are so ungainly. (And a camel, too, has strange beauties and symmetries that disclose themselves only gradually.) The King James Bible—the "A.V.," or Authorized Version, as it was known when I was made to attend school services in England—is the product of one of the most intense committee meetings of all time. And its effect on our vernacular and literature is probably as deep and as lasting as that of its near contemporary, the canon of William Shakespeare himself. In *Notes of a Native Son,* James Baldwin explained his own passion for language and liturgy in this laconic way:

> I hazard that the King James Bible, the rhetoric of the storefront churches, something ironic and violent and perpetually understated in Negro speech—and something of Dickens's love for bravura—have something to do with me today, but I wouldn't stake my life on it.

The presence of this superb text in everyday idiom is not a coincidence, and nor is its implied association with irony and violence—two of the resources of the oppressed. For many centuries, it was exceedingly dangerous to try to translate the Good Book into a language that the people could understand. Like the secret work of Emmanuel Goldstein in *Nineteen Eighty-Four,* the Bible was the possession of an inner-party elite, and its arcana were part of the stage management of priestcraft. The Protestant Reformation, assisted by the spread of printing, built on the banned fourteenth-century English manuscript translation by John Wycliffe, and made steady efforts to disseminate the Word in intelligible form. Miles Coverdale and William Tyndale (such Hawthorne-like names) were the sixteenth-century pioneers: Tyndale was strangled and burned by the clerical authorities for his pains in 1536 (he had been especially hounded by "Saint" Thomas More, that persecutor for all seasons), and his friend and deputy John Rogers was sent to the stake by Queen Mary. But successor editions were produced by English Calvinists in Geneva and—perhaps so as not to be outdone—by English Catholics in Reims and Douai. (The Geneva one was the version borne by the Pilgrims to Plymouth Rock.)

Thus, King James's conclave of scholars and divines was not working with a *tabula rasa* when it began scrutinizing the translations from Hebrew and Greek in 1604. It did, however, have to bear in mind a few political imperatives. The once refulgent reign of Queen Elizabeth had come to a stale and frustrated end in the preceding year, and a new monarch had been imported from Scotland, emerging from the rather questionable uterus of the old queen's former rival, the amorously notorious Mary, Queen of Scots. James I was known to be very ugly and somewhat bloodthirsty (he liked hunting both witches and deer). He was also known for a very high degree of mentality and education. Among his attainments, like that of Julien Sorel in *The Red and the Black,* was the ability to memorize the whole of the Bible in translation and to recognize any passage from its pages the moment he was shown it.

Hermeneutics was politics in those days, and to an acute degree. Henry VIII had broken with Rome, but Catholicism was still a power in the land, and the 1552 Thomas Cranmer prayer book—that other great quarry of English religious phraseology and precept—had been a compromise between the High and Low versions of Christianity. A fresh synthesis was required for a new form of nation-building monarchy that aimed at uniting England and Scotland, and at instating the divine right of kings without actually saying so too loudly. (One of the many, many everyday expressions that we derive from the text is the phrasing "the powers that be," which—please do not forget—are said by Paul in his Epistle to the Romans to be "ordained of God.")

Adam Nicolson's re-creation of this context is beyond praise. In *God's Secretaries,* he brings off a brilliant freehand portrait of an England more rich yet insecure, more literate yet superstitious, more urban yet still rural in rhythm, more unified yet riven with factions. The years of the King James translation were also those of the first stage productions of *Othello, Volpone, King Lear* and *The Tempest,* none of these being exactly free of reference to the crisis of authority and the role of conscience. Nobody could possibly have guessed it, but the civil war and the Puritan Revolution were only a few decades into the future. Sir Oliver Cromwell, the member of Parliament for Huntingdon and subsidizer of Virginia settlements, gave a banquet for the new King James at his country mansion. If Nicolson knows what the four-year-old eldest son of the house was doing on that auspicious day, he doesn't tell us.

The men who met at Hampton Court to furnish the new kingdom with a new Bible were themselves men stranded partway between superstition and knowledge. Lancelot Andrewes, the dean of Westminster and leading Protestant divine of his day, believed that the plague in London was a punishment from God all right, and argued that this must be so because the effects of the pestilence were not indiscriminate. (He was, in other words, halfway toward making an epidemiological observation.) Many of his colleagues were in favor of a broad reconciliation between Puritans and Catholics, until the Guy Fawkes Gunpowder Plot was unearthed in November 1605. Nicolson, the author most recently of *Sea Room,* about life in the Hebrides, compares this to Sept. 11, 2001, in establishing a connection, in some minds, between religious affiliation and political disloyalty. Fawkes was ruthlessly tortured into making a confession that implicated a "Romish" network, but you didn't have to be a papist to be racked in England in those days.

Given all this distraught theological and political context, the extraordinary fact about the eventual Authorized Version is its relative mildness and, to employ a neologism, its accessibility. Nicolson does some fine work in demonstrating the overlap with the Tyndale translation and also the ways in which retranslation can confer something of the numinous. Here is Tyndale:

> Thys ys my commaundement, that ye love togedder as I have loved you. Gretter love then this hath no man, then that a man bestowe his lyfe for his frendes.

And here is the reworking:

> This is my Commaundement, that ye loue one another, as I haue loued you. / Greater loue hath no man then this, that a man lay downe his life for his friends.

The superior resonance of the second lies in its more ringing certainty and assertiveness. This work was refined and prepared in order to be heard and memorized, by a congregation still largely illiterate, and to be recalled in time of trouble or of need. Print was secondary: no doubt the audience of the later misprinted 1631 edition, when instructed by Exodus 20:14 that "thou shalt commit adultery," understood that a "not" had been omitted at the press rather than in Sinai. Nicolson's book is, perhaps unintentionally, a proof that the word of God is not immutable. Further proof of this is available from another quarter, in the flat banality of the so-called New English Bible, whereby the committees of English and American Protestantism came together three and a half centuries later, and threw a pearl away richer than all their tribe.

THE NEW YORK TIMES BOOK REVIEW,
MAY 18, 2003

JEWISH POWER,
JEWISH PERIL

Two old Jewish men are sitting on a park bench in Berlin in the early 1930s. Things are not yet so bad, but that doesn't mean they won't get worse. One of the two is solemnly reading a Jewish newspaper. The other is scanning a Nazi newspaper, and laughing out loud. Finally, the first man stops reading and says, "It's bad enough that you read that pro-Hitler rag. But to laugh at it!"

The second responds with a shrug. "What if I read your paper? It tells me about Jewish windows being broken, Jewish shops boycotted, Jewish children beaten up in school. So . . . if I read the Hitler paper it tells me that we Jews control the whole world."

L ike all jokes on this subject, the above story involves a dangerous flirtation with bad taste, with tragedy, and with irony. Irony has been an essential constituent of Jewish life ever since Maimonides wrote that, while the Messiah will one day come, "he may tarry." That shrug—half hopeful and half pessimistic—is present in Woody Allen and in Lenny Bruce. And the tragic element is so raw and so recent that there isn't any need to go over it. American Jews may be the most successful minority in American history, which is as much as to say that they are the most successful minority ever. But no other ethnicity has ever had to witness the physical destruction of perhaps one-third of its entire membership, carried out by a highly civilized European country that had been the model for assimilation, and involving the deliberate state murder of children. Still, no other American minority can also claim a stake in a local super-state of its very own, at the other end of the Mediterranean, where for the first time in history Jews can debate whether it would be proper to employ nuclear weapons on the Sabbath.

As I began to write this article, synagogues had been firebombed in several French towns and in one north London suburb, and a suicide assassin had massacred Jews who just minutes earlier had arrived from synagogues for a Passover dinner in the Israeli coastal town of Netanya. In response, American Jews in California had taken out an advertisement urging Woody Allen and others to boycott the Cannes Film Festival, on the grounds that the days of Vichy were back. Similar themes were being stressed by many Jewish and Israeli writers, who spoke darkly of the imminence of another Holocaust.

Very often recently, this "Never Again" note has been struck by liberal and even radical Jews who seem to regret their former softness. Nat Hentoff, civil libertarian and longtime friend of the civil-rights movement, told *New York* magazine that "if a loudspeaker goes off and a voice says, 'All Jews gather in Times Square,' it could never surprise me."

I have to say that if such a voice were ever raised or broadcast, I would be much more than surprised, and very much more than shocked. I also think I could count on a very large number of Jews failing to report to Times Square, and an even larger number of non-Jews willing to support this refusal. Perhaps I should say here that I am related on my mother's side to this ancient argument and that, according to the Law of Moses, the Israeli Law of Return, and the Nuremberg laws, I can be counted as a member of the ancient tribe. This isn't much use, either to the tribe or to myself, since I don't believe there is a single word of truth in either Exodus or Genesis, would never consider asking a Palestinian to move out and make room for me, and do not believe that the human species is subdivided into races.

I maintain that I have the best evidence of Darwin and DNA on my side, as well as many recent anti-Biblical and anti-mythical discoveries made by Israeli archeologists. Ze'ev Herzog, professor of archeology at Tel Aviv University, has concluded that "the Israelites were never in Egypt, did not wander in the desert, did not conquer the land in a miliary campaign, and did not pass it on to the Twelve Tribes of Israel. Furthermore, the united monarchy of David and Solomon, which is described by the Bible as a regional power, was at most a small tribal kingdom." (Archeological myths are often the most toxic. The legend of Masada involves believing in a positive and noble aspect of the story that Jewish resistance to Rome culminated in a suicide-murder.)

Nonetheless, I like to think that I would be despised or hated by any movement defining itself as anti-Semitic. And on my shelf is an American Nazi pamphlet, denouncing the "Zionist Occupation Government" (or "ZOG") that covertly rules these United States. This illiterate screed isn't just a joke: it comes from the same swamp as those who murdered the Jewish radio host Alan Berg in Denver in 1984, and ultimately from the same mind-set that produced the atrocity in Oklahoma City.

In these hate-clotted pages I am—for the first and only time in my life— listed with both Henry Kissinger and Norman Podhoretz as a member of the

Jewish/Zionist conspiracy. As in the case of the tale with which I began: who knew I had such power?

Nativist and Christian though that 1989 pamphlet is, it was written partly in praise of the Ayatollah Khomeini. And the most horrifying recent development on the international scene is the emergence, in the Arab and Muslim world, of the debauched myths and falsifications of medieval Christianity. Saudi Arabian and Egyptian and Palestinian sources, some of them official, have been circulating *The Protocols of the Elders of Zion*, and reviving the accusation that no Passover meal is complete without the blood of a non-Jewish child to thicken the dough for the matzos. It is degrading even to argue with this kind of thing: the *Protocols* have been repeatedly and conclusively shown to be a fabrication, originating in the witch trials of the Middle Ages and updated for the modern world via the reactionary secret police of the Russian czars and the publishers of *Mein Kampf*. (In neither circle, incidentally, were Arabs or Muslims regarded very highly.)

Here again we find a version of the same sick joke: the Jews are supposed to be diabolical and clever enough to plot a secret world rule, and stupid enough to write the whole plan down. But please don't let the title fool you. The hideous cunning of the whole thing is that, in the secret book of their private deliberations, the "Elders" never mention Zionism or Palestine at all. The Jews' plan is that, from being the most despised and reviled minority in history, they go straight to a worldwide takeover and supreme power. Just like that. (The scary plot is hatched, according to this hoax, at midnight in the Jewish cemetery in Prague, near the later resting-place of Franz Kafka.)

Confronted with the re-appearance of this filthy libel, even Jews who inhabit global and regional superpowers such as the United States and Israel, can be pardoned for feeling edgy. Anti-Semitism is not like other prejudices. Many white people do not like other people with supposedly African genes, but they don't accuse them, or even suspect them, of taking over Wall Street as a prelude to world domination. Nor do they accuse them of murdering Jesus Christ (one of the emptier accusations against the Jews, I have always thought, since if Christ hadn't been killed there would be no Christianity, and presumably the Christians think that god had some say in the decision to offer his only son). Some Protestants think that Catholics form a secret society. Some Catholics think that Freemasons form an invisible government. Many secular crackpots believe that the Illuminati or the Trilateralists or the Knights Templar are really running the world.

But anti-Semitism is a kind of venomous distillation of all this conspiracy mania, and it is directed at a group which, when it can't be attacked as a race, can be indicted as a religion. Or, when it can't be attacked as a capitalist plutocracy, can be arraigned as the evil genius behind Communism. Or, and in each case, both. The Nazis portrayed Jews both as bloated profiteers and as gaunt, sinister Bolsheviks.

This infection occurs in almost all societies, and breaks out at the oddest times, and is derived from paranoia. It is completely evidence-proof. (*The Protocols* were endorsed by *The Times* of London in 1920 and later reprinted and distributed all over the United States by Henry Ford, though no increase in missing children at Passover-time had ever been reported.) Jew-hatred has a special appeal to the quasi-educated and the pseudo-intellectual, as well as to the ignorant who fear modernity and the big city. It is more like a form of mental disorder, or collective hallucination, than a form of racism.

Though there are societies, such as India, where it has never been a problem, and the United States has seemingly been successfully inoculated against it, there are grounds for thinking that it is somehow ineradicable. Certainly this is what the Zionist movement believes.

To many others, also, it now seems self-evident that the presence of this sort of toxin is proof enough by itself that the state of Israel needs an unqualified defense. Most of the anxious propaganda about anti-Semitism earlier this summer was mobilized in favor of General Ariel Sharon, or by the supporters of Benjamin Netanyahu, who thinks that Sharon is a sissy. But how obvious is this connection when you come to examine it?

The Protocols were fabricated by hired anti-Jewish reactionaries in Paris, almost certainly in 1897 or 1898, according to *Warrant for Genocide*, Professor Norman Cohn's magisterial 1966 study of the subject, and certainly between 1894 and 1899. What else was happening at that precise moment in history? France was being convulsed by the case of Captain Alfred Dreyfus, a Jewish army officer who had been framed for treason. In this, the mother of all French scandals, the issue of justice for a single Jew had split the army, the church, the press, the parliament, and the whole society.

A Viennese Jewish journalist named Theodor Herzl, covering the trial, was so appalled by French mobs yelling against the Jews that he decided to call for all Europe's Jews to abandon the sick continent and seek their own national home. He founded the movement known as Zionism in 1897. His slogan was that "a land without a people" should be a national home for "a people without a land." In other words, he made the serious mistake of asserting that Palestine was effectively uninhabited.

This huge miscalculation was overlooked by some Jews because of the terrible pogroms in the late 1880s, which had driven millions of refugees out of czarist Russia. A handful of the religious among them wanted to go to Jerusalem, where Jews were scarce, but the majority opted for exile in the "Christian" world. Not everybody in Western Europe or America was pleased to see these new arrivals. In Britain, for example, in the first years of the twentieth century, a Conservative politician named Arthur Balfour made a political reputation by opposing "alien" Jewish immigration.

Meanwhile, in 1899, Dreyfus had been pardoned, which meant that for the first time a Christian European nation had decided that the right of a single Jew under the law was worth a national climb-down. But Herzl's petitioning and campaigning continued, through the energy of his disciple (and Israel's first president), Chaim Weizmann, and extended itself through the First World War. In 1917 it culminated in the anti-Semite Balfour issuing "the Balfour Declaration," which is the effective founding document of the state of Israel. Balfour was not the first or last anti-Semite to urge Jews, in effect, to clear off to Palestine or to Uganda or Cyprus or Madagascar or other remote isolated places briefly considered by Herzl himself as alternative "homelands." An old slogan of anti-Zionist and leftist Jews was that, "when Jew-baiters say 'Jews get out,' the Zionists offer to be the travel agents."

And this does not exhaust the irony. The British Cabinet at the time contained only one Jewish member, Edwin Montagu, and he was passionately opposed to the declaration on the grounds that (a) it was a capitulation to anti-Semitic bigotry, with its suggestion that Palestine was the natural destination of the Jews, and that (b) it would be a grave cause of alarm to the Muslim world.

Balfour's wording had included the proviso that "nothing shall be done which may prejudice the civil and religious rights of existing non-Jewish communities in Palestine," but not even the most committed Zionist will claim that that part of the promise has been kept. The fact must be faced: even if *The Protocols* had never been confected, and even if the settlers in Palestine were Dutch or British, there would still be an Arab nationalist resistance to the loss of their land.

Much of this history has been forgotten, because of the unimaginable disaster which later overwhelmed European civilization and very nearly annihilated European Jewry. However, a respect for truth requires one to remember that for the first three decades of the argument the only serious anti-Zionists were Jewish. There were leftist Jews who thought that the Arabs of Palestine were being done an injustice. There were Orthodox Jews who thought Zionism was a blasphemy, because no return to Jerusalem was possible before the arrival of the Messiah. And there were liberal assimilationist Jews who thought that the future of the Jewish people lay in the Diaspora throughout the Western world, the scene of all its triumphs from Spinoza to Einstein. (Those Jews who today boycott the *New York Times* for being bleeding-heart about the Palestinians would smack their brows if they could see how Arthur Hays Sulzberger kept the whole American Zionist movement at arm's length before and even during the Second World War.)

Between about 1942 and 1948, the American Council for Judaism enjoyed wide support for its anti-Zionist arguments (it is still worth reading Thomas Kolsky's scholarly history of the period, *Jews Against Zionism*). Be serious and ask what is more likely: that Nat Hentoff is right and America will intern and exterminate its Jewish population, or that Israel will succeed forever in governing resentful Arabs? The first outcome is to the very highest imaginable degree improbable. The second is simply impossible.

In a recent essay for the Jewish weekly *Forward* in New York, for which I ought to say I have been an occasional book reviewer, the liberal pro-Israeli critic Paul Berman detected a certain coarsening among those who take the Palestinian side. He was able to cite some disgusting examples of euphemism, concerning the hellish tactic of suicide-murder, among Western intellectuals who were ready to explain the murder of children as a symptom of "despair."

He even detected concessions to anti-Semitism in the pages of *The New York Review of Books*—which might be described as the flagship of secular liberal Judaism—particularly in the anti-Sharon essays it had published from

Professor Tony Judt of New York University. Yet when it came to it, Berman was unable to cite any explicitly anti-Jewish propaganda in such sources. "It is unintended inferences," he concluded somewhat lamely, "that seem to me the most frightening of all."

Well, let's agree by all means that there are reasons enough for hypersensitivity. I, for example, always think I can tell something from the mere way that a person pronounces the word "Jew." (The longer he takes to pronounce it, the more on guard one should be.) Harold Abrahams in *Chariots of Fire* says memorably of prejudice that you "catch it on the edge of a remark."

Nonetheless, there is a danger in overprescribing, as well as underdiagnosing.

If everything is anti-Semitic, then the term loses its vital distinction. In a recent debate with a rabbi from the Simon Wiesenthal Center, I ridiculed the idea that Vichy and Kristallnacht have resurfaced in France.

First, it's probably not true. But second, and hardly less important—what would be left to say if these horrible phenomena really did *occur*? I care enough about the issue to keep my hatred pure, and to reserve it for those who truly merit it.

In April there was a huge demonstration in Washington, D.C., in favor of the Palestinians. To the astonishment of many bystanders, in the front rank of this demonstration stood a phalanx of bearded and hatted ultra-Orthodox Jews.

They carried the flag of the P.L.O. and waved placards denouncing Zionism root and branch. They were not for a two-state solution: they were for a Palestinian state from the Jordan to the Mediterranean. These are the members of Neturei Karta. For them, the Messiah will indeed tarry, in fact won't even bother to call in advance, until the bogus atheist state of Israel has disappeared. (You can read about anti-Zionist Hasidim in Chaim Potok's 1967 novel *The Chosen*, or view them in the movie of the same name.)

I have seen these people before, in Brooklyn and in the Mea Shearim quarter of Jerusalem, where they spit on the Israeli flag. I hung around with them at the demonstration for a while, collected some of their arcane literature, and noticed the more usual contingents of left and liberal and secular Jews who oppose the occupation, some of them wincing as hoarse and furious young Arabs shouted "*takbir!*" invoking Islam and jihad. I realized again why this long story has no neat or tidy resolution: maybe no resolution at all.

If the insane sickness of Fascism were to strike the "Christian" world again, and all the Jews had to flee—the six million or so American Jews, the 600,000 in France, the large populations in Argentina, Russia, Canada, Ukraine, and Britain—there would be no room in Palestine unless the state of Israel were to approximately double its size as well as to evict many if not all of the three million Muslim and Christian Palestinians. (A repellent option, with whose advocates Sharon himself has flirted.)

One could hardly expect this to be tolerated even by the most moderate Arabs, who are in enough of a rage as it is (and not entirely because of the circulation of *The Protocols*, either). This would not be the only assimilation problem: the Israeli writer David Grossman points out that, as it is, more Israeli Arabs speak Hebrew than American Jews.

If, on the other hand, there were to be a peace agreement which led to the dismantling of the settlements, and the settlers had to be "assimilated" within a smaller Israel, an even more Zionist movement would spring up among the former colonists, who would start to dream—and not just to dream—of a "return" to the lost West Bank homeland of Hebron and Nablus.

This would be the perfect counterpart to the scheme in Philip Roth's 1993 novel, *Operation Shylock*, where Israeli-born Jews dream of liberation and escape by rejoining the Diaspora.

Meanwhile, having promised safety to the Jews by means of a state in Palestine, the Israeli government issues almost daily warnings of the imminent destruction of the whole community. Having proposed Zionism as a means of declaring proud independence from fluctuations in Gentile goodwill, Israel has become utterly reliant upon foreign aid—especially an annual American subsidy of $3 billion—in endless battle with its neighbors.

And, having proposed Zionism as a cure for anti-Semitism, Israel recruits the support of anti-Semitic fundamentalists such as Pat Robertson and Billy Graham, who see the Jewish state as a prelude to the conversion of the Jews, to be followed happily enough by Armageddon and the consigning of the nonconverts to hell.

Some of these ironies are in Israel's favor: the kids who burned those French synagogues this past spring were lumpen Arab immigrants trying to make a crude and violent point about Palestine, and at least France's leading anti-Semite, Jean-Marie Le Pen, has promised to deport all of them.

But some of the ironies were not helpful: there is no decent way to compare destitute Arab refugees in Gaza to the members of the SS, as Menachem Begin used to do. One sign of modern anti-Semitism is the obsessive, nasty need of some people to compare Israel to Nazi Germany. It would actually be good if all sides dropped this outrageous analogy, which is designed to cheapen something, namely the Shoah, or Final Solution, the memory of which must not be abused.

The survival of the Jewish people has for centuries been a means of taking the moral temperature of a society. Those who take that temperature are quite rightly conditioned to notice even a slight elevation. It is sometimes said that all Jews must have a bag mentally packed, ready to flee. To the extent that this is true it will, alas, always be true. The creation of a Jewish state, it can now be argued, merely restates an old dilemma in fresh terms. Neither Israel nor messianism can cure the irrational.

Myself, even as a wretchedly heretic and bastard member of the tribe, I perhaps conceitedly think that there may be something to the cliché about Jews' being inherently and intuitively smart. Smart enough to see that if ethno-religious nationalism isn't good for other people, it may not even be good for the Jews. Smart enough to doubt the divinity of antique man-made scrolls. Smart enough even to see that the Promised Land may be a secular multi-ethnic democracy, none the worse for being a second home to many other wanderers and victims, too. America, in a word. The best hope and, yes, perhaps the last one.

VANITY FAIR, SEPTEMBER 2002

THE FUTURE
OF AN ILLUSION

K arl Marx was neither a determinist nor a vulgar materialist and never said that religion was "the opium of the people." What he did say, in his *Critique of Hegel's Philosophy of Right*, was that it was at once the expression of inhuman conditions and the protest against them: "the heart of a heartless world; the sigh of the oppressed creature; the spirit of a spiritless situation." Secular criticism, he said, had endeavored to "pluck the flowers from the chain, not in order that man shall wear the chain without consolation but so that he may break the chain and cull the living flower." It was only in this context and with these metaphors that he described religion as an opiate, and even then not as we would now define a mind-dulling (or mind-expanding) "controlled substance," but rather as an analgesic on the Victorian model.

On his analysis, the likelihood that religion would ever wither away or go into a decline must be reckoned as very slight. However, the possibility of its becoming a private belief or a purely personal source of comfort—rather than a matter of state and society—should not be dismissed either. Freud only extended this idea in his celebrated essay "The Future of an Illusion," by pointing out the extraordinarily close correlation between doctrines of immortality and redemption, and the inextinguishable human desire to defeat or transcend death. For him, faith was ineradicable as long as humans were in fear of personal annihilation—a contingency that seems likely to persist. But the strength and tenacity of the belief did not make it any less of an illusion

The moral superiority of atheism (and also of what I prefer to call anti-theism and has been called miso-theism) is less often stressed than its intellectual superiority. The intellectual advantage hardly needs elaboration: we do not normally accept unprovable assertions at face value, however devoutly they are maintained, and we possess increasingly convincing explanations of matters that once lay within the province of the supernatural. Skepticism and inquiry and doubt are the means by which we have established such a civilization as we possess; professions of sheer faith are a hindrance to investigations both moral and material.

However, there are some moral claims for atheism that may be worth putting forward. First, and most conspicuously, the atheist cannot be entirely happy with his conclusion. To be resigned to death and extinction is not always a consolation even to the Stoic—though it does have its satisfactions. Among these satisfactions, at any rate, one can include the reasonable certainty that mere wish-thinking did not help to stack one's intellectual deck. Second, the atheist can expect to be free of the pervasive solipsism that disfigures religious thought. If an earthquake should occur, or a comet fill the sky, he can be sure that this development is not all, indeed not at all, about his own brief existence and vain human aspirations. W. H. Auden put it deftly when he wrote (as a hopeful Anglican):

> *Looking up at the stars, I know quite well,*
> *That for all they care, I can go to hell.*

We live in a time when physics is much more awe-inspiring than any faith or any man-made deity, and when Galileo's realization—that the solar system is not earth-centered—has itself been eclipsed and re-eclipsed, so that we can see the solar system itself as a dim and flickering bulb in an unimaginable sweep of galaxies and constellations. Paradoxically, it is those who calmly recognize that we are alone who may have the better chance of investing human life with such meaning as it might be made to possess.

Those who decide to try and lead ethical lives without an invisible authority are also 'blessed' in another way, because they do not require a church, a priesthood, or a reinforcing dogma or catechism. All that is needed is some elementary fortitude, and the willingness to follow the flickering candle of reason wherever it may lead. Despite many recent fluctuations in religious fervor and allegiance, the evidence is that millions of adults now live this way (probably including in their number a fair proportion of the congregations at churches, mosques, and synagogues). The Dutch, by some accounts, now have an actual secularist majority. In Northern Ireland recently, despite British government inducements to register as Protestant or Catholic in the census—if only on the false promise of compensation for past wrongs—12 percent of respondents declined to adopt a confessional allegiance. For me, however, the country with the most impressive and intelligent secularist movement is India—most recent victim of the stupidity and cruelty of mobilized faith.

Those who write about religion and who tell me that it stands for, or substitutes for, various nationalist or emotional or historical needs, are telling me what I already know and what nobody is trying to deny. Those who maintain that it is a strong and continuing force in human affairs are simply bashing their shoulders against an open door: I knew that too. Those who write about religion and tell me that "God does not merely create something other than himself—he also gives himself to this other," are claiming to know something that they cannot possibly know. If I made a concession in an argument with the religious, it would be this: I am willing to admit that there may be unknowable things. It's a poor return for this admission to be told that the devout already know the mind of god. That was the ground of argument to begin with—and what's the point of an ineffable deity if he can be so readily comprehended by banal mammals like ourselves? At least the faithful should be expected to display a little reverence here. But apparently they can't wait to seize their little shred of local and temporal authority.

And why is that? Their god already controls the past and the future, and has dominion over paradise and hints on how to get there. His kingdom, as the Christians say, is not of this world. But in which world does religion actually exact the demand for obedience? In this one. How confoundedly odd.

Now you may choose to tell me that Osama bin Laden (say) is upset about Jerusalem and Mecca and Medina, and still raw about the Crusades, and that this analysis of his agitation explains his appeal. What could be more intelligible, or more trite? But how would it explain his theology? According to him, all is decided by heaven, and the true believer is assured eternal luxury and congratulation: a vast promise compared to the brevity and vicissitude of this vale of tears. Versions of this fantasy appear in all creeds, with discrepant degrees of literal-mindedness depending on the date and on the society.

If I truly had such a belief, it would make me happy, or at least would have a chance of doing so. But does it bring contentment to its adherents? Not at all! They can know no peace until they have coerced everyone else into sharing their good news. Does this argue for confidence in the belief? Not self-evidently. My provisional conclusion, then, is that the religious impulse lies close to the root of the authoritarian, if not the totalitarian, personality.

Some obvious connections can't avoid notice even from the most casual observer: religious absolutism makes a good match with tribal feeling and with sexual repression—two of the base ingredients of the fascistic style. This is also true of the "secular" forms taken by the religious mentality. Ostensibly irreligious despotisms based on faith and praise and adoration invariably take the form of cult worship. North Korea today manifests this idolatry to an extent not attained even by Hitler or Stalin or Mao. But this observation does not just mean what many take it to mean—that fanaticism or tyranny can take an atheist form. It means, rather, that fanaticism and tyranny have a strong if not ineluctable tendency to take a theistic form. The connection between Stalin and the predecessor system that regarded the Czar in the light of the divine is fairly obvious. China and especially North Korea can be shown to have modeled their precepts of authority on Confucianism. The Japanese emperor-worshiping militarists took the principles of Zen as their inspiration and employed them as a training manual. (See the fascinating new study *Zen at War*, written by Brian Victoria, a Buddhist savant.) Hitler was a pagan in some ways but he got the Roman Catholic bishops to celebrate his birthday from the pulpit every year. The other fascist leaders in Europe—Mussolini, Pavelic in Croatia, Franco in Spain, Salazar in Portugal, Horthy in Hungary—were in more or less explicit alliance with the Vatican, and one of them (Father Tiso in Slovakia) was actually in holy orders.

Ah, but what about Martin Luther King, Jr., and Gandhi? I would reply, first, that if religious believers are not willing to accept the connection between faith and horror as necessary, they should be careful in proposing any close connection between faith and good works. The emancipation of black America and the independence of India were not sacred causes: they were fought for by many people of no religion (and opposed by many people of profound faith). No supernatural commitment was or is necessary in either case, and no religious claim is vindicated by it. Take the references to god out of Dr. King's speeches and they lose none of their moral force. Take the ostentatious Hinduism out of Gandhi's worldview and you increase the chance that sectarian fratricide in India could have been averted. In neither outcome, in any case, can it sensibly be argued that god intervened in human affairs.

Again, those who wish that he would had better be careful what they ask for. If their god can claim credit for miracles, then he cannot avoid responsibility for many other drastic occurrences. I would think it base and illogical to argue that suffering disproves the existence of god: there seems to be no ground for connecting the two ideas in the first place. But if I were arguing for the existence of a god, I would be careful to avoid citing happiness or good fortune, lest I arouse that same base and illogical (and corollary) thought in the minds of the unconvinced.

If Karl Rahner really said that "the mystery enfolds [me] in an ultimate and radical love which commends itself to [me] as salvation and as the real meaning of [my] existence," then why should he not be asked how anybody can know this? His statement is inoffensive enough: it does not propose a jihad or a crusade or an Inquisition. But it is circular and meaningless. So is his related claim that "The world receives God, the infinite and the ineffable mystery, to such an extent that he himself becomes its innermost life." This is just as interesting as being told by some saffron-cloaked mendicant that all things are part of the great whole. Few of us have not had some moment of "transcendence": a feeling that there is more to life than the strictly material. And few of us have not been tempted by harmless superstition: a sensation that something may have happened for a purpose. However, nobody has proposed any nontautological reason to suppose that this is more than an emotion, and it is quite possible to survive cheerfully enough, once having recognized that the problem of interpretation that superstition proposes has no resolution.

I was being intentionally gentle when I referred to superstition as "harmless." I suppose I mean that it is forgivable to be impressed by, say, apparently fateful coincidences, or moments of unusual beauty in the natural order. However, while credulity and solipsism are to be found in every person, it is not usually thought advisable to praise someone for his credulous and solipsistic aspects. It is, rather, the work of education and civilization to train the mind to employ reason and to respect evidence, and to train the individual to be modest. Somebody claiming to detect a divine design in respect of himself may phrase the idea in terms of humility, even submissiveness. But this false modesty is, as always with false modesty, a symptom of the most majestic self-centeredness. ("Don't mind me—I'm just busy doing god's work.") In individuals, I must say that I find this mainly irritating. But by all means let them devote some of their day to prayer and reflection, and to an awareness of the transience of all things.

Religion, however, is not the recognition of this private and dutiful attitude. It is its organized eruption from the private into the public realm. It is the elevation and collectivization of credulity and solipsism, and the arrangement of these into institutional dogma and creed. It is the attempt to decide what shall be taught, what shall be allowed by way of sexual conduct and speech and even thought, and what shall be legislated. And it is the attempt to make such decisions beyond challenge, through the invocation of a supernatural authority.

In many places, the attempt to do these things has been implicitly accepted as a resounding failure as well as a historical outrage, and it will be noticed that those societies that honor pluralism and liberty the most are those that have learned to keep religion in bounds. However, there are constant efforts to undo the secular state and it is important for us never to forget what happened, and what happens, when these attempts are successful.

A word in closing on the "anti-theist" position.

I discover when I read the claims of even the more meek Tillich-like theologians that I am relieved that they are untrue. I would positively detest the all-embracing, refulgent, stress-free embrace that they propose. I have no wish to live in some Disneyland of the mind and spirit, some Nirvana of utter null completeness. Religion's promise to deliver this is in my opinion plainly false. But what it can deliver me is the prospect of serfdom, mental and physical, and the chance to live under fantastic and cruel laws, or to be subjected to frantic violence.

Nobody asserts that there is a straight line of connection between faith and murder and slavery. But that there is a connection is undeniable.

When I analyze the sermons of bin Laden, I cannot see how his claim to divine authority and prompting is any better or any worse than anybody else's. And I am not content to dispute his conclusions only with people who share his essential premise.

DAEDALUS, SUMMER 2003

The Gospel According to Mel

> But he was wounded for our
> transgressions, he was bruised for our
> iniquities: the chastisement of our
> peace was upon him; and with his
> stripes we are healed.
>
> —ISAIAH 53:5

> But I can't think for you.
> You'll have to decide
> whether Judas Iscariot had God on his side.
>
> —BOB DYLAN, "WITH GOD ON OUR SIDE"

> 'e's not the Messiah! 'e's a very
> naughty boy!
>
> —TERRY JONES AS MANDY COHEN IN
> MONTY PYTHON'S LIFE OF BRIAN

One must concede this much to Mel Gibson, who has invested $25 million of his own money to direct, produce, and co-write *The Passion of the Christ:* a movie (due in theaters February 25, Ash Wednesday) that purports to show what the last twelve hours in the life of Jesus were truly like. Most representations of the Crucifixion are softly devotional and sentimental, showing a patient and mournful-looking young man in a highly uncomfortable position. The large majority show him in a loincloth, though this detail in other religious painting and iconography does not always conceal what you might suppose. (It was often put there by devout illustrators to conceal the subject's navel: a far more awkward physical feature from their point of view because it invited unsettling questions about what sort of birth he had had.) Only Grünewald's Isenheim Altarpiece (1515) shows us unsparingly what a man might look like in the expiring stages of a protracted death by torture, and even then the clear biblical evidence that Jesus was exposed naked on the Cross was considered too much for mortals to bear.

Gibson keeps the rag of decency in place but otherwise goes way beyond what has so far been attempted in painting, sculpture, and film. We are shown someone being flogged to ribbons, kicked and beaten, reviled and humiliated, before being brutally hammered into place on a beam and left to die of exposure and slow asphyxiation. I don't know which sources Gibson consulted for this graphic exercise: Hyam Maccoby's history *Revolution in Judaea* contains the best account known to me of the details of Roman capital punishment. That book's dispassionate tone makes it, if anything, somewhat harder to read. The horror and the terror of crucifixion were not reserved just for religious zealots. Thousands of the followers of the Thracian gladiator Spartacus went the same way, and Howard Fast's novel *Spartacus* contains this reflection:

> Once, long after this time, a Roman slave was placed upon the cross, and after he had hung there for twenty-four hours, he was pardoned by the emperor himself, and somehow he lived. He wrote an account of what he had felt on the cross, and the most striking thing about his account was what he had to say on the question of time. "On the cross," he said, "there are only two things, pain and eternity. They tell me that I was on the cross only twenty-four hours, but I was on the cross longer than the world has existed. If there is no time, then every moment is forever."

"Pain and eternity." Gibson's film is fascinated with the first, to an almost lingering and lascivious degree, but it is unsubtly angled toward the second. To illustrate what I mean, let me pose a question. The reaction of a morally normal human being, on witnessing a sadistic episode in progress, is to intervene to stop it. Does Gibson intend us to hope for this, even as he shows us the extremes of anguish? (We use the word "excruciating" for a good reason.) Of course he does not. One has to positively want it to go on and on, all the way, every cut of the lash and every bloody footprint and every rusty nail, until the very bitterest end. At least one has to desire this if one believes in the film's "agenda"—which is a clumsy, melodramatic attempt at the vindication of biblical literalism.

How do we know that we ought not to interrupt the Roman butchers or their rabbinical Jewish allies? According to the film's bannering of the verse from Isaiah above, even though that very verse is couched mainly in the past tense, we must still quench our natural compassion because this atrocity was foretold. It is prophesied and so it must be fulfilled. From the opening passages of the first New Testament Gospel (the Gospel according to Matthew) the story of the life of Jesus is interspersed with verses like this one: "Now all this was done, that it might be fulfilled which was spoken of the Lord by the prophet" (Matthew 1:22). In other words, those who were composing the Gospels were simultaneously checking off the conditions for the manifestation of something inevitable and inescapable. And they also knew how the story must end, because that terminus was divinely mandated. In still other words, this man was killed—if we accept the story—by nobody but his father. He went to Jerusalem to die, and for no other reason but to keep that unpostponable appointment. All the human actors in the drama were playing roles previously allotted to them by heaven: no "responsibility" in its true or usual sense can attach to anyone.

This clear reading of the legend has been obscured for many years by Verses 10–11 of Chapter 19 of the Gospel according to John:

> Then saith Pilate unto him, Speakest thou not unto me? Knowest thou not that I have power to crucify thee, and have power to release thee?
>
> Jesus answered, Thou couldest have had no power at all against me, except it were given thee from above: therefore he that delivered me unto thee hath the greater sin.

Unscrupulously employed, this highly ambiguous verse—ambiguous because it's by no means plain who has done the "delivering"—has caused the most appalling harm. For many centuries, Jews living in Christian societies were well advised to stay indoors at Easter time because violent sermons were preached that blamed them in perpetuity for deicide, or awarded them the collective responsibility for the murder of "the Christ." (In Greek, this is another word for "the Messiah," whose first, not second, coming many Jews are still grimly awaiting.) Pogroms and lynchings were incited in the name of Christianity, and vulgar spectacles such as the famous Passion play at Oberammergau, in Bavaria, depicted Jews as sinister, homicidal conspirators. It was not until the time of Pope John XXIII and the reforms of the Second Vatican Council, in the 1960s, that the Roman Catholic Church explicitly repudiated the "Christ-killer" slur against the Jewish people. That's a long time to wait when you remember that Rome's own theology, and almost every other verse of the four Gospels, makes God the Father the true author and designer of the Crucifixion.

Mel Gibson is an odd man, and has been getting odder. In *Signs*, which would be on any list of the ten worst films of the past decade, he played an ex-priest who recovers his faith after seeing little green men. More recently, and fired up by the directorial itch, he restricted the pre-release screenings of his movie to selected groups of Christian and Jewish conservatives. This didn't always immunize him from criticism. At a showing in Washington, D.C., there was a searching question from a conservative Episcopalian. Why, this man wanted to know, had the film made so much of the subtitled and notorious words from Saint John quoted above, while, to drive the point home for the uninstructed, the camera had been dwelling on the face of the Jewish high priest Caiaphas? Gibson jumped excitedly from his front-row seat and said, "It's in the Bible! Who here didn't know it was in the Bible?" Gibson appears to believe, from the many interviews he has given, that the Gospels were written by eyewitnesses and that this is all the research he needs. It may come as a shock to him to find that the Gospels were composed a long time afterward, by many hands, and in Greek, and that biblical literalism would have to mean that Jesus's own disciples were not strictly Christian since (a) they could not read and (b) they could not in any case have read the New Testament. Then we have Saint Matthew's account of the Crucifixion, where at the moment of death there was a terrible earthquake, a rending of the veil in the Jewish temple, "and the graves were opened; and many bodies of the saints which slept arose, and came out of the graves after his resurrection, and went into the holy city, and appeared unto many." These rather conspicuous events, which among other things would seem to make resurrection something of a commonplace, were entirely missed by Saint John, or at any rate unreported by him, and appear not at all in the only written historical record, which was by Flavius Josephus. Nor are they all shown in *The Passion of the Christ*, even though they are "in the Bible."

But many things are "in the Bible," and one can tell a good deal from what people choose to select. In this film, James Caviezel has been picked to play a heartthrob Jesus (no evidence at all for that, except in the ancient text of *Jesus Christ Superstar*), and he doesn't shriek or beg or defecate during his martyrdom, which means that for all the special harrowing whipping-and-nailing effects the thing is only pseudo-realistic. In Cecil B. DeMille's *King of Kings* also, the Jews came off badly, and by the time of *The Greatest Story Ever Told*,

John Wayne could assume the part of a Roman centurion. (Cued to say, "Truly this man was the Son of God," and told to "try it with a little more awe," the Duke pulled himself together and said, "Aw, truly this man was the Son of God.") In this fluctuation of sinister bad taste and kitsch good taste (of which *Life of Brian* is the undoubted moral summit), where does Mel rank?

Comes the question: Did Gibson know, or not know, what he was doing with his evocation of John 19:10–11? His father is a renowned Catholic-extremist crackpot who speculates wildly about the untruth of the Holocaust and who believes that the current Pope is a heretic and a "Koran kisser," but at least the Bible teaches us to be wary of blaming sons for the sins of their papas. However, Gibson himself is a financial angel to a Catholic splinter group that rejects the Second Vatican Council and employs only the Latin Mass. He has even built a church for this sect, conveniently located for the many sinners near Malibu. And he tells us that the sources for his script were the New Testament (presumably in English, into which it wasn't translated until a few hundred years ago) and the later work of two nuns. The first of these women, Mary of Agreda, was a figure in seventeenth-century Spain who wrote that the Jewish culpability for the murder of Jesus "descended to their posterity and even to this day continue(s) to afflict this group with horrible impurities." The second, Anne Catherine Emmerich, is better known. She was a nineteenth-century German, one of those who brooded for so long and so morbidly on the Crucifixion that she claimed to have received the stigmata—the bloody wounds in hands and feet that are for some people the sign of the true devotee. She also told of a vision in which she saved an old Jewish lady from purgatory. This woman had "confessed" that Jews would slaughter Christian children and use their infant gore to thicken the Passover matzo. This "blood libel," an even more depraved allegation than the Christ-killing one, was a powerful toxin in medieval demagogy and was later much exploited by the Nazis. You can look it up today on the Web sites of jihad. The Syrian defense minister, Mustafa Tlas, has authored a vile book entitled *The Matzo of Zion*, repeating the "charge."

The lacerating detail in which the torture of Jesus is portrayed in the film, it seems to me, is a way of diverting attention from these alarming elements of reactionary propaganda. It isn't all that hard to upset Jews, as Gibson must have known he would, and it's even possible to suspect him of doing so in order to create a climate of emotional publicity. I don't know if that's worse than his attachment to crude theocratic dogma. Some sequences in the movie may have been toned down as a result of criticism from Jewish sources, and this might turn out to be the worst outcome of all. There are many people—check out a fan Web site for *The Passion of the Christ* if you don't believe me—who would like nothing better than to say that the Jews got to Mel. He has hinted something of the sort himself, in a thuggish attack on Frank Rich of the *New York Times* ("I want to kill him. I want his intestines on a stick . . . I want to kill his dog"). Gibson has also said that "modern secular Judaism wants to blame the Holocaust on the Catholic Church" and that with the Caiaphas scene "they'd be coming after me at my house, they'd come kill me." Mel's people bragged that the Pope himself had endorsed the film—a claim that the Vatican now disowns. Maybe the Jews got to His Holiness as well? Perhaps such paranoia is Gibson's excuse for announcing that *The Passion* was really directed by "the Holy Ghost": what Jewish mob would dare to take revenge on that authority?

But the one-note chorus of official American Jewry has been yet another depressing aspect of this "row." Remember—the Vatican now fully concedes that the death of Jesus cannot be laid at the door of all Jews in subsequent ages. That's no more than common sense, even if it did take centuries to assert itself. But nobody can claim that the Jewish clerical hierarchy in Judea at the time did not desire that this rabble-rouser be put to death. On that point, at least, all the supposed Gospel accounts concur. And the greatest Semitic sage of all, Maimonides, was later to write that the Jewish high priests had done exactly the right thing in defense of their faith. Jesus had plagiarized much Jewish learning and teaching and claimed it as his own, had practiced sorcery and magic by claiming to heal the sick and by such tricks as making the spirits of devils enter into the bodies of swine, and had made the further and fantastic claim that he was the Messiah, or Son of God. No more appalling heresy could be imagined, and the Jewish punishment for heresy was every bit as absolute as that of any other monotheistic sect. Their religious authorities, however, did not then have the power of crucifixion, so they left that task to the Roman occupiers. By its own narrow and fanatical standards, the Sanhedrin was quite right to do so, just as the Christian authorities were acting consistently when they used the whip and the pyre and the rack and the wheel on millions and millions of non-Christians and heretical Christians in the years thereafter. (Rome was merciful compared with the Crusades and the Inquisition and the conquistadores, though I don't think a Gibson epic on any of these is ever likely to be made. He prefers anti-English crowd-pleasers, such as *Gallipoli* and *Braveheart* and, even lower, *The Patriot*.) If Christian orthodoxy is valid, then Judaism is futile: a pointless hanging-about for the arrival of the Messiah, who has already shown up. Why not just admit this, instead of whining with Abe Foxman of the Anti-Defamation League about negative stereotypes and all the rest of the self-pitying babble? If the Jewish leadership had any guts, it would turn on those who taunt it with "Christ-killing" and say, "Yeah, all right, since you keep mentioning it, we did you a favor. Judas too. Where would your faith be without us?" This would have the effect, however, of giving away the open secret that religion is man-made. For some reason, we are assumed to need protection from such a revelation.

It makes no difference at all that Jesus himself was "ethnically" Jewish. (In the movie he is sometimes even laughably called "rabbi.") Nor does it make any difference that he spoke Aramaic rather than Hebrew. The Jewish prayer for the dead, the Kaddish, is still recited in Aramaic, as is the Kol Nidre, the prayer said on the eve of Yom Kippur. I have also heard Aramaic spoken by Maronite Catholics on Cyprus and by Syrian Muslims outside Damascus. Roman soldiers would have spoken a dialect of Greek rather than Latin, so Gibson's use of and misuse of ancient tongues is a further layer of mystification.

The "truth" is that religious Christians and Jews could still both be wrong. Jerusalem may not be a "holy city" at all, but just an archaeological site that inspires bad behavior. There could be an afterlife and no god, or a god and no afterlife. Even an alleged resurrection doesn't prove, in itself, that the teachings of the resurrected one are true. (Think of the random resurrections in Matthew 27:52–53.) Miracles prove nothing on their own; Pharaoh's magicians could perform them with ease, or so the Bible says. Most of all: stop and ask yourself seriously why the church took nearly two millennia of human time before it would admit the obvious—that people not alive in those days could not be implicated in a first-century execution. Now, how and why could this concession possibly have taken so long, and been made so reluctantly? Quite simply because, if the Jews are not implicated in those events, then why should anyone else be? And if succeeding generations cannot be bound by a quasi-mythical account of a ritual killing, then the entire business collapses. This is why Catholic fundamentalists like Gibson cannot bring themselves to leave the Jews out of it. Small revisions lead to larger ones: there's no such thing as being a little bit heretical. Thank god for that, at least.

VANITY FAIR, MARCH 2004

III. WAR

Before September

The Struggle
of the Kurds

I f you take a plane from Istanbul and fly southeastward to Diyarbakir, you stay in the same country. But you leave Europe for the Middle East, and you enter the world of the Kurds. In Diyarbakir, a boiling, teeming city enclosed within ancient walls made of forbidding black basalt, the Kurdish flag is prohibited and use of the Kurdish language restricted. So elevator boys and waiters were being careful when whispering to Westerners like myself: "This is not Turkey . . . this is Kurdistan. Diyarbakir—*capital* of Kurdistan. . . . We are not Turks . . . we are Kurds."

I visited a coffee shop with my new friend Hasan, a young Kurd who had agreed to show me his city. I watched as he looked around in disgust through the plumes of tobacco haze and took the proprietor to one side. Within seconds the loud cassette music had been replaced by another tape, more wild and mournful sounding—but not until the boss had cast a swift glance down the street. Taking the best table, Hasan—a man of relatively few words— explained: "Stupid Turkish music. I told him play some good Kurdish tunes."

I had come in search of the Kurds, a people who in 1991 had been abruptly and cruelly promoted to center stage by their battle against Saddam Hussein's regime and by the sympathy felt in the West for those who had suffered longer than the Kuwaitis from Saddam's ambitions. For months I would travel among them, trying to make sense of where this ancient people fit in the modern world.

Who are the Kurds? They number twenty-five million and are scattered from the Middle East to Europe, North America, and Australia, which makes them one of the largest ethnic groups in the world without a state of its own. Once nomadic, most are now farmers or have migrated to cities.

Like the majority of their neighbors, most Kurds are Sunni Muslims; a few are Jews or Christians. Their language is fractured—like the Kurds themselves—by region and dialect, but it is distinct from Turkish, Persian, and Arabic. They are neither Turks, nor Persians, nor Arabs, and they regard their own survival as proof in itself of a certain integrity.

For more than 2,000 years, travelers to the heart of Kurdish country have reported on the blue or green eyes and fair hair seen among the Kurds—and on their fierceness. Four centuries before Christ, as the Greeks were retreating from the Persians toward the Black Sea, Xenophon recorded that they were harassed along the way by Kardouchoi, people who "dwelt up among the mountains . . . a warlike people . . . not subjects of the King." Most modern scholars agree that this is a reference to the Kurds.

Some three million Kurds live in the region of Iraq they call Free Kurdistan, in the mountains where Turkey, Iran, Syria, and Iraq come together. Here, since the humbling of Saddam, the Kurds have established the largest and most populous area of autonomy in their modern history: an area of some 15,000 square miles where Kurds are giving orders, collecting taxes, holding rudimentary courts, and conducting their own parliamentary elections, primarily between the two major parties, Jalal Talabani's Patriotic Union of Kurdistan and Masoud Barzani's Kurdistan Democratic Party. But the Kurds seldom speak with one voice; indeed the positions of the two parties have often shifted. Today the central issues are: Should the Kurds sign a limited autonomy agreement with Saddam (the Barzani view) or should they hold out for more territory and more political concessions (the Talabani position)?

When I arrived in Free Kurdistan, in the spring of 1991, there was a swath of trouble and grief on every side. To the south, Saddam's forces were mustering again to reassert central control. To the north, the Turkish authorities maintained that Turkey was one nation and that Kurds were part of the Turkish family. To the east, the Kurds of Iran chafed under the rule of the mullahs as they had under the shah. To the west, in Syria, the Kurds were some distance from full citizenship; in Lebanon and beyond they were in diaspora.

The Kurds have survived like other large minorities, by sniffing the wind and being adroit at the business of tactics. While in large parts of the West the

Kurds are hailed as tough, romantic, and dashing, it isn't unusual to hear them described by their immediate neighbors as downright uncouth, oil greedy, and for sale to the highest bidder.

To the impatient, proud regional powers that already enjoy statehood, the Kurds are *in the way*. In the way of Saddam's dream of a greater Babylon, glory of the Arabs. In the way of Turkey's plan to earn international respect by modernizing and assimilating the Kurdish provinces. In the way of Iran's scheme for a republic based on Shiite Islam. In the way of Syria's wish to make a militarized nation out of a patchwork of religious and ethnic minorities.

The Kurdish national motto, with origins older than anyone can remember, is simply: "The Kurds have no friends."

In the months just after the gulf war ended in March 1991 it was still dangerous to visit Iraqi Kurdistan, so I enlisted the help of an armed escort hardened by months of guerrilla fighting. Hoshyar Samsam, who knew this country well and had been the personal bodyguard of Jalal Talabani, was taking care of me. He calmly conducted me through bomb-shattered villages and deserted towns. He foraged for me in an area blighted by famine and helped me dodge Iraqi patrols. He looked as if he could carry me if the need arose, and I wasn't sure it might not. He had a fierce, beaming face and huge hands. His hair was reddish and his eyes blue-green. I asked him to tell me his story.

Hoshyar was born to a peasant family in the hills near Kirkuk, the oil capital of Iraqi Kurdistan. He had been brought up on ancestral tales of Kurdish suffering and defiance and had carried this formative memory with him when he left home for Baghdad to study engineering.

In the great Kurdish uprising that followed Desert Storm, Hoshyar was an enthusiastic militant, and a photograph of President George Bush in a jogging outfit was gummed proudly to the windshield of his Toyota jeep. After the first exhilarating days of the revolution—"We took our great city of Kirkuk, without any help from anyone"—he had been caught up in the defeat, exodus, and massacre that captured world attention.

"What about your family?" I asked.

Hoshyar's answer was slightly shrugging. He is a *peshmerga*—in the Kurdish term of honor, one who has made an understanding with death. He was married to the struggle and had no time for domesticity. His relatives were extended all over the hills of the area and scattered between the refugee camps and shelters that dot Iraqi Kurdistan today. "Maybe, after victory, I have my own family."

The Kurds might well have broken and dispersed by now if it weren't for the strength of their family tradition. Everyone seems related to everyone else; it's also sometimes true. Cousins, for example, are encouraged to marry so that farms and orchards can stay in the family. In the squares and streets, men would keep asking photographer Ed Kashi to take pictures of their children. The Kurdish family is the nexus of their solidarity and survival. Even this, though, is linked to "the struggle." An old man we met in the village of Khalifan was sitting with his submachine gun hung over the back of a chair and watching his grandsons frisking about. When I praised their charm and friendliness, he beamed. "Yes," he said. "They will make good soldiers."

Even among the Kurds who live in seemingly normal circumstances, there are the daily reminders of reality.

In the old city of Diyarbakir, for instance, a foreign visitor can leave the noise and smoke of the street, pass through thick walls opening on to a shaded courtyard, and settle in at one of twenty tables at the Trafik Çay Bahçesi, a tea garden. Children play on brightly painted swings and slides nearby. Young men and women hold hands, chat, and loll away the warm autumn afternoon over bottled Coke or small glasses of thickly sweetened tea. The carefree mixing of the sexes comes as a reminder that we are deep in Kurdistan, where—unlike much of the Middle East—women have traditionally not been secluded or veiled.

Fadime Kirmizi, a law student in her early twenties, comes in, accompanied by her brother. They find a table where the light is good and settle down with her law books. He quizzes her through the afternoon.

The afternoon's serenity is regularly broken by fighter jets screaming overhead, one after another, buzzing the city before returning to their Turkish Air Force base. To an outsider the jets seem a pointed reminder to the Kurds that they do not really belong. Yet to most of the Kurds I met, the attitude seemed to be expressed in the thought, what are the Turks doing in *their* country?

* * *

Today's Kurds find themselves caught between their ancient culture and the rush of the twentieth century. At an embassy dinner in Turkey I was seated next to an Iranian woman. Her father was a banker, and she was married to an American, and when she heard of my interest in the Kurds, she exclaimed: "How fascinating! Of course, Khomeini treated them very badly, and they have resisted very bravely. But don't you find them really very—you know—*primitive?*"

In Shaqlawah, a beautiful but run-down town in northern Iraq that serves as a guerrilla headquarters for Free Kurdistan, I was witness to another demonstration of the same attitude.

It was early in June 1991, and the barren "negotiations" between Saddam and the Kurds were being conducted in the nearby town of Arbil. A hand-picked Iraqi intelligence officer had been sent to Shaqlawah to escort rival leaders Talabani and Barzani to the meeting. Lieutenant Colonel Zeid, as he was called, arrived in an immaculate dark green uniform with carefully straightened black beret.

I was eyeing Lieutenant Colonel Zeid when a hoarse and raucous voice broke in. It belonged to a Kurd named Malazada, an unkempt local balladeer with a shell-shocked aspect. Impromptu, he stepped forward and began a long free verse recitation for the occasion. He went on and on, and the lieutenant colonel's clipped mustache began to writhe impatiently. Siamand Banaa, a public spokesman for Barzani's Kurdistan Democratic Party, touched my arm. "You'll have to excuse old Malazada," he whispered. "He's just missing a few strings, as we say."

I appreciated the courtesy, but I rather liked the tolerance of the Kurds, who were willing to stall their big meeting for an old man whose liking for the village epic did no harm. In many ways I was miles and years away from his shaggy, verbose, bucolic style and his horizon bounded by tribe and the rhythms of seasons. The sight of the lieutenant colonel, who thought of these folk as barbarians, reminded me that many outwardly advanced types have taken little from development except technology, which they have employed for barbarous purposes.

* * *

All across Iraqi Kurdistan you can drive for miles, map in hand, and mark off each succeeding heap of stones as the place where a village once stood. One by one the Iraqis dynamited or bombed or poisoned these communities in the name of repressing Kurdish insurgency and shifted their inhabitants into relocation centers. You can still see those too, bleak and menacing blockhouses, hemmed in with wire, where people who had known no master were confined and supervised. The Kurds have been hardened by the digging up of mass graves; estimates of the missing and dead range from 100,000 to 300,000. A United Nations report concluded that the atrocities committed by Saddam's regime were "so grave and . . . of such a massive nature that since the Second World War few parallels can be found." Yet in this landscape of blasted and deserted hamlets there are two sites that all the Kurds insist you must see: Qalat Dizah and Halabjah.

Qalat Dizah's turn came in June 1989. As a large market town near the Iranian border, it may have shown an independence of spirit that annoyed Iraqi military planners. They made an example of the place by bringing in the bulldozers and the dynamite. After the expulsion of the population—perhaps 70,000 individuals—the city was leveled house by house. Only the trees were left standing.

By the time I arrived, many of the former inhabitants, finding life insupportable in the refugee camps over the border, had returned to squat in the ruins of Qalat Dizah. A single tiny dispensary, run by a depressed doctor named Osman Salim, tried to hold the line against malaria, typhoid, and malnutrition. They were Osman's daily enemies, and he was combating them with almost zero resources.

"Exactly *nothing* has been done for the people of Qalat Dizah," he told me, complaining that the storied Western relief effort—which would eventually deploy millions of dollars in a hugely successful operation—had not yet trickled down here. The survivors faced another harsh winter, with unclean water and poor food and not nearly enough of either.

Not even this was enough to prepare me for the town of Halabjah, a community that has the same resonance for the Kurds as does the Warsaw Ghetto for the Jews or Guernica for the Basques. The town became suddenly and horribly famous on March 16, 1988, when it was almost obliterated by Iraqi bombs and its people were savaged by nerve gas and other poison agents.

"I saw the planes come," Amina Mohammed Amin told me through an interpreter. "I saw the bombs fall and explode. I tried to get out of town, but then I felt a sharp, burning sensation on my skin and in my eyes."

Mrs. Amin then did something that astounded me. Without warning, she drew up her voluminous dress and exposed her naked flank. Her whole left side, from mid-calf to armpit, was seared with lurid burns. And they were *still* burning.

"The Red Crescent took me to a hospital in Iran," she said, "and then I had five months in a London hospital. But the burns need to be treated every day." Even as we spoke, her daughters began applying salves to the exposed area. It was hard to look, and hard not to look.

Mrs. Amin said that twenty-five members of her family had been killed that day, which was a terrible figure even if you allowed mentally for the way Kurds talk of extended families. Nizar Hassan, the chief physician at the hospital, told me later that the town lost 5,000 people in the attack, out of a total population swollen by refugees to 70,000. (Later estimates pushed the doctor's body count above 6,000.)

I found one of the causes of the horror in a blitzed building. Here, lodged in a basement corner where it fell from an Iraqi Air Force bomber, was a wicked-looking piece of hardware with stencil markings on its side. Worried about fallout from the Halabjah escapade, the soldiers of Saddam had entered the town and carried off all the evidence. Or almost all of it. There was the bomb, and there were the survivors. Halabjah would, after all, be remembered.

You can't take much from people who have nothing to lose, yet I was impressed at how the Kurds make the best of hopeless situations. They are tough and adaptable, which is perhaps the key to their longevity in this war-ravaged region. Their resilience may face its latest test sometime this summer. Iraqi troops have been massing just outside Free Kurdistan, held at bay by fighter planes of the post-Desert Storm coalition. When that air cover is withdrawn, it is likely that the Kurds will again be under direct attack.

I was resting near the town of As Sulaymaniyah, then held by Iraqi troops. We were roasting a lamb for dinner. In every direction the land looked naked and lunar, stripped of life. It was hot. I wondered, out loud, if there was any beer in this wilderness.

"Beer," said one of my Kurdish bodyguards. "The Englishman wants beer!"

One of the fighting men dropped what he was doing and walked up to me. "How many Saddams you have?" he asked.

"Many Saddams," I replied.

We were talking money. Some of the bills in Iraqi currency are printed with the portrait of Saddam Hussein, leading the Kurds to joke incessantly about "dirty money."

"For fifty Saddams," the guerrilla said gravely, "I can bring quite a lot of beer."

I peeled off sixty—it seemed no time for penny-pinching—and my man vanished into the dark. He was back in an hour, lugging an old sack containing cans of frosted Western ale.

"Ali, how on earth?"

Ali smiled, revealing nothing, but I suspected that he had struck a deal with a bored Iraqi guard in town.

A few days later, passing the war-scarred settlement of Rawanduz on our way back to the Turkish border, I saw other evidence of Kurdish enterprise. The owner of a roadside café had scrounged canned goods from somewhere and kept them chilled in a mountain stream, ready for sale. Small boys sold Western cigarettes still in their cellophane-wrapped packages. (How had they gotten them?) Families sat eating, half in and half out of cannibalized cars and trucks that were kept going on God knows what. The café proprietor and his wife were singing away, dishing up kabobs in exchange for fistfuls of Saddams.

These people had been bombed and routed, but they had come back and were evidently enjoying their moment of independence. Kurds, once regarded as suspicious of strangers, now took every Westerner as a friend.

"You will tell of us?" asked the old cook, as I pressed my last Saddams on him. "Tell people not to forget?"

The Kurds usually make their appearance in other peoples' narratives by virtue of a readiness to quit their mountain fastness and engage in battle. But their tendency is to go back to the mountains as soon as war is over.

Unfortunately, the Kurds live in an area that is strategically important to three great modern nationalisms, Turkish, Arabic, and Persian, and that is enormously rich in the two great natural resources of oil and water. The tendency of nationalism is to try to assimilate minorities and to invent a new "nation" such as Iraq (which is actually three communities, the Sunni Muslim ruling group, the southern Shiite Muslim majority, and the northern Kurds, mostly Sunni, rolled into one uneasy state). And the tendency of Middle Eastern politics is to establish control over oil fields and headwaters, not just for their own sake but before anyone else does.

The Kurds themselves have certain fundamental similarities. All are survivors. All are well acquainted with dispersal and persecution. But I began to discern variations in their status throughout the region. In Jerusalem, for instance, there is a small but prosperous middle class of Jewish Kurds who live in peace. In Beirut, however, Kurds are the lowest of the low. A large Kurdish community has been in Lebanon since the beginning of this century, but on the identity card that Kurdish immigrants must carry, the words "domicile under review" appear in the space for citizenship. This puts the Kurds into a category of seasonal or migrant workers. In Lebanon the Kurd is almost always a menial, depicted by Lebanese novelist Elias Khoury as a faceless toiler and random victim.

Stateless in a state where statehood is itself a tenuous thing, Lebanese Kurds have thrown their support to the Kurdistan Workers Party, or PKK. This is a Marxist organization run by an enigmatic figure named Abdullah Öcalan, with a camp in Lebanon's notorious Bekaa Valley. Here the PKK operates under Syrian protection, carrying on a guerrilla war against Turkey. Syria provides an umbrella for the same reason that umbrellas are always provided—water. In Turkish Kurdistan the huge new Atatürk Dam allows the Turks to control the flow of the Euphrates River before it crosses the Syrian frontier. Anxious for leverage, the Syrian regime uses the Kurds to remind the Turks not to exploit this advantage.

Those in the rank and file of the PKK seem unaware that they are foot soldiers in the game of nations. Jawan and Soubhi, two young people who met me in Beirut, conducted me through a series of safe houses (never as reassuring as the phrase suggests, especially in Beirut). All my questions, they said, could be answered when I met the man they call Apo—Uncle: Abdullah Öcalan.

When I arrived at the camp known as the Mahsum Korkmaz Academy, for a PKK member who died in a battle in Turkey, I found hundreds of young people in well-cut, olive drab military fatigues, much more disciplined and military in aspect than any of the local militias, or indeed than either the Syrian or Lebanese Armies. Men and women mixed freely, a change from the monastic character of peshmerga camps in Iraq.

Hearing English spoken, I soon found myself talking with Milan, an olive-skinned teenager who had come from Australia, where her Kurdish parents had gone for work. Now she was a soldier in the war against Turkey.

"I'm trying to forget I ever knew English," she said. "All I care about now is Kurdistan." Unlike rival Kurdish parties in Iraq that seek autonomy within that nation, the PKK calls for a separate Kurdish state spanning the existing borders of Iraq, Syria, Turkey, and Iran. As if to prove her dedication, Milan had just been to a Maoist-style "self-criticism session," held under an awning just off the hot square at the camp's center. Face alight with belief, she invited me to watch rehearsals for the forthcoming PKK fiesta. In a few days tens of thousands of Kurds would converge on the camp for dances and speeches, with *Serouk Apo*—Apo the Leader—the guest of honor.

Apo himself, whom I met later that day, is a stern critic of the Kurdish people and their attachment to tradition. "We are a feudal society," he told me, "and our leaders have been chieftains who betray us. Our cultural and political level is low." He pointed to dark moments in the Kurdish past, such as the role played by Kurdish mercenaries in the Turkish slaughter of the Christian Armenians in 1915. He said that the Kurds were victims of the divide-and-rule mentality and could always be counted on to fight among themselves. There was some truth to all this, but Apo's own chieftain-like appearance and the tame eagle tethered rather eccentrically to his desk didn't inspire the absolute confidence he demanded.

An experienced Kurd can tell his grandchildren of betrayal by colonial Britain and France, of promises made by Iran, Iraq, Syria, and Turkey to support the Kurds for as long as they were fighting only on the rival's territory, of interventions in Kurdistan by Israel to weaken Arab nationalist regimes, and of promises made by both cold war superpowers that turned out to be false.

Ever since President Woodrow Wilson incorporated promises for Kurdish autonomy into his Fourteen Points following World War I, the Kurds have traditionally looked to the United States as their deliverer from old injustices. George Bush appeared to sympathize with their cause during Desert Storm, yet his subsequent lack of support has left them baffled. Western politicians seem unable to appreciate the depth of the Kurdish yearning for a homeland. I sat with Jalal Talabani, leader of the Patriotic Union of Kurdistan, at his guerrilla headquarters in northern Iraq. He was telling me about the city he was most fiercely contesting with Saddam Hussein. "Kirkuk," he declared, "is our Jerusalem."

Lacking an alternative homeland of any kind, Kurds can emigrate, but they can't escape. In the grim factory belt that stretches between the Spandau and Charlottenburg areas of Berlin, Kurds work to produce the brand name goods of Osram, Siemens, and Volkswagen. The German government doesn't recognize them as Kurds but only as the Turkish passport holders that they are. They tend to cluster in rundown areas like Kreuzberg.

My guide to this world was a young man named Bayram Sherif Kaya, born in Germany of Kurdish parents who emigrated from southeastern Turkey. He divided his day between a Kurdish-language radio station, a kindergarten for Kurdish children, and various Kurdish relief organizations, all of which he helped run. "Fortunately I speak perfect German and I look European, so I don't have the problems that most of our people have."

Bayram doubts that he can go home again. "We are watched by the Turkish Embassy, which hates Kurdish nationalism. We are watched by Turkish extremists, who believe all Kurds are dogs. We are attacked by German fascists who shout '*Ausländer raus*—Foreigners out!' and paint it on our walls."

All over Kreuzberg, with its squatters and rent-controlled communes, were the slogans of different Turkish and Kurdish political factions. I paid a visit to Hînbûn, a women's center in Spandau that was originally founded to teach literacy but now serves as a sort of community center in hard times. "Most of the Kurds here come from one single town called Muş, in the Lake Van region of eastern Turkey," I was told by Aso Ağace, a Kurdish woman who works at the center. "Often they can speak German but not write it, so they need help with form filling, and they need help with the schools, which don't recognize Kurdish as a language."

Hînbûn is a counterpart to the male-dominated side of Kurdish life, in that it is for women only and acts as a support group. It tries to make Kurdish housewives and women workers feel more secure. "People are afraid," Aso Ağace told me. "We have also seen pressure from the Turkish Consulate on the municipal government of Berlin, which used to help us distribute our literature." Here, too, one found a sort of transplanted ghetto solidarity. The problem, as ever, was that of trying to survive as Kurds, while not seeming alien to a larger society.

It is difficult for an outsider to learn the essentials of the Kurdish cultural style. For one thing, although most Kurds who are Muslims adhere to the Sunni sect, some are Shiites; still other Kurds practice one of several indigenous religions. In addition, the Kurdish language is divided by dialects and subdialects. Kurds in northern Iraq, eastern Turkey, and the former Soviet Union speak Kurmanji, while those in western Turkey speak Zaza; in southern Iraq Sorani prevails, in Iran the Guran and Laki dialects. This problem of Babel is an impediment to Kurdish identity. Nonetheless, all Kurds can recognize Kurdish. Scholars at the Institut Kurde in Paris are at work on a Kurdish-French dictionary of about 50,000 words.

While this codification goes on, the mass of Kurds keep together with a sort of musical vernacular. During my sojourn in Iraq, for example, everyone was glued to cassette tapes by singer Juwan Hajo, a Syrian Kurd whose productions are bootlegged all over the region. And in Diyarbakir the cassette business proved so popular that the Turkish authorities relaxed their ban on Kurdish music—the ban that my friend Hasan had so casually defied. Kurds who have made the United States their home live in communities from California and Texas to Brooklyn, New York, where the Kurdish Library and Museum acts as a focal point for Kurdish affairs and crafts.

Most of them live in and around San Diego, where they began settling after the collapse of another Kurdish revolt in Iraq in 1975. The late Mustafa Barzani, father of political leader Masoud Barzani, came to the U.S. first, followed by a few hundred of his retinue.

A community leader sponsored a social evening for me in the suburb of Chula Vista. Though almost all present had made good lives for themselves, they struck me as stranded in time, compelled to watch the sufferings of their kinsmen from afar. They had all recently been, once more, taken up as a cause during the gulf war, and then dropped. There was much wistful talk, over tea and cakes, of the way it had been fashionable to be a Kurd during Desert Storm and of how newspapers never sent photographers any more.

"We are known as a refugee people," said Jamal Kasim, who runs a trucking business. He's a burly, smiling fellow who doubles as California spokesman for the Kurdistan Democratic Party. "So our image depends on the daily and weekly news," he went on. "People are generally friendly, and they sympathize with Kurds, especially since Halabjah, but Americans these days are not so interested in foreign affairs, and there are many who do not like immigrants of any kind."

Yet again, it seemed, the Kurds had pitched their tents in a difficult environment—the San Diego-Tijuana border, with its daily flux of illegals and its mounting anxiety over language, culture, and integration. (One local Kurd, I later found, had resolved the problem of his own assimilation by landing a job with the U.S. Border Patrol.)

Our gathering in Chula Vista included a food store manager, an architect, a freelance journalist, and two computer engineers. Only one guest was unemployed. The two computer engineers worked for Ted Turner; one of them, Alan Zangana, was very proud of his company's having colorized "a film you may have seen called *Casablanca*."

Successful as they were, though, I noticed again the absence of women, a tender subject that caused a mini-controversy when I brought it up. Alan Zangana picked up an argument I had been hearing off and on since I had innocently asked, back in Shaqlawah, where all the women had got to. One of my Kurdish guides then took to pointing every time he saw a female, as if to vindicate the good name of Kurdistan, "Look. There is one. Now are you satisfied?" It is easy for Westerners to mistake the Kurds for backward fundamentalists, but Alan maintained that it was high time that women played an equal role in the political struggle. Nobody exactly disagreed, although I had the sense that I had stumbled into an argument they would have again.

* * *

I had almost abadoned my dream of finding a "typical Kurd" when I was introduced to Sheikh Talib Berzinji of Los Angeles. "Sheikh" is an honorific title; in the old country his family claimed descent from the Prophet Muhammad. Talib himself, with his leonine head and ample military mustache, is from the area of As Sulaymaniyah. He had been a follower of Mustafa Barzani—"Ah, the old general!"

He now divides his time between running a laundry service in Los Angeles, which he must do to make a living, and writing and translating plays, which he would do full-time if he could. He has translated *The Merchant of Venice* into Kurdish.

But his days are filled with the endless responsibilities of being a Kurd. The old sheikh explains to journalists and radio interviewers who the Kurds are and how long they have been fighting. He has to raise money for refugees. He has to think of his extended family back in the perilous mountains. A spread of the hands: "You see how it is."

If I had started my quest by talking to Sheikh Berzinji, a lot of what he said would have seemed either mysterious or self-pitying. But now I saw the stages through which he had passed. The Kurds are homeless even at home, and stateless abroad. Their ancient woes are locked inside an obscure language. They have powerful, impatient enemies and a few rather easily bored friends. Their traditional society is considered a nuisance at worst and a curiosity at best. For them the act of survival, even identity itself, is a kind of victory. The old man, holding on to his Kurdishness in a choice of hostile or indifferent environments, is the Kurd for all seasons.

NATIONAL GEOGRAPHIC, AUGUST 1992

THUNDER IN
THE BLACK MOUNTAINS

I suppose," I said, gesturing in a polite conversational manner at the fabulous escarpment of peaks that rose behind us, "that it's the mountains that have made Montenegro unconquerable." The priest with whom I was lunching lowered his piece of fresh-killed lamb. "No," he admonished me emphatically. "It is a site only for the eroticism of the wolves." There is true power in really good bad English, and I was halfway to getting the point but perhaps looking baffled, because the priest decided to throw euphemism to the winds. "For the fucking of the wolves, with the other wolves. Only for this." In other words, he was saying, nobody really wants to conquer Montenegro. It's the place that god forgot, the end of the earth, a wasteland of violence and poverty given over to lupine copulation. (I later learned that in the local vernacular there is actually a word—*vukojebina*—which is used pungently to denote the location of a wolves' motel.)

This is deep Balkans: a den of banditry and haunt of clans, with a "black" economy conjured from smuggling and extortion. If I had been told, of our delicious if basic lunch, that it was black lamb slaughtered by gray falcon, I would have been inclined to believe it. The "Black Mountain." *Crna Gora.* Montenegro. In whatever language you render it, the very name has a slightly Ruritanian ring (and the goings-on at the old Montenegrin court in fact inspired Franz Lehár to write *The Merry Widow*). But between the grimness and tragedy, and the operetta-scale farce, is being written the likely final chapter in the whole demented project of Greater Serbia. The final fratricide of the Milošević wars will probably take place here, the endgame of a half-diseased and half-romantic national frenzy.

Ten years ago, there were six republics within federal Yugoslavia. Two of them—Slovenia and Croatia—split away as soon as they could, suffering light and heavy bombardment respectively from the Serb-dominated Yugoslav army (J.N.A.). Macedonia and Bosnia followed suit, with catastrophic consequences for the latter. Only Montenegro decided voluntarily to stay with Serbia, and to lend a drapery of illusion to the existence of a "Federal Republic of Yugoslavia"—the nightmare state of which Slobodan Milošević is still the "president." Montenegrins are close kin to Serbs and have a shared history of arduous and bitter resistance to the Turks, and to Islam. It was Montenegrin forces who were noticeable and aggressive in the hellish shelling and looting of the ancient Dalmatian city of Dubrovnik in 1991. It was a psychotic Montenegrin extremist—the failed shrink Radovan Karadžić, now wanted for war crimes—who acted as Milošević's surrogate leader in Bosnia. Milošević's own father was from Montenegro. The current "prime minister" of rump Yugoslavia, Momir Bulatović, is a Montenegrin. For practical purposes, Montenegro has been Serbia's jackal over the past ten years. But now, and against all expectations, a probable majority of Montenegrins want out of Yugoslavia and an end to Milošević's rule. It is as if Austria, having united with Germany in the Anschluss of 1938, had opted to reclaim its independence in 1944.

Land Without Justice was the harsh title given by the heroic Yugoslav dissident Milovan Djilas to his 1958 memoir of a Montenegrin childhood and youth. But it can be a mistake to stress only the bleak history of blood feuds and "ancient hatreds." The rocky interior of Montenegro, it is true, is arid and pitiless and impoverished, and enlivened chiefly by amorous yelpings from the wolf population. But on the coast around the luminous Gulf of Kotor there are gemlike cities that once paid allegiance to Venice, with gorgeous Catholic and Orthodox churches existing in amity. (The little town of Perast, a sort of micro-Venice complete with campanile and its own pair of miniature islands, is one of the most exquisite as well as one of the most friendly places in which I have ever set foot. It was there that I casually mentioned to a complete stranger the absence of any pictures of President Slobbo. "Milošević—son of a whore!" was his immediate reply: the better for being uttered in the Italian slang *figlio di puttana* that you often encounter along this coast. Out on the crystalline Adriatic water, a Serbo-Yugoslav gunboat provided a floating reminder of who is still in charge, as well as of the fact that Montenegro, for now, is

Serbia's only coastline.) Then, after a journey up through the heartbreaking ranges, you can come to the cool and elegant antique royal capital of Cetinje. Here, amid the lime trees and wide walking streets and little piazzas, you can find a moment of old Europe as if preserved in aspic or amber. Before 1914, Montenegro was an independent kingdom. To this day Cetinje boasts, whether locked and shuttered or sometimes transformed into arts schools or music rooms, the former embassies and legations of Austria-Hungary, imperial Russia, and all the other powers that came to ruin in 1914. I happened to be there on the fourth of August, the eighty-fifth anniversary of the British Empire's declaration of war on Germany, and paid a call on the building where a plaque announced HIS MAJESTY'S LEGATION. The faded old villa-cum-mansion now did duty as a conservatoire. But though I spent a long moment gazing back through the looking glass at the lost world of pre-deluge Europe, I had come on exactly the right day to look forward—to the day when Montenegro will ask for its independence to be restored, and recognized again.

On his visit to Cetinje in 1929, Evelyn Waugh played up the Ruritanian angle strongly, mocking the tiny Parliament building for having been "the legislature by day and the theater by night." He also stressed the Corsican and Sicilian ethic, noting the number of daggers and pistols for sale and dryly suggesting: "Most likely the owners were saving up to buy cartridges for a stolen army rifle, and so snipe the neighbors in a more deadly manner from behind their pig-styes." The man I had come to meet could have represented, at first glance, either the comical or the sinister side of this caricature. He was understood to be "close" to the independence-minded young president of Montenegro, the thirty-seven-year-old Milo Djukanović. But he held no formal position and he wouldn't be quoted by name. He also looked—though I had heard him described as a "spin doctor"—as if he had spent a night in the open in an especially louche *vukojebina*. "Wolfish" was a word that leapt immediately to mind. The experience was much more like an encounter with a watchful dissident than one with the unofficial spokesman of a government. However, he turned out to speak with passion and authority, and everything he predicted to me came true, so I am glad that I took so many notes as we lowered our questing muzzles into the slivovitz.

"The Fascist idea of 'Greater Serbia' is now dead," he announced without preliminaries, "It is impossible without the nucleus of Montenegro." He was himself, he said, a full-blooded Serb (a number of Montenegrins announce themselves as such) but a Montenegrin patriot first and foremost. "And since 150,000 Montenegrins also live in Serbia, our very existence is an argument for dissolving Yugoslavia and replacing it with a confederation." (This might sound like a contradiction, but bear in mind my analogy above of Austrian nationalism as opposed to German supernationalism.)

There were free elections in Montenegro last year, which the anti-Milošević forces won in spite of intimidation from armed pro-Belgrade elements. So, said my friend, "Milošević can never be president here again. Nor does he control any local ethnic forces who could help him try his usual tactic of racial partition." Then he told me what was going to happen. "In two or three days, the Montenegrin government will make a series of demands to Belgrade. We will ask for the name Yugoslavia to be scrapped and replaced by 'Commonwealth of Serbia and Montenegro.' We will ask for full control over all our armed forces, and for complete economic independence. We shall also propose a one-chamber parliament with equal rights for Montenegro, and a distinct and convertible Montenegrin currency." I put the most obvious question: What if Milošević refuses this amputation of his authority? "In that case we will hold a referendum on full independence, no sooner or later than next year." A day later, the Montenegrin authorities did make precisely this series of demands, tightening up the last point a bit by giving Milošević only six weeks to reply and announcing that if he responded in the negative there would be a referendum on complete independence this fall.

Some people think that President Milo Djukanović is bluffing. But I would not be so sure. As a former Milošević protégé and well-tailored leader of the Communist Youth, he has seen the dank and desperate Serb-dominated leadership from the inside and has come to appreciate that Montenegro is now shackled to a corpse. On the streets of his capital, and at airports and border posts, he is daily reminded that Montenegro cannot long endure half Serb and half free. The military is controlled from Belgrade, while the local police and militia are loyal to him. A volatile situation of "dual power" obtains. Several examples illustrate the point. During the Kosovo war, Belgrade attempted to establish martial law in Montenegro, and called up young Montenegrins to fight. The local authorities ignored the draft law, and Dragan Soć, the minister of justice, who received his own call-up papers, walked defiantly past the military court each morning on his way to work, giving a disrespectful salute. Djukanović invited members of the Muslim and Albanian minorities into his Cabinet, and allowed 70,000 Kosovo refugees onto Montenegrin soil. Not content with this snub to Milošević, he permitted leading Serb dissidents to take refuge in his autonomous republic, and permitted the circulation of anti-Milošević leaflets and magazines, many of which found their way back to Belgrade.

"Above all," I was told determinedly by the audacious Milka Tadić at the offices of *Monitor*, the leading magazine of the democratic opposition, "above all, and for the first time, Montenegro refused to fight in a Serbian war. We helped Milošević in Bosnia and Croatia, but these latest massacres are all his own, and for the first time our people were not shielded by the state from knowing all about them. Everyone can see what a horrible crime it was—if only because they were not involved." Now, she said with a triumphant smile, Montenegro has recognized the international court at The Hague, and has promised to cooperate with it. "So, can you imagine a 'federal republic' where the president cannot pay a visit to the sister republic, because he would have to be arrested and deported to stand trial for war crimes?" The offices of *Monitor* were bombed twice by pro-Milošević thugs during the Bosnian war: I can tell she had waited a long time for the chance to say this. And no, she said with a shrug, it's not dangerous to speak that way, or "not anymore."

Ms. Tadić, editor of *Monitor*, is not in the least like a wolf. She's more like a fox. And she's tall. Montenegrins are extremely tall—to my eye the tallest people in Europe. Taller than the Danes. I met Tadić in Podgorica, the relatively hideous and sprawling and purpose-built capital that was once Titograd. But one reason the old ex-capital of Cetinje had seemed such a miniature was that its inhabitants gave me the impression that they walking around on stilts. Since Montenegro has about 650,000 inhabitants, while Serbia boasts 10 million or so, it may be a huge psychological advantage to call on so many lofty people, with such a long martial tradition. (Down on the coast is the homeland of antiquity's Illyrian warrior queen, Teuta. Teuta is a favorite birth name for Albanian girl babies.)

As I write, Milošević has not personally replied to the Montenegrin *démarche*. His chief political henchman, the ultra-chauvinist Vojislav Šešelj, is, however, making blood-and-thunder speeches, saying that the J.N.A. will intervene by force in Montenegro "like the Americans would if California tries to go away." Mr. Šešelj's Chetnik militia has never lost a battle against civilians and was involved in some of the foulest work in Bosnia and Kosovo. I wonder, though, how it would acquit itself in battle against tough Montenegrins who are kith and kin. The talk in cafés and bars in Podgorica is just the sort of hushed conversation one used to hear in the banana republics of Central America, revolving eternally around the question "Which way will the army go?" Milošević keeps his Second Army in Montenegro, and its commanding officers are loyal to him as far as anyone can tell. But the mid-level of the officer corps is thought to contain many who are sympathetic to independence, or are unwilling to risk another dustup with NATO, or are just leery of being the last man killed in defense of an obviously doomed regime. During the Kosovo war, Montenegrin forces stood off Milošević's soldiers in a confrontation over Kosovar refugees, and this test of wills was as heady as it was novel. Just as one cannot make a child grow smaller, so the momentum and appetite for autonomy increase with the experience of it.

Montenegro is in an advanced and hectic stage of being a little bit pregnant. You can see it in the emerging battle of the colors: green, red, black, and white—the Montenegrin rainbow. Montenegro lost its independence in the First World War by impulsively siding with Serbia, by suffering Austro-Hungarian occupation as a result, and then by submitting to a 1918 plebiscite on joining the new kingdom of Jugoslavia. In fact, it was the only state on the Allied side in 1914 that went on to lose its independence at the end of the war. Serb troops were on hand to make sure that the 1918 plebiscite went the right way. Those who opposed the Anschluss had to mark ballot papers in green, and have ever since been known as *zelenasi*, or "the greens." The pro-Serb elements were white, or *bjelasi*, when white was the Russian shade for counterrevolution. Today, when you see a spray-paint slogan supporting Milo Djukanović, it will be lettered in vivid green, even though he and his rivals both used to prefer red. Montenegro was the reddest of the old Jugoslav republics: solid for the

WAR • BEFORE SEPTEMBER

wartime Communist partisans and with a very high proportion of party members until the very end of Titoism. Now, however, pro-Belgrade slogans tend to be scrawled in black. This is partly the historic color of Fascism—which is apt enough—but also reminds people that the local Orthodox prelate, a thickly furred old hooligan named Amfilohije Radović, has been a rhapsodic supporter of Serb ethnic cleansing. And, just to clarify matters, green in the Balkans is the traditional color for Muslims—whose mosques have not, in Montenegro, been dynamited and defiled as they have everywhere else that is in range of Greater Serbia's guns.

Anyway, when Milo Djukanović took his oath of office as Montenegro's president in January of last year, he did so in the ancient former capital of Cetinje and not in the "official" seat of government. So that old geopolitical cliché—"the family of nations"—may be about to welcome a tiny new member. Did I say welcome? The NATO powers, including the United States, have been very grudging and hesitant about attending the baptism, or even acknowledging the conception and parturition. Pompous noises are made by the State Department about the "territorial integrity" of the former Yugoslavia, as if that bastard and hybrid were being kept alive by anything but a death-support machine. (Milka Tadić said that she'd argued the point with Clinton at the July summit in Sarajevo, and as her eyes flashed and her Amazonian limbs flexed, I wondered for an instant how he'd coped with the real local version of a "strong woman.") Everyone knows why Europe and America are dithering: if Montenegro "goes," then there is no Yugoslavia, and if there is no Yugoslavia, then there is no state for Kosovo to be a legal part of, and there are timorous statesmen who hope that this highly spiced and heavily booby-trapped question does not come up on their watch. But might it not be nice if, just for this once, there was a crux in the Balkans that did not take our diplomatic masters completely by surprise? This one has been coming for a long time: coming like Christmas, coming like a heart attack. There's no excuse for being unprepared. When wolves couple, it's dramatic and impressive and the more modest and reticent animals hardly dare peek. A wolf divorce is more seldom seen, but worth some serious attention for all that.

VANITY FAIR, NOVEMBER 1999

VISIT TO
A SMALL PLANET

The North Korean capital, Pyongyang, is a city consecrated to the worship of a father-son dynasty. (I came to think of them, with their nuclear-family implications, as "Fat Man and Little Boy.") And a river runs through it. And on this river, the Taedong River, is moored the only American naval vessel in captivity. It was in January 1968 that the U.S.S. *Pueblo* strayed into North Korean waters, and was boarded and captured. One sailor was killed; the rest were held for nearly a year before being released. I looked over the spy ship, its radio antennae and surveillance equipment still intact, and found photographs of the captain and crew with their hands on their heads in gestures of abject surrender. Copies of their groveling "confessions," written in tremulous script, were also on show. So was a humiliating document from the United States government, admitting wrongdoing in the penetration of North Korean waters and petitioning the "D.P.R.K." (Democratic People's Republic of Korea) for "lenience." Kim Il Sung ("Fat Man") was eventually lenient about the men, but not about the ship. Madeleine Albright didn't ask to see the vessel on her visit last October, during which she described the gruesome, depopulated vistas of Pyongyang as "beautiful." As I got back onto the wharf, I noticed a refreshment cart, staffed by two women under a frayed umbrella. It didn't look like much— one of its three wheels was missing and a piece of brick was propping it up— but it was the only such cart I'd see. What toothsome local snacks might the ladies be offering? The choices turned out to be slices of dry bread and cups of warm water.

Nor did Madeleine Albright visit the absurdly misnamed "Demilitarized Zone," one of the most heavily militarized stretches of land on earth. Across the waist of the Korean peninsula lies a wasteland, roughly following the 38th parallel, and packed with a titanic concentration of potential violence. It is four kilometers wide (I have now looked apprehensively at it from both sides) and very near to the capital cities of both North and South. On the day I spent on the northern side, I met a group of aging Chinese veterans, all from Szechuan, touring the old battlefields and reliving a war they helped North Korea nearly win (China sacrificed perhaps a million soldiers in that campaign, including Mao Anying, son of Mao himself). Across the frontier are 37,000 United States soldiers. Their arsenal, which has included undeclared nuclear weapons, is the reason given by Washington for its refusal to sign the land-mines treaty. In August 1976, U.S. officers entered the neutral zone to trim a tree that was obscuring the view of an observation post. A posse of North Koreans came after them, and one, seizing the ax with which the trimming was to be done, hacked two U.S. servicemen to death with it. I visited the ax also; it's proudly displayed in a glass case on the North Korean side.

A local phrase book, entitled *Speak in Korean*, has the following handy expressions. In the section "On the Way to the Hotel": "Let's Mutilate U.S. Imperialism!" In the section "Word Order": "Yankees are wolves in human shape—Yankees / in human shape / wolves / are." In the section "Farewell Talk": "The U.S. Imperialists are the sworn enemy of the Korean people." Not that the book is all like this—the section "At the Hospital" has the term *sol-saga* ("I have loose bowels"), and the section "Our Foreign Friends Say" contains the Korean for "President Kim Il Sung is the sun of mankind."

I wanted a spare copy of this phrase book to give to a friend, but found it was hard to come by. Perhaps this was a sign of a new rapprochement with the United States, or perhaps it was because, on page 46, in the section on the seasons, appear the words: *haema-da pungnyoni dumnida* ("We have a bumper harvest every year").

I was hungry when I left Pyongyang. I wasn't hungry just for a bookshop that sold books that weren't about Fat Man and Little Boy. I wasn't ravenous just for a newspaper that had no pictures of F.M. and L.B. I wasn't starving just for a TV program or a piece of music or theater or cinema that wasn't cultist and hero-worshiping. I was *hungry*. I got off the North Korean plane in Shenyang, one of the provincial capitals of Manchuria, and the airport buffet looked like a cornucopia. I fell on the food, only to find that I couldn't do it justice, because my stomach had shrunk. And as a foreign tourist in North Korea, under the care of vigilant minders who wanted me to see only the best, I had enjoyed the finest fare available.

North Korea is a famine state. In the fields, you can see people picking up loose grains of rice and kernels of corn, gleaning every scrap. They look pinched and exhausted. In the few, dingy restaurants in the city, and even in the few modern hotels, you can read the *Pyongyang Times* through the soup, or the tea, or the coffee. Morsels of inexplicable fat or gristle are served as "duck." One evening I gave in and tried a bowl of dog stew, which at least tasted hearty and spicy—they wouldn't tell me the breed—but then found my appetite crucially diminished by the realization that I hadn't seen a domestic animal, not even the merest cat, in the whole time I was there. (In a Pyongyang restaurant, don't ever ask for a doggie bag.) Nobody knows how many North Koreans have died or are dying in the famine—some estimates by foreign-aid groups run as high as three million in the period from 1995 to 1998 alone—but the rotund, jowly face of Kim Il Sung still beams down contentedly from every wall, and the fifty-eight-year-old son looks as chubby as ever, even as his slenderized subjects are mustered to applaud him. Kim Jong Il, incidentally, has been made head of the party and of the army, but the office of the presidency is still "eternally" held by his adored and departed dad, who died on July 8, 1994, at eighty-two. (The Kim is dead. Long live the Kim.) This makes North Korea the only state in the world with a dead president. What would be the right term for this? A necrocracy? A thanatocracy? A mortocracy? A mausolocracy? Anyway, grimly appropriate for a morbid system so many of whose children have died with grass in their mouths.

Even in former days, Korea was known as the "hermit kingdom" for its stubborn resistance to outsiders. And if you wanted to create a totally isolated and hermetic society, northern Korea in the years after the 1953 "armistice" would have been the place to start. It was bounded on two sides by the sea, and to the south by the impregnable and uncrossable DMZ, which divided it from South Korea. Its northern frontier consisted of a long stretch of China and a short stretch of Siberia; in other words its only contiguous neighbors were Mao and Stalin. (The next-nearest neighbor was Japan, historic enemy of the Koreans and the cruel colonial occupier until 1945.) Add to that the fact that almost every work of man had been reduced to shards by the Korean War. Air Force general Curtis LeMay later boasted that "we burned down *every* town in North Korea," and that he grounded his bombers only when there were no more targets to hit anywhere north of the 38th parallel. Pyongyang was an ashen moonscape, it was year zero, Kim Il Sung could create a laboratory, with controlled conditions, where he alone would be the engineer of the human soul.

During my sojourn in this lab, I got an idea of why the more it remains the same, the more it changes. In the past few years, the hermetic seal has broken and is now leaking in all directions. Take those fearsome cases of anti-American xenophobia with which I began. The uniformed guards who gave me a tour of the U.S.S. *Pueblo* asked for five dollars to add my visit to the schedule (the ship is normally off-limits) and wanted to score a couple of packs of American cigarettes when the tour was done. The same *pourboire* worked wonders during my visit to the DMZ. In the basement of my hotel, a casino had been opened by Chinese riffraff from the gambling capital of Macao, who once tried to stop me from playing blackjack because I was wearing peasant sandals and was thus improperly attired. In a karaoke bar in downtown Pyongyang, while I regaled the customers with a spirited rendition of "Girls Just Wanna Have Fun," "La Bamba," and, as the night wore on, "Proud Mary," my Korean friends preferred the soothing banality and individualism of "Yesterday" and—a solid favorite—"My Way." (There's a special plangency to the line about facing the final curtain.) One night I snuck off for a sauna and massage. For nearly an hour I was alone and unsupervised with a Korean civilian. But I couldn't make much of it, because she didn't speak English and also chose to numb me with techniques that seemed more like Tae Kwon Do than massage. As I took my aching joints back to the hot tub, I saw one of my guides materializing, naked and glistening through the steam. When our eyes met we conceded unspokenly that we'd both gone above and beyond the call of duty.

* * *

Playing pool with Korean officials one evening in the Koryo Hotel, which has become the nightspot for foreign businessmen and an increasing number of diplomats (to say nothing of the burgeoning number of spies and journalists traveling under second identities), I was handed that day's edition of the *Pyongyang Times*. At first glance it seemed too laughable for words: endless pictures of the "Dear Leader"—Little Boy's exalted title—as he was garlanded by adoring schoolchildren and heroic tractor drivers. Yet even in these turgid pages there were nuggets: a telegram congratulating the winner of the Serbian elections; a candid reference to the "hardship period" through which the country had been passing; an assurance that a certain nuclear power plant would be closed as part of a deal with Washington. Tiny cracks, to be sure. But a complete and rigid edifice cannot afford fissures, however small. There appear to be no hookers, as yet, in Pyongyang. Yet if casinos come, can working girls be far behind? One perhaps ought not to wish for hookers, but there are circumstances when corruption is the only hope.

The external changes have been much more dramatic, and it's by means of these hints that those on the inside can at last begin to guess what's going on in the big world. The Soviet Union has vanished, and its Russian successor no longer wants to buy North Korean goods at the old fraternal rates. China, which once had a lower standard of living than North Korea, is now booming. All along the northern border, even Little Boy's frontier guards can see that the lights are on all night in China across the Yalu and Tumen Rivers, while blackouts and shortages are the common lot on the North Korean side. (The power cuts out continually in North Korea. The lights went off even while I was touring the U.S.S. *Pueblo*, which is a showpiece.) The Yanbian prefecture of China's Jilin Province is largely Korean-speaking, and at least a quarter of a million famine-refugees have crossed the border at great risk and are hiding among their kin. This is unprecedented; nobody knows the effect of the "feedback"—a grim term under the circumstances—among the relatives left behind. But, for the first time since the foundation of the North Korean state, a dissident movement is beginning to put out tiny shoots among the hunger exiles, many of whom cross and recross the stricken frontier areas.

Most important of all, though, is the sudden thaw from the South. Kim

377

Dae Jung, this year's Nobel laureate for peace, is a man much more deserving of adulation than either Fat Man or Little Boy. I'm proud to say that I know him slightly. When he returned to South Korea from exile in 1985, having survived imprisonment and kidnapping and at least one assassination attempt, carried out by the dreaded Korean Central Intelligence Agency, I went along with him and was a witness to his arrest by the military junta at Seoul airport. By dint of truly astonishing bravery and patience—he had to "win" an election that was overturned by the generals before he was allowed finally to succeed—Kim Dae Jung has put an end to half a century of dismal and sordid military/police dictatorship on the southern half of the peninsula. It's no longer possible for the North Koreans to claim that the "other" regime is a colonial puppet held in place by American troops.

Kim Dae Jung has wagered everything on what he calls a "sunshine" approach to his austere and backward northern neighbor. Everybody's breath was caught by his visit to Pyongyang last June, and by the reunions of sundered families that followed it. There is even talk of building a direct road and rail link between the South Korean capital of Seoul and Pyongyang—something that would have been unimaginable a year ago.

Sooner or later, all talk among foreigners in Pyongyang turns to one imponderable subject. Do the locals really believe what they are told, and do they truly revere Fat Man and Little Boy? I have been a visiting writer in several authoritarian and totalitarian states, and usually the question answers itself. Someone in a café makes an offhand remark. A piece of ironic graffiti is scrawled in the men's room. Some group at the university issues some improvised leaflet. The glacier begins to melt; a joke makes the rounds and the apparently immovable regime suddenly looks vulnerable and absurd. But it's almost impossible to convey the extent to which North Korea just isn't like that. South Koreans who met with long-lost family members after the June rapprochement were thunderstruck at the way their shabby and thin northern relatives extolled Fat Man and Little Boy. Of course, they had been handpicked, but they stuck to their line.

There's a possible reason for the existence of this level of denial, which is backed up by an indescribable degree of surveillance and indoctrination. A

North Korean citizen who decided that it was all a lie and a waste would have to face the fact that his life had been a lie and a waste also. The scenes of hysterical grief when Fat Man died were not all feigned; there might be a collective nervous breakdown if it was suddenly announced that the Great Leader had been a verbose and arrogant fraud. Picture, if you will, the abrupt deprogramming of more than 20 million Moonies or Jonestowners, who are suddenly informed that it was all a cruel joke and there's no longer anybody to tell them what to do. There wouldn't be enough Kool-Aid to go round. I often wondered how my guides kept straight faces. The streetlights are turned out all over Pyongyang—which is the most favored city in the country—every night. And the most prominent building on the skyline, in a town committed to hysterical architectural excess, is the Ryugyong Hotel. It's 105 floors high, and from a distance looks like a grotesquely enlarged version of the Transamerica Pyramid in San Francisco (or like a vast and cumbersome missile on a launchpad). The crane at its summit hasn't moved in years; it's a grandiose and incomplete ruin in the making. "Under construction," say the guides without a trace of irony. I suppose they just keep two sets of mental books and live with the contradiction for now.

I saw exactly one picture of Marx and one of Lenin in my whole stay, but it's been a long time since ideology had anything to do with it. Not without cunning, Fat Man and Little Boy gradually mutated the whole state belief system into a debased form of Confucianism, in which traditional ancestor worship and respect for order become blended with extreme nationalism and xenophobia. Near the southernmost city of Kaesong, captured by the North in 1951, I was taken to see the beautifully preserved tombs of King and Queen Kongmin. Their significance in F.M.-L.B. cosmology is that they reigned over a then unified Korea in the fourteenth century, and that they were Confucian and dynastic and left many lavish memorials to themselves. The tombs are built on one hillside, and legend has it that the king sent one of his courtiers to pick the site. Second-guessing his underling, he then climbed the opposite hill. He gave instructions that if the chosen site did not please him he would wave his white handkerchief. On this signal, the courtier was to be slain. The king actually found that the site was ideal. But it was a warm day and he forgetfully mopped his brow with the white handkerchief. On coming downhill he was confronted with the courtier's fresh cadaver and exclaimed,

"Oh dear." And ever since, my escorts told me, the opposite peak has been known as "Oh Dear Hill."

I thought this was a perfect illustration of the caprice and cruelty of absolute leadership, and began to phrase a little pun about Kim Jong Il being the "Oh Dear Leader," but it died on my lips. And there is more than just callousness and fatalism to the Confucian style. It was noticeable, during the visit of Kim Dae Jung, that Little Boy observed Confucian etiquette, deferring to his senior at all points and even respectfully adjusting his pace to that of the older man. Similarly, rather than seem too ambitious in taking the succession after his father's death, he delayed his assumption of formal power and decreed a three-year mourning period for the departed—the pious Confucian maximum. Even the two national flowers—the Kimilsungia and the Kimjongilia—reflect this relative modesty. The Kimilsungia is a gorgeous orchid. The Kimjongilia is a fairly humble member of the begonia family.

Still, the fervor and single-mindedness of this deification probably have no precedent in history. It's not like Duvalier or Assad passing the torch to the son and heir. It surpasses anything I have read about the Roman or Babylonian or even Pharaonic excesses. An estimated $2.68 *billion* was spent on ceremonies and monuments in the aftermath of Kim Il Sung's death. The concept is not that his son is his successor, but that his son is his *reincarnation*. North Korea has an equivalent of Mount Fuji—a mountain sacred to all Koreans. It's called Mount Paekdu, a beautiful peak with a deep blue lake, on the Chinese border. Here, according to the new mythology, Kim Jong Il was born on February 16, 1942. His birth was attended by a double rainbow and by songs of praise (in human voice) uttered by the local birds. In fact, in February 1942 his father and mother were hiding under Stalin's protection in the dank Russian city of Khabarovsk, but as with all miraculous births it's considered best not to allow the facts to get in the way of a good story.

It was once said of Prussia that it wasn't a country that had an army, but an army that had a country. And North Korea is a garrison state, a society organized for war. I took a trip on the Pyongyang subway (between the "Resurrection" stop and the "Glory" stop, both of them ornately decorated *á la Moscou*) and noticed that the escalator took me down to an almost thermonuclear depth; it's a bomb shelter. In the countryside are long and oddly straight roads with almost no vehicles on them; these must be emergency landing strips and airfields. You see military uniforms on about every tenth person. Partly this is a means of additional regimentation for the society, and partly it's a solution to the unemployment problem. (The Korean People's Army doesn't look so frightening when you see it stripped to the waist and digging ditches with worn-out tools, as I did on the road to Nampo, the country's main port.) But a gigantic part of the budget still goes for heavy weapons, missile technology, and nuclear power plants.

Like some Lilliput masquerading as Brobdingnag, North Korea likes to bluff the rest of the world and force it to ask, Would this regime be prepared to immolate itself and others to make a last, dying point? The baroque secrecy of the culture and the arcana of its rituals help to give the impression that it might be capable of anything. I witnessed the same "Mass Games" in the colossal May Day Stadium that were, a week or so later, put on to impress Madeleine Albright. Here is how the impression is created.

First, you have to picture the outcome of a ten-year collaboration between Busby Berkeley and Leni Riefenstahl. The entire floor of the amphitheater is suddenly filled with hypnotizing phalanxes of men, women, and children (proof on their own of a totally drilled society). With bewilderingly faultless choreography, and to the strains of kitsch light-opera music, people form and re-form into the shapes of Mount Paekdu—complete with blue lake—a raging sea, and a map of the Korean peninsula. On the other side of the arena, a wall of humanity executes the most expert and versatile flash-card displays, turning on a dime from a refulgent and embossed portrait of the Fat Man to a scene of flowers or factories. Every now and then, the sentimental and the folkloric are punctuated, to the accompaniment of massed searchlights and skull-splitting chords, by the image of a granite-jawed soldier with flamethrower and bayonet, or—and this was the climax—by that of a great rocket lofting into the sky. It was at this point that Little Boy turned to Albright with a smile and said, "Don't worry. We won't test any more of them."

Was this a threat or a promise? Perhaps it was a bit of both. By behaving sullenly, North Korea has gotten attention and aid and even respect. But it remains Lilliput. Don't lose a sense of proportion: it could not conquer the South, which has more than twice its population, and it certainly could not govern the South even if it could conquer it. North Korea would actually be shattered into fragments and paved over once again if it even tried a war with the United States and its regional allies. And it would not have a friend in the world, which it did last time with the slightly reluctant support of Stalin and Mao. The whole "threat inflation" directed at this distraught Oz-like regime is either slightly paranoid or slightly cynical. The idea of America building a huge, hypothetical, costly "missile shield" to ward off Little Boy is an especial absurdity. His projectiles are antique and inaccurate, and he wouldn't live to see the first one splash down if he ever did decide to go mad.

But *is* he mad, as we used to be told he was? From a society and state where the human personality has been ruthlessly erased, and one individual character obscenely exalted, there arises a recurrent question. Are we dealing with a giggling and sadistic playboy, or with a slight oddball who has a bizarre and thwarted need to become a Hollywood *auteur* and perhaps possesses latent Gorbachevian tendencies?

Again it could be both. South Korean intelligence blames Little Boy for the bombing of an airliner and for an explosion which killed several members of the South Korean Cabinet. These outrages occurred back in the 1980s, during the rule of Fat Man, so it doesn't seem likely that Little Boy could have been allowed to commit them on his own. What he did do, on his own initiative, was kidnap a South Korean movie star and have her brought to Pyongyang for his cinematic appreciation. The only people who can be said to "know" Kim Jong Il are Choi Un Hoi, whose screen performances so ravished and captivated him, and her husband, the director Shin Sang Ok. In 1978 they were snatched by Little Boy's agents in Hong Kong. The concept in the mind of the Dear Director was not a fate worse than death for the wife, but a collaboration on celluloid. Shin spent five years in a North Korean jail for refusing to make any propaganda movies; when released he was told he could have creative and artistic control. The couple spent some quality face time with their host, made him some films, and in 1983 managed to tape-record some of his table talk. So we know that he likes splatter movies (*Friday the 13th* is an all-time favorite), but also that he admires Liz Taylor and especially her work in *Butter-field 8*. He maintains lavish postproduction and dubbing facilities and is especially proud when he can get his name on a film credit, which he usually can.

He was also quite outspoken on matters political. The tape, which seems genuine, has him saying that, "after having experienced about thirty years of socialism, I feel we need to expand to the Western world to feed our people." He adds that the current system gives people no incentive to work, and that South Koreans have reached college level while North Koreans are still in kindergarten. However, he is aware that reforms would threaten the basis of his father's state. "When China opened up a bit, the first thing the people learned was not technology. Instead, the young people grew their hair long and grew mustaches. They were interested in superficial things. This stems from the emptiness of themselves, and the socialist system. We are in the same situation as China."

Choi and Shin's old kidnapper has since published a book—*Kim Jong-Il on the Art of the Cinema*—a copy of which I was able to find (not without a searching glance from my minder) in a Pyongyang bookstore.

There's much turgid propaganda and boilerplate, but one or two heartfelt observations as well. Robert Altman could surely endorse the following:

> A film which merely aims to make a profit by showing off the stars' faces, cannot be real art . . . There cannot be a genuine creative spirit, and the beautiful flower of art cannot bloom where actors sell their faces, and even their souls.

In another of his recent works, *Abuses of Socialism Are Intolerable*, Little Boy surprised me by confronting head-on the notion that Korean socialism was "totalitarian," "barracks-like," and "administrative and commanding." These words appear, with emphasis, on almost every page. Of course, the muscular prose of the master polemicist makes short work of the accusations. But most North Koreans are never permitted to know what the outside world thinks of their system. They are told instead that the rest of humanity pulses with love for Fat Man and Little Boy. Could there be a coded message here?

If so, it may not be the only one. The most hysterical and ridiculous and grandiose attempt to persuade the North Koreans that the whole world is with them is to be found in the "International Friendship Exhibition," a colossal marble pagoda among the beauties of Mount Myohyang, about two hours' drive north from the capital. Built at remorseless expense (and much of it underground, like a lot of North Korean institutions), it houses more than 61,000 gifts, bestowed on the Great Leader and the Dear Leader by foreign heads of state, delegations, and random celebrities. Every schoolchild is brought here at least once, to be assured that Kim Il Sung was an international statesman without peer.

On one level, it is a giant museum to the death of Communism and dictatorship. There are two huge railway carriages—one from Stalin and one from Mao—which commemorate the days when state socialism was something made of wrought iron. Vanished politicians and even vanished regimes are featured: here is a stuffed bear's head from Nicolae Ceausescu and a bust from East Germany. Capitalist despots are well represented, too, including Zia ul-Haq of Pakistan and General Suharto of Indonesia (who also presented a pair of chimps to the national zoo, where they joined a warthog from Robert Mugabe). Every now and then, amid the bric-a-brac of onyx ashtrays or mounted hunting rifles, one finds a gem. A silver box, with the CNN logo, from Ted Turner and Jane Fonda. An English version of Kim Il Sung's essays, with a foreword by Eldridge Cleaver, from Harrison Salisbury of the *New York Times*. A white crane sculpture, listed as given by "The Religious Leader of the United States." Who he? My inquiry is met with polite astonishment. Why, Billy Graham of course. He and his sons are here all the time.

The four entrance doors are made from solid copper and weigh four tons apiece. Shift sixteen tons and whaddaya get? A stuffed crocodile, beamingly upright and proffering a cocktail tray, from the Sandinistas. I began to get the giggles, imagining that Kim Il Sung had thousands and thousands of dotty aunts and batty uncles, and had solemnly resolved to keep every one of their rubbishy birthday and Christmas presents in case they ever came to call.

However, in the smaller adjacent building, devoted to the gifts received by Little Boy, we find a whole new note being struck. Almost every present and tribute is from a foreign business. Plaques from British insurance companies are prominent, for some reason. Most astonishing, though, is the main room, which is given over to the trophies of the recent summit with Kim Dae Jung. Vast, shiny wide-screen TV sets and computer monitors, bearing the logos of Samsung and Daewoo. A limousine—interestingly called a Dynasty limousine—from Chung Ju Yung, the founder of Hyundai. Mr. Chung also gets his picture displayed, with a smiling Little Boy. The whole room is a shrine to consumer capitalism. What must the North Korean visitors think as they are paraded around the exhibits and shown goods they have never seen? Their faces give nothing away. But if this is not a hint about a possible future, perhaps along the lines of the "two Chinas," I don't know what would be.

Suppose we picture North Korea as a gigantic film set, with everyone a con-scripted extra. The sole director feels he needs more scope. But he doesn't quite want to share power with the larger studio system, and thus sacrifice his autonomy. I went to the official film studios, which are nowhere near as luxu-rious as Little Boy's private facilities. They consist of a series of huge back lots populated by listless and bored people. On the whole expanse of one million square meters, nothing was being shot. The entire place wore an air of com-plete torpor. One abandoned set represented a street in Seoul, the South Korean capital, in the early 1960s. The street, intended obviously to suggest decadence, featured some bars and a brothel and a cinema advertising Marilyn Monroe in *The Seven Year Itch*. After spending some time in Pyongyang, I thought, Boy, I could use a little of *that*.

But then, quitting the back lots for downtown Pyongyang, I suddenly real-ized that the whole place is for show. It's an "as if" society. Uniformed female traffic cops do pirouettes at intersections, though there are no cars. Newspapers come out, though they contain no news. Restaurants produce menus of non-existent dishes. At the airport, there are barely any planes. In the national art gallery—they understand that you have to *have* a national art gallery—almost all the paintings are of the same two people. In the Palace of Children—a for-bidding structure with no play space—I found a class of tiny Koreans solemnly learning Morse code under the supervision of an adult. He unblinkingly beep-beeped and they doggedly transcribed the dots and dashes. Nobody has told them that the international community abandoned Morse two years ago.

* * *

Worst of all was the Great People's Study Hall, a huge book depository erected on one side of Kim Il Sung Square. It cost, I was proudly told, $100 million. There are desks, card catalogs, shelves; it's free and open to the "public"—it's just what it would be like if Pyongyang had a public library. But almost all the books seemed to be by or about Fat Man and Little Boy, and though I was informed that there was an edition of *Les Misérables* in Korean, it couldn't be produced. (Why did they volunteer *that* one?) On every floor there is a room where, I was told, a professor sits and makes himself available for questions. I was even pointed to a door behind which such a professor sat. What a great idea! Since journalists are not allowed, I was visiting Pyongyang in my other guise, that of university lecturer. I asked if I could put a question to the professor. Instant panic. "There's no time—you'll miss the rest of the tour." No, that's O.K., I'm not in a hurry. "But he's a social-science professor." Fine—I've got just the question for him. "But he specializes in political economy." Good. After a lot of fluttering and (on my part) a certain smiling obstinacy, my guide knocked and opened the door. A small man looked up from behind a large desk. The desk was bare. He seemed *petrified*, as if caught masturbating or harboring impure thoughts about the Dear Leader. There was a long anxious exchange in Korean, after which I was told that, unfortunately, the professor answered only questions about Kim Il Sung as a geographer. I have to admit that I could not think of any, and I also realized that the man's discomfort was acute. "Such pity," said my guide soothingly. She meant "Such a pity," but I agreed nonetheless.

It would be nice to think that the menacing aspects of North Korea were for display also, that the bombs and reactors were Potemkin showcases or bargaining chips. On the plane from Beijing I met a group of unsmiling Texan types wearing baseball caps. They were the "in-country" team from the International Atomic Energy Agency, there to inspect and neutralize North Korea's plutonium rods. Not a nice job, but, as they say, someone has to do it. Speaking of the most controversial reactor at Yongbyon, one of the guys said, "No sweat. She's shut down now." Nice to know. But then, so is the rest of North Korean society shut down—animation suspended, all dead quiet on the set, endlessly awaiting not action (we hope) or even cameras, but light.

VANITY FAIR, JANUARY 2001

HAVANA CAN WAIT

I n La Bodeguita del Medio, a drink shop on Calle Empedrado, in the Cathedral quarter of Old Havana, where Ernest Hemingway used to absorb his *mojito* thirst quencher before moving on to his daiquiri at the nearby Floridita restaurant, there is an inscription in the visitors' book. *"Viva Cuba Libre!"* it reads. *"Chile espera."* The words "Cuba Libre" also connote a cocktail—a fang-crumbling and nauseating blend of rum and Coke—but one can be reasonably certain that the author of the scrawl was not toasting his hosts in that way, because the signature of Salvador Allende follows, with the date of June 28, 1961. At that time, Allende was a fairly obscure Chilean physician with a rising reputation in opposition politics. Six and a half years later, he dispatched personal emissaries to the Chile-Bolivia border to help rescue the tattered rabble who had survived Ernesto Che Guevara's suicide mission to the Andes. Three years after that he was elected president of Chile and, as his first act, broke the embargo against Cuba by restoring relations and inviting Fidel Castro for a state visit. In September 1973, Allende was murdered in the presidential palace in Santiago, on the orders of the same General Pinochet he had promoted to be his army chief.

As I downed my own melancholy *mojito*—these days a rather standardized and automatic concoction of weak rum and limp leaves of mint—I could hear the street musicians outside, offering routine versions of that still-beautiful ballad to Che: "Hasta Siempre Comandante" ("Forever Commander"). In London, General Pinochet, now eighty-four, was about to undergo medical tests to determine his fitness to stand trial for crimes against humanity. In

Chile, Ricardo Lagos, sixty-one—an old associate of Allende's—stood a fighting chance of winning the presidency in a runoff. And in Old Havana—this was the turn and cusp of 1999—they were marking the centenary of Hemingway's birth on one hand and hawking T-shirts of Guevara to the same tourists with the other. I veered nostalgically between the ironies of history and the importance of being either Ernesto.

As if to confirm his mooring in a time warp, Fidel Castro, seventy-three, had decided that January 1, 2000, was not the beginning of a new millennium. Determined as ever to remain at an angle to the rest of the world, he announced that the true year would be 2001. This eccentric if mathematically correct gesture had a surreal feel on an island where official figures and statistics mean almost nothing, and where the revolution climaxed on New Year's Eve 1958. I was staying in the faded palace of the Hotel Nacional, that harborfront resort where Graham Greene's hapless British pseudo-agent Wormold survived a poisoning plot in *Our Man in Havana*, and where Mob summits occurred before Mob rule flamed out, as in the best-remembered moments of *The Godfather Part II*. The placards in the lobby summoned me to celebrate not the closing of a thousand-year epoch but the opening of Year 41 of La Revolutión. Forty-one: the unarguable onset of middle age.

Cuba. The very name—short, pungent, yet romantic—has ineffaceable associations. Cuba—the place where the United States received a foretaste of Vietnam in its humiliation at the Bay of Pigs. Cuba—where the missiles of October gave the world its longest and steadiest look at the nuclear furnace when that hellish door swung briefly open in 1962. Cuba—home base to the gangsters who clustered around J.F.K. and may even have killed him. Cuba—whose exiled fanatics were caught in the Watergate building. Cuba—whose troops inflicted the salutary military defeat on the South African forces in Angola. Cuba—an island, like Ireland, which refuses to accept its real size and weight in the world, and whose writers and poets and musicians populate our imagination. Can such a place undergo a graceful menopause, like a veteran of some Buena Vista reunion?

Middle age can be vigorous and affirmative—oh, that I would see forty-one again—but Cuba today exists in a state, and as a state, of suspended animation. The leadership emphasizes this in ways of which it may not even be aware. REVOLUTIONARIES FOREVER YOUNG proclaims a billboard of Castro's long-ago guerrilla associates, their bushiness and trimness making a bold contrast to the Maximum Leader's paunch and thinning fur. (People call him "Fidel," but I find I can't, since I don't know the guy.) Even the endless hysterical rallies outside the U.S. Interests Section on the Havana waterfront, for the return of six-year-old Elián González from Miami, contain a forlorn attempt to reanimate a lost and rebellious childhood. For a better clue to the true position of affairs, look up the statement made by the kid's divorced father. Naturally, I can provide for him here in Cuba, the man said. Don't I work in the tourist-services industry?

At first look, the word *espera* in Allende's message seems to mean "hopes," as in *esperanza*. But it actually means—Spanish being such an ironic language—"waits." To wait is to hope, of course, and in some ways to hope is to wait. But, at present, Cuba just waits. And while it waits, it sells itself to pass the time. What it waits for and what it hopes for may both be radically different from what it gets.

In the seaside town of Cojimar, the setting for *The Old Man and the Sea*, the aging and practiced charmers at La Terraza can spot a gringo scribbler from several furlongs away. Out come the folkloric appurtenances: the photos of Hemingway with Castro; the giant fish gaping at the lens; the sepia shots of Anselmo Hernandez—"The Old Man" or "Old Santiago" himself—who died in Miami. Then there's the ancient captain to be visited a few blocks away: Gregorio Fuentes, who kept Ernest's boat in the water and who on the day I met him was approaching his 103rd birthday. In another week, he would have lived in three centuries. Amazingly raddled and wattled, he nonetheless executed a very strong handshake and immediately lit and puffed upon the truncheon-size Cohiba that the photographer and I had brought as an anniversary tribute. Things were, he opined, in general, in the hands of God. (I always love the wisdom of ancient mariners and peasants.) Round the corner dwells Raúl Corrales, the dapper and silvered veteran who photographed The Revolution—always somehow capitalized in ordinary speech—and who is a full member of the system's cultural elite. He, too, was willing to receive guests and to submit to reverent curiosity. Then it was back to the bar and to a series of delicious but costly pledges to international friendship. I've done this routine before, yet this time was slightly different in that everyone, at every stage, hit me up for money. (I slightly exempt Captain Fuentes, whose son put the squeeze on me on his behalf, but then, at age 102 one is entitled to say, like Castro himself, *"Yo no soy marinero, soy capitán,"* and let others do the soliciting.)

"This is a country," says one of my oldest comrades on the island, "where everybody is on the take." Old people sell lavatory paper, square by square, at the doors of public bathrooms. Avid vendors of everything jostle outside the hotels. Ungifted street musicians remove their fingers from their instruments as soon as they see a hand drift toward a pocket. Girls—and boys—strike up conversations, only to reveal that they don't just like you for your mind or even—this is especially hurtful—for your body. It seems a long, long time since Guevara was in charge of the national bank, signing the currency notes with a contemptuously scrawled "Che," or since there was serious public discussion of the abolition of money. (This Utopian aspiration has been at least partially realized, since the Cuban peso note would now be refused even by those whose job in life it is to sell lavatory paper by the sheet.)

They are waiting, all of them. In the sweet little town of Viñales, in the rural province of Pinar del Río, a beautiful girl persuades me that her restaurant is the best. "The finest pork in Cuba." She insists on showing me the grill, where whole pigs lie marinating. She presses a porcine sample on me, full of crackle and taste. It's delectable, which is just as well, since there's nothing else on the menu save the black bean–white rice combo known as Moros y Cristianos ("Moors and Christians"). At this point I detect, from the silver Star of David round her neck, that she is neither Moorish nor Christian but Sephardic. "Oh, yes," she responds brightly. "My family was from Jerusalem and we expect an Israeli tour party today." And her job is to sell fresh hot pig from dawn to dusk. Easy to tell what she's waiting for. She's waiting for Miami—not for her to visit it, but for it to visit her.

In the town's main square, there's a little sociopolitical set piece, like those you can still see in some parts of Italy and Greece and eastern Germany. On one side, the Communist Party office, with faded red flags and curling posters.

On the other, a church, with garish icons and a wooden shelf of tracts. Between them, a sort of armed truce, and in the square, young couples and old people taking the air and making the *paseo* ("promenade"). Across the road stands a bookstore, next to the workers' club. It is laden with flyblown Bulgarian and East German editions of a decade ago, diluted with a few cheap versions of children's classics and—on the topmost display—some furtive works on sexual hygiene. I handle a dusty copy of *History Will Absolve Me*, the bravura speech that Fidel Castro made from the dock before being imprisoned in the dreaded Isle of Pines penal colony in 1953. In the second paragraph he says:

> He who is speaking abhors, with all his being, childish conceit, and nei-
> ther by his temperament nor by his present frame of mind is he
> inclined toward oratory or toward any kind of sensationalism.

The speech goes on for eighty-one pages: arguably the shortest and best one he ever gave. For over four decades now, this great *solipsista* has monopolized the microphone for rhetorical marathons of several hours. I decide I must have the pamphlet. It costs an exorbitant amount in dollars, exacted from me by a wispy old lady who wears a heavy crucifix. She has a waiting attitude, also.

I first came to Pinar del Río province in 1968, wondering if the news about the Cuban Revolution could really be true. And some of it was. It was true, for example, that official racism had been abolished. (In the grisly old days, even the dictator Batista was refused membership in certain clubs on the grounds that his hide was insufficiently pink.) It was also true that illiteracy had been almost eradicated, and that no Cuban with any illness had to live in fear. Moreover, much of the rest of Latin America was sweltering under uni-formed despotisms like that of Somoza, and these juntas enjoyed the most cynical indulgence in Washington. Salvador Allende was not the only intel-lectual or idealist to see Havana as a beacon. There were aspects of the society I didn't like—the boring emphasis on sports and on military virtues, for instance, and the inculcation of compulsory enthusiasm, reminded me of a boarding school. Even worse, the Castro leadership that year decided to endorse the Soviet invasion of Czechoslovakia, and thus to betray its own stand against superpower bullying.

Bad enough. But now look. The only leader in Latin America who always wears a military uniform, and who steadfastly and on principle refuses elections, is Fidel Castro. Cuban citizens are forbidden by law to use hotels reserved for the rich and may not even enter many stores and pharmacies which trade only in dollars. After forty years, there are few senior black faces in the supposed "leadership." Many doctors have been trained, but they are paid less than the hotel doormen or policemen in the segregated tourist districts. The regime publishes a daily newspaper which all the literates can read, yet I cannot improve on the description of it given by the late Argentinean editor and dissident Jacobo Timerman, who described his morning encounter with that same paper as "a degradation of the act of reading." (One old man in Hemingway's Cojimar came close when he told me that "if you listen to the radio you don't need the newspaper.") No intellectual or idealist voyages to Cuba anymore in search of debate or passion or enlightenment: the best book ever written on the expunging of mental life on the island was, paradoxically if you like, written by the Chilean writer Jorge Edwards, who was Allende's first accredited ambassador to Cuba. (The book is called *Persona Non Grata*, because not even his status as an envoy from Allende's socialist Chile prevented Edwards from being unceremoniously chucked out for his friendship with independent-minded intellectuals.)

"Seventh-rate citizens in our own country." So I was told by Miriam Leiva, one of the small but increasing number of open, declared oppositionists. Until a few years ago, she and her economist husband worked in the Cuban foreign service, and were last stationed in the embassy in Belgrade. ("Easy to see that Milosevic was turning into a Fascist," she remarks calmly of the man who is defended in the official Cuban press almost every day.) Fired for the expression of deviant views, the couple hang on in a tiny windowless apartment in the Playa district of Havana, surviving by a bit of translating here, a bit of writing there—and by waiting.

"If Karl Marx were a Cuban, he would be in jail or in Miami," says Dr. Oscar Espinosa, Leiva's fifty-two-year-old husband. " 'From each according to his abilities—to each according to his need.' That's the old slogan. But the average salary here is eleven dollars a month, and only the army and the bureaucracy get what they need." Slowly emerging behind the Fidelist flourishes and slogans is a system not unlike that in China, where capitalism and profiteering are permitted but democracy and free expression are not. You might call that the worst of both worlds. "We are told to have faith," he comments sardonically. "And in our language the word for faith is *fe*. So now we say that faith is literally f.e.—*familia exterior*, or 'family outside.' Only those with relatives in Florida can beat the system." The good doctor goes on to point out that this, too, leaves black Cubans at the bottom of the heap, because they are the least likely to have cousins in Miami. They get to cut the cane and roll the cigars, which remain Cuba's chief products, just as in Batista's day.

On the following afternoon, Leiva takes me to meet Elizardo Sanchez, the public face of Cuban dissent. Now fifty-five, he lives in a moderate-size family villa, overrun with guests and relatives for New Year's Day. Chicken wire protects the porch and the windows from stone-throwing and spitting mobs, who were trucked to his door by the regime as "volunteers" until a short while ago. (Since Sanchez began to receive international human-rights prizes, and also calls from visiting statesmen, the gallant spontaneity of the crowd appears to have declined somewhat.) Here is a man who knows how to play a waiting game. Like most of the native and domestic dissidents—and in colossal contrast to the Miami exile leadership—he is a veteran social democrat with a background in the pre-Castro Communist Party. His ideological mainspring broke, as did that of so many, with the crushing of Alexander Dubcek's Prague experiment in 1968. After he signed a protest against Cuban endorsement of that atrocity, he lost his job as a professor of philosophy, went in and out of jail, and was subjected to various slanders and indignities. Now he collects lists of political prisoners, monitors the press, and lives in the few inches of protection that are afforded by friendship with a handful of correspondents and diplomats. He dryly hands me a card, and I notice only later that his telephone number has the words "*si funciona*" printed after it in parentheses.

"There are no death squads in Cuba, and no political murders," he says. "But we do have a closed society, and we do have a political oligarchy which exploits the workers. There's no free press, no free trade unions, no Red Cross inspection, no right to leave the country or to leave it and return." Side by side on his crammed bookshelves are the memoirs of Gorbachev and a long history of the eclipse of Franco in Spain. Which model, I ask him, does he think is more likely? "Well, the regime is in its terminal and moribund stage. It cannot last. The only question is how it will change. The *grupo duro* [hardliners] in Miami denounce me for saying this, but I believe that Fidel Castro should lead the transition. If he does not, we could see social breakdown, violence, uncontrolled emigration, revenge . . ."

In spite of the squalid and cramped and frustrated lives that most of them are forced to lead—it's amazing to see the sheer abject slumminess of the streets in the very center of Havana—the Cuban people are so welcoming and so decent that it's hard to picture them turning nasty. Yet I was warned time and again that there exists a large underground reservoir of acidity and resentment—against the system of informers, against the tourist apartheid, against the shortages and bullying, and against the endless, dreary, nonuplifting speeches. Last year, the U.S. Interests Section interviewed candidates in a lottery for 16,000 travel documents. Known colloquially as El Bombo, or the raffle, this offer was printed in the Cuban press. More than 500,000 applications were immediately received. Given that applicants had to be between the ages of eighteen and fifty-five, given that an application to leave is not always considered a friendly act by the regime, given that only one application per family is considered, and given that the total population is 11 million, this was something like a proposal for a mass evacuation of the island. Of those howling at official "Return Elián" rallies outside the U.S. Interests Section, many must have been expressing a repressed desire to join him.

On an earlier visit to Cuba during the Gorbachev era—and, boy, how Castro despised Gorbachev—I happened to be reading Ralph Ellison's *Invisible Man*. I underlined a striking sentence where, recalling a potent college president under whom he had studied, Ellison wrote, "Whether we liked him or not, he was never out of our minds. That was a secret of leadership." It all keeps coming back to Fidel Castro, who is now, with a mixture of defiance and complacency, preparing to celebrate the departure of the ninth American president since he took power. The part he plays, in the imagination of his subjects and of his foes, is almost totemic. But he, too, is a mere mortal mammal, and he, too, must be waiting for something, even if it's only the end. "I can propose a title for your article," says Elizardo Sanchez. "Why not call it 'Chronicle of a Transition Foretold'?" Gabriel García Márquez, who has somewhat prostituted himself for Castro, believes in historical irony as much as historical inevitability. On either grounds, I think I'd still prefer to title it "The Autumn of the Patriarch," because if autumn comes, can The Fall be far behind?

VANITY FAIR, MARCH 2000

THE CLINTON-
DOUGLAS DEBATES

S peaking to an audience on Martha's Vineyard a few days after ordering the destruction, by a volley of cruise missiles, of a factory in Khartoum, Bill Clinton was at his huskiest. Worse, he was at his most confiding:

> I was here on this island up till 2:30 in the morning, trying to make absolutely sure that at that chemical plant there was no night shift. I believed I had to take the action I did, but I didn't want some person who was a nobody to me—but who may have a family to feed and a life to live and probably had no earthly idea what else was going on there— to die needlessly.

At the time, I remember being both nauseated and impressed. Nauseated by the mock-compassionate and pseudohumanitarian bilge that the man was uttering. (It was around the thirty-fifth anniversary of Dr. King's celebrated address to the March on Washington, so he was milking his famous "comfort level around black Americans" on top of the usual lip-biting horror show. How better to commemorate Dr. King than by committing random mayhem in Africa and then blubbering to African-Americans?) And impressed, almost as never before, by the absolute contempt he shows for his listeners, and the pathetic transparency of his mendacious devices. Glance at the above sentences and you will see a president and commander in chief essentially saying that the Al-Shifa plant in Khartoum must have been a chemical-weapons facility because, among other reasons, it wasn't even guarded at night.

Now Rob Reiner tells a mutual friend that he remembers what Michael Douglas says, while attempting to get Annette Bening to disrobe in that forgettable movie *The American President*. Seeking, as who indeed would not (we all do it, all presidents have done it, well almost all, let's have no sexual McCarthyism, it's no big deal, how would you like to be asked about this stuff?), to get into the underwear of a female lobbyist by exposing his human and thoughtful and reflective side, Douglas tells her:

> Somewhere in Libya right now, a janitor is working the night shift at Libyan intelligence headquarters. And he's going about doing his job because he has no idea that in about an hour he's going to die in a massive explosion.

When Ronald Reagan did this sort of thing, recycling lines from bad movies to justify policies—like Star Wars—that were wicked as well as fantasy-driven, there were expressions of polite concern. But that was then. As a matter of fact, a huge appropriation for a Star Wars program was contained in Clinton's much-ballyhooed budget deal, but I notice that subject, too, has been dropped by the intelligentsia.

Actually, one poor and anonymous man was randomly killed in the rocketing of Sudan. I don't suppose that the president has lost a wink of sleep over him, although he may well have had a family to feed and undoubtedly a life to live and most certainly had no earthly idea what was going on, or indeed what had hit him. Moreover, a very large number of people are going to die, or are dying now, as a direct result of the destruction of a poor nation's chief producer of medicines and agricultural pesticides. And everyone knows how this works in an underdeveloped country; it is the children and the old people and those who are already sick who die when the vaccines and the antibiotics and even the analgesics fail to show up. I look at Bill Clinton's face—when I can force myself to do it—and ask: "People were put to death to save that?"

This is, as far as I know, the only time in recent history when a president has made war on civilians for a contemptibly obvious personal and political motive and escaped without any protest from the traditional stage army of the good. And it's not as if, as in precedent cases, the ghastly truth only emerged after a leak, or a lapse of time. Four of the five members of the Joint Chiefs of Staff were excluded from the hurried decision to bomb, and as Seymour Hersh, who has tried brilliantly to ventilate the subject, put it recently, those men "had an explanation for why they were cut out. They were cut out because they would have said 'no.' "

Most of the evidence for their doubts was in plain view right away, and quite a few ordinary civilians were so "ironic" and "cynical" that they even gaily mentioned *Wag the Dog* on the day of the bombing itself. But irony and cynicism, as people have an interest in forgetting, are not mere mannerisms, or "coping skills" for dealing with the postmodern. They originate in hardwon and dearly bought experience. What if, dear sir or ma'am, your apt cultural reference to a recent clever and weightless motion picture turns out not to need those smirking "air-quotes" you are so goddamned fond of? What if you are speaking, or have come upon by accident, the literal truth? As soon as the implications of this question became plain, individuals who had seldom got anything so right in their whole lives dropped the ironic act and went back to being obedient citizens who didn't like Ken Starr, either, and wanted to move the country forward, or at any rate to "move on."

The presidential "approval ratings" actually went "up" a bit after Cruise Missile Day. ("A bounce," we were coldly assured, is the customary reward for such operations, and no more or less than the president deserved.) I have become intrigued by these same ratings. People tell me confidently that the "numbers" express satisfaction with the economy, and also dissatisfaction with moral conservatism. The collectors of these numbers must be jolly good at their "job." I sometimes wonder what it would take to bring them down (the numbers, I mean). People were unmoved, we were told, by the campaign finance scandal as well. They were unmoved by Bosnia, too. But they must have liked something about Clinton of Khartoum, or they wouldn't have awarded him any extra points. Myself, I have concluded on no better evidence that the masses look upon politics as a private matter. Why shouldn't they? Meanwhile, it's not *Wag The Dog*, stupid. It's *The American President*.

THE NATION, NOVEMBER 16, 1998

AFTER SEPTEMBER

WE'RE STILL STANDING

W ell, I won't see Barbara Olson again.

This brave, tough, clever lady just had time to call her husband, the solicitor general, before the civilian plane she had boarded, American Airlines flight 77 to Los Angeles, was guided at inhuman speed into one of the five wings of the Pentagon. According to Cable News Network, Barbara said on her cellphone that the passengers had been herded into the rear of the plane, and that their captors and raptors were armed only with knives. He had time to tell her what had already happened to the World Trade Center. So she knew what was coming. This is where one crosses the frontier of the humanly imaginable.

It was a day for the macrocosmic and the microcosmic. From one view, the whole of lower Manhattan engulfed in stench and fumes, as if Charles Manson had been made God for a day, and as if the capital of the modern world had been plunged into utter darkness. From another perspective, the view of a young Ground-Zero cameraman named Fairbanks, who pointed his lens into the heavens and captured something almost beautiful: the underside of a silver jetliner as it sailed in blue sky into the flank of a noble skyscraper.

"Look at that!" said the chubby blonde girl at the United Airlines ticket counter where I was struggling, as she pointed over my shoulder at the airport TV screen. "That" was the slow-motion collapse of the second tower of the World Trade Center, while it briefly held its shape, even while crumbling to atoms, and resembled a peeled banana sculpted from smoke before dissolving into eddies of filth. The girl was laughing, partly from nerves. Other people in the departure lounge were confessing guilt as they watched greedily to see again the long shot of the plane arcing into the building, and the plume of red and gold flame. One knew objectively that this lovely projectile was packed with shrieking or frozen captives, but one also knew that this was an image to which the mind would recur, and recur again. (At least, that's how I was thinking until I kept seeing Barbara Olson plunging into a reinforced concrete fortress in Virginia.)

One of Tom Clancy's pulp novels ends with the picture of a tailfin protruding from the wrecked dome of Capitol Hill. One of my favorite American moments is when the late shuttle from New York comes in to Washington at dusk, wheeling over the Hill and giving a stirring view of the White House, before showing off the presidential memorials along the Tidal Basin and even featuring an aerial view of the Pentagon before touching down. I now realize that I shall never be allowed to see this magnificent, fragile panorama ever again. That flight-path is no more. From now on, our lives as travellers will be dominated as never before by the security man, the expert, the professional and the assessor of risk. And again, oscillating between the big picture and my own solipsism, I can recall getting engaged to be married in the old "Windows on the World" restaurant at the top of the World Trade Center, and going to the Social Security office on a lower floor to get my first social security number as an immigrant. It was a structure that helped define Manhattan, and therefore the future. That someone should be able to humble such a pinnacle, snuff out such a beacon . . .

But in the small town outside Seattle, where I was when I heard the news, people made rather a point of not getting excited. At lunchtime in the main local joint, not one table raised its voice on the matter. (In cities with big towers, like Seattle itself and Chicago, there was more imaginative sympathy.)

Most reaction yesterday consisted of either understatement or overstatement.

It is unlikely in the extreme that the hideous criminals will be impressed either by the closing of public buildings in states on the Pacific coast (to take one response at the low or ineffectual end) or by promises from Senator John McCain to treat the atrocity as an act of war (to give an instance of big talk at the higher end).

* * *

Badly fallen between the low and the high stool was President Bush, at least in the opinion of every citizen I overheard. Caught on an out-of-town trip, he first said he was heading right back to the White House and then diverted his own plane to Nebraska for a rethink. One or the other of these maneuvers, I would have said, but not both (his eventual speech, only made at the very end of the day, was somewhat corny and insipid). Meanwhile, it was scarcely reassuring to learn after the fact that the Congressional leadership and the First Lady had been whisked to undisclosed locations.

While the citizens of New York were inhaling dust and giving blood, in other words, the political Establishment was hastily activating its own self-insurance skin-saving program for Doomsday.

If Doomsday ever does come, it will probably not be heralded by any advance intelligence from the CIA either. And, if it takes anything like the form it did yesterday, it will not be something that can be forestalled by sci-fi lasers and missile defenses.

One has to face the hitherto incredible: a gang or a government was able to prepare a near-calamitous strike against the United States, complete with pilots and pirates and superb coordination, and to do it not from outside the borders of the country but from within it. And not a note of warning was sounded or registered. The Japanese at Pearl Harbor did not use kamikaze pilots; yesterday's "day of infamy" needed only four civilian aircraft, stolen from the victim nation, while providing no enemy bold enough to accept the responsibility of being struck in return.

There will be a great deal of pugnacious talk to be endured in the next few days. Much of what is said by the cable bombardiers will be worthless, or bluff. But the overused words "civilized world" seem to me appropriate. You could see the civilized world in the streets of Manhattan yesterday, as people of all faiths and shades kept calm, kept moving, kept in touch and kept up their solidarity. This is a strength that the sadists and fanatics do not possess and cannot emulate.

I mentioned Tom Clancy a moment ago. What we saw yesterday were the last frames of the disaster movie that never gets made; the unimaginable sequence that occurs when James Bond drops the ball or Harrison Ford loses his grip. This is what it would be like without a happy ending or an action hero. And yet, everyone is still basically standing (forgive me, Barbara) and there has been no panic or lynching or looting. Almost everybody interviewed in New York seemed to have been brought up on programs about British phlegm during the Blitz.

There may be some laughter in hell, but those who willed this nightmare and sent others out to perpetrate it might be wondering peevishly why they haven't evoked more agony and distress. Let us hope to keep them wondering.

EVENING STANDARD, SEPTEMBER 12, 2001

THE MORNING AFTER

One day into the post-World Trade Center era, and the question "how" is still taking precedence over the question "why." At the presidential level, the two questions appear to be either crudely synthesized or plain confused, since George Bush has taken to describing the mass murder in New York and Washington D.C. as "not just an act of terrorism but an act of war." This strongly implies that he knows who is responsible; an assumption for which he doesn't care to make known the evidence. Instant opinion polls show the same cognitive dissonance at the mass level. Most people, when asked if they agree with the president about the "war" proposition, reply in the affirmative. But in follow-up questions, they counsel extreme caution about retaliation "until all the facts are in." This means, in ordinary words, that they have not the least idea whether they are at war or not.

Over the years since the seizure of the American embassy in Tehran in 1979, the public has become tolerably familiar with the idea that there are Middle Easterners of various shades and stripes who do not like them. The milestones of this—the marine barracks in Beirut, the Gulf War, the destruction of PanAm flight 101—actually include a previous attack on the WTC in 1993. And on that occasion, the men convicted of the assault turned out to have backgrounds in a western-sponsored guerrilla war—actually a jihad— in Afghanistan.

Osama bin Laden had pretty good name-recognition among American news consumers even before Tuesday's trauma. He's already survived a cruise-missile attack ordered by President Clinton in 1999 (in the same cycle of attacks that destroyed a Sudanese aspirin factory in the supposed guise of a nerve-gas facility). Bin Laden is perhaps unlikely to die in his bed, but his repeated identification as a "Saudi millionaire"—we thought the Saudi Arabians were on our side—makes consistency in demonisation rather difficult; the image somehow doesn't compute.

My friend Hussein Ibish of the Arab-American Anti-Discrimination Committee tells me that there have already been cases of random violence against Arab-owned shops. But on the whole, it's been remarkable to see how such crude response has been kept to a minimum. The television repeatedly shows film of Palestinian youths applauding the attacks in New York, but instantly "balances" it with a calm and reasoned appeal from the telegenic Dr. Hanan Ashrawi. Mayor Rudolph Giuliani's Tuesday evening press conference in Manhattan—one of his very best and almost the first occasion on which any hard information was provided to the public—was notable in the same way. He tersely promised extra police protection to Arab and Muslim citizens, and dismissed any thought of vigilantism.

With cellphones still bleeping piteously from under the rubble, it probably seems indecent to most people to ask if the United States has ever done anything to attract such awful hatred. Indeed, the very thought, for the present, is taboo. Some senators and congressmen have spoken of the loathing felt by certain unnamed and sinister elements for the freedom and prosperity of America, as if it were only natural that such a happy and successful country should inspire envy and jealousy. But that is the limit of permissible thought.

In general, the motive and character of the perpetrators is shrouded by rhetoric about their "cowardice" and their "shadowy" character, almost as if they had not volunteered to immolate themselves in the broadest of broad blue daylight. On the campus where I am writing this, there are a few students and professors willing to venture points about United States foreign policy. But they do so very guardedly, and it would sound like profane apologetics if transmitted live. So the analytical moment, if there is to be one, has been indefinitely postponed.

In any case, the question of "how" is for the moment the more riveting one. Did the murderers have accomplices within the airport security systems? Have there been "sleepers" here for years? How did the coordination work? How near did we come to losing the White House? And—more nerve-rackingly— has all the venomous energy been spent in this one climactic assault?

During the cold war, it was often said that the United States faced an unsleeping foe that was "godless." I don't think it's sufficiently recognized how important this one word was, and how much it is missed. The holy warriors, as these seem to be, are an entirely different proposition. The United States as a country has no fixed position on Islamic fundamentalism. It has used it as an ally, as well as discovered it as an enemy. It could not bomb Saudi Arabia or the United Arab Emirates, even if it found conclusive proof that the hijackers and assassins had actually trained there. So what does the president mean when he says so portentously that "we shall make no distinction between the terrorists and those who harbor them"? It looks like a distinction without a difference, and gives a momentary impression of being decisive, while actually only confusing the issue.

As I write, fighter planes are the only craft in the sky over New York and Washington, and indeed, the rest of the country. The National Guard is on the streets. The Atlantic and Pacific coasts are being ostentatiously patrolled by large and reassuring Navy vessels. Not only does this deployment do absolutely no good today (it has about the same effect as the newly imposed ban on curbside baggage check-in at airports), but it would have made absolutely no difference if it had started last Sunday.

Yes, it does give the impression that we are "at war," all right. But being on manoeuvres is not the same as warfare, and "preparedness" and "vigilance" are of little value if they contribute to the erection of a Maginot Line in the mind.

THE GUARDIAN, SEPTEMBER 13, 2001

AGAINST RATIONALIZATION

I t was in Peshawar, on the Pakistan-Afghanistan frontier, as the Red Army was falling apart and falling back. I badly needed a guide to get me to the Khyber Pass, and I decided that what I required was the most farouche-looking guy with the best command of English and the toughest modern automobile. Such a combination was obtainable, for a price. My new friend rather wolfishly offered me a tour of the nearby British military cemetery (a well-filled site from the Victorian era) before we began. Then he slammed a cassette into the dashboard. I braced myself for the ululations of some mullah but received instead a dose of "So Far Away." From under the turban and behind the beard came the gruff observation, "I thought you might like Dire Straits."

This was my induction into the now-familiar symbiosis of tribal piety and high-tech; a symbiosis consummated on September 11 with the conversion of the southern tip of the capital of the modern world into a charred and suppurating mass grave. Not that it necessarily has to be a symbol of modernism and innovation that is targeted for immolation. As recently as this year, the same ideology employed heavy artillery to destroy the Buddha statues at Bamiyan, and the co-thinkers of bin Laden in Egypt have been heard to express the view that the Pyramids and the Sphinx should be turned into shards as punishment for their profanely un-Islamic character.

Since my moment in Peshawar I have met this faction again. In one form or another, the people who leveled the World Trade Center are the same people who threw acid in the faces of unveiled women in Kabul and Karachi, who maimed and eviscerated two of the translators of *The Satanic Verses* and who machine-gunned architectural tourists at Luxor. Even as we worry what they may intend for our society, we can see very plainly what they have in mind for their own: a bleak and sterile theocracy enforced by advanced techniques. Just a few months ago Bosnia surrendered to the international court at The Hague the only accused war criminals detained on Muslim-Croat federation territory. The butchers had almost all been unwanted "volunteers" from the Chechen, Afghan and Kashmiri fronts; it is as an unapologetic defender of the Muslims of Bosnia (whose cause was generally unstained by the sort of atrocity committed by Catholic and Orthodox Christians) that one can and must say that bin Ladenism poisons everything that it touches.

I was apprehensive from the first moment about the sort of masochistic e-mail traffic that might start circulating from the Chomsky-Zinn-Finkelstein quarter, and I was not to be disappointed. With all due thanks to these worthy comrades, I know already that the people of Palestine and Iraq are victims of a depraved and callous Western statecraft. And I think I can claim to have been among the first to point out that Clinton's rocketing of Khartoum—supported by most liberals—was a gross war crime, which would certainly have entitled the Sudanese government to mount reprisals under international law. (Indeed, the sight of Clintonoids on TV, applauding the "bounce in the polls" achieved by their man that day, was even more repulsive than the sight of destitute refugee children making a wretched holiday over the nightmare on Chambers Street.) But there is no sense in which the events of September 11 can be held to constitute such a reprisal, either legally or morally.

It is worse than idle to propose the very trade-offs that may have been lodged somewhere in the closed-off minds of the mass murderers. The people of Gaza live under curfew and humiliation and expropriation. This is notorious. Very well: Does anyone suppose that an Israeli withdrawal from Gaza would have forestalled the slaughter in Manhattan? It would take a moral cretin to suggest anything of the sort; the cadres of the new jihad make it very apparent that their quarrel is with Judaism and secularism on principle, not with (or not just with) Zionism. They regard the Saudi regime not as the extreme authoritarian theocracy that it is, but as something too soft and lenient. The Taliban forces viciously persecute the Shiite minority in Afghanistan. The Muslim fanatics in Indonesia try to extirpate the infidel minorities there; civil society in Algeria is barely breathing after the fundamentalist assault.

Now is as good a time as ever to revisit the history of the Crusades, or the sorry history of partition in Kashmir, or the woes of the Chechens and Kosovars. But the bombers of Manhattan represent fascism with an Islamic face, and there's no point in any euphemism about it. What they abominate about "the West," to put it in a phrase, is not what Western liberals don't like and can't defend about their own system, but what they *do* like about it and must defend: its emancipated women, its scientific inquiry, its separation of religion from the state. Loose talk about chickens coming home to roost is the moral equivalent of the hateful garbage emitted by Falwell and Robertson, and exhibits about the same intellectual content. Indiscriminate murder is not a judgment, even obliquely, on the victims or their way of life, or ours. Any decent and concerned reader of this magazine could have been on one of those planes, or in one of those buildings—yes, even in the Pentagon.

The new talk is all of "human intelligence": the very faculty in which our ruling class is most deficient. A few months ago, the Bush administration handed the Taliban a subsidy of $43 million in abject gratitude for the assistance of fundamentalism in the "war on drugs." Next up is the renewed "missile defense" fantasy recently endorsed by even more craven Democrats who seek to occupy the void "behind the president." There is sure to be further opportunity to emphasize the failings of our supposed leaders, whose costly mantra is "national security" and who could not protect us. And yes indeed, my guide in Peshawar was a shadow thrown by William Casey's CIA, which first connected the unstoppable Stinger missile to the infallible Koran. But that's only one way of stating the obvious, which is that this is an enemy for life, as well as an enemy of life.

THE NATION, SEPTEMBER 20, 2001

N ot all readers liked my attack on the liberal/left tendency to "rationalize" the aggression of September 11, or my use of the term "fascism with an Islamic face," and I'll select a representative example of the sort of "thinking" that I continue to receive on my screen, even now. This jewel comes from Sam Husseini, who runs the Institute for Public Accuracy in Washington, D.C.:

> The fascists like Bid-Laden could not get volunteers to stuff envelopes if Israel had withdrawn from Jerusalem like it was supposed to—and the U.S. stopped the sanctions and the bombing on Iraq.

You've heard this "thought" expressed in one way or another, dear reader, have you not? I don't think I took enough time in my last column to point out just what is so utterly rotten at the very core of it. So, just to clean up a corner or two: (1) If Husseini knows what was in the minds of the murderers, it is his solemn responsibility to inform us of the source of his information, and also to share it with the authorities. (2) If he does not know what was in their minds—as seems enormously more probable—then why does he rush to appoint himself the ventriloquist's dummy for such a faction? Who volunteers for such a task at such a time?

Not only is it indecent to act as self-appointed interpreter for the killers, but it is rash in the highest degree. The death squads have not favored us with a posthumous manifesto of their grievances, or a statement of claim about

Palestine or Iraq, but we are nonetheless able to surmise or deduce or induct a fair amount about the ideological or theological "root" of their act (Husseini doesn't seem to demand "proof" of bin Laden's involvement any more than the Bush administration is willing to supply it) and if we are correct in this, then we have considerable knowledge of two things: their ideas and their actions.

First the actions. The central plan was to maximize civilian casualties in a very dense area of downtown Manhattan. We know that the killers had studied the physics and ecology of the buildings and the neighborhood, and we know that they were limited only by the flight schedules and bookings of civil aviation. They must therefore have been quite prepared to convert fully loaded planes into missiles, instead of the mercifully unpopulated aircraft that were actually commandeered, and they could have hoped by a combination of luck and tactics to have at least doubled the kill-rate on the ground. They spent some time in the company of the families they had kidnapped for the purpose of mass homicide. It was clearly meant to be much, much worse than it was. And it was designed and incubated long before the mutual-masturbation of the Clinton-Arafat-Barak "process." The Talibanis have in any case not distinguished themselves very much by an interest in the Palestinian plight. They have been busier trying to bring their own societies under the reign of the most inflexible and pitiless declension of shari'a law. This is known to anyone with the least acquaintance with the subject.

The ancillary plan was to hit the Department of Defense and (on the best evidence we have available) either the Capitol Dome or the White House. The Pentagon, for all its symbolism, is actually more the civil-service bit of the American "war-machine," and is set in a crowded Virginia neighborhood. You could certainly call it a military target if you were that way inclined, though the bin Ladenists did not attempt anything against a guarded airbase or a nuclear power station in Pennsylvania (and even if they had, we would now doubtless be reading that the glow from Three Mile Island was a revenge for globalization). The Capitol is where the voters send their elected representatives—poor things, to be sure, but our own. The White House is where the elected president and his family and staff are to be found. It survived the attempt of British imperialism to burn it down, and the attempt of the Confederacy to take Washington D.C., and this has hallowed even its most mediocre occupants. I might, from where I am sitting, be a short walk from a gutted Capitol or a shattered White House. I am quite certain that in such a case Husseini and his rabble of sympathizers would still be telling me that my chickens were coming home to roost. (The image of bin Laden's men "stuffing envelopes" is the perfected essence of such brainless verbiage.) Only the stoicism of men like Jeremy Glick and Thomas Burnett prevented some such outcome; only those who chose to die fighting rather than allow such a profanity, and such a further toll in lives, stood between us and the fourth death squad. One iota of such innate fortitude is worth all the writings of Noam Chomsky, who coldly compared the plan of September 11 to a stupid and cruel and cynical raid by Bill Clinton on Khartoum in August 1998.

I speak with some feeling about that latter event, because I wrote three *Nation* columns about it at the time, pointing out (with evidence that goes unrebutted to this day) that it was a war crime, and a war crime opposed by the majority of the military and intelligence establishment. The crime was directly and sordidly linked to the effort by a crooked president to avoid impeachment (a conclusion sedulously avoided by the Chomskys and Husseinis of the time). The Al-Shifa pharmaceutical plant was well-known to be a civilian target, and its "selection" was opposed by most of the Joint Chiefs and many CIA personnel for just this reason. (See, for additional corroboration, Seymour Hersh's *New Yorker* essay "The Missiles of August.") To mention this banana-republic degradation of the United States in the same breath as a plan, deliberated for months, to inflict maximum horror upon the innocent is to abandon every standard that makes intellectual and moral discrimination possible. To put it at its very lowest, and most elementary, at least the missiles launched by Clinton were not full of passengers. (How are you doing, Sam? Noam, wazzup?)

So much for what the methods and targets tell us about the true anti-human and anti-democratic motivation. By their deeds shall we know them. What about the animating ideas? There were perhaps seven hundred observant followers of the Prophet Muhammed burned alive in New York on September 11. Nobody who had studied the target zone could have been in any doubt that some such figure was at the very least a likely one. And, since Islam makes no discrimination between the color and shade of its adherents, there was good reason to think that any planeload of civilians might include some

Muslims as well. I don't myself make this point with any more emphasis than I would give to the several hundred of my fellow Englishmen (some of them doubtless Muslims also) who perished. I stress it only because it makes my point about fascism. To the Wahhabi-indoctrinated sectarians of Al Qaeda, only the purest and most fanatical are worthy of consideration. The teachings and published proclamations of this cult have initiated us to the idea that the tolerant, the open-minded, the apostate or the followers of different branches of The Faith are fit only for slaughter and contempt. And that's before Christians and Jews, let alone atheists and secularists, have even been factored in. As before, the deed announces and exposes its "root cause." The grievance and animosity predate even the Balfour Declaration, let alone the occupation of the West Bank. They predate the creation of Iraq as a state. The gates of Vienna would have had to fall to the Ottoman jihad before any balm could begin to be applied to these psychic wounds. And this is precisely, now, our problem. The Taliban and its surrogates are not content to immiserate their own societies in beggary and serfdom. They are condemned, and they deludedly believe that they are commanded, to spread the contagion and to visit hell upon the unrighteous. The very first step that we must take, therefore, is the acquisition of enough self-respect and self-confidence to say that we have met an enemy and that he is not us, but someone else. Someone with whom coexistence is, fortunately I think, not possible. (I say "fortunately" because I am also convinced that such coexistence is not desirable.)

But straight away, we meet people who complain at once that this enemy is us, really. Did we not aid the grisly Taliban to achieve and hold power? Yes indeed "we" did. Well, does this not double or triple our responsibility to remove them from power? A sudden sheep-like silence, broken by a bleat. Would that not be "over-reaction"? All I want to say for now is that the under-reaction to the Taliban by three successive United States administrations is one of the great resounding disgraces of our time. There is good reason to think that a Taliban defeat would fill the streets of Kabul with joy. But for the moment, the Bush administration seems a hostage to the Pakistani and Saudi clients who are the sponsors and "harborers" the president claims publicly to be looking for! Yet the mainstream left, ever shuffling its feet, fears only the discomfort that might result from repudiating such an indefensible and humiliating posture. Very well then, comrades. Do not pretend that you wish to make up for America's past crimes in the region. Here is one such crime that can be admitted and undone—the sponsorship of the Taliban could be redeemed by the demolition of its regime and the liberation of its victims. But I detect no stomach for any such project. Better, then—more decent and reticent—not to affect such concern for "our" past offenses. This is not an article about grand strategy, but it seems to me to go without saying that a sincere commitment to the secular or reformist elements in the Muslim world would automatically shift the balance of America's up-to-now very questionable engagement. Every day, the wretched Arafat is told by Washington, as a favor to the Israelis, that he must police and repress the forces of Hamas and Islamic jihad. When did Washington last demand that Saudi Arabia cease its heavy financing of these primitive and unscrupulous organizations? We let the Algerians fight the Islamic-fascist wave without saying a word or lending a hand. And this is an effort in which civic and social organizations can become involved without official permission. We should be building such internationalism whether it serves the short-term needs of the current administration or not: I signed an anti-Taliban statement several months ago and was appalled by the eerie silence with which the initiative was greeted in Washington. (It ought to go without saying that the demand for Palestinian self-determination is, as before, a good cause in its own right. Not now more than ever, but now as ever. There are millions of Palestinians who do not want the future that the pious of all three monotheisms have in store for them.)

Ultimately, this is another but uniquely toxic version of an old story, whereby former clients like Noriega and Saddam Hussein and Slobodan Milosevic and the Taliban cease to be our monsters and become monstrous in their own right. At such a point, a moral and political crisis occurs. Do "our" past crimes and sins make it impossible to expiate the offense by determined action? Those of us who were not consulted about, and are not bound by, the previous covert compromises have a special responsibility to say a decisive "no" to this. The figure of six and a half thousand murders in New York is almost the exact equivalent to the total uncovered in the death-pits of Srebrenica. (Even at Srebrenica, the demented General Ratko Mladic agreed to release all the women, all the children, all the old people and all the males above and below military age before ordering his squads to fall to work.) On that occasion, U.S. satellites flew serenely overhead recording the scene, and

Milosevic earned himself an invitation to Dayton, Ohio. But in the end, after appalling false starts and delays, it was found that Mr. Milosevic was too much. He wasn't just too nasty. He was also too irrational and dangerous. He didn't even save himself by lyingly claiming, as he several times did, that Osama bin Laden was hiding in Bosnia. It must be said that by this, and by other lies and numberless other atrocities, Milosevic distinguished himself as an enemy of Islam. His national-socialist regime took the line on the "towel-heads" that the Bush administration is only accused, by fools and knaves, of taking. Yet when a stand was eventually mounted against Milosevic, it was Noam Chomsky and Sam Husseini, among many others, who described the whole business as a bullying persecution of—the Serbs! I have no hesitation in describing this mentality, carefully and without heat, as soft on crime and soft on fascism. No political coalition is possible with such people and, I'm thankful to say, no political coalition with them is now necessary. It no longer matters what they think.

THE NATION ONLINE, OCTOBER 8, 2001

A REJOINDER TO
NOAM CHOMSKY

The two related questions before the house are these. Can the attacks of September 11 be compared to an earlier outrage committed by Americans? And should they be so compared?

Noam Chomsky does not rise much above the level of half-truth in his comparison of the September 11 atrocities to Clinton's rocketing of Sudan. Since his remarks are directed at me, I'll instance a less-than-half-truth as he applies it to myself. I "must be unaware," he writes, that I "express such racist contempt for African victims of a terrorist crime." With his pitying tone of condescension, and his insertion of a deniable but particularly objectionable innuendo, I regret to say that Chomsky displays what have lately become his hallmarks.

I have a very clear memory of the destruction of the Al-Shifa chemical plant in Khartoum on August 20, 1998, and of the false claim made by the administration that it had sought out and destroyed a nerve gas facility that was linked to Osama bin Laden's shady business empire. I wrote a series of columns in *The Nation*, dated October 5, October 19, and November 16, 1998. The first one of these was recirculated on the web by *Salon* magazine. I then wrote an expanded essay for the January 1999 issue of *Vanity Fair*. And the chapter in my book *No One Left To Lie To*, titled "Clinton's War Crimes," is a summary and digest of all the above. I quoted Tom Carnaffin, the British engineer who had helped construct the plant. I quoted the German ambassador, Werner Daum, who had recently toured it. I interviewed one of the world's leading authorities on inorganic chemistry, Professor R. J. P. Williams.

I interviewed Milton Bearden, a retired CIA station chief. My conclusions, which were stated earlier and at greater length than by any of the journalists cited by Chomsky, were that the factory was a medical and pharmaceutical facility, unrelated in any way to the holdings of bin Laden, and that this could and should have been known in advance. In any case, I argued, the United States had no right to hit Sudanese territory without at least first requesting an inspection of the plant. In short, as I put it, several times and in several different ways, "only one person was killed in the rocketing of Sudan. But many more have died, and will die, because an impoverished country has lost its chief source of medicines and pesticides." As I also phrased it, the president had "acted with caprice and brutality and with a complete disregard for international law, and perhaps counted on the indifference of the press and public to a negligible society like that of Sudan."

Thus I think I am indeed "unaware," with or without Chomsky's lofty permission, of my propensity for racist contempt. Since Chomsky reads *The Nation* and seems to have a clip-file on Al-Shifa, he is in a position to know my views if he cares to. I think I can say without immodesty that I wrote more, and earlier, about this scandal than any other person. I also helped the late John Scanlon in preparing the basis for a lawsuit by the owner of the factory, Saleh Idris, seeking compensation from the U.S. government. That suit is still active.

I have to say that I didn't get an unambiguous response from the left at the time, because there were those who were uneasy at the allegation that Clinton had "wagged the dog." (The bombing took place as Miss Lewinsky was returning to the grand jury, and secured Clinton a nauseating "bounce" in the opinion polls.) It was felt in some "progressive" quarters that to make too much of the atrocity was to "give ammunition" to the Republicans. I may be mistaken, but I don't remember Noam Chomsky circulating the news of the war crime when it would have made any difference. Certainly not with the energy he does now—by way of a comparison with the massacres in New York and Washington and Pennsylvania.

How exact is this comparison? Chomsky is obviously right when he says that one must count "collateral" casualties, though it isn't possible to compute the Sudanese ones with any certainty. (And he makes a small mistake: The Sudanese regime demanded at the UN only that there be an on-site inspection of the destroyed factory—a demand that the United States resisted, to its shame.) But must one not also measure intention and motive? The clear intention of the September 11 death squads was to maximize civilian deaths in an area renowned for its cosmopolitan and multi-ethnic character. (The New York Yemeni community alone is "missing" some two hundred members, mainly push-cart vendors in the nearby streets.) The malicious premeditation is very evident and manifest: The toll was intended to be very much higher than it was. And I believe I have already pointed out that the cruise missiles fired at Sudan were not crammed with terrified civilian kidnap victims. I do not therefore think it can be argued that the hasty, politicized and wicked decision to hit the Al-Shifa plant can be characterized as directly homicidal in quite the same way. And I don't think anyone will be able to accuse me of euphemizing the matter.

(Incidentally, the *New York Times* for October 2 carried a report on page B4. The World Bank now estimates that the shock suffered by the international economy as a result of September 11 will have the following effects on poorer societies. "It is estimated that 40,000 children worldwide will likely die from disease and malnutrition and 10 million people will fall below the bank's extreme poverty line of $1 dollar a day or less as a result of slower economic growth." No doubt Chomsky will wish to factor this in. Or will he prefer to say that the World Bank is the problem in the first place? His casuistry appears to be limitless.)

In a brilliant article in *The New Yorker* for October 12, 1998 ("The Missiles of August"), Seymour Hersh reconstructed the decision-making that led to the Al-Shifa raid. He found that four of the five Joint Chiefs had been kept in the dark about it, as had Louis Freeh of the FBI, who was then in Africa investigating the ghastly bombings of two neighboring U.S. Embassies. I was myself able to find several senior people at the State Department and the CIA who had urged against the strike at the time and who could prove it, and would let their own names be used for quotation. It was as near to a purely presidential decision, replete with Strangelovian opportunism, as could be. Never mind for now whether this strengthens my case for trying Clinton—a case that Chomsky makes without realizing it. How fair is it to say that "the United States" decided in advance on all those Sudanese deaths? It might be fairer than one might like, but it still wouldn't come up to the Al Qaeda standard.

As one who spent several weeks rebutting it, and rebutting it in real time,

I can state that the case for considering Al-Shifa as a military target was not an absolutely hollow one. (One of the main Sudanese opposition groups, for example, had identified it as a bin Laden facility engaged in the manufacture of nerve gas.) In one way this makes little difference, because Clinton never demanded an inspection and because a nerve gas plant can't be folded like a tent and moved overnight. So that what was committed was certainly an aggression. However, at least a makeshift claim of military targeting could be advanced: President Clinton and his contemptible Defense Secretary Cohen did not boast of having taught Sudanese civilians a lesson. Furthermore, the Sudanese regime had been sheltering and nurturing Osama bin Laden, had been imposing its own form of Islamic dictatorship and has in other respects a filthy record. And two embassies had just been blown up in Kenya and Dar es Salaam, with the infliction of very many hundreds of African civilian casualties, by men in bin Laden's network. (It's not specially pointful to this argument, but Chomsky's touching belief in the then-imminence of regional peace strikes me as naïve.) I thus hold to my view that there is no facile "moral equivalence" between the two crimes.

But this by no means exhausts my disagreement with Chomsky. Suppose that we agree that the two atrocities can or may be mentioned in the same breath. Why should we do so? I wrote at the time (*The Nation*, October 5, 1998) that Osama bin Laden "hopes to bring a 'judgmental' monotheism of his own to bear on these United States." Chomsky's recent version of this is "considering the grievances expressed by people of the Middle East region." In my version, then as now, one confronts an enemy who wishes ill to our society, and also to his own (if impermeable religious despotism is considered an "ill"). In Chomsky's reading, one must learn to sift through the inevitable propaganda and emotion resulting from the September 11 attacks, and lend an ear to the suppressed and distorted cry for help that comes, not from the victims, but from the perpetrators. I have already said how distasteful I find this attitude. I wonder if even Chomsky would now like to have some of his own words back? Why else should he take such care to quote himself deploring the atrocity? Nobody accused him of not doing so. It's often a bad sign when people defend themselves against charges which haven't been made.

To be against rationalization is not the same as to be opposed to reasoning. By all means we must meet the challenge to our understanding. I think that the forces represented by Al Qaeda and the Taliban are fairly easy to comprehend, but not very easy to coexist with. I also believe that we would do well to take them at their word. I even believe that it is true that September 11 was a hinge event. Chomsky gives me the impression of regarding it as an inconvenience. With some irritation and impatience, he manages to assimilate it to his pre-existing worldview, and then goes on as if nothing much had happened. I think it would be flattering to describe this as an exercise in clarification. And I think it also contains a serious danger of euphemism, in that it purportedly connects the mass murder of our fellows to causes (such as the emancipation of the Palestinians from occupation) which are much better considered in their own right. To propose the connection is inevitably to flatter Al Qaeda, even if only indirectly. If I seem to exaggerate, then pray consider this passage from page 39 of Chomsky's most recent book: *A New Generation Draws The Line: Kosovo, East Timor and The Standards of the West*:

> The huge slaughter in East Timor is (at least) comparable to the terrible atrocities that can plausibly be attributed to Milosevic in the earlier wars in Yugoslavia, and responsibility is far easier to assign, with no complicating factors. If proponents of the "repetition of Bosnia" thesis intend it seriously, they should certainly have been calling for the bombing of Jakarta—indeed Washington and London—in early 1998 so as not to allow in East Timor a repetition of the crimes that Indonesia, the U.S., and the UK had perpetrated there for a quarter-century. And when the new generation of leaders refused to pursue this honorable course, they should have been leading citizens to do so themselves, perhaps joining the bin Laden network. These conclusions follow straightforwardly, if we assume that the thesis is intended as something more than apologetics for state violence.

Here, the pretense of remorseless logic degenerates into flat-out irrationality. "These conclusions follow straightforwardly"? The accusations against Milosevic are "plausible"? A year ago it would have been possible to notice the same thing that strikes the eye today: Chomsky's already train-wrecked syllogisms seem to entail the weird and sinister assumption that bin Laden is a ventriloquist for thwarted voices of international justice. (For more on this, see an excellent forthcoming essay on Chomsky's work in *The American Prospect*, authored by Professor Jeffrey Isaac of the University of Indiana, to whom I am indebted.)

If there is now an international intervention, whether intelligent and humane, or brutal and stupid, against the Taliban, some people will take to the streets, or at least mount some "Candle In the Wind" or "Strawberry Fields" peace vigils. They did not take to the streets, or even go moist and musical, when the administration supported the Taliban. But that was, surely, just as much an intervention? An intervention, moreover, that could not even pretend to be humane or democratic? I had the same concern about those who did not object when the United States safeguarded Milosevic, but did protest when it finally turned against him. Am I supposed not to notice that these two groups of "anti-interventionists" are in fact the same people?

Concluding, then. I have begun to think that Noam Chomsky has lost or is losing the qualities that made him a great moral and political tutor in the years of the Indochina war, and that enabled him to write such monumental essays as his critique of the Kahan Commission on Sabra and Shatila or his analysis of the situation in East Timor. I don't say this out of any "more in sorrow than anger" affectation: I have written several defenses of him and he knows it. But the last time we corresponded, some months ago, I was appalled by the robotic element both of his prose and of his opinions. He sought earnestly to convince me that Vaclav Havel, by addressing a joint session of Congress in the fall of 1989, was complicit in the murder of the Jesuits in El Salvador that had occurred not very long before he had landed in Washington. In vain did I point out that the timing of Havel's visit was determined by the November collapse of the Stalinist regime in Prague, and that on his first celebratory visit to the United States he need not necessarily take the opportunity to accuse his hosts of being war criminals. Nothing would do, for Chomsky, but a strict moral equivalence between Havel's conduct and the mentality of the most depraved Stalinist. (He's written this elsewhere, so I break no confidence.) I then took the chance of asking him whether he still considered Ed Herman a political co-thinker. Herman had moved from opposing the bombing of Serbia to representing the Milosevic regime as a victim and as a nationalist peoples' democracy. He has recently said, in a ludicrous attack on me, that the "methods and policies" of the Western forces in

Kosovo were "very similar" to the tactics of Al Qaeda, an assertion that will not surprise those who are familiar with his style. Chomsky knew perfectly well what I was asking, and why, but chose to respond by saying that he did not regard anybody in particular as a co-thinker. I thought then that this was a shady answer; I now think that it may also have been an unintentionally prescient one. I don't believe that any of those who have so anxiously sought his opinions in the past three weeks have felt either inspired or educated by them, because these opinions are a recipe for nothingness. And only an old admiration should prevent me from adding, nothingness at the very best.

THE NATION ONLINE, OCTOBER 15, 2001

J ust once more, and then we'll really have to get on with more pressing business. I could subscribe myself at any time to any of the following statements:

- An Arab child born in Nablus should have no fewer rights in his or her homeland than a Jewish child born in Flatbush.
- The United States of America has been the patron of predatory regimes on five continents.
- The United States of America exports violence by means of arms sales and evil clients.

You can probably fill in a few extras for yourself. However, none of the above statements means the same thing if prefaced with the words: "As Osama bin Laden and his devout followers have recently reminded us . . ." They wouldn't mean the same thing politically, that is to say, and they wouldn't mean the same thing morally. It's disgraceful that so many people on the periphery of this magazine should need what Noam Chomsky would otherwise term instruction in the elementary.

Here are two brief thought experiments that I hope and trust will put this degrading argument to rest. Both of them, as it happens, involve the date September 11.

I have long kept September 11 as a day of mourning, because it was on that date in 1973 that Salvador Allende was murdered and Chilean democracy assassinated along with him. We know all the details now, from the way the giant corporations subsidized subversion to the way that U.S. politicians commissioned "hit jobs" and sabotage. It took the Chilean opposition many years of patient struggle to regain their country and their democracy, and the small help I was able to offer them is one of the few things in my life of which I can be proud. There was one spirited attempt to kill Augusto Pinochet himself during this period, with which I had some sneaking sympathy, but on the whole the weaponry of terror (death squads, car bombs, the training of special killers) was in the department of horror employed by Chilean and U.S. officials working for, or with, the dictatorship. And now Chilean dignity has been restored, and Pinochet himself is a discredited and indicted figure, spared the rigor of law only for humanitarian reasons. We may even live to see justice done to some of his backers in Washington, though the holding of breath would be inadvisable.

I don't know any Chilean participant in this great historic struggle who would not rather have died—you'll have to excuse the expression—than commit an outrage against humanity that was even remotely comparable to the atrocities in New York, Washington and Pennsylvania. And I think I'll leave it at that, since those who don't see my point by now are never going to do so.

There are others who mourn September 11 because it was on that day in 1683 that the hitherto unstoppable armies of Islam were defeated by a Polish general outside the gates of Vienna. The date marks the closest that proselytizing Islam ever came to making itself a superpower by military conquest. From then on, the Muslim civilization, which once had so much to teach the Christian West, went into a protracted eclipse. I cannot of course be certain, but I think it is highly probable that this is the date that certain antimodernist forces want us to remember as painfully as they do. And if I am right, then it's not even facile or superficial to connect the recent aggression against American civil society with any current "human rights issue."

Why not pay attention to what the cassettes and incantations of Al Qaeda actually demand: a holy war in which there are no civilians on the other side, only infidels, and a society of total aridity in which any concept of culture or the future has been eradicated?

One ought to be clear about this: The Ottomans who besieged Vienna were not of that primeval mentality. But the Wahabbi fanatics of the present century are. Glance again at the trite statements I made at the beginning of this column. Could Osama bin Laden actually utter any of them? Certainly not. He doesn't only oppose the entire Jewish presence in Palestine; he opposes the Jewish presence in *America*. He is the spoiled-brat son of one of our preferred despotisms and the proud beneficiary of the export of violence. Why, then, do so many fools consider him as the interpreter of their "concerns," let alone seek to appoint their ignorant selves as the medium for his?

Thanks to all those who demand that I tell them what is to be done. As the situation develops, they may even ask themselves this question as if it really demanded a serious answer. We certainly owe a duty to Afghanistan's people, whose lives were rendered impossible by the Taliban long before we felt any pain. We might even remember that the only part of Iraq where people are neither starving nor repressed is in the Kurdish area, now under international protection as a result of public pressure on Bush Senior's vaunted "coalition." (See especially David Hirst's two engrossing reports from northern Iraq in the London *Guardian* of August 1 and 2: Hirst himself is probably the most consistently anti-imperialist journalist in the region.) But wait! That might mean that one could actually *do* something. Surely we are too guilt-stained for that?

Thanks also to all those who thought it was original to attack me for writing from an "armchair." (Why is it always an armchair?) As it happens, I work in a swivel chair, in an apartment on the top floor of one of Washington's tallest buildings. In the fall of 1993 the State Department's Office of Counterterrorism urgently advised me to change this address because of "credible" threats received after my wife and daughter and I had sheltered Salman Rushdie as a guest, and had arranged for him to be received at the cowering Clinton White House. I thought, then as now, that the government was doing no more than covering its own behind by giving half-alarmist and half-reassuring advice. In other words, I have a quarrel with theocratic fascism even when the administration does not, and I hope at least some of my friendly correspondents are prepared to say the same.

THE NATION, OCTOBER 22, 2001

THE ENDS OF WAR

The United States of America has just succeeded in bombing a country back out of the Stone Age. This deserves to be recognized as an achievement, even by those who want to hasten past the moment and resume their customary tasks (worrying about the spotty human rights record of the Northern Alliance is the latest thing). The nexus that bound the Taliban to the forces of Al Qaeda, and that was symbolized by the clan relationship between Mullah Omar and Osama bin Laden, has been destroyed. We are rid of one of the foulest regimes on earth, while one of the most vicious crime families in history has been crippled and scattered. It remains to help the Afghan exiles to return, to save the starving and to consolidate the tentative emancipation of Afghan women.

When Julius Nyerere sent his forces across the border of Uganda in 1979 he announced that Tanzania was defending itself under international law against repeated attacks from Idi Amin. If the Amin regime fell as a consequence, he continued, that was all to the good. (Idi Amin did indeed fall and has since been hiding in Jeddah, under the protection of our delightful Saudi allies. He, too, claims to be a spokesman for the oppressed Muslims of the world.)

No possible future government in Kabul can be worse than the Taliban, and no thinkable future government would allow the level of Al Qaeda gangsterism to recur. So the outcome is proportionate and congruent with international principles of self-defense.

This is the best news for a long time. It deserves to be said, also, that the feat was accomplished with no serious loss of civilian life, and with an almost pedantic policy of avoiding "collateral damage." The hypocritical advice of the Pakistani right wing (keep it short, don't bomb, don't bomb during Ramadan, beware of the winter, leave Kabul alone) was finally ignored as the insidious pro-Taliban propaganda that it actually was. Those ultraleftists and soft liberals who repeated the same stuff—in presumable ignorance of its real source and intention—could safely be ignored then and needn't be teased too much now. The rescue of the Iraqi Kurds in 1991 taught them nothing; they were for leaving Bosnia and Kosovo to the mercy of Milosevic; they had nothing to say about the lack of an international intervention in Rwanda. The American polity is now divided between those who can recognize a new situation when they see it, and those who cannot or will not.

This brings me to the other piece of great recent news. Apparently unimpressed by those who maintained that the Al Qaeda death squads were trying to utter a cry for help about the woes of the world's poor (a dismal song I must say I haven't heard being sung so much lately), Judge Baltasar Garzón has put the Spanish wing of this gangster network into custody. We know this judge is not soft on crime, because he helped open the new era of universal jurisdiction by issuing a warrant for the arrest of General Pinochet. He has now gone one better, by telling Attorney General Ashcroft that arrest and detention work only when they are used to enforce the rule of law. No country that respects these norms will deliver prisoners to a country that does not respect them. Military tribunals that take evidence in secret and that have the power to impose the death penalty are, by definition, not up to recognized international standards. Perhaps Ashcroft learned these techniques of jurisprudence from the abattoir regimes, like those of Chile and Guatemala, that the American right has so long defended. It will be very interesting to see how this near-perfect confrontation plays out. Of course, those who were soft on the original crimes will get correspondingly less of a hearing as the debate goes on.

I learn with complacency that I have been excommunicated from the left. Edward Herman, in a recent cyber-anathema, expels me because I am "rushing toward the vital center, maybe further to the right, with termination point still to be determined." He states pityingly that I apparently "cannot understand that attacking supposed rationalizations for X may be de facto rationalizing for Y." I must say I think that last bit is a touch obvious. Herman, along with several other of my correspondents, doesn't like it when I agree with certain conservatives or (let's be fair) when they agree with me. Well, I could have replied in just those terms to Herman as long ago as the Bosnia and Kosovo wars. At that time, the majority of the American right, from Kissinger to Gingrich and Forbes, were opposed to U.S. intervention. In the post-September 11 hostilities, Pat Buchanan and Oliver North have warned against American "imperial" tactics, and David Duke has traced the Al Qaeda motive to the pre-existing violence of Zionism. Why did I not turn these guns on Herman? Because the reasoning would be too puerile and the attempted association too reminiscent of the methods of Stalinism. I suppose, though, that these are the very elements that recommend such "arguments" to him.

Some readers may have noticed an icy little missive from Noam Chomsky, repudiating the very idea that he and I had disagreed on the "roots" of September 11. I rush to agree. Here is what he told his audience at MIT on October 11:

> I'll talk about the situation in Afghanistan. . . . Looks like what's happening is some sort of silent genocide. . . . It indicates that whatever, what will happen we don't know, but plans are being made and programs implemented on the assumption that they may lead to the death of several million people in the next—in the next couple of weeks . . . very casually with no comment . . . we are in the midst of apparently trying to murder three or four million people.

Clever of him to have spotted that (his favorite put-down is the preface "Turning to the facts . . . ") and brave of him to have taken such a lonely position. As he rightly insists, our disagreements are not really political.

THE NATION, NOVEMBER 29, 2001

PAKISTAN:
ON THE FRONTIER
OF APOCALYPSE

PESHAWAR, NORTH-WEST FRONTIER PROVINCE,
OCTOBER 20, 2001

I used to love the city of Peshawar, which lies near the Pakistani-Afghan border and commands the superb approaches to the Khyber Pass. Its name derives from the Sanskrit for "city of flowers," and, combined with its frontier-town status, this conveys a sense of openness and spaciousness: a vast crossroads under a great vault of sky. But this trip was different. In the first few weeks of the "coalition war"—just as it was becoming plain that the war would not be brief—Peshawar felt enclosed, brooding, almost hermetic. This was partly because the frontier was shut to all but a few smugglers and nomads and Taliban infiltrators. It was also because the city was choked with people: exiles and refugees whose camps ringed the city. These huddled masses cook with wood—further denuding Pakistan's already poorly husbanded forestry—and at evening the normally pristine air was heavy with acrid smoke, catching at the tear ducts and the back of the throat. To this element of stifling atmosphere was added another: the air of menace that now accompanies the close of evening prayers. All-male crowds, with no outlet for their emotions after listening to inflammatory sermons from the mullahs or the Jamaat-Ulema-i-Islami Party demagogues, spilled out of the mosques and displayed what I can only call an attitude. (In a town once famed for its latitude and tolerance, prudent women are wearing the hideous and enveloping burka in the Afghan neighborhoods.) I chose this devotional moment, one choking evening at dusk, to get out of my car in an Afghan bazaar and approach a vendor of Osama bin Laden T-shirts. I wanted half a dozen for friends, and though I normally will pay rather than haggle, I was not going to

437

part with the two hundred rupees that the startled tradesman demanded for each item. Fifty was my limit, and I was prepared to be British about it.

I have never been so swiftly and completely surrounded. It was as if, in this formerly cosmopolitan city, they had never seen a foreigner before. "Why you want these?" Faces right in mine, fingers and hands prodding and pushing me. "You like Osama?" "Of course. He is my brother." "He is your *brother?*" "All men are my brothers." Much jeering and sneering, and then: "Why you not scared? Why you show money here?" "Why should I be scared? Muslims do not steal from guests." I experienced a peripheral vision of writhing, baffled beards and mustaches. As a rule, I resent reading feverish journalistic accounts of swarthy locations; I avoid using non-human terms such as "teeming" or "seething," and I have often been received with exquisite hospitality in the poorest parts of the Islamic world, but this was different. As elsewhere in Pakistan, there was a miasma of self-pity mingled with self-righteousness. It takes hysterical and contradictory forms: thus one is instructed loudly that "everybody knows" the Jews blew up the World Trade Center—even though bin Laden is praised in the very same heated breath for doing it himself. The mullahs tell people that the Taliban are correct to ban all pictures and photographs and television and film, because the representation of the human form is profane. But the T-shirts displaying bin Laden's oddly epicene features are on sale right outside the mosque . . . In the English-language papers you can read well-written denunciations of this foul and vicious mood, in articles composed by brave Pakistani dissidents and secularists. But the press reaches only a fraction of the population of 145 million, 57 percent of whom are illiterate.

It was a few miles from here, at the border post in Torkham, at the head of the Khyber Pass, that my old friend, Ahmed Rashid, Pakistan's best and bravest reporter, actually witnessed the birth moment of our current world crisis. He had just been covering the Soviet withdrawal from Afghanistan in April 1989 and was lying on a patch of grass waiting for the border post to open when:

> suddenly, along the road behind me, a truck full of Mujaheddin roared up and stopped. But those on board were not Afghans . . . The group was made up of Filipino Moros, Uzbeks from Soviet Central Asia, Arabs

from Algeria, Egypt, Saudi Arabia and Kuwait and Uighurs from Xin-jiang in China . . . Under training at a camp near the border they were going on weekend leave to Peshawar . . . They had come to fight the jihad with the Mujaheddin and to train in weapons, bomb-making and military tactics so they could take the jihad back home.

That evening, Ahmed met Lieutenant General Hamid Gul, then head of Pakistan's now notorious Inter-Services Intelligence (ISI) and a dedicated Islamic ideologue. "I asked him if he was not playing with fire by inviting Muslim radicals from Islamic countries, who were ostensibly allies of Pakistan. Would these radicals not create dissension in their own countries, endangering Pakistan's foreign policy?" Gul's reply is worth giving: "We are fighting a jihad and this is the first Islamic international brigade in the modern era. The communists have their international brigades, the West has NATO, why can't the Muslims unite and form a common front?"

I disagree slightly with Ahmed's emphasis; it would be more accurate to say "Muslim reactionaries" than radicals. (The historic essence of Fascism is the most retrograde people using the most revolutionary rhetoric.) And I wish that those in the West who harbor softheaded illusions about Muslim grievances could see and hear General Gul (rhymes with "ghoul"). He is not an oppressed peasant. He is Pakistan's Pinochet: a militaristic and privileged thug, fattened for many years on American subsidies. He was much in evidence around Islamabad during my recent stay, calling for an end to the American intervention in Afghanistan. Too many people, he said, had already died. This must have been the first time in his career that he had expressed the smallest concern about civilian casualties.

But then, there is a certain hypocrisy inscribed in the very origins and nature of "Pakistan." The name is no more than an acronym, confected in the 1930s at Cambridge University by a Muslim propagandist named Chaudhri Rahmat Ali. It stands for Punjab, Afghania, Kashmir, and Indus-Sind, plus the suffix "-stan," meaning "land." In the Urdu tongue, the resulting word means "Land of the Pure." The country is a cobbling together of regional, religious, and ethnic nationalisms, and its founding, in

1947, resulted in Pakistan's becoming, along with Israel, one of the two "faith-based" states to emerge from the partitionist policy of a dying British colonialism. You may notice that there is no *b* in the acronym, even though for the first two decades of its existence Pakistan forcibly enclosed East Bengal (now Bangladesh) and still includes the restive and reluctant province of Baluchistan. The *P* comes first because Pakistan is still the property of the Punjabi military and feudal elite, but the thing might as easily be rendered as "Akpistan" or "Kapistan," depending on whether the battle to take over Afghanistan or Kashmir is to the fore.

Unlike India, which fought tenaciously for independence for many decades (until 1947), Pakistan cannot claim any glorious history of struggle as its birthright. It is the product of a carve-up, against the wishes of a majority of the subcontinent's population. The carve-up was a hasty improvisation, designed to cover the retreat of the exhausted British, and achieved largely behind closed doors between the last viceroy, Lord Mountbatten, and Mohammed Ali Jinnah, the ambitious exclusivist leader of the subcontinent's Muslim minority. Jinnah is still revered, Eastern European-style, as the great teacher and leader and unquestionable founder of the state. Fifty-four years later, there are almost as many Muslims in India as in Pakistan; the battle over the status of Kashmir is one of the deadliest and most volatile on the planet, and the resulting arms race, which now includes nuclear weaponry, consumes the budgets of two poverty-racked countries. Meanwhile, Pakistan is in a state of perpetual strife among its different regions and their rival Sunni and Shiite Islamic populations, while the 1971 Bangladesh war—in which a Muslim army put a Muslim population to the sword—is still memorable as one of the great horrors of the post-1945 period. Far from being a "Land of the Pure," Pakistan is one of the clearest demonstrations of the futility of defining a nation by religion, and one of the textbook failures of a state and a society. But the fanatics by definition do not learn from their mistakes. (Santayana was correct in describing a fanatic as one who re-doubles his efforts when he has lost sight of his aims.) The battle is now on to mutate Pakistan one stage further, and to set up a totally Muslim state where once there was just a state for Muslims. It is this lethal tussle *between* Muslims—to impose Koranic or Shari'a law by force across the Islamic world—that has already claimed terrible casualties in two major American cities.

* * *

The Pakistani capital, Islamabad, is an architectural expression of the state's artificiality. Not even built until after 1947, it is an Asian Brasília, with wide and impersonal boulevards connecting great palaces of bureaucracy. Its street names are ciphers of numbers and letters. It is also very handy to Rawalpindi, the headquarters garrison town of the Pakistani armed forces. Anyone wanting to mount a coup has only to drive his tanks a few blocks. Pakistan has been a fiefdom of the military for most of its short existence: as was once said of Prussia, it is not a country that has an army but an army that has a country. (On roadsides and at traffic circles, the typical monuments are tanks or fighter planes set in concrete, or replicas of the mountain under which Pakistan's first nuclear device was detonated.) In Rawalpindi itself, the genial regimental atmosphere of the British days—symbolized by the aptly named Flashman's Hotel—is now somewhat overlaid by the signs of influence from West Point and Langley. The ISI, originally set up in 1948 by a British officer named Major General Cawthorne, who "stayed on" after partition, has more recently become an expensively Americanized apparatus. But the big subject of whispered conversation during my stay was this: Did the United States still call the shots? Who was the client and who was the puppet? What if the shadowy "enemy we can't see" is made up partly of our supposed friends?

The atmosphere of intrigue and bad faith, in the hotel lobbies of Islamabad and in the discreet and luxurious villas of the city's fat cats, was even more nauseating and obfuscating than the hot fumes of Peshawar. An average day in this sterile, furtive town would consist of a morning spent in the Marriott Hotel's corridors (and in its "deniable" rip-off basement bar), followed by a briefing at the Foreign Ministry, the regular farce of the press conference at the Taliban embassy, and then a soirée at some private palazzo (where at least the Scotch was free, and imported, rather than emitted from some diesel-engine off-the-record distillery in Quetta). One morning I encountered not just one but two representatives of the much-ballyhooed King of Afghanistan, the octogenarian potentate who has not set foot in his country for twenty-nine years and who doesn't really speak its main language. (He pronounces in a Persian dialect favored by the elite.) One of these monarchical envoys, Rahim Sherzoy, gave me a business card inscribed with an address in Fremont, California. His cohort, the oft televised and word-lessly suave Hedayat Amin-Arsala, looked like Sidney Greenstreet with a goatee and exuded all the charm of pre-war Monte Carlo. Bringing the fissile elements of Afghan tribalism together is at the best of times like herding cats (and feral cats too, if I may say so without disrespect). The idea of the tribes rallying to this brace of eight-piece suits seemed like a pipe dream, and a dream from one of those aromatic pipes in Peshawar at that. Serious forces, such as the heroines of RAWA (the Revolutionary Association of the Women of Afghanistan, which actually defies the Taliban in Kabul and Kandahar), are not encouraged to join the discussion, because the Pakistani Army really, really doesn't like them.

From this Casablanca moment I proceeded to the torpid, scrofulous building that still housed the Taliban embassy. Not wishing to be too polite to the bored and turbaned character who oversaw visa requests, I made myself diffi-cult over the application form. "It says here, after the space for my name, 'Son of' . . ." He confirmed that this was so. "What if I was a daughter? Is there another form for women?" I wish I had a Polaroid of the spite and contempt on his face at hearing this question (to which the answer was "No"). At a later Taliban-embassy press conference, their ambassador, Mullah Abdul Salam Zaeef, was at pains to ridicule Secretary of State Colin Powell's mention of "broad-based" and "moderate" Taliban elements. There were, said this sneering envoy, no broad-based people in his party's ranks. I, for one, was ready to believe him. The Taliban were asking for large cash bribes to take reporters on shepherded tours across to Kandahar, and I didn't feel like paying up that day. So it was off to the Foreign Ministry briefing, given by a sharkskin smoothy named Riaz Mohammad Khan, who, I must say, had better English than his daily-briefing counterparts in Washington. I had a rude question for him too. That morning's *Dawn* newspaper had carried a small item about wounded Taliban fighters' being brought across the Pakistani frontier for medical treatment and then returned fit for duty. Was this the act of an ally, and if they could cross, why could not journalists cross as well, rather than have to depend on the Taliban's purchased hospitality? Mr. Khan would not be drawn out on part two of my question, but he replied to the first part, saying that Pakistan had always recognized whatever government was in power in Kabul, even the one installed by the Red Army. Yes, but Pakistan hadn't invited wounded Russian soldiers for medical treatment and then sent them tenderly back to the front line . . . Later that week, Maulvi Jalaluddin Haqqani, one of the Taliban's military commanders, appeared in Islamabad honored and unmolested, and announced matter-of-factly that his "guest" Osama bin Laden was still "living in complete safety." He met with high Pakistani officials and repeated his assertion, and then returned home contentedly. If the United States Embassy felt impotent while watching this insufferable display, it was at pains to conceal the fact.

In the evening, at a sumptuous dinner in the home of a local tycoon, I met the even smoother if not ultimately smooth Shaukat Aziz, who is Pakistan's finance minister and a longtime *grand fromage* at Citibank. He was newly returned from Washington, where it didn't hurt that as a friend of Treasury Secretary Paul O'Neill's he could effectively negotiate Pakistan's enormous foreign debt out of existence. Mr. Aziz is used to this kind of thing—he was on hand for former prime minister Benazir Bhutto at a time when her husband was convicted of stuffing Swiss banks with chunks of the Pakistani treasury—but, even so, he must have felt on this occasion that all his birthdays had come at once. In the 1980s, Pakistan got a blank check from the U.S. to combat the Russians, and spent much of the check in building up the Taliban. Now it is getting another check and a brand-new interest-free mortgage in order to pretend that the Taliban are its enemy. It just doesn't *get* any better than this.

I think the roots of the all-pervasive anti-Americanism spring exactly from this mendicant's-begging-bowl arrangement. Pakistanis know that they are bought and paid for, and so the way to assert pride is to spit in the face of those who have owned and used them. (Something of the same pathology applies in the case of our former Afghan mercenaries.) Thus to self-righteousness and self-pity is added the third charm of self-hatred. An especially toxic example of this degraded relationship was the subtext of conversation at the very same dinner. For years during the cold war, the United States had pretended in public that Pakistan had not manufactured its own nuclear weapons. This had permitted a lavish military-aid budget to continue to be approved by Congress. But now we know all about the Pakistani nuclear arsenal. We just don't quite know who controls it. What if the next short march from Rawalpindi to Islamabad were to bring the missiles and the warheads into the itchy hands of General Gul? Nobody at the table was sure that the president, General Pervez Musharraf, had insurance he trusted against this contingency. And, indeed, a few days later I learned that three of Pakistan's top nuclear scientists had been discovered to have quite close connections with the Taliban. The sinister trio—Sultan Bashiruddin Mahmood, Mirza Yusuf Baig, and Chaudhry Abdul Majid—were taken in for "questioning." I would dearly like to know what the questions—and the answers—were.

This may be the great unintended consequence of Osama bin Laden's world-shaking fanaticism. His intense need to do something immediate and apocalyptic has quite possibly saved us, at least for now, from the takeover of Pakistan by the cadres of the ISI and its clones—which are the Taliban, the Pakistani religious parties, and Al Qaeda. Until a few months ago, these factions stood a sporting chance of winning power, with Musharraf as their front man. But he turned out to be so much of a front man that he is now willing to be stroked and "turned," and to act as a front man for Washington instead. "He's such a simple guy," it was said by the Pakistani elitists at this dinner. "He likes to drink, and he has an eye for the wives of brother officers. The hardliners thought he was a pliable puppet, and they were right; he's anybody's pliable puppet." The danger of an Al Qaeda nuke has passed, for now. But if you want to write your congressman about anything, write him and ask what's being done to neutralize that arsenal for good.

Tiring of the provincial and surreptitious mood in the capital, and having already exposed myself to the Afghan, or "Akpistan," frontier, I decided to try to see "Kapistan" as well. You need military permission to visit the Pakistani-held part of Kashmir, and the army eventually agreed to take me to what is the near-certain flash point of a coming war that could well become an Asian Armageddon. (In one of his most recent broadcasts, bin Laden's noisy deputy Sulaiman Abu Ghaith put Kashmir in the top four Al Qaeda causes, right after Afghanistan, Palestine, and the U.S. presence in the Arabian peninsula.

They want a holy war against "the Hindus" as well as the Christians, and the Jews, and the secularists. This is one of the many ways that the gang repays years of Pakistani support and protection.)

Look at any atlas and you can see that Kashmir is the keystone in the arch of Indo-Pakistani confrontation. Its frontier is long and arduous, and extends all the way through the Himalayas, touching Afghanistan and nearly Tajikistan before reaching China. A good stretch of this frontier is known as "the Line of Control" and is a heavily armed military demarcation, drawn at the cease-fire point of the last Indo-Pakistani war. In 1990 there was almost another war, when Pakistan became convinced of an impending Indian attack and readied a nuclear strike to offset New Delhi's vast superiority in men and armor. Officials in Washington who were involved in the crisis still turn pale when they recall that the pre-emptive strike was aborted with frighteningly little time on the clock. Things have, you will be relieved to know, gotten much, *much* worse since then. For one thing, the Kashmiri militants who contest India's rule over a Muslim-majority province have abandoned nationalist rhetoric and tactics and opted instead for jihad. A few days before I arrived— on October 1, to be precise—they had blown up the Kashmiri State Assembly in Srinagar, the capital city of Indian Kashmir, killing almost forty people in a suicide car-bomb-attack. Discovering Al Qaeda supporters among the plotters, the Indians had responded by shelling Islamist camps across the Line of Control, and so the Pakistani Army was eager to show me the consequences of Indian "aggression."

Muzaffarabad, the capital of Pakistani Kashmir, is a hill town of surpassing beauty and one of the settings for Paul Scott's marvelous "Raj Quartet." Here one finds that the same Raj still breathes, because the only subject of conversation is the still-unfinished business of the partition of 1947. It isn't resolved yet! It's gone nuclear instead. I cursed the ghost of Lord Mountbatten once again as I sat and interviewed Sardar Sikander Hayat Khan, the Buddha-bellied and white-mustachioed old lion who is prime minister of the Pakistani-run statelet. He, like his father before him, has been at it ever since the waning days of the Empire. The issue was stale when the United Nations was founded. Almost in a trance of repetition, he recited the litany of ancient woes, and pretended not to speak proper English only when he was asked a pointed question. The question he wouldn't answer was whether he knew how the bin Laden forces managed to make their way across the border to India.

This very same topic struck the Pakistani military commander in the sector as a mystery of Elmore Leonard or Agatha Christie proportions. How do these blighters do it? The Pakistani Army has stern and consistent control over the whole area and doesn't allow tourists or journalists to make unauthorized visits. Martial law is effectively in force. Carrying weapons is forbidden. The terrain is very mountainous and thickly forested and seamed with gullies and ravines. In fact . . . ah, yes, that must be it. These unauthorized elements are obviously dragging their rocket launchers and heavy weapons across unmonitored bits of the border at night. That's if they are doing it at all, which is not officially admitted. A problem, sir, indeed. A real enigma. So I am assured, in British-military English, by Brigadier General Muhammad Yaqub, commander of "the Mujahid Battalion," also known as "the Shaheen," or falcons, in the Chakoti sector of the front. He and his men have taken me by jeep as far as a jeep will go, and then on foot through some trenches and dugouts that remind me of the Somme, to a position where I can wave at the Indian soldiers who are dug in hard behind embrasures and entrenchments on the opposite hill. Marks of shellfire on the walls of Chakoti tell their own story.

Tea and biscuits are served and I am given a highly tendentious briefing. "Look, in 1970 the Indians helped the Bangladeshis to rebel against Pakistan," Yaqub says. "So we would be morally justified in helping the Kashmiris to revolt against India." Well, are you doing so? "Not exactly; their freedom struggle is internally generated." But no fewer than sixty-four medals were awarded to Pakistani soldiers after they were found in highly suspicious company on the other side of the Line of Control in May 1999, just after a summit meeting had taken place between India and Pakistan. To this the brigadier prefers to give no reply. And what about bin Laden's infiltrators, who throw acid in the faces of unveiled Kashmiri women and mount suicide attacks in Srinagar? "It is India's responsibility to stop them crossing the frontier, if indeed they do cross it," says Yaqub. (Back in Islamabad, the Foreign Ministry spokesman, Riaz Mohammad Khan, had managed to insinuate that the Indians were actually behind the October 1 bombings in Srinagar, in an effort to win the sympathy of Colin Powell for their cause.) It's true that India has long been a backer of Afghanistan's Northern Alliance, and it's also the case that Indian policy in Kashmir is semi-colonial, but once again it is Pakistani hypocrisy that is truly breath-catching.

From "Akpistan" to "Kapistan": The Pakistanis tried to make Afghanistan into a province or a colony so they could have "strategic depth," as they called it, for the real confrontation in Kashmir. The result is the near Talibanization of Pakistan and the spillover of the fundamentalists into Kashmir itself. Standing on this remote and lovely hilltop I feel certain that I am getting a curtain-raiser preview of the terrain on which the world's first nuclear exchange will inevitably occur. Every other British-sponsored divide-and-quit partition has led either to another partition or to another war, or both. This will be both, and on a scale of grand opera. It's not a cheerful thought to be taking back to Islamabad.

But Islamabad is not a cheerful place to which to return. There was a warning of all this, as far back as 1983, when Salman Rushdie published the best-ever novel about Pakistan, *Shame*. Many readers remember the dense paragraph in which he tried to delineate a wounded civilization, striving to write

about the bandits on the trunk roads who are condemned for doing, as private enterprise, what the government does as public policy; or about genocide in Baluchistan; or about the recent preferential awards of State scholarships, to pay for postgraduate studies abroad, to members of the fanatical Jamaat party; or about the attempt to declare the sari an obscene garment; or about the extra hangings—the first for twenty years—that were ordered purely to legitimize the execution of Mr. Zulfikar Ali Bhutto; or about why Bhutto's hangman has vanished into thin air, just like the many street-urchins who are being stolen every day in broad daylight; or about anti-Semitism, an interesting phenomenon, under whose influence people who have never met a Jew vilify all Jews for the sake of maintaining solidarity with the Arab states which offer Pakistan workers, these days, employment and much-needed foreign exchange; or about smuggling, the boom in heroin exports, military dictators, venal civilians, corrupt civil servants, bought judges . . .

In 1989 it was the Pakistani fundamentalist fringe which first shed blood in the streets over the publication of *The Satanic Verses*, igniting a chain of violence that transmitted the neurotic energy of Muslim fundamentalism from Eastern territories to Western capitals. That, I felt at the time, was also a warning. Now there is another Pakistani Islamist party, even more extreme than its predecessor. There is also the Sepah-i-Sahaba militia ("Soldiers of the Companions of the Prophet"), a Sunni Muslim Kalashnikov gang that does battle with its Shiite rival, the Sepah-i-Mohammad ("Soldiers of Mohammad"). As ever with the faithful—rather like the Christians in Northern Ireland—just come see how the believers love one another. One of these goon squads then turned the Kalashnikovs on Pakistan's Christian minority, drowning a whole congregation in blood on October 28. So it goes. An 800-page biography of Pakistan's founder, the aforementioned Mohammed Ali Jinnah, is too careful to make any mention of the way he always spoke with his unveiled sister at mass meetings, or of the fact that his second wife was a non-Muslim. A movie producer who tried to make a feature film stressing the same facts was accused of having Salman Rushdie as his scriptwriter, and was subjected to chilling threats. From a state merely *for* Muslims to a full-on theocratic state is a bigger change than most Westerners can yet appreciate.

As I was making ready to leave Peshawar, I went along the old Jamrud Road and paid to unlock its Christian cemetery, which is where the dead of British times are interred behind a brick wall and under a canopy of shade trees. The place is much dilapidated, but one can still see the regimental symbols and the sad old grave markers from lost campaigns. I truly wanted to be the first writer to visit Peshawar and not quote Rudyard Kipling, but as I walked alone through the marble memorials I remembered some long-forgotten lines and couldn't help myself:

> *And the end of the fight is a tombstone*
> *white with the name of the late deceased,*
> *And the epitaph drear: "A Fool lies here*
> *who tried to hustle the East."*

And of course from that it's only a step to the imperishable verses of Kipling's "Arithmetic on the Frontier." The gates of memory swung open fully: my father's father had been a soldier in pre-partition India.

> *A scrimmage in a Border Station—*
> *A canter down some dark defile—*
> *Two thousand pounds of education*
> *Drops to a ten-rupee jezail*

With its unconsoling conclusion, about the military proportions between locals and intruders:

> *Strike hard who cares—shoot straight*
> *   who can—*
> *The odds are on the cheaper man.*

All week, within a few miles of where I was standing, American warplanes had been wheeling and diving over Afghanistan in an effort to disprove that very arithmetic. The equivalents of the old single-shot jezail rifles were powerless against the swift, silvery F-16s. The cheaper men could make no impression on the lancing, laser-guided missiles and bombs. And two of the pilots, I learned from a man who had just come to Islamabad from the deck of the U.S.S. *Carl Vinson*, were females. I felt a momentary need to go to the Taliban embassy and say, "It's your worst nightmare, you bastards. She's pissed, she's packing, and she's headed for you."

But the United States government, in exaggerated deference to its Islamic "allies" in Saudi Arabia and elsewhere, took its time making public boasts about its women fliers. Whereas among the faded British graves there were many affecting headstones recording the deaths of wives and children. The British may have used some Sikhs and other local troops, but they came to stay, and they did a lot of their own fighting and dying. What is to become of an empire that relies on mercenaries to take its risks on the ground?

Still more sobering was the thought: What if some of those hirelings secretly want you to lose? In every silky statement from General Musharraf about the need for a short—in other words: limited—war, and in every nuance of the Pakistani official posture, I was sure I detected the local version of Schadenfreude. An American humiliation would preserve the Afghan assets built up by General Gul, and keep the pressure off Kashmir. It would also mean further subsidies and debt forgiveness, because an "ally" cannot be abandoned after so many presidential pledges have been made. The tail could wag the dog indefinitely. But the only people I met who had really hoped for an American success against the Taliban were local secular leftists who had relatives in Britain or America.

As I arrived at Islamabad airport to take my leave, a huge bomb had just been found and detonated in the parking lot. Who knows who put it there, or why? On Pakistan International Airlines it is still permitted to smoke, but not to order a drink. And there are now obligatory Muslim prayers played on takeoff. So I may have been in a sour mood as I quit the country. An artificial nation, born out of manipulation and middleman tactics, had managed to switch sides twice, first to the Taliban and Al Qaeda, and then with undignified haste to the Anglo-American coalition. In both cases, its oligarchy had used and misused the money of the too trusting American taxpayer. At every stage of the counterattack against the Taliban, General Musharraf had intensified his unhelpful demands: don't fight during Ramadan, don't let the Northerners take Kabul . . . Oh, and give us some costly hardware after all we've done for you. (Nobody I spoke to was in any doubt that it was "rogue" Pakistani intelligence agents who had tipped off the Taliban to capture and murder the legendary Abdul Haq, as he slipped across the Afghan border to try and coordinate the resistance.) Meanwhile, the failing Pakistani state had been revived to prosecute another war in Kashmir. Unfortunately, this could not be described as an unintended consequence of the emancipation of Afghanistan. I slumped in my airline seat, uttered a secular prayer for the victory of the coalition, and realized that we'd all be back here again before long.

VANITY FAIR, JANUARY 2002

SADDAM'S
LONG GOOD-BYE

Your own choice of a high moment, if I may invite it, from David
Lean's *Lawrence of Arabia?* Let's agree to exempt the resplendent
scene of flogging and implied rape, which is the cheapest kind of
Orientalism. ("You're just Florence of Arabia," as a cynical cameraman on the
set once phrased it to Peter O'Toole.) That may leave us to choose among the
bitter trek by hardened freedom fighters across the desert, the pitiless
bombing of Arab tents by Ottoman aircraft, the sabotage of the Hejaz railway
by guerrilla warriors, the orgiastic massacre of the retreating foe by Lawrence
and his overenthusiastic volunteers, and the quagmire or quicksand that
engulfs his young "friend" Daud. For me, though, the climax has always been
the anticlimax. Having taken Jerusalem and then Damascus, the Arab forces
begin to quarrel and bicker, and to look with glittering annoyance upon their
Western allies and patrons. Chaos, tribalism, and egomania overwhelm the
grand enterprise. The British general Allenby watches cynically as the revolt
peters out, giving the natives just enough time to pillage and loot, so as to
wreck their own chances. And then the Arabs leave the city and fade back into
the sand dunes, and out of history. What else could one expect?

In June 1976, I spent a while in the National Museum in Baghdad, doing
some amateur research on the legend of Gilgamesh, King of Uruk, for a friend
who hoped to write an opera on the subject. My guide was a poised and polished man named Mazen al-Zahawi—a professional "minder" for the regime,
it is true (he also took me to meet the notorious assassin and saboteur Abu
Nidal, then living openly as a guest of the Baath Party), but a fine companion

for all that. He was partly Kurdish and wholly gay. He lived in the former Nazi German Embassy residence near the Tigris—an elegant enough house—and invited me to dinner with a publisher friend of his who lived on a houseboat. There he told me that his favorite recreation was to improvise a Mesopotamian version of Wilde's *The Importance of Being Earnest*, with himself in the part of Lady Bracknell. Dear Mazen went on to become Saddam Hussein's interpreter, because of his superb English, and I wondered how long he'd survive. (Not all that long: he was tortured to death on a whim and then denounced for being a queer.) I mourn him terribly, along with many other brave and witty Iraqi and Kurdish friends. But I think he might rather be dead than have seen the recent vandalizing and desecration of the museum and the National Library. Is it profane to care as much for artifacts as for people? What are we defending when we talk about civilization?

It may seem like a small thing, even a trivial thing, but I spent an appreciable bit of my time in the early months of 2003 arguing just one point with people in Washington. Whatever you do about Iraq, or in Iraq, please don't use "Desert" in the code name. Everything is wrong with that designation. This is not a land of dunes and camels, as Bush Sr.'s "Desert Storm" and Clinton's "Desert Fox" condescendingly implied. It is a highly evolved and complex society. It is the site of Babylon and Ur and Babel, and the womb of the founding myths of civilization. (In *Gilgamesh* we read of a man who built a boat to survive a predicted flood.) Some of the very earliest Christian places are to be found there, and until 1948 there were more Jews in Baghdad than there were in Jerusalem. And our folklore doesn't come from the brothers Grimm: it originates with Sinbad, Scheherazade, and Haroun al-Raschid.

Among the better reworkings of these ancient tales was one by Somerset Maugham. It begins, "Death Speaks."

There was a merchant in Bagdad who sent his servant to market to buy provisions and in a little while the servant came back, white and trembling, and said, Master, just now when I was in the market-place I was jostled by a woman in the crowd and when I turned I saw it was Death that jostled me. She looked at me and made a threatening gesture; now, lend me your horse, and I will ride away from this city and avoid my fate. I will go to Samarra and there Death will not find me. The merchant lent him his horse, and the servant mounted it, and he dug his spurs in its flanks and as fast as the horse could gallop he went. Then the merchant went down to the market-place and he saw me standing in the crowd and he came to me and said, Why did you make a threatening gesture to my servant when you saw him this morning? That was not a threatening gesture, I said, it was only a start of surprise. I was astonished to see him in Bagdad, for I had an appointment with him tonight in Samarra.

As I went grinding up the road from Kuwait to southern Iraq in March, in the first few days after a gigantic, mechanized Anglo-American-Australian-Polish army had passed along the same route, I had a similar sense of keeping an unpostponable date. I was watching the closing moments of a war that had begun on August 2, 1990, when the armed forces of Saddam Hussein smashed in the opposite direction across the Kuwaiti frontier. That conflict had supposedly ended on February 27, 1991, with the official restoration of Kuwaiti sovereignty. But it had smoldered on for more than a dozen years, like a fire deep in a bad old mine, and was only now being brought to a conclusion.

I went on a fairly easy day-trip, organized by the Kuwait Red Crescent Society, to deliver supplies to the people of Safwan. This is the town inside Iraq which could claim the faint privilege of being one of the first centers of population liberated from Saddam's control. It lies not far from the port of Umm Qasr, the harbor by which "the coalition" aimed to open the hermetic state to the magnificence of the sea and the munificence of humanitarian aid. Conscripted dolphins were sporting in the blue waters of Umm Qasr, gaily employing their sonar to detect Saddam's mines, but in Safwan there was a scene of aridity, stagnation, and misery. As our relief convoy arrived, with upbeat stencils and slogans on the sides of the trucks, I swiftly realized that it had been fatuous to hope for a greeting of sweets and flowers.

At first, the baked fields around the town appeared inactive, if not depopulated. Then a group of children materialized, waving and scampering. Soon it seemed as if people were rising by magic from the dusty furrows and hillocks. Within moments, the convoy was halted by the sheer press of numbers, and a yelling throng was pushing so close that it prevented the rear doors of the trucks from being opened. After a nasty, undignified scuffle in which some limbs were broken, the Kuwaiti relief workers began to toss the precious cartons out onto the heads of the mob, as if supervising frenzy-time in some badly run zoo. I don't remember witnessing a more dispiriting scene. The "Arab street," whether for or against, is no prettier than any other scene of crowd emotion.

Older people were shoved to the rear, as were the less aggressive children, so one had the chance to talk. On the whole, it was the children who were most enthusiastic about the new arrivals. One of them did an astonishing impression of a helicopter gunship firing down, and then gave an emphatic "thumbs up" signal. (Generally, children provide the cheer-up moment in situations like this, so I disliked myself for noticing how many of them had pinched, acne-studded, wolfish faces.) Several of the grown-ups, though, manifested acute resentment and annoyance. "Why do you photograph us like animals?" said one man, shaking with displeasure. "Here—this is how it should be done." And he produced from under his robe an Iraqi-government ration book, which with the help of my translator I deciphered as a list of his meager entitlements, as a father of four, from the local Baath Party. Gesturing furiously to the winner-take-all grabfest a few hundred yards away, the old boy made it volubly plain that this was not his idea of a fair deal. But he also made it clear that he didn't much like Kuwaitis. A reek of envy was evident: Iraqis have been told for decades that their southern Arab neighbors are rich and fat and fit only to be despoiled of their inherited oil wealth. For this man and others, it was shameful to be the recipient of charity from such a depraved source.

'Boosh, Boosh!" was still the piping chant of the toddlers and the younger boys, even if some of them did distract the photographers and cameramen by this means, cunningly enabling other kids to circle behind and grab wallets and water bottles. A Kuwaiti woman, who hadn't wanted to dismount from the bus, found her privacy and modesty invaded by a small lad who never-theless proffered a sharp knife. A little earlier, a man named Ajami Saadoun Khlis, who had lost a son and a brother to Saddam, had wept unendingly in the presence of a journalistic colleague of mine, and said, "You just arrived. You're late. What took you so long?" But this, too, was a version of impotence and animosity and humiliation. I found several men—all the women hung back throughout, many of them winding their veils ever closer—who openly praised Saddam Hussein. "He is the only Muslim leader." "He is the only Arab who is a soldier." These were, admittedly, slavish quotations from repetitive regime propaganda, but they were being uttered several days after Saddam's army had dissolved or fled, and they obviously weren't being voiced in the hope of an extra handout.

Another man, wearing a red-and-white headdress, took my sleeve. "Yesterday I saw a British soldier shoot two small children just here on this road." This was a British sector, and there were British military police in the town, so I asked him to tell me more about it. "He shot them with an M-16." I offered to take his complaint to a nearby British officer, even though I know that British forces don't carry M-16s, whereupon he became somewhat evasive and silken. "All right, then," I said. "Forget the officer. Where are the bodies?" "We buried them right away." "And as for the funeral?" "There wasn't time." At this point my companion and interpreter, a vast bear-shaped Palestinian whom I shall call Omar, touched my arm and said, "Come along, Mr. Christopher. These people are all liars."

The Iraqi who had spoken was certainly a liar, and a poor one as well as a mean and low one, but something in me wanted to resist Omar's conclusion. Or perhaps to explain it away. The townspeople of Safwan didn't owe me an explanation. They certainly didn't owe me a welcome, or a friendly pelting with the rose petals they didn't have. They really did live in something like a desert. On previous visits to Iraq, I had been embarrassed by the hospitality of those who had much less than I did. On this trip, I felt awkward for the opposite reason. But on this occasion, after all, the soldiers, the relief workers, and the reporters outnumbered the population. Should the locals have put on a feast for people who were casually throwing them food? Especially when what they most wanted, and most often mentioned, was water? In the end, even when it takes a vain form or a truculent or sullen shape, pride is an essential part of self-respect. As I departed, a titanic convoy began to roll by. It took forever to pass me, with its massive squadrons of earthmovers, ditchdiggers, tanks, and armored cars, feeding one of the longest supply lines in the whole story of warfare, already stretching all the way to the suburbs of Baghdad. By agreement, the soldiers of the coalition do not fly their national flags on the soil of Iraq. Good. But there was no mistaking their origin, and they roared by the dwarfish mud-brick dwellings without looking to left or right.

I realized that I had seen something faintly similar in my past. It was in Romania in 1989, when the Caligula regime of Nicolae Ceausescu was overthrown by the army and the people. I was in Transylvania and had with me some photographs of the late dictator with his awful wife, Elena, lying riddled with bullets on the floor. Nobody, for the first few days, could believe these pictures to be genuine. It was unthinkable that a man who had occupied the skulls of his people for so long could really be dead. Surely some vampire-like trick had been pulled? And, in the ground-down wasteland of southern Iraq, only the old could remember any time before Saddam. The colonization of the mind still persisted, with trauma right below the surface. It would take more than a few M.R.E. handouts (jambalaya flavor preferred) to dispel this waking and sleeping nightmare.

Just a few months previously, the inhabitants of Safwan had been forced to celebrate not just a 100 percent national vote for Saddam Hussein, the sole candidate in a presidential referendum, but a 100 percent turnout as well. What's it like to endure such a sadomasochistic ritual? There are two ways of surviving these challenges to self-respect. One is the Mafia syndrome, where you play along with the local bosses and learn a shitty way to smile, and the other is the Stockholm syndrome, where you take a tiny consolation out of the "security" the boss can provide. Even the children of Safwan had picked up these elementary lessons.

It had taken me a few days to attain my paltry journalistic ambition of setting foot, however briefly, on the soil of newly liberated Iraq. And the eventual experience had been anticlimactic, to say the least. But I gradually came to appreciate that I had been on "liberated" territory the entire time. Thirteen years previously, the whole of Kuwait had been appropriated by force as the nineteenth province of an expansionist Iraq. Arab and Muslim countries had fought and invaded each other before, inflicting casualties of the kind that would be called "barbaric" if imposed by Westerners, but not until 1990 had one Arab state simply abolished the existence of another. The reminders were on every hand. A few miles from Safwan, the Rumaila oil field was burning. The field itself straddles the Iraq-Kuwait border, and was one of the prizes coveted by Saddam in 1990. It has more than 400 oil wells, 9 of which had been ignited by retreating Baathists in the first hours of the recent war and some of which were still ablaze as I crossed the border. The heat is so infernally intense that it turns sand into glass around the wellheads, while the sky darkens with choking plumes (as with the ghastly, quasi-medieval siege tactic of flammable oil ditches, set off in Basra and Baghdad by the literally "last ditch" black-shirted diehards of the regime). But in 1991, and in defeat, Saddam had ordered the blowing of more than 600 wells, and flooded the Gulf by opening the pipelines. The reprise was a sputtering, closing version of the original conflagration.

The futile sabotage of March 2003 was not comparable to the petro-holocaust of February-March 1991 in point of its scale, but it helped rephrase the whole idea of a war that's "all about oil." Here is a sadistic leader who, if he can't annex the oil for himself, will put it to the torch and toxify the entire regional environment. One experienced the same pungent recollection when responding to the almost daily air-raid warnings over Kuwait City. At unpredictable intervals, Iraq discharged missiles at its former colony. The generic term for these is "Scuds," though it's not always clear what make or type of weapon is involved. Kuwait City is in theory the best-defended capital in the world when it comes to "missile defense," and the new generation of Patriot interceptors is designed to destroy warheads instead of knock them down, leaving only shards to be analyzed. So we were kept intriguingly in the dark as to whether these were the fabled Al Samoud or Al Ababil missiles—in other words, whether they were missiles with a range already banned by the United Nations (or whether the Hans Blix rules didn't actually ban missiles fired at nearby Kuwait). Their effect on the ground was the same: at the first wail of the sirens the people rushed to the shelters, and the press corps made a point of looking tough and indifferent. I saw one brief exception to this in late March, when the sirens sounded at midday during a driving sandstorm, and nobody could see anything in the sky. The two high-altitude explosions could be heard almost before the sirens gave the alert, and I did notice a few reporters wrestling with their expensive gas-mask equipment in the streets. Through the disagreeable atmospheric mixture of pelting sand and burning oil, one could discern no plan or strategy emanating from Baghdad. What was the point of these raids?

A single missile hurled from the Iraqi north was useless unless it had a chemical or biological payload. And we were continually assured, raid by raid, by the specially trained Czech Chemical Protection Battalion that was "in country," that the wreckage bore no toxic trace. The damn things were practically innocuous. The worst night was the last one I was there, when what seemed to be a Chinese-built Silkworm cruise missile managed to get under the radar and strike a downtown shopping mall. (Iron rule: The one that is successful is the one that doesn't trigger the sirens.) But that effort had less force than a car bomb would have had. The same was true of the shell that whistled over our relief buses as we paused at a roadblock, and banged loudly into the landscape off to our left. It was at the same time vicious and meaningless.

We were parked and pulled over, just near the Mutlaa Ridge. This encampment is traversable by way of Highway 6, a long straight road which connects Kuwait City to southern Iraq. In 1991 it had been the scene of a terrible and disfiguring atrocity committed by the allied forces. A huge convoy of retreating Iraqis had been straggling back from Kuwait as Baghdad radio announced their withdrawal. It was laden with every refrigerator, television set, and item of food or clothing that the late occupiers had been able to carry off with them. This sluggish, crawling monster was caught right out in the open by pilots flying off the deck of the U.S.S. *Ranger*. They bombed the front of the convoy to prevent it from going any farther, and they bombed the rear of it to prevent it from retreating. And then they bombed it some more.

The aircrews later breezily described the experience as a turkey shoot, comparable to strafing the road to Daytona Beach during spring break. For hours, while the ship's P.A. system blasted the Lone Ranger theme, they hastened back for fresh loads and roared off to dump the fragmentation bombs and to unleash armor-piercing incendiary rounds on the helpless thieves below. The resulting carnage and carrion are imperishably described in *Martyrs' Day*, Michael Kelly's book about the "first" Gulf War. (Mike would be killed on April 3, on the very outskirts of the Baghdad airport, while riding with the United States Third Infantry Division. He has a monument in the hearts of many friends, Iraqi and American, but this book is his best memorial.)

On the Mutlaa Ridge, I came to realize again that I was covering the end of the longest short war, or the shortest long war, that the United States has ever fought. It was in Safwan in 1991, after the eviction of Saddam Hussein from Kuwait, and as the Shia people of southern Iraq were mounting a desperate intifada, that Allied and Iraqi generals met for a permanent cease-fire.

A transcript of the meeting tells the whole story. Lieutenant General Sultan Hashim Ahmad, representing the Iraqi side, had a request:

> We have a point, one point. You might very well know the situation of the roads and bridges and communications. We would like to agree that helicopter flights sometimes are needed to carry some of the officials, government officials or any member that is needed to be transported from one place to another because the roads and bridges are out.

To this clever request, the victorious General Norman Schwarzkopf felt able to give a magnanimous response. As long as none of Saddam's choppers flew over American positions, he replied, there was "absolutely no problem." Hashim Ahmad could scarcely believe his luck, as the transcript shows:

> Schwarzkopf: "I want to make sure that's recorded, that military helicopters can fly over Iraq. Not fighters, not bombers."
>
> Hashim Ahmad: "So you mean even helicopters that is [sic] armed in the Iraqi skies can fly, but not the fighters?"
>
> Schwarzkopf: "Yeah, I will instruct our Air Force not to shoot at any helicopters that are flying over the territory of Iraq where we are not located . . ."

And then the rain of horror from the sky as the Baath Party and its airborne gunships restored order, cleared a space for the special police squads and Republican Guard, slaughtered as many as 60,000 Shia civilians, shelled the holy sites of Najaf and Karbala, and recaptured all of the other places whose names have lately become familiar to a mass readership, or in some cases familiar again.

But, for the powerless, immiserated population of Safwan, on the day I saw them, it was about twelve years since they'd seen it all before. The big, happy, friendly, gullible Western officers; the fat smiles; the sly grins; the done deal— all déjà vu. Much depended on how smart the second wave would be. A few miles up the road, in the city of Qalat Sukkar, the Marines of 2003 arrived with an interpreter and guide named Khuder al-Emiri, who had led a rebellion in the town in 1991 and then escaped with his life. He had been working in

Seattle ever since and had volunteered to help with the intervention. He was well liked, and he knew his way around. If there had been more of that kind of intelligent preparation, there could have been much less looting and panic and revenge. But as I write this, I am numb with misery about the torching and plundering of the National Museum and the National Library of Baghdad: a disaster to be compared to the Mongol desecrations of antiquity. Yet what if we, and our Iraqi and Kurdish allies, had put an end to the Saddam system in 1991?

I was in Iraqi Kurdistan that summer, and when I look at my old notes and photographs I start to quiver. Here it all is. The victims of chemical bombing in the city of Halabja, some of them with injuries that were still burning and festering. Villages voided and scorched by Saddam's ethnic cleansing, in a darkened landscape that seems to stretch to hell and back. White-faced refugees and defectors from the South, telling stories of oppression that harrow the soul. But also the triumphant parades of cars and trucks, their occupants chanting "Boosh, Boosh," pictures of Bush Sr. on the windshields. Exiles returning, at first nervous and tentative and then delighted, from years of enforced emigration. And the odd encounter with laconic 40 Commando Royal Marines, manning the strongpoints on the road. (I have a note of Captain Michael Page and Lieutenant Dominic May in the town of Amadia, telling me "some of Saddam's chaps tried something on our perimeter after nightfall. They rather came off second, though.") Without their presence, and that of other soldiers, the gunships might have finished the annihilation of Kurdistan that year, too.

"Bushistan," they called it then, half in jest and half in tribute. I don't think there's a single picture of Bush Sr. in the region these days. And where are you now, Hoshyar my friend, and all the other brave men who more or less carried me across those streams and mountains? Were you by any chance right to be cynical about superpower patronage? Would you have bothered if you thought that Saddam was going to get another dozen years?

Those twelve years were eaten by the locusts. The trunk of the tree of Iraq was allowed to rot, and its branches to wither. And all the time, a huge and voracious maggot lay at the heart of the state. Trade turned into a racket, the market was monopolized by the mafiosi, the sanctions screwed the poor and fattened the rich, and palaces with gold shithouses were constructed to mock the slumdwellers and the conscripts. A class of lumpen, uneducated, resentful losers was bred. When the Great Leader wanted to be popular, as on the grand occasion of his last referendum, he declared amnesty for the thieves, rapists, and murderers who were his natural constituency. To his very last day, he continued to divide and rule: to pump gangrene and pus into the society, disseminating lies and fear and junky religious propaganda. And there his bastard children were when the opportunity for hectic destruction and saturnalia presented itself.

The evidence of this in Kuwait was everywhere, and still horribly fresh, even after the passage of thirteen years. Here are the places used as dungeons and execution chambers for fellow Arabs and Muslims. Here is the place where Sheikh al-Fahd Ahmed al-Jabir, the most pro-Palestinian man in the country's leadership, was shot down by the Baathist invaders. Here is the citizens' committee, which to this day seeks information on the hundreds of Kuwaiti P.O.W.'s taken off in blindfolds and never seen again. Here is where the Kuwaiti libraries and museums were gutted. Iraq promised at the UN to give compensation and accounting for these and other depredations, but never did. It was for all this, and not just because of the morbid ambition to acquire weapons of genocide, that Saddam brought ruinous sanctions on his luckless country.

There was a clinging stench of wickedness left behind, and it was traceable to one nameable individual. General Ali Hasan al-Majid, a cousin of Saddam Hussein himself, was placed in charge of the occupation of Kuwait for four of those atrocious months. He had earned this rough promotion with some gusto, having commanded the ethnic cleansing of Iraqi Kurdistan between 1987 and 1988, during which time he boasted openly of using chemical techniques to suppress the population. ("I will kill them all with chemical weapons," he can be heard saying on a notorious tape. "Who is going to say anything? The international community? Fuck them . . ." Alas, his low opinion of the international community was correct—or at least it was then.) His media nickname—"Chemical Ali"—was entirely too jaunty. He was on every human-rights "Wanted" list in the world, for murder and torture and rape. And in March of 2003 he was appointed to command the southern region of Iraq, and to hold it for Saddam. An easy way to get a facial expression to change, in the flyblown streets of Safwan, was to mention the name of either man. There was no mistaking the abrupt flash of panic and insecurity that came into the eyes.

Kurdistan, Kuwait . . . and then the pitiless destruction of the independent habitat of the marsh Arabs near Basra, where the dirty smoke from the immolation of their ancestral territory had been visible from the space shuttle Endeavour. Somewhere way up the road north of Safwan, there was a rendezvous with this crime family that couldn't be put off any longer. In early April, outside Basra, Ali Hasan al-Majid was (I hope and believe) shredded by a laser-guided missile that was much more selective and scrupulous than the 1991 bombings and strafings had been, and millions of Iraqis and Kurds made a holiday in their hearts. As for Saddam himself, they had to make do with graven images. And not very far from the clan's hometown of Tikrit is a once lovely city on the banks of the river Tigris, containing the tombs of two great imams and a spiral minaret that is one of the region's wonders. In the ninth century, when many Europeans were dressed in skins, it was the shining capital of the Abbasid dynasty. I say "once lovely" because it has more recently become the site of the most inspected "facility" in Iraq, a plant that at one point produced an officially admitted 4,000 tons of mustard gas, VX, sarin, and other nightmarish chemical agents. Samarra is the name of the town, in case you are curious, and it's been waiting for the appointment for a very long time.

VANITY FAIR, JUNE 2003

A LIBERATING EXPERIENCE

A nd what about the Communists?" I ask Ambassador L. Paul Bremer, the United States administrator of the occupation of Iraq. He sits in an office that is not so much absurdly colonial as positively and ridiculously colonial, in a gargantuan marbled palace still surmounted by four great sculpted heads of Saddam Hussein. Efforts to humanize or down-size this context—such as Mr. Bremer's desert boots, which don't match his monogrammed "LPB" shirt, or the folksy desk-plaque that reads "Success has a thousand fathers"—only succeed in emphasizing it. But a few days prior to our meeting, he had announced a twenty-five-person "Governing Council" for the country, one of the named persons being Hamid Jameed Mousa, sec-retary of the Iraqi Communist Party. Well, says Bremer, the party has a long record of brave opposition to Saddam Hussein, and represents a good slice of the population, and Mr. Musa has shown signs of learning from history and understanding the importance of market reforms. Mr.Bremer spent many years working at the office of Kissinger Associates, and he must be the first alumnus of that outfit to have used American military power to instal a Communist leader in a Third World provisional government.

Don't bother visiting Baghdad today if you are too easily upset by contra-dictions. Irony and negation are the everyday currencies. For example, Iraq as a place, and Iraq as a country, is the special territory of archaeologists. Turn over a spade in the sand near Babylon, or Ur, or Nineveh, and you may come upon a pottery shard from the dawn of antiquity. People have been digging up Mesopotamia for generations. And the modern state of Iraq is partly the creation of British archaeology buffs: its borders were drawn by that eccentric explorer Gertrude Bell, and many of its greatest sites were carefully classified by Sir Max Mallowan, husband of Agatha Christie. (With this pair of seasoned eccentrics I once took a highly bizarre punting trip in Oxford.)

Of late, though, unearthing in Iraq has given way to something more like exhumation. The Saddam Hussein regime had a morbid mania for burying things, and people. The task of the most recent Western occupation has not been the relatively jolly if intricate one of analyzing and classifying the different layers of civilization. It has been one of disinterring the evidence of modern barbarism. Here are just some of the objects, and subjects, dug up before and during my most recent visit to the country:

- On 25 June it was disclosed that an Iraqi scientist named Mahdi Obeidi, the former chief of Iraq's uranium-enrichment program, had led American investigators to a spot in his back yard. In this place, in 1991, he had buried several components of a gas centrifuge, used for uranium enrichment, along with a two-foot stack of blueprints. The burial had been personally ordered by Saddam's younger son, Qusay, and the trove had survived several waves of inspections.

- On 29 June, near the town of Kirkuk, eight million dollars in cash were dug out of the garden of Abdel-Mahmoud Hamid al-Tikriti, Saddam Hussein's former personal secretary. Also recovered were a million dollars worth of jewelry belonging to Saddam's wife. Within a few weeks, Mr. al-Tikriti himself was given the disagreeable task of helping to identify the bodies of Uday and Qusay, the gruesome twosome of the old regime, before they could be interred in their turn.

- A senior analyst for the U.S. Department of Defense told me that, in the run-up to the war, Iraqi forces were spotted by satellite as they buried MIG-25 aircraft in the desert. "A plane that's been buried in the sand is never going to fly again," he said. "So why did they do it?"

- On 13 May American forces were called to a place near the town of Al-Hilla in southern Iraq, where local people had begun frenziedly searching through a mass grave. The remains of at least 3,000 individuals were brought to the surface, and a thousand or so of them were fairly swiftly identified by relatives. But it is estimated that there could be as many as 15,000 Iraqis buried at this place alone: eye-witnesses from the horrific repression of 1991 report seeing three truckloads of victims, three times a day, for a month, being unloaded there. A pre-dug pit awaited them, and they were marched into it before being shot and then buried or, in many instances, buried alive. There are sixty-two such sites already identified in southern Iraq alone. While I was in northern Iraq, the Kurdish and American authorities uncov-ered several more, including one that seemed to be reserved—in some deranged gesture of selectivity, perhaps—for the corpses of women and babies only. Digging is going to be an occupation in Iraq for some time to come.

To the Al-Hilla site I actually went myself. A calm and dignified Iraqi physician named Dr. Rafed Fakher Husain was being assisted by Major Al Schmidt, a reservist from New Jersey who is an FBI investigator in civilian life. Rows and rows of plastic bags were lying on the ground, tagged with personal items and identifying papers to help grieving families reclaim their loved ones. It was feared that the low water-table in the area had decomposed or washed away many of the bodies, but the search was still persisting. Where unearthing had been completed, the ground had been blessed and was now considered holy. All cultures have a natural horror of desecration, which is why *Antigone* is the most powerful of the plays of Sophocles. But Creon had only ordered one body to lie profanely unburied: Saddam Hussein consigned hundreds of thousands of his people to be gnawed by wild beasts or to rot without mourning or cere-mony. "We lived without rights," said the doctor. "And without ideas." The latter formulation seemed even more potent for its quiet understatement.

In Iraq in July the heat easily touches 120 degrees at mid-day, and a sour, gritty wind was blowing across the scene. This breath-catching temperature, plus the sun-screen lotion that one must continuously apply, plus the drenching per-spiration, means that a sort of crust or carapace forms on the skin. I'd become relatively used to this nasty paste on my person, and to the idea that showers in a country with a shattered water-supply are few and far between. But as the dirt clung and caked in my hair and inside my shirt, I began to cringe at the idea that I was being glutinously coated in the dust of a mass grave. It wasn't the time or the place to make a point of my own private revulsion, but if you can imagine feeling tainted in that way and unable to get clean, you have an inkling of the Iraq that Saddam has left to us. The whole society is clawing its way out of a shallow grave.

For the past year, most of the debate about American-sponsored "regime change" was intently focused on the question: "What if it fails?" What if Saddam's elite troops fight to the last? What if there are myriad civilian casualties? What if—a mantra of the anti-war forces, by the way—hideous weapons of mass destruction are unleashed? What if, in the fog and chaos of war, the Turks invade the north of Iraq, the Israelis seize the chance to expel all the Palestinians, the Arab "street" rises as one, all pro-Western regimes are overthrown and Al Qaeda gets the boost of a lifetime? What about the potential million-and-a-half refugees and the impending humanitarian disaster? I am sure that some critics will have the grace to recognize their own former arguments in this list. But now there is a new surly note being struck: does a fresh "quagmire" loom as a "guerrilla resistance" exacts a regular toll of American lives?

That still leaves another question, which is equally pressing and dramatic, if not indeed more so. "What if it works?" What if the intervention is a success? What if the Iraqi and Kurdish peoples, released from their surreal imprisonment and humiliation at the hands of a psychopathic crime-family, can draw themselves up to their full height? And what if the United States and its allies can be tough and smart enough to help this process, yet clever enough to know when it's complete?

I didn't really understand what the two familiar words "military superiority" can mean until I made my second visit to Iraq this year. There isn't anything within a thousand miles of Baghdad that can even consider taking on the United States armed forces, far from home as they may be. Command of the air is absolute, both from high up in the sky, and at helicopter level lower down. So is command of the adjacent waters, and of the river system within the country, and of the huge nexus of bases in neighboring countries. Control of the oilfields was established in the first days of the war: in the case of Kurdistan with the help of a strong and well-disciplined indigenous army which is far more gung-ho, and much more pitilessly anti-Saddam, than any outsider can be.

Against this are pitted the absolute scum of the earth. First, one finds the remnant of the so-called "Fedayeen Saddam": a cruel militia which used to be employed filling in those mass graves and performing other lowly tasks, and which has never lost a battle against civilians. Its ranks were already augmented before the war by imported "jihad" fighters from other countries, who have assisted the Ba'ath Party in its mutation from pseudo-secularist fascism into full-fledged Islamic dogmatism. The fanatics of the sole party meet the fanatics of the sole deity: a recent Saddamist "resistance" leaflet in Baghdad spoke of "One Leader. One Nation. One God," and the rhetoric generally is the drone of "martyrdom" and "the infidels." It was to keep this gang going that the treasury of the beggared country was looted just before its former tormentors went "underground" themselves. Almost every week, caches of gold ingots or U.S. dollars are recovered by American soldiers using sophisticated sensors and ever-more eager informants, but the going rate for an "operation" against these same American soldiers can go as high as a thousand bucks in cash. (An "operation" is a shot in the back with a throw-away weapon, or perhaps a hastily-rolled grenade, and it is offered to lumpen or criminal elements who can really use the money. Thus, Ba'athism meets jihad meets Mafia. They may employ superficially guerrilla tactics, but they are really comparable to the Contras: the scabs of the *ancien regime.*) Meanwhile, Wahhabi recruiters from Saudi Arabia are making their appearance, as are some gaunt characters allied with the theocrats of Iran, so the elements of bin-Ladenism and Khomeinism are making common cause.

But the political point of regime-change in the first place was to put these regional forces off-balance and out of temper, and this time—for a change—the violence is taking place on what they consider to be "their" turf. How right are they to believe that Iraq is, or can be, theirs? I flew over Baghdad several times, at night, in a Black Hawk helicopter. The lights were coming back on, and you can see why people compare the vivid sprawl to that of Los Angeles. Every now and then, an arc of red tracer fire could be seen, or the flash of an explosion. The chopper crews joked on the intercom at the sight of this negligible stuff. Yet only once since the occupation began has there been a real barrage, and that was the extraordinary fusillade of joyous tracer and rifle fire that greeted the news of the death of Uday and Qusay. More rounds were fired that night than on all the other nights combined and doubled. Bear that in mind.

I don't want to sound like Clint Eastwood here, though actually General John Abizeid and I have Clint in common. The new commander of American forces, a Lebanese-American who speaks fluent Arabic and has a degree in Middle East studies from Harvard, was used by Eastwood as a role-model for an exploit in *Heartbreak Ridge*. (It's the moment when he commandeers a bulldozer at Grenada airport and turns it into a battering ram.) And my apartment in Washington was used as a location by Clint for the shooting of *Absolute Power*. I hesitate to mention this tenuous celluloid bond when I meet the General for lunch at the Al Rasheed hotel in Baghdad, but when I do bring it up he moves swiftly to downplay it. "Yeah, I was as tall as Clint Eastwood," says this rather compactly-shaped officer, "until I came out here." This is actually his second time in Iraq. As a battalion commander, he helped supervise the protection of the Kurdish zone after the first Gulf War in 1991, and used to go and talk to the Iraqi officers along the cease-fire line. Everything was negotiable, he recalls, until you brought up the name of Saddam Hussein and saw their faces go rigid with fear.

It would probably surprise as many Americans as Iraqis to find an Arabic-speaking intellectual in charge of the intervention in Iraq. If he wasn't so modest (and so suspicious of the press) he could make himself a media star overnight. He prefers to deal in paradox. Most people think of progress in terms of the cessation or diminution of violence. For Abizeid, violence from the other side can be a sign of progress. It means the enemy is rattled. Their sabotage is directed at success—at new power lines, functioning oil-wells, co-operative Iraqi mayors and officials. But still, more Iraqis want to join the Coalition forces than want to fight them. "Don't ever underestimate what an Iraqi fighting for Iraq can bring to the table. He knows who's bad and who's good." Meanwhile, the task of American forces is not to measure themselves in "boots per square meter" but to downsize to a point that is "lighter, more mobile and more agile."

It takes the press a long time to catch up to this idea, but when you meet a battlefield officer in Iraq you are not encountering a grizzled, twitchy veteran of Cambodia or El Salvador, who talks out of the side of his mouth and loves the smell of napalm in the morning. As often as not, you are dealing with someone who cut his or her teeth in political-humanitarian rescue in Bosnia, Haiti, Kosovo or Afghanistan. Their operational skills are reconstruction, liaison with civilian forces, the cultivation of intelligence and the study of religion and ethnicity. They like to talk about human rights and civil society, not body-counts or "interdiction." I think of Lieutenant Colonel Bill Mayfield of the 173rd Airborne in Kirkuk, who had the job of arbitrating a tense turf-war between local Arabs and Kurds, in a district where Kurds had historically been "cleansed" and where they were inclined to take informal revenge by grabbing Arab property. He went and found some local Arab and Kurdish attorneys, convened a meeting between the two sides, roughed out some common ground and established a truce that is still holding.

In the Mosul-Nineveh district, American forces had held an election for a local council and produced a governing body made up of Arabs, Kurds and Turkomans, with representation from the Christian and Yezidi religious minorities. I sat in on a meeting of this group, which was made up chiefly of educators and civil servants. The mayor, Ghanim Al Basso, was a former Ba'ath party member and senior army officer who had made the cut, however, because his brother had been executed for trying to assassinate Saddam Hussein. The discussion positively fizzed with regional pride: Mosul is famous for its old university, and its inhabitants cherish the renown they enjoy for their outspokenness. Smartly-uniformed new Iraqi police were on the streets, right under the balcony from which Saddam was once filmed discharging his famous shotgun into the air. The university was back in business, and the 101st Airborne was showing it how to connect to the World Wide Web; a privilege it had long been denied. Down the road towards Nineveh, biblical home of Jonah, American soldiers had taken over Saddam's luxurious local palace and were splashing in its pool and cooking fried chicken with the help of a friendly Iraqi staff. The palace had originally been built on land stolen from the university and the plan was to return this property, with the palace as a bonus, to the academy. We were then just twelve hours away from the Mosul rendezvous with Uday and Qusay: intelligence officers told me even then that they were getting more raw information than they could sift or process, and were being scrupulous in screening out tips that might involve grudges or revenge. This is, in every sense, a smart army.

In fact, what is happening in today's Iraq is something more like a social and political revolution than a military occupation. It's a revolution from above, but in some ways no less radical for that. I haven't seen anything like it since the Portuguese army overthrew the fascist dictatorship in Lisbon in April 1974, and sent what it called "dynamization" teams out into the countryside, to try and dislodge the torpor and backwardness of decades. Local people are getting used to the sight of professional young American women, white and black and Hispanic, efficiently on patrol. Police cadets are receiving instruction in civil and human rights. Satellite dishes are proliferating and the newsstands are full of fresh publications, many of them lurid and sensational. Baghdad and Basra international airports are being spruced up to resume civilian traffic for the first time in years. A new currency is being printed without the ubiquitous face of the despot. In the course of a few hours spent loitering in the bustling courtyards of Bremer's palace, I ran into civilian advisors who were supervising voter registration and a census, rebuilding the electrical generators that now run at close to melting-point, reopening the long-closed Iraqi National Museum and irrigating the parched and drained habitat of the southern marshes, dried out and burned by Saddam Hussein in an ecocidal attempt to punish the stubborn resistance to his awful will. (By the way, driving through Baghdad one day I was amazed to come upon a demonstration against pollution sponsored by the local Green Party. Perhaps Iraq will ratify the Kyoto Treaty before the United States does.)

Back in March and April, a lot of ink was wasted on the question of hearts and flowers. Would Coalition forces be greeted with joy, or not? I myself wrote for this magazine from the grimy southern frontier town of Safwan, where the inhabitants barely had a pulse and didn't know which way things were going. Well, if you want to see a truly joyous welcome you should have flown with me on a Chinook helicopter last July, to see the reception that Paul Wolfowitz and Baroness Nicholson received when they flew to the desolate town of Al Turabeh, east of the Tigris and about twenty miles from the Iranian border. In this region, an area the size of New Jersey had been turned into desert by Saddam's vengeance on the Marsh Arabs, but the inhabitants still made beautiful ark-like houses out of woven reeds, and anchored them on the land. Two out of seven marshes were being irrigated again, and the ecstatic display from the population (especially for the Baroness, who championed their cause in Parliament during the lean and arid years) could not possibly have been faked. In the cities of Najaf and Karbala, holy places of Shi'a Islam, Wolfowitz's convoy was attended by swarms of waving and cheering children wherever it went, and greeted by local councils who employed the word "liberation" without affectation or embarrassment. Who knows what the mood will be like a year from now? But I insist that I saw all this with my own two eyes, and I would never have known of it if I had relied on the grudging and defeatist mainstream press.

Want to know how to create an "incident" in today's Iraq? Here's how I managed it. I accompanied Paul Wolfowitz to a meeting of the new city council in Najaf. The interim governor of the region, Haydar al Mayalli, greeted him by saying: "You have done tremendous things for Iraq. You still have a heavy responsibility for our country. You have commitments that must be fulfilled. We are grateful that you have opened the door to democracy and freedom." The gathering proceeded in this vein (I thought it was going to be all male until the door opened and a willowy form, draped head to toe in black, swept in carrying a smart leather briefcase and took her seat. A security nightmare, of course, but I suppose people get to know her by her walk.) After the discussion was over, our convoy got ready to head for the airport. I remarked that it would seem a shame if we didn't find time to pause at the shrine to Imam Ali, which is the holiest site in Shi'a Islam. So we made a stop, still greeted by friendly locals, outside the golden dome in the center of the city, and exchanged a few "salaam aleikums" with the passers-by. No weapons were flourished by Americans in the vicinity and nobody tried to enter the mosque: respects were paid and we moved on. But hours later a furious crowd gathered, incited by a man named Moqtada Sadr, who claimed that a plot was on foot to surround his office and arrest him. Mr. Sadr is a local Shi'a demagogue who hasn't been picked to serve on the predominantly Shi'a Governing Council, and he might be downcast if he knew how little intention there was of taking him so seriously. His brand of Khomeini-style theocracy has its fans in the region, but too many people have relatives or friends in Iran, or have been there to study, for there to be much enthusiasm for a mullah-type regime on the Tehran model. That model is in any case in deep trouble with its own population. It was actually local ayatollahs who ended up dispersing Moqtada Sadr's rumor-driven mob, but the press reports I later saw made it look as if there had been a near "Death To America" insurgency. This all arises in part from the feeble reluctance of the media to challenge anybody with apparently "Islamic" credentials, no matter how spurious.

And so to the North. One of the greatest pleasures in life is that of visiting liberated territory. Twelve years ago in Iraqi Kurdistan, I received a great deal of kindness and hospitality from the local population, who cheerfully shared the nothing that they had, and put me up in the charred ruins that they then inhabited. This time was different. To move up into the Kurdish hills is not just to escape the baking heat and misery and dislocation of the plains. It is to travel years forward into a possible Iraqi future. The roads are smooth, the landscape cultivated and (slowly but surely) the oilwells are pumping. There are four female High Court judges. Gas stations, clogged by long lines elsewhere, look as if they were in Holland or Connecticut. Well-dressed Kurdish police and militia stand guard at intersections, and Americans hardly bother to wear their flak-jackets. It was easy to connect to the internet and, finally, to have a long shower, before being offered a serious cocktail and a meal featuring five different kinds of lamb. At the reception given by President Mahsoud Barzani, in a manicured villa and garden as opposed to the shell-pocked ruin in which I had last seen him, I met my old friend Dr. Barham Salih, who is prime minister of the adjacent Kurdish region. Once highly clannish and even fratricidal, the Kurds have shown that they can transcend their differences once they have an autonomy worth defending. Barham was in tip-top form, wondering why the Americans didn't ask for a few companies of Kurdish fighters to take part in the hunt for Saddam. "No shortage of motivation," he remarks. But even here the conversation is overlaid by talk about interment and disinterment: not only has a new mass grave been opened at Hatra, near Mosul (this is the one apparently reserved for mothers and children) but a huge mound of cadavers has been unearthed in the far south of the country, near the Saudi border, and apparently the remains include many fragments of Kurdish dress. This could be the long-sought clue to the whereabouts of the hundreds of male villagers of Barzan, taken off on trucks in 1988 and never seen again. There seemed little point in driving them so far away just to shoot them: there are persistent rumors that they were used as live subjects for weapons experiments. There's no celebration in today's Iraq that doesn't take place under a shadow like this.

Even better than visiting liberated territory is visiting liberated friends. In Washington last year I had lunch with Muni al-Khatib, a fine Iraqi gentleman of the old school who had resigned from his country's diplomatic service the moment he heard that Saddam Hussein had become president. He was then just beginning to think that, after a quarter-century of exile, he might get home again. With slight embarrassment, he told me that what he missed most was the particular scent of the orange-groves along the Tigris. These, he shyly maintained, smelled better than orange-blossom anywhere else. I lost touch with him during the war. Entering the newly-reopened Foreign Ministry in Baghdad one flaming-hot day in July, I heard a voice: "Have you forgotten me so soon, Christopher?" "Muni! How are the orange-groves?" He was deputy foreign minister, and has since become secretary general to the Governing Council. Oddly satisfying.

I also went to pay a call on Ahmad Chalabi, founder of the Iraqi National Congress. He has moved himself into a preposterous villa, designed to look half-Chinese palace and half-Japanese pagoda, and resulting in a synthesis that is all kitsch. The place used to belong to Saddam's abysmal cousin, Barzan al-Tikriti, and it shows. When I arrived, Chalabi was receiving a delegation from the Sudanese community in Baghdad, who hoped to bring about "regime change" in their own benighted country. In the remaining time I spent there, he was waited upon by large and deferential groups of businessmen, lawyers, mullahs and other petitioners. His aides told me that this procession never ceases. He was beginning to look just a little bit like a pasha, dispensing advice and patronage. I hope it doesn't get to him.

Kanan Makiya once had to publish *The Republic of Fear,* his path-breaking anatomy of the Ba'ath regime, under a pseudonym. He had to do the same with *The Monument,* a haunting study of the public architecture—"part Nuremburg, part Las Vegas"—of Saddam's Baghdad. The "monument" of the title is one of the most offensive things, visually and aesthetically, that I have ever seen. It consists of an arch, higher than the Arc de Triomphe, formed by two massive forearms that, clutching matching swords, emerge from the ground. These limbs are based on a plaster-cast of Saddam's own arms. From near each wrist protrudes a giant metal peanut-bag, torn open to spill out a cornucopia of military helmets. These helmets, each with a shrapnel or bullet hole, were gathered from dead Iranians in the calamitous Gulf War, and they form something like a carpet of skulls. The same arch, and the same filthy skull-effect, is repeated about a half-mile away so as to form two ends of a triumphal procession route. When Saddam was in power, this was used for spectacularly intimidating parades. Now, it looks merely tawdry and nasty.

And it is here that Kanan Makiya is hoping to create his museum of Ba'athist atrocities: a library of remembrance and respect. To meet this brave, modest, honest intellectual, back in his home-town at last, was another moment of quiet confirmation. There are perhaps four million Iraqis who have been condemned to live in exile. They have acquired a host of skills and qualifications, and have been living for the most part in democratic societies. If they can be drawn home, Iraq will rise again.

Think of the talent and quality that has been buried under the rubble. At a dinner given by the Governing Council I had the honor of being placed next to Judge Dara Nor al Din, a man of unthinkable courage who, as a member of the Iraqi Court of Appeals, had had the nerve to hold one of Saddam's edicts unconstitutional. He was promptly flung into Abu Ghraib prison, a horror jail in the desert outside Baghdad. He didn't make too much of his experiences, but a few days later I visited Abu Ghraib for myself. I badly wanted to leave after ten minutes: the mind refuses to imagine what it would be like to be there indefinitely. Stinking little cells into which prisoners were packed like vermin in the stifling heat, with a steady and brutish execution rate to keep the numbers under control. I was shown a huge shed with a long bar over a deep pit: there was room for several nooses to be in use at the same time. The lowest estimate of deaths in this one jail is 30,000. More spadework, more digging, more hellish disinterment. . . .

I don't doubt that, with more excavation and more analysis of captured blueprints, it will emerge that Saddam always intended to reconstitute his WMD program. He never complied with pressing UN resolutions, even at the last, and it seems distinctly improbable that he expelled the UN inspectors in 1998 in order to embark on a crash program of unilateral disarmament. I have no patience with those who grant this madman the presumption of innocence, or with those who granted it earlier. The Ba'ath regime was often underestimated, in its dangerous capacity for aggression, by Western intelligence. (The CIA refused to believe that Saddam was going to invade Kuwait in 1990, and nobody came near to guessing how close he then was to the acquisition of a nuclear bomb.) Still, the fact remains that the Bush and Blair administrations decided that it was easier to scare the voters than to try and persuade them, and simpler to stress the language of "threat" than the discourse of human rights or the complexities of the Genocide Convention. Greatly to their shame, neither Bush nor Blair ever readied a bill of indictment, for war crimes and crimes against humanity, that could have been used as a warrant for intervention. They did not want to re-open the wretched file on their countries' past collaboration with Saddam. This deceitful condescension has tainted a noble cause, I hope not irretrievably.

There's a term of art that is employed by all Coalition spokesmen in Iraq, whether civil or military. When they refer to any new development, whether it is an Iraqi police department or a new court system or a soon-to-be formed local militia, they always say that it's been "stood up." Thus, we've "stood up" a council in such and such a town. Once or twice, I thought I detected a faint note of bluffing here, as if scenery was being erected and nobody dared to sneeze. But consider the options. Iraq cannot go back to Ba'athism. It is incredibly unlikely to opt for an Islamic theocracy, given a state where no faith or faction has absolute predominance. It is too rich, actually and potentially, to collapse into penury. And it is emerging from a period of nightmarish rule to which anything would be preferable. So dare to repeat, in spite of everything, the breathless question: What if it works?

VANITY FAIR, OCTOBER 2003